Socialist Authority

SOCIALIST AUTHORITY

The Hungarian Experience

PETER A. TOMA

PRAEGER

New York
Westport, Connecticut
London

Library of Congress Cataloging-in-Publication Data

Toma, Peter A.
  Socialist authority.

  Bibliography: p.
  1. Hungary—Social conditions—1945– .
2. Hungary—Politics and government—1945– .
3. Hungary—Economic conditions—1968– .
4. Socialism—Hungary. I. Title.
HN420.5.A8T65   1988   306′.09439   87–11775
ISBN 0–275–92602–8 (alk. paper)

Library of Congress Catalog Card Number: 87–11775
ISBN: 0–275–92602–8

First published in 1988

Praeger Publishers, One Madison Avenue, New York, NY 10010
A division of Greenwood Press, Inc.

Printed in the United States of America

The paper used in this book complies with the
Permanent Paper Standard issued by the National
Information Standards Organization (Z39.48–1984).

10 9 8 7 6 5 4 3 2 1

Contents

PART I: REAL VERSUS IMAGINARY SOCIAL CONTRACT

PART II: WHO GETS WHAT, FOR WHAT?

PART III: THE HEDONISM OF AUTHORITY

PART IV: NEW SOCIETY WITH OLD TRADITIONS

List of Tables and Figures

TABLES

FIGURES

List of Abbreviations

CC	Central Committee
CLC	Constitutional Law Council
CMEA	Council for Mutual Economic Assistance
FISz	Independent Youth League
GMK	Enterprise Work Association
CPH	Communist Party of Hungary
HSWP	Hungarian Socialist Workers' Party
KISz	Independent Youth League
MASZEK	Entrepreneur
NCTU	National Council of the Trade Unions
NEM	New Economic Mechanism
NPP	National Peasant Party
OTP	National Savings Bank
PJT	Civil Legal Associations
PPF	Patriotic People's Front
RFE	Radio Free Europe
SP	Smallholder Party
SDP	Social Democratic Party
SzOT	National Council of Hungarian Trade Unions
WTO	Warsaw Treaty Organization

Introduction

This book is about "authority" as it pertains to individuals and groups of people living in socialist Hungary, who explicitly or tacitly permit the ruling elite to make decisions for them over certain issues, thus permitting important choices to be determined for them. Hence, whereas on the one hand [socialist] authority includes the voluntary granting of permission to decide certain shared issues and joint actions by the [communist] party members and its auxiliary mass organizations, on the other hand it also includes the reluctant acceptance of rules imposed on a feeble majority by the power elite of the central authority, which not only controls decision making over major economic issues concerning production, investment, wages, and prices, but also claims "the right of self-elected power, content totally to dispose of the lives, habits, ambitions, inclinations, future and even physical existence of individuals."[1] In Hungary, as elsewhere in the world, ruling authorities are now being challenged in all areas of human life. Many of the questions now being asked about the nature and function of authority are similar to the ones asked in the labor movement before and shortly after World War I, when V.I. Lenin reinterpreted Marxism to tailor its application to a peasant-dominated rural Russia. In many ways, progressive theoreticians in Hungary, as elsewhere, are attempting to rediscover Karl Marx as a source of socialist ideas to guide the present decision makers in their challenge to cope with a technocratic age and the problems caused by modernization.

The breakdown and diffusion of authority structures, the impotence of governments, the advent of economic disarray in the technologically advanced societies, the persistence of poverty in the developing countries, the lack of coherence in global, regional, and national systems, the intractability of the arms race, the disregard for international law and treaty obligations, and the overall decline of civility—all are symptomatic of the profound crisis of authority on a global level.[2]

In a shrinking, turbulent world of interdependence, no nation, large or small, rich or poor, can escape the influences of transnational politics. The actors in the international arena are not only the sovereign nation states, but intergovernmental and nongovernmental organizations, including economic cartels and terrorist hijackers. The rise of multinational corporations and the need to maintain employment levels for income benefits have opened up new opportunities for the international division of labor to compete on a cost and quality basis in the manufacturing of consumer goods for the international market. Hungary, like some other socialist countries, successfully negotiated with multinational capitalist firms to locate several production units in its territory, in spite of the very different property and production relations that prevail in its socialist system. In other words, in an attempt to modernize, for the past two decades Hungary has entered the competitive world market in search of all the opportunities and benefits it has to offer. Of course, success in this competition is measured by low production costs, high productivity, and high quality of work. Therefore Hungary, like other countries competing in the international market, must provide stimuli and incentives to achieve the above attributes in order to become a successful competitor. Consequently the process of modernization has required structural and attitudinal changes in the social character of Hungary, which has unleashed all sorts of new social problems as well as needs and demands to accommodate the changed relations between individuals and groups toward institutions of authority. Because the ruling elite looks upon unsanctioned individual or group needs as illegitimate and dangerous—as seeking a reassertion of capitalist values— it reserves the right to determine, control, and meet all social needs in accordance with the priorities established, in the name of the people, by the party [that is, by the leaders of the Hungarian Socialist Workers' Party]. As Charles Lindblom put it, the major tasks of the party are "to mold the behavior of citizens into patterns that support rather than obstruct the regime, and to maintain the obedience of government officials to top leadership."[3] This role of the party is, however, considered by several party theoreticians old fashioned and inadequate to meet the challenges of modernization in today's world. Many of them feel that the party must reacquire its original Marxist role to permit greater participation in the decision-making process, greater decentralization and pluralism of power to encourage grassroot socialist democracy as well as civil liberties. They argue that private property is not the crucial issue;[4] the important political issues are the mode of distribution and allocation of the surplus value and the prevention of injustices through exploitation. In other words, the key issue for the critics is how to combine economic planning, which is necessary to achieve tolerable equality and social justice, with the freedom and individual autonomy that arises only from pluralism and free choice.[5]

It is not my purpose in this book to try to settle the dispute between the advocates of participatory socialist democracy and pluralism on the one hand, and the advocates of central authority as the only qualified members of society able to express the interests of the entire nation, on the other. Instead, it is to consider the actual changes that have taken place in the economic, social, and political structures of Hungarian society, and then to analyze the implications of these changes for individual autonomy and citizenship. My starting point is that political authority has remained at least formally a separate sphere from economic activity, especially in the second economy. Since 1968 (when the New Economic Mechanism [NEM] was introduced), the Kádár regime has successfully used political authority to change the economic relations that have prevailed since the communists gained power in 1947; and in recent years these have mostly been in the direction of trying to give the economic sphere a slightly greater degree of self-regulation through the means of private initiative. I will argue that the reasons for these attempts were to achieve social change and technological modernization (especially in the rural areas) of the country while maintaining an improved standard of living, social satisfaction, and political stability. But I will also argue that these economic and social changes (as well as the modest political ones), were induced to some extent by the prevailing favorable climate for multinational corporations, by the internationalization of production, and by the reappearance of mass unemployment and the reassertion of market principles in the world economy. Furthermore, I suggest that the economic success of the reforms in Hungary triggered new demands for political liberalization or reforms, which caused concern at the 13th Party Congress in 1985 to draw a clearer demarcation line between political authority and economic activities (or reforms) in the country. Thus the ultimate question before the decision-making authorities is whether or not it is possible to continue with economic reforms without making commensurate allowances for political reforms. The answer to this question, however, is beyond the scope of this book.

At this juncture it is appropriate to ask whether the Hungarian party elite is autonomous in determining the role individuals and groups play in the decision-making process. Ever since November 4, 1956 (when the Soviet army crushed the so-called Hungarian "Freedom Fighters"), the Kádár regime has been held accountable to the Kremlin leaders, who reserve the right to reinvade if the country deviates from the Soviet-approved policies. This unwritten law is in essence what is also known as the Brezhnev doctrine, which justified the Soviet invasion of Czechoslovakia in August 1968 to "save" socialism from the "enemies" of the "socialist community." Thus the Hungarian party elite and the sovereign government are, in effect, a subordinate power, in Hobbesian terms, and the Kremlin leaders and the Soviet government the superior power in the socialist community. In spite of the restrictions imposed on Hungary by the Soviet elite, a close scrutiny of the economic and social (and to a limited extent also political) changes will reveal that the quality of life and lifestyle of most Hungarians has improved considerably during the period of NEM, especially since the mid-1970s.

The Hungarian success story has not gone unnoticed in the world electronic and print media or in the scholarly literature. Credit in most instances is attributed to the economic reforms.[6] While it is accurate to maintain that the NEM is the catalyst for the improved conditions (especially economic ones) prevailing in Hungary today, the question, which this book attempts to answer, still remains: why was the NEM introduced by the Hungarian party elite in 1968 and why has it become a success when other socialist countries (e.g., Czechoslovakia) could have but failed to adopt the Hungarian model for restoration after a major upheaval? Scholars who have researched the subject offer all kinds of explanations for the liberalization process in Hungary, but most findings are incomplete and some are based on circumstantial evidence. Zvi Gitleman, for example, has reluctantly concluded that the Hungarian success can be attributed to external factors because "Kádár's restoration efforts were made at a time of political experimentation in the USSR, while Husak's reign [in Czechoslovakia] is paralleled by a more conservative Soviet leadership."[7] Similarly Jiri Valenta attributes the Hungarian success to the external environment when he states that "reformism under Khrushchev actually helped to advance Kádár's normalization process in Hungary.... Another factor that favored Kádár's policies was the Soviets' perception of the domestic situation in Hungary, particularly the memory of the bloody conflict of 1956 when the Soviets suffered several thousand casualties.... A third reason for Soviet tolerance was Kádár's personality."[8]

While these explanations have certain merit, the increased economic and cultural relaxation accompanied by gradual political liberalization in Hungary cannot be explained without an understanding of the complexity of the Hungarian social character, which this book attempts to emphasize in the last chapter. The model of the Hungarian social character put forward in the final chapter is submitted with caution and intellectual modesty as an alternative to various approaches and theorizing about the limits of autonomy and freedom of choice imposed on individuals and groups in Hungary, to guide our research toward greater empirical investigation, and to advance new hypotheses about the nature and dynamics of national communism. This chapter reveals not only the sources and causes for change from a centralized to a pluralistically oriented concept of authority, but also the skill of adaptation of socialism in Hungary to changed conditions that have created a new political culture of "socialist pragmatism" with its own subculture consisting of unsanctioned practices of an underground economy.

Through a series of case studies, based on interviews (with about 500 individuals representing a cross-section of white- and blue-collar workers of the Hungarian society with emphasis on urban population) supported by hard data (derived from surveys and additional interviews conducted by various Hungarian institutions), one of the chief aims throughout the book will be to differentiate between theory and practice of socialist authority in an analysis of how the people of Hungary have learned to circumvent the restrictions imposed by the authorities and to survive both internal and external pressures of bureaucratic socialism. In order to get to the bottom of the motivating force and the shrewdness of both the rulers and the ruled, it was deemed necessary to illustrate the intricate relationship in some detail with case studies, so that the reader unfamiliar with the present Hungarian socioeconomic culture could more readily understand the nuances involved in the daily interactions among the members of the Hungarian society. All occurrences and situations in these cases are real; only the names have been changed in order to protect the interviewed subjects. Although the narrative of some of the events may appear to be uncomplimentary or derogatory, there was no intent to defame or ridicule any individuals or institutions either as members of the party or because they represent positions of authority. As a disclaimer, this author would like to state unequivocally that corruption, bureaucratic red tape, abuse, discrimination, crime, and other social ills of society are not confined to Hungary or to socialist systems alone. For example, injustices and political intrigues at institutions of higher learning can be found as easily in Tucson, Arizona, as they can in Budapest, Hungary; only the labels of the institutions and their actors are different—the motivations, objectives, and methods, however, are the same.

Throughout the book "man" is used generically and only for stylistic convenience. Actually the meaning includes men and women—human beings of either gender. Soft data (i.e., attitudinal information) are corroborated by hard data derived mainly from the Central Statistical Office in Budapest and primary sources of various types. Because there is no intent to make this treatise a theoretical discourse of the merits of the ideological tenets of Marxism-Leninism, a summary of the ideas of Marx and Lenin are presented here only for orientation or background purposes, and therefore they may appear to some sophisticated scholars as simplistic or over-generalized. For similar reasons, to assist the curious reader with a background to the prevailing conditions in Hungary, what follows is an historical sketch rather than a complete history of the Magyars.

HISTORICAL SKETCH

While the intent here is not to rely on geopolitical determinism as an explanation of history, there are certain environmental factors that impinge on Hungary's socioeconomic and political developments. Because of favorable soil and climatic conditions, Hungary has remained until fairly recently a rural society with its population ranging from horse breeders and shepherds to peasants, farmers, and agricultural workers. Even after the industrialization of Hungarian society most of the population still lives in village-type settlements with close ties to agricultural activities and rural customs. Since defeat in WWI, when "it lost two-thirds of its territory and population,"[9] Hungary has been a landlocked country. As a result, Hungary lost most of its natural resources and was forced to rely on agricultural activities, for which the Great Plains (Alföld, located east of the two main rivers, the Danube and the Tisza), which were once a large steppe, are best suited.[10] Industrialization and urbanization in Hungary, which began in the second half of the nineteenth century, followed the topography and the environmental conditions, as well as the peculiarities of socioeconomic and political conditions prevailing in the country. Thus urbanization can be found in the industrialized half of the central highlands in northwest Hungary, stretching from Miskolc through Budapest to Györ.[11]

Before invading the Danubian basin in the ninth century A.D., the ancestors of the Hungarian people were nomadic herdsmen and warriors who roamed the territory of the Khazar empire between the Don and Volga rivers near the Black Sea. They were organized in a loose confederation of archer tribes known collectively as the Turanian peoples of Asia, who mingled with a variety of cultures, plundering towns and villages in search of booty and territory to colonize. In the 870s, according to legend, the chiefs of seven tribes chose the strongest tribe, the Megyer (later known as the Magyar), and its chief, Álmos, to lead them to a new home. Hungarian historians have designated 896 A.D. as the year the Magyars, under the leadership of Árpád (son of Álmos), conquered the territory roughly equivalent to the present area of Hungary. Under the rule of the Magyars, the seven tribes evolved from a pagan society of wandering raiders, mercenaries, and cattle breeders to a Christianized, feudal, agrarian society.

The princedom of Hungary became an apostolic kingdom in 1001 A.D., when (Saint) Stephen I, who had previously converted the "nation" to Christianity, received the royal crown from Pope Sylvester II. Subsequently, the kings of the House of Árpád consolidated the feudal order in Hungary. In 1241, the Mongol hordes of Batu Kahn devastated the country, which was later rebuilt under the leadership of the great King Béla IV. During the reign of King Matthias (Corvinus) of Hunyad (1458–1490), Hungary became one of the leading cultural centers in Europe.

Other highlights of Hungarian history include the year 1520, when invading Turkish armies from the Balkans won the battle at Mohács. This defeat caused the disintegration of medieval Hungary. The country was thereafter divided in three: the largest subdivision fell under Turkish rule; the northern and western regions yielded to the German emperors from the Austrian House of Hapsburg, who became the recognized kings of Hungary; and Transylvania became an "independent princedom" under the Turkish Protectorate. Between 1683 and 1699 imperial Austrian troops combined with native Hungarians to drive the Turks out of both the areas of direct rule and the "protectorate."

The Turkish domination was followed by that of the Hapsburgs, whose yoke the nation was unable to throw off, despite several uprisings. The national freedom war of 1703–1711, led by Ferenc Rákóczi II, ended in defeat, as did the 1848 war for independence, led by Lajos Kossuth. In 1867 the Hungarians concluded a compromise agreement with the House of Hapsburg that marked the beginning of the Austro-Hungarian monarchy.

During the half century of the Austro-Hungarian Empire, Hungary remained a feudal aristocracy ruled by magnates and the gentry. Industry was weak, commercial policy protected the interests of the landlords, the administration was corrupt, and the countryside was economically underdeveloped. More than half the population of the country was illiterate. The national minorities, who constituted a majority of the population, were deprived of all their rights, which in the final analysis proved to be the principal cause of the disintegration of the empire. Ironically, it was the assassination of Franz Ferdinand and his wife in Sarajevo on June 28, 1914, that plunged Hungary into World War I; not because the Hungarians loved their archduke and were willing to die for a (Magyarophobe) Hapsburg, but because they believed in Magyar supremacy and territorial integrity of the empire. The coalition government headed by Count Michael Károlyi, which followed the reign of the last Hapsburg king (Karl), tried desperately to turn doomsday into Kingdom come. However, the Károlyi government was unable to resolve any of the major problems facing the new republic (establishing peace, carrying out agrarian reform), and there was general unrest and deprivation throughout the country. Under such conditions, Bolshevism, which had been brought to Hungary by prisoners of war returning from Russia, gained a substantial following in industrial areas. Against this background, one sudden blow brought down the whole, precarious structure of Hungarian democracy. On March 20, 1919, the armistice commission in Budapest informed the government that it must relinquish still more territory to newly-created neighboring states. Károlyi could not and would not accept these terms. Negotiations between the Social Democrats and the Communists were initiated to deal with the problem. The following day, March 21, 1919, the Károlyi government was forced to resign and the Hungarian Soviet Republic was formed. Under its commissar of foreign affairs, Béla Kun, the socialist–communist coalition government allied itself with Lenin and the Soviet Union and opted to support world revolution. In so doing, the regime hoped to salvage "Saint Stephen's kingdom" from complete destruction by the Entente forces who were backing Czechoslovakian and Rumanian claims to Hungarian territory. Although Kun's army successfully withstood initial attacks by the Czechs, on August 6, 1919, the Rumanian army marched into Budapest and the 133–day Hungarian Soviet Republic came to an end. The cruelty and the number of victims of the "Red Terror" of Béla Kun were surpassed only by those of the "White Terror" of Rear Admiral Miklós Horthy von Nagybánya (supreme commander of the Hungarian National Army, which had fought alongside foreign forces to defeat the Kun regime).[12] By 1920 Hungary had lost not only the war and the greater part of its territory, but also all aspirations for democracy. After the demise of the Kun regime, Hungary became a kingdom without a king; the Hapsburgs were prohibited by law from assuming the throne. On March 1, 1920, the Hungarian National Assembly made Horthy regent of the Hungarian kingdom and thus began a period of authoritarianism that lasted for a quarter of a century.

The Horthy regime restored the traditional values, institutions, and authorities that had evolved under the feudal, monarchical system. Belief in God and country as well as in the sanctity of family ties and private property were placed above everything else; the rights of "gentlemen" over the common people were reaffirmed. The Hungarian upper (or ruling) class—comprising remnants of the old aristocracy, landowners, higher-level members of the clergy, military leaders, and industrialists—constituted about 6 percent of the post-1920 population. The middle class—consisting of bureaucrats, professionals, and business people—constituted about 8 percent of the population. About 37 percent were workers and artisans, and 49 percent belonged to the peasantry. Social stratification was based on such attributes as ancestry, race, wealth, type of residence, and national origin. The prevailing spiritual outlook or "Zeitgeist" of the country before World War II was chauvinistic, religious, introverted, and traditional.[13]

The secret ballot was not reestablished until 1939, but by this time Hungary was already moving into the Nazi camp. For its collaboration,

Hungary received from Hitler approximately 80,000 square kilometers of "lost territory" with about six million inhabitants. "Great Hungary," as it was called during the war, reciprocated by rendering diplomatic as well as military support to the Axis Powers.[14]

Following the Nazi attack on the Soviet Union in 1941, Hungary ordered a contingent of about 350,000 soldiers to fight against the Russians. However, the Soviet victory at the battle of Stalingrad in February 1943 demoralized the Hungarian army and forecast the ultimate defeat of Germany. In the autumn of 1944, when the Soviet army was pushing through the Carpathian Mountains, Admiral Horthy made an attempt to surrender to Moscow, but he was seized by the Gestapo and forced to abdicate. The Nazis installed a puppet regime of fascist fanatics under the direction of Ferenc Szálasi, leader of the Hungarian Arrow Cross Party. The Szálasi government committed the Hungarians to fight with the Nazis until the end of World War II.[15]

In December 1944 the Soviet army laid siege to Budapest. At the same time (and with encouragement from the Soviet army), the Hungarian communists—most of whom had lived in exile in the USSR until 1944— met at Debrecen and established a Provisional National Assembly composed of a communist-controlled coalition of four nonfascist parties (Smallholder, Social Democratic, National Peasant, in addition to Communist). This Assembly formed a Provisional National Government with General Béla Dálnoki-Miklós as premier. (Dálnoki was the only general under Horthy who succeeded in surrendering to the Soviet army in October 1944.) It was with representatives of this government that the three Allied Powers signed an armistice in Moscow on January 21, 1945.[16]

The cost of the war in Hungarian lives (nearly one-half million military casualties) and material (40 percent of the national income) was staggering. Budapest was besieged for two months. Only Warsaw, Stalingrad, and the German cities suffered such horror and destruction. In April 1945, when the Russian army drove the German and Hungarian armies into Austria, the towns and villages as well as the people of Hungary had been totally devastated. Although Hungary was ostensibly governed by an Allied Control Commission composed of British, American, and Soviet representatives, in reality it was under the control of the occupying Soviet army. By Article 22 of the 1947 Peace Treaty (Soviet—Hungarian Peace Treaty), the Russians were in full occupation until the treaty came into force in September 1947.

At the end of World War II, Hungary had a semi-feudal agrarian economy and a rigid class structure. There had been almost no industrial development since the disintegration of the Austro-Hungarian Empire. In 1945, more than three times as many people were employed in agriculture as in industry; industrial workers accounted for only 21 percent of the labor force. The main reason for this was that the country's inter-war ruling elite had consisted of large landowners interested in the preservation of the status quo, rather than industrialization.

Under the Horthy regime, almost a quarter of Hungary's arable land belonged to a few estates of 500 hectares or more, which were owned by only 0.1 percent of the landholders, including the Catholic church. Because of these conditions, land reform and industrialization were the two main objectives pursued by the Hungarian communists after the Soviet army began to drive out the Nazis in 1944.

The program advocated by the Provisional National Government had been prepared well in advance of the armistice by the Hungarian communists in exile, under the auspices of the Soviet party leaders, and propagated by the Hungarian Communist Party (HCP) ever since its reemergence in November 1944. The purpose of the program was to implement national-democratic revolution; the Stalinists applied similar strategies to other Eastern European countries. When the Soviet army took Debrecen in December 1944, there were less than 3,000 Hungarian communists in liberated Hungary. (Most of them had been in exile in the Soviet Union during the Horthy regime.) By the end of World War II, communist party membership was 150,000; by March 1947 it had risen to 650,000; and by the time it merged with the Social Democratic Party in 1948, the HCP had an estimated 1,500,000 members.[17] The Hungarian Communist Party was the first to start organizing life and popular power; it was the only party capable of mapping out a democratic revival. It invited the other parties, which were slowly organizing, to accept its program and to cooperate in its fulfillment.[18] The primary task of the Hungarian communists after the war was to build communist strength across the country. In practice this meant organizing a communist mass party controlled by a communist elite; the placing of administrative power in the hands of the communist-controlled Committees of National Liberation; the formation of a new people's security system and army, built on the Soviet model; the prohibition of the revival of the political parties and organizations that had represented reactionary interests in prewar Hungary; a systematic purge of the political, economic, and cultural life of the country; the expulsion of the German minority; and other measures enabling the Hungarian communists to consolidate their control.

For example, after the Hungarian Communist Party machine had become well established (that is, after December 1944), the Soviet Military Command allowed only the leaders of nonfascist parties to organize; the result was a progressive democratic coalition (the National Independence Front) that included the Social Democratic Party (SPD), the National Peasant Party (NPP), and the Smallholder Party (SP), in addition to the HCP. Cooperation among the leaders of the three noncommunist parties dated back to May 1944, when Hungary was occupied by Nazi Germany. Furthermore, as early as October 10, 1944, the HCP and the SDP agreed to pursue a united front policy against reactionaries and to merge the two parties eventually. With regard to the systematic purge of undesirable political elements, between 1945 and 1946 approximately 25,000 Hungarian citizens were tried as war criminals by the people's courts; about 2 percent of them received the death penalty. Between January 1945 and March 1, 1948, a total of 39,514 Hungarians were brought to trial for political crimes, and 19,273 were convicted.[19]

In their well-organized bid for power, the communists first created pressure from below through the agitation of "the masses" and then exerted pressure from above through the influence of communist-dominated governmental units and the initiation of legislation. Both types of pressure kept the opposition constantly on the defensive. The aim of this "pincer tactic" was to force rivals to yield to pressure from both above (the National Independence Front, representing political unity) and below (the workers and peasants, representing national social and economic unity) so that adversaries could eventually be manipulated into a vulnerable position for the final assault. The Stalinists applied the pincer tactic throughout Eastern Europe. In Hungary the final seizure of power occurred on June 13, 1948, when the expurgated rump of the Social Democratic Party was absorbed by the Hungarian Communist Party. On that date, Hungary began a systematic transition from capitalism to socialism with no organized opposition in sight.[20] Between 1945 and 1948 the Hungarian communists skillfully employed the pincer technique described above in a complex process of power struggle. Aided by Soviet authorities, they kept alive the struggle against the former fascists and collaborators, against black marketeers and opportunists, against those hostile to Hungarian friendship with the Soviet Union, and against the landed class of large-estate owners. As a matter of fact, while fighting was still going on in March 1945, one of the first acts of the Provisional National Government was the declaration and implementation of a land reform. Under the communist minister of agriculture, Imre Nagy, and the chairman of the Land Reform Council, Péter Veres, more than a third of the agricultural land of Hungary was distributed among some 640,000 small or new farmers.[21] "The peasants who had thus been given land put their confidence in the working class and its revolutionary party."[22]

At the same time the communists encouraged private enterprise within certain bounds, and through their auxiliary organizations and the cooperation of leftwing Social Democrats, they rallied support for greater civil, political, and economic rights for all strata of Hungarian society. The Hungarian Communist Party did not promote "class struggle" on such issues as "reactionary forces," the slow pace of legislative work, sabotage, espionage for a "reactionary power," and the so-called conspiracy against people's democracy until several months after the first, national, postwar parliamentary elections, which took place in November 1945.

Because of their increasing efforts and hard work, the communists were confident of victory at the polls. Nevertheless, to play it safe, they decided to hold municipal elections before November in Budapest, where they anticipated the support of the working class. (Two-thirds of Hungary's manufacturing industry and the majority of the country's working class were concentrated in and around Budapest at that time.)[23] The strategy backfired: in the October 7 municipal elections, the Smallholder Party, which represented small farmers, Catholic clergy, and an assortment of political opportunists, received 51 percent of the vote, making the two workers' parties (the HCP and the SDP) and the National Peasant Party members of the minority. After this defeat, Marshal Voroshilov, head of the Allied Control Commission, in an effort to exert some control over the November election, tried to coerce the leaders of the Smallholder Party into accepting a common list of the four coalition parties that specified a predetermined number of seats—at first 45 percent, then 47.5 percent—but they refused to commit their party to anything beyond the promise that, whatever the results of the November election, the Smallholders would continue to work within the coalition of the National Independence Front.[24] Hungarian and foreign observers have agreed that the first parliamentary elections were freely conducted by secret ballot. The Smallholder Party won 57 percent of the seats in Parliament. For the next two years the aim of Smallholder leaders (such as Ference Nagy and Béla Kovács), was to prevent further sovietization of Hungary. The aim of communist and Soviet policy in Hungary, however, was to break the Smallholders' power and to speed up the development of a Hungarian "People's Democracy." Communist pressure on the Ferenc Nagy government was well coordinated. What the Hungarian Communists could not achieve through the leftwing bloc of the National Independence Front—a political alliance of the HCP, SDP, NPP, and the National Council of Trade Unions—the Soviet occupation authorities accomplished for them.

The first significant attempt to weaken the Smallholder Party in Parliament came in January 1946, when the leftwing block sponsored a bill for the nationalization of mines.[25] Although the Smallholder Party had enough votes to block the passage of the bill, it failed to do so because its leftwing members had threatened to bolt the party (which they eventually did in July 1947). Two months later, the SP's leaders again yielded to the demands of the leftwing bloc of the National Independence Front and convinced the party to expel (on the basis of trumped-up charges) 21 of its members holding seats in Parliament. The leftwing bloc made more demands: support of land reform; state control over banks and heavy industry; nationalization of the flour mills; the Three-Year Plan; struggle against conspirators, exploiters, and speculators; and many others.[26] The climax of the SP's crisis came late in February 1947 with the arrest of Béla Kovács, general secretary of the Smallholder Party. Soviet security forces arrested Kovács on February 26, 1947; they charged that he had organized espionage on behalf of a foreign power, against the Soviet army. It was later revealed that this was a trumped-up charge, but at the time it was accepted at face value. After his arrest, Kovács was held in captivity in the Soviet Union. (He did eventually return from his Soviet internment; in October 1956 he participated in Imre Nagy's government, and after the Soviet invasion he joined the Hungarian refugees in the West.) Before his deportation, however, he was reported to have incriminated his friend, Ferenc Nagy.[27] In May 1947, while Nagy was in Switzerland, Soviet authorities produced "evidence" against him. The inevitable result was the expulsion of Nagy and most of his associates from the Smallholder Party. Ferenc Nagy was succeeded by a fellow traveler, Lajos Dinnyés.

In early June 1947, Hungary was invited to participate in the Marshall Plan. However, after Soviet authorities had exerted considerable pressure against participation, the Dinnyés government rejected the plan, and on August 1, the implementation of the Hungarian Three-Year Plan began. In December 1946 the Central Committee of the HCP had announced an overall plan for the development of the national economy and had put out the directives of the Three-Year Plan for national reconstruction. The plan was endorsed by the leftwing bloc within the National Independence Front and a segment of the Smallholder Party, which made open agitation against the plan by Nagyists futile. Thus, the country embarked on a state-planned economy that, according to the former director of the Agricultural Research Institute, the late Ferenc Erdei, "became a highly effective weapon of socialist transformation."[28] Thereafter the National Planning Office had the right to demand the death sentence for proven sabotage of the plan, and the National Bank gradually assumed control of industry, foreign trade, and savings and loan institutions. By the end of March 1948, 73.8 percent of the industrial workers in Hungary had become state employees.

In the summer of 1947, Hungary made preparations for new parliamentary elections. The communists were so confident of victory that they encouraged all parties to go to the polls on separate lists. They also initiated a new electoral law that disqualified voters who had been convicted of offenses against the republic or against democracy. As a result, six percent of the electorate, or 333,000 persons, lost their right to vote. In comparison to the first national elections, the elections of August 31, 1947, were a fraud. The Hungarian Communist Party, which received almost 23 percent of the vote, became the largest party in Parliament. Its success was due largely to support received from the Soviet army and to such underhanded tactics as stuffing ballot boxes, voting more than one time, and other irregularities. The Smallholder Party received only 15.4 percent of the vote, primarily because after a July split, the party represented only one faction—the leftwing—at the polls.

Two months before the August 31 election, communist authorities had sanctioned the formation of six opposition parties to assure that the anti-Marxist vote would be divided among various factions; these parties were the Independence Party, the Democratic People's Party, the Hungarian Workers' Party (referred to by the communists as the Radical Party), the Freedom Party, the Independent Hungarian Democratic Party, and of course, the Smallholder Party. However, before the election, the rump of the Smallholder Party joined the leftwing coalition. As a result, the opposition parties together received only 1,955,419 or 39 percent of the votes as against 3,042,919 or 61 percent cast for the government groups. The Social Democratic Party polled 14.9 percent and the National Peasant Party 8.3 percent of the electorate.[29] Thus, in the new Parliament, the leftwing bloc held 271 seats whereas the opposition held only 140 seats. In contrast to the 2-to-1 split in the legislature, the new government itself was 100 percent leftwing; the opposition had no representation in it whatsoever. The new regime of the National Independence Front therefore encountered no opposition when it adopted and proceeded to implement the communist program for Hungary's socialist development. Although all major programs were based on parliamentary legislation, government continued to be largely by decree. For example, on March 26, 1948, all factories that had more than 100 employees as of August 1, 1947, were taken over by the state.[30] In fact, this appropriation was the culmination of policies carried out by leftwing members of the SDP under the direction of Árpád Szakasits. First as vicepremier and later as president of the republic, Szakasits was instrumental in converting the National Independence Front into a communist-front organization. Since, in the bipolar system of the National Independence Front government, Social Democrats were the pivotal factor, the anti-communist Smallholders, eager to win Social Democratic support on specific issues (e.g., wage policy, land reform, educational policy, and religious tolerance), were willing to yield to certain Social Democratic demands, even though after November 1947 these demands represented Communist interests.

The postwar Social Democratic Party served both as a catalyst of the communist consolidation of power and as a national unifier in the political arena of new Hungary. Considering the strength of the prewar SDP, especially in the labor movement, the reason for organizing two postwar workers' parties (HCP and SDP), instead of just one, becomes obvious. Because the HCP had been outlawed in August 1919, following the brutalities of the White Terror, the SDP became the only labor outlet for political socialization in Hungary between the two wars.[31] The pre-World War II (or old) SDP ceased to exist during the Nazi occupation of Hungary in 1944. To capture the support of the more than 100,000 union members who had belonged to Social Democratic unions before the war and to prevent rightwing leaders from usurping the potential power of the Social Democrats, leftwing leaders (supported by the Soviet army and the communists) built a new SDP, which in reality became an indispensable tool of communist strategy. Between 1945 and 1948 the voting strength of the SDP fluctuated between 112,000 and 325,000. Without SDP support, communist pressure from above would have been a fiasco and the "peaceful" seizure of power in June 1948, unattainable.[32]

The socialist transformation period between the June 1948 *Gleich-schaltung* and August 20, 1949, when the Constitution of the Hungarian People's Republic was adopted, was effectively used by the communists to win over to their side the "orphans" of capitalism and to consolidate the power of the dictatorship of the proletariat. To achieve these ends, the communists employed the following means: they initiated a new agricultural program, which led to collectivization and the organization of state farms; they expanded the network of state schools and welfare organizations; they converted the National Independence Front into the People's Front of National Independence (which meant replacing the alliance of political parties with mass organizations such as the National Council of Trade Unions, the Federation of Working Youth, and the Hungarian Federation of Democratic Women); they removed all "enemies of the people" from responsible positions in the state; and, on May 15, 1949, they held a new election. This time the single list of candidates of the People's Front received 95.6 percent of the total votes cast (the rest were either opposition votes—about 3 percent—or votes invalidated on technical grounds);[33] thus the election legitimized the power the communists had acquired in May 1947. After May 1949 the road was open for the communists to travel with full speed toward the complete establishment of a monopoly of power in Hungary.

NOTES

1. See F. Fehér, A. Heller, and G. Márkus, *Dictatorship Over Needs* (London: Basil Blackwell, 1983), 260.

2. See James N. Rosenau, "A pre-theory revisited: World politics in an era of cascading interdependence," *International Studies Quarterly* 28 (1984): 245–305.

3. Charles Lindblom, *Politics and Markets: The World's Political–Economic Systems* (New York: Basic Books, 1977), 242.

4. Marx argues that "property" is a mode of inter-human relationship; he therefore rejects undifferentiated human entities as abstract individuals and insists on identifying their real attributes as workers, peasants, or capitalists—in a social context—for it presupposes the division of labor. Hence his aim is to show that production by its very nature relates to inter-human modes of contact. Hence the social contract among the workers/producers.

5. See Mihály Vajda, *The State and Socialism* (London: Allison and Busby, 1981), 74–75.

6. See, for example, Rudolf L. Tökés, "Hungarian reform imperatives," *Problems of Communism* 33 (1984): 1–23.

7. Zvi Gitleman, "The politics of social restoration in Hungary and Czechoslovakia," *Comparative Politics* 13 (1981); 206–207.

8. Jiri Valenta, "Postintervention normalization," in *Communism in Eastern Europe*, edited by Teresa Rakowska-Harmstone (2nd ed.; Bloomington: Indiana University Press, 1984), 347–48.

9. Hungary's territory was actually decreased from 325,000 square miles to 92,607 and her population from 20,900,000 to 7,800,000; Paul Ignotus, *Hungary* (New York: Praeger, 1971), 154.

10. Only 11 percent of the iron ore and 15 percent of the timber supply remained within the new borders. See Ivan T. Berend and György Ránki, eds., *Underdevelopment and Economic Growth: Studies in Hungarian Economic and Social History* (Budapest: Akadémiai Kiadó, 1979), 111.

11. Adapted from Chapter 1 written by this author in Peter A. Toma and Ivan Volgyes, *Politics in Hungary* (W.H. Freeman and Co., 1977), pp. 2–8, and is reprinted here with the permission of the publisher.

12. For comparative figures, see Franz Borkenau, *World Communism: A History of the Communist International* (New York: Norton, 1939), 130.

13. For the aggregate cited data, see Károly Nagy, "The impact of communism in Hungary," *East Europe* 18 (March 1969): 11–17.

14. In 1945 Hungary again lost all of the territory she had regained during World War II.

15. M. Simai and L. Szücs, *Horthy Miklós titkos iratai* [Nicholas Horthy's Secret Documents] (Budapest: Kossuth Könyvkiadó, 1962); and M. Ádám, G. Juhász, and L. Kerekes, *Magyarország és a második világháború* [Hungary and the Second World War] (Budapest: Kossuth Könyvkiadó, 1961.) According to Vincent J. Esposito, *A Concise History of World War II* (New York: Praeger, 1964; p.400), 140,000 Hungarian soldiers were killed during the war.

16. Hugh Seton-Watson, *The East European Revolution* (New York: Praeger, 1961), 105.

17. See Ernst C. Helmreich, ed., *Hungary* (New York: Praeger, 1957), 125–26.

18. Ferenc Erdei et al., eds., *Information Hungary* (New York, London, Budapest: Pergamon Press, 1968), 289.

19. Jenö Lévai, "The war crime trials relating to Hungary," in Randolph L. Braham, ed., *Hungarian Jewish Studies*, Vol. 2 (New York: World Federation of Hungarian Jews, 1969), 253–96.

20. Erdei, *Information Hungary*, 297.

21. R. R. Betts, ed., *Central and South East Europe* (London: Royal Institute of International Affairs, 1950), 291.

22. Erdei, *Information Hungary*, 291.

23. Ibid., 193.

24. H. Seton-Watson, *The East European Revolution*, 193.

25. "The transference of German assets in Hungary to the USSR (see Article 28 of the Hungarian Peace Treaty) meant that the latter also acquired a dominant interest in the development of Hungarian bauxite mining. Hungarian–Soviet companies were founded to monopolize all river and air transport, and the country's oil development...." Betts, *Central and South East Europe*, 109.

26. Erdei, *Information Hungary*, 293–97.

27. Betts, *Central and South East Europe*, 106. See also *The Truth About the Nagy Affair* (New York: Praeger, 1959); and H. Seton-Watson, *The East European Revolution*, 199. Seton-Watson erroneously claims that Kovács died in prison.

28. Erdei, *Information Hungary*, 297. Cf. György Ránki, *Magyarország gazdasága az elsö 3 éves terv idöszakában* [Hungary's Economy During the First Three-Year Plan] (Budapest: Közgazdasági es Jogi Könyvkiadó, 1963).

29. See Bennet Kovrig, *Communism in Hungary. From Kun to Kádár* (Stanford: Hoover Institution Press, 1979), 218.

30. Erdei, *Information Hungary*, pp. 297–298. See also Betts, *Central and South East Europe*, p. 110.

31. See Miklós Lackó, *Ipari munkásságunk összetételének alakulaśa 1867–1949* [The Formation of Our Industrial Workers' Movement, 1867–1949] (Budapest: Akadémiai Kiadó, 1961); and C.A. Macartney, *October Fifteenth: A History of Modern Hungary, 1929–1945*, 2 vols. (Edinburgh: Edinburgh University Press, 1957 and 1961).

32. Erdei, *Information Hungary*, 298. See also Stephen D. Kertész, "The methods of communist conquest: Hungary 1944–47," *World Politics* 3 (October 1950): 20–54; Jozsef Révai, "The character of a people's democracy," *Foreign Affairs* 28 (October 1949): 143–52; U.S. House of Representatives, 80th Congress, Select Committee on Communist Aggression, Special Report No. 10, *Communist Takeover and Occupation of Hungary* (Washington: D.C., GPO, 1948).

33. *Magyar Nemzet* (May 18, 1949).

PART I
REAL VERSUS IMAGINARY
SOCIAL CONTRACT

1
Socialist Democracy and Socialist Authority

Currently the Hungarian elite is attempting to rediscover the "democratic" and "humanistic" elements of Marxist socialism while maintaining its loyalty to the Leninist principles of authoritarianism. The road to developed socialism, conditioned by Marxist-Leninist ideology and Hungarian realities, is paved with terra incognita and thus experimentation is a common phenomenon, recalling a British cliché, "muddling through." There are dialogues about "socialist democracy," "pluralism," "grassroots participation in decision making," even the abandonment of the "monopoly of power" by the party. Hungarian socialist theory is being scrutinized not only by "outsiders" in a quiet way, but by the "insiders" (communist ideologues) as well.

Since for Marx, communist society will be determined by the specific conditions under which it is established, and these conditions cannot be predicted in advance, Marx's sketches of future society are few and open to interpretation. He said practically nothing about the way in which the transformation from capitalism to communism will occur. Marx's discussions of future society are austere and restrained. This limitation is imposed on Marx by his own epistemological premises and, of course, the fact that his analysis of capitalism dealt with a nineteenth instead of a twentieth century population in a different stage of development. Consequently it was Lenin who took it upon himself to fill the existing gap and therefore he formulated certain ideas but only about the first stage of socialist development—the dictatorship of the proletariat. Although he considered himself a true disciple of Marx, critics charge that Lenin turned Marxism upside down with his modifications and manipulations, making the political aspects of communist theory primary and socioeconomic issues secondary.

It should be made clear that the concept of socialism represents the only political philosophy acceptable to the Hungarian regime, which professes to base its policies, strategies, and tactics on the principles of Marxism-Leninism. According to these principles, the Hungarian Socialist Workers' Party (HSWP) is the leading and guiding force of Hungarian society and the nucleus of its political system and all state and public organizations. Its members are known as Communists and as such have pledged their support to communist comrades at home and abroad. They are committed to defend and promote the principles of Hungarian socialist theory.

THE IDEAS OF MARX AND LENIN

Before we can address the issue of socialist theory in Hungary, it is imperative to identify—at least in a simplified fashion—the ideas of its principal founders: Karl Marx and Vladimir Ilyich Ulyanov, better known as Lenin.[1]

The theories of Marx revolve around two fundamental themes: the primacy of human productive activity, in the course of which one comes to interact with oneself, with other human beings, and with nature; and the materialist conception of history, also known as dialectical materialism—a phrase coined by his collaborator and benefactor, Friedrich Engels. While the first theme focuses on the condition of the individual (as "species being") and his relationship to labor, productivity, creativity, and alienation, the second concentrates on the condition of society and such concepts as substructure versus superstructure, division of labor, class, and class conflict.

Human beings, states Marx, are by nature driven to productivity: they *must* work, they *must* produce. Labor, defined by Marx as productivity and creativity, is the very essence of human personality. One expresses oneself, realizes oneself, in one's labor; to put it differently, one lives one's life in one's labor. As such, labor, productivity, and creativity represent the epitome of human fulfillment. They are not to be seen as burden or drudgery. According to Marx, labor is an expression of human personality; as such, it should be a voluntary expression. Accordingly, in the ideal society—a society of economic abundance and no surplus value—human beings, Marx asserted, should have freedom to express themselves as they see fit and as they please.

Throughout history, according to Marx, labor has involved compulsion and force because of the clashing interests in the mode of production; the productive and creative personality has been exploited, oppressed, dispossessed, and brutalized. In other words, throughout the historical development of capitalism human creativity has led to human alienation. Marx argued that the reason man is alienated from the activity of his own labor is the fact that man engages in forced labor, which is an act against human nature. Therefore, in Marx's view, in order to be human one must labor voluntarily. Marx maintained that under capitalism, man has been alienated from the products of his own labor. The main reason, again, is that man's productive activity is no longer voluntary self-activity, man is no longer a creative being; according to Marx, he is forced to sell his labor for the production of commodities. Marx also maintained that under capitalism man is alienated from other human beings who come together to form society because *forced labor* transforms society into a collection of individuals—all production robots. Finally, because of forced labor, man is alienated from nature; nature, too, is exploited and ravaged for someone else's advantage or profit. In summary, then, Marx argued that there is a fundamental gap between human essence—voluntary productive activity—and human existence—forced and alienated labor. Hence, the only solution to the problem of dehumanization, according to Marx, is revolution. Marx's assumption was that the elimination of alienation would return man to an ideal condition of voluntary and spontaneous productivity and creativity. Insofar as man is a "productive being," he is a reflection of the economic system in which he finds himself. Hence, to change man, one must change the economic foundation of society.

All human society, according to Marx, has two main components: a substructure and a superstructure. The substructure consists of material, economic forces that are institutionalized and therefore constitute the "social relations of production." The material, economic forces are not only the most important in human society, but they also determine the shape of the superstructure, which consists of all other aspects of society: politics, ideologies, ideas, religion, art, and culture. The superstructure, therefore, is secondary and derivative, reflecting as it does the substructure upon which it rests, which in turn represents the interests of the ruling class.

According to Marx's materialist interpretation, each stage of history is characterized by a distinct mode of production, a distinct set of classes, and conflict among those classes. In each phase of history, therefore, the primary means of social change is class struggle culminating in revolution. What is unique about the proletarian (world) revolution (which, by the way, is according to Marx *spontaneous* and will occur only when world capitalism has exhausted itself and brought about its own self-destruction) is that it leads to the abolition of private ownership of the means of production—and hence of class, class struggle, and the state.

Following a short period of the dictatorship of the proletariat, the transition of a classless society is completed; mankind, we are told, reaches a utopia of harmony, peace, and abundance.

Since it is not our task here to examine whether or not Marx's ideas are riddled with serious fallacies, or whether or not Marx's scientific principles are idealistic expressions of wishful thinking, let us now turn to the main ideas of V.I. Lenin and examine his contribution to socialist theory in Hungary.

Repeatedly invoking Marx's own dictum that "theory is a guide to action," Lenin made a series of concrete changes in Marxist doctrine. He modified Marx's interpretation of history by adding a substage called "imperialism"; he changed Marx's concept of world revolution to a protracted revolution in both advanced and developing countries; he rejected Marx's idea of spontaneity by insisting on the vanguard of the proletariat, namely the communist party; and he modified Marx's concept of the state by stipulating the necessity for a "socialist political apparatus." Let us explain.

In 1916, Lenin, in *Imperialism: The Highest Stage of Capitalism,* offered an explanation of why, contrary to Marx's expectations, capitalism had not collapsed. Lenin's central thesis was that, unforeseen by Marx, capitalism had undergone a basic transformation by becoming international in scope. National capitalism, in other words, had not collapsed because it had broadened its scope by becoming international, that is, imperialist. Thus, imperialism for Lenin was synonymous with "international capitalism." Having exhausted the domestic markets, according to Lenin, capitalism turns to international markets. This is accomplished by the capitalist state through colonization. The capitalist search for colonies, according to Lenin, is bound to lead to a series of wars and conflicts, which will mark the collapse of capitalism. According to Lenin, there will be wars between capitalist states and the peoples of the colonies who at some point in time will rise in armed stages to overthrow their foreign oppressors. The socialist countries, whose emergence Lenin saw over the horizon, as it were, will render full support to the peoples of the colonies. There will be, of course, said Lenin, wars among the capitalist powers themselves because as time goes on there will be less and less to colonize. These conflicts and wars then, Lenin prophesied, will bring about the end of capitalism. Lenin's concept of imperialism, therefore, altered Marx's idea of a world proletarian revolution caused by economic factors—and, in a protracted way, by allowing for the occurrence of proletarian revolutionary movements in developing countries (where the economic conditions for revolution are absent), promoted revolutions that are carried out by political means only.

According to Lenin, there are *two* types of communist revolutions: those occurring in advanced capitalist countries and those occurring in underdeveloped colonial lands. In both types, it is the role of the "vanguard of the proletariat"—the communist party—to organize, mobilize, and lead the discontented masses against the capitalist ruling class. Communist revolutions in less-developed countries go through two stages of development. The first stage, called "bourgeois-democratic," involves the alliance of the proletariat (meaning the leadership of the communist party) with all social forces, classes, and groups that for whatever reason oppose imperialism. In other words, communists form a "united front" with all social strata that, inspired by nationalists and democratic sentiments, oppose the status quo. It should be pointed out that with Lenin, the exploitation of the nationalist sentiment in the service of communism becomes a hallmark of communist theory and practice.

Having engineered a bourgeois-democratic revolution and having consolidated sufficient power, the second stage of the Leninist proletarian revolution is set in motion. The proletariat now turns on its former allies, persecutes and eliminates them and thus, through the "proletarian-socialist" revolution, the communist party takes over the reins of government.

The communist party, according to Lenin, is the only instrument capable of bringing political consciousness to the proletariat. It is the only instrument capable of organizing, mobilizing, and leading the proletariat in the political and armed struggle as well as in the legal and illegal struggle. Although elitist in nature, the communist party cannot separate itself from the masses; the party must appeal to their self-interest and emotions, persuade them to identify the party's interest as their own, rally them to the cause, draw them to revolutionary action, deploy and coordinate their energies toward the realization of revolutionary objectives. Lenin, like Marx, believed that man's personal outlook and identity can be changed during the course of socialist development from the dominant role of national-ethnic or religious associations to economic class identification—more specifically, to the class of toilers, or the proletariat.

The party must have cohesion, solidarity, discipline, control, and above all, *unquestioned command and leadership.* Factionalism and dissent cannot be permitted or tolerated. The party, therefore, is a monolithic organization. Any minority views or challenges to leadership the party must not allow—the party must periodically purge itself of all "opportunist" and "deviationist" elements.

At the social level, the Leninist principle governing party organization is "democratic-centralism." The centralism of this concept means a rigid hierarchy extending from the top to the bottom. The lines of authority (running downward) and of responsibility (running upward) are inflexible and absolute. Every higher level has absolute authority over every lower level and every lower level is absolutely responsible to every higher level. The "democracy" part of democratic centralism suggests that at each level, party members have an opportunity to engage in discussion and debate before decisions are made. In effect, however, all decisions for any one level of the party organization are made by party leaders at the immediately higher level. Parenthetically, it can be argued that "democracy" is simply a means of creating an illusion of participation and decision making, thereby keeping party members pacified, if not content.

Because of the protracted nature of the proletarian revolution, Lenin departed from Marx to argue that the state as a political apparatus will continue to exist after the dictatorship of the proletariat has been completed. Besides, Lenin argued, socialism in the world was still threatened by the multitude of capitalist states. However, even after the conquest of world capitalism, Lenin argued, the construction of a communist society of abundance, too, requires the political power of the state. Thus the state as an oppressive organ does not wither away, as Marx argued.

Although Lenin considered himself a loyal disciple of Marx, he changed Marx's ideas so drastically that some of his contemporaries accused him of establishing the dictatorship over, rather than of, the proletariat and of ruthlessly disregarding Marxist analysis of economic forces. Thus the changes Lenin introduced are viewed by some as an abandonment of Marx; but others view them as a development of Marx (e.g., contemporary ideologues in socialist countries —hence their reference to "Marxism-Leninism").

Lenin viewed the Marxist call for spontaneous and successful risings of the oppressed against the oppressors as weak and untenable and, therefore, replaced it with the political formula of protracted revolutions led by the communist party. Economic analysis was important to Lenin, to be sure, but far more important were such political considerations as class alliance and united front, leadership, and organization of the party, socialist state, and socialist construction. Although in theory the social base of Leninism is internationalist, in practice, however, Lenin turned Marxism into a national enterprise, and as such there is as much friction between communist countries today as there is between any other groups.

HUNGARIAN THEORY OF SOCIALISM

What has been stated so far about Marx's and Lenin's ideas of socialism is also inherent in Hungarian socialism, which for the purposes of harmony and allegiance to the USSR and other socialist countries in the world functions under the label of "Marxism-Leninism." As alluded to in the Introduction, our task in this book is to examine Hungarian socialism only insofar as the ramifications of the issue of socialist authority in Hungary are concerned; therefore, only those aspects of socialist theory that have relevance to the issue of socialist authority will be discussed in this chapter. In this regard, Marx's labor theory of value will be important in our consideration; so will the principles of substructure and superstructure in Hungarian society. However, the Hungarian interpretation of Lenin's ideas about party monopoly, class alliance, united front, and socialist construction will reign supreme.

At the outset we should point out that all reasoning, argumentation, and explanation of issues by Hungarian writers concerning socialism are couched in references and documentations to Marx and Lenin; therefore, it would be difficult to identify any of the writings and pronouncements by members of the Hungarian elite as original ideas. What is original about them is the formulation of the issues confronting Hungarian society today and the interpretation of Marxism-Leninism as ideological tenets providing the answers to these challenges and problems. For the same reason, any definitions of Hungarian socialism are simply reflections of Marxism-Leninism. Because Lenin regarded social ownership of the means of production as the backbone of socialism, most Hungarian ideologues use this explanation as a key to operationalize their definition of socialism. For example, György Aczél, head of the HSWP Institute of Social Sciences and a member of the Politburo, is of the opinion that "a society can be called socialist when a new political system and mechanism come into being on the basis of the new conditions of ownership."[2] Or, as Valéria Benke, a former member of the party's Politburo and editor-in-chief of *Társadalmi Szemle* (the theoretical journal of HSWP) states, "Socialism is a system which ultimately promotes equality of society, in the division of labor and the distribution of incomes as well as in the style of living and culture."[3] What is inherent in all definitions is the fact that the historical objective of socialism remains the welfare of workers and the material, intellectual, political, and moral progress of the people. Hence the Hungarian socialist leaders begin with the assumption that "perfect, complete Marxism does not, cannot, and will never exist,"[4] and therefore theory is subject to adaptation to realities, or, in Aczél's own words, "the teaching of Marxism-Leninism is implemented in every area of life always according to the specific needs of the Hungarian situation."[5]

Socialist theory in Hungary starts out with the assumption that "socialism is not complete, and by its nature, it will never be; it is still a system in a stage of becoming, in the process of formation and continuous evolution."[6] Hungary's socialist development is in transition from a stage of intermediary economic development to a stage of building "developed socialism" or, as György Aczél put it, "to switch from extensive industrial development to the intensive development of the economy." This new stage of socialist development requires new methods and approaches from both the superstructure and the substructure of the Hungarian society. It demands inventiveness, independence, increased and improved productivity, a higher degree of organization, a favorable attitude toward innovation, and greater risk-taking on the part of socialist enterprises. From government authorities it requires a clear definition of specific goals and improvement of the system of regulating economic management, education and training, the cultural processes, and guidance of research and development activities.

Developed socialism also requires a radical rearrangement of factors of production. Whereas during the stage of industrialization the focus of economic policy has been on investment projects and the supply of raw materials and energy, the new stage of socialist development focuses on the human resource—its quality—which constitutes the social relation of production. The latter presupposes substantial transformation in conscience, in living conditions, and in work habits of the members of Hungarian society. In other words, the emphasis during the stage of developed socialism is on *qualitative* improvement of working conditions and moral ways of life of the people in Hungary. Since there are no specific guidelines for this stage of development that can serve as points of reference, similar to the previous stages of socialist development, Hungary is cautiously probing and experimenting with new ideas tailored to Hungarian realities but always justified (or rationalized) by quotations from Marx and Lenin. As the following chapters indicate, while Hungary faces many and serious problems, the country is well balanced today, and most people in Hungary enjoy a relatively better lifestyle than their counterparts in other countries of the socialist community.

Another assumption of socialist theory in Hungary is that the achievement and problems of socialist development must be examined within the context of internal and external changes and challenges to Hungarian political and economic practice. In other words, developed socialism or intensive economic development in Hungary, as the next stage, is also very much dependent on world economic development, and therefore Hungary, like all socialist countries, must be interested in overcoming, not aggravating, the current world economic crises. Not to do so would mean to slow down the process of socialist development and encounter more serious problems on the road toward that goal. "Socialist countries whose world economic contacts are considerable have proved sensitive to the crises of the capitalist world economy"[7] because these crises have coincided with the switch to intensive economic development in the socialist economies, and this has made it necessary to stop unprofitable production and start on speedy transformation of the structure of production. This transformation is made more difficult by the need to adjust to more unfavorable terms of trade and intensified competition. Moreover, "since we have got over the illusions that socialism can finally outstrip its rival [capitalism] within a short time, we are also aware that 'peaceful coexistence' and cooperation will be part of an operational historical program as long as antagonistically opposed social systems exist."[8]

Hungarian ideologues are in agreement that Hungary's present problems and difficulties are caused in large part by external economic conditions—exports and the pricing system in the international market—that have changed abruptly, and that therefore Hungary's economic policies and work style must change respectively to meet those challenges. Not to do so spells a disaster similar to what has occurred in Poland, where "distortion in economic policy triggered the political crisis of 1980 because the former leadership failed to react at the right time to the changes in the world market."[9] Thus the plea by some theoreticians is for widening the base of "socialist democracy," which, they believe, would lead to more efficient economic management and more effective decision making by government authorities.[10]

Although democratic centralism is fundamental to communist party leadership, the ruling elite of the Hungarian society argues that "democracy must be extended and not restricted."[11] What Aczél and others mean by this is improved flexibility among decision makers, more efficiency and competitiveness among managerial groups, and a closer relationship between HSWP and the masses of workers organized in trade unions and other social strata under the umbrella of the "united front." Having learned from the lessons of the period of the "personality cult" and the suppression of the counterrevolution of 1956, the party, we are reminded, "knowingly builds on control by the masses and consistently strives to subject itself, or rather its decisions, to mass control."[12] It is frequently pointed out that while the party leads in socialist construction, socialism cannot be the cause of the members of HSWP alone. Nonparty members, according to Hungarian socialist theory, may fill any office or function in the state apparatus except party offices. 'Democracy' is perceived as a comprehensive exchange of views and participation in 'society-framing-action' (not authoritative decision making) by working masses, public opinion, party members, and those who are not—in party and mass organizations, in parliament and the local government councils, in the forums of shop-floor democracy, in various trade unions and professional associations, and in the entire system of institutions of this [Hungarian] society.[13] In other words, in the newest stage of socialist development, "democracy" has been expanded so the political system can recognize and deal with the various diverging—and in some cases conflicting—interests and views prevailing in contemporary Hungarian society. This type of socialist democracy is still *centralized,* but within the context of new socialist values: "the party and Marxism-Leninism enjoy no monopoly but hegemony. However, hegemony is not less than monopoly."[14] This implies the recognition that Hungarian society is not ideologically homogeneous, that there is ideological diversity, but at the same time it also means that the party and the ideology of Marxism-Leninism are the only institution and ideology playing a decisive role in the authoritative decision-making process. Or we can state the problem this way: If Hungarian society has an ideology—as it does: Marxism-Leninism—then that ideology serves socialism and holds a hegemonic position.

Democracy also implies that the credibility and survival of Marxism-Leninism in the present stage of developed socialism in Hungary is dependent on constant pulse-taking of the mood of the social strata and on frequent debates with groups of different persuasions. The task of the ruling elite is not more law enforcement, but speedy response to public opinion and more effective use of persuasion toward their critics in a complex society. It is for this reason that HSWP has intensified its policy of alliances in this ideologically heterogeneous Hungarian society. The famous slogan by the secretary general and chairman of the Politburo of the Central Committee of HSWP, János Kádár—"He who is not against us is with us"[15]—serves as an imperative for the party to cooperate with all those who—irrespective of their way of thinking—are not opposed to the socialist system, accept its constitutional order, and contribute their labor to the building of a socialist society—*even if their opinions on a whole range of subjects differ*. Of course, just as centralism controls democracy, the supremacy (or hegemony) of the party and its ideology are nonnegotiable. Or as György Aczél succinctly put it: "Let no one expect us to treat as allies those who, counting on the deterioration of our situation, aim to undermine our achievements and trample on our laws."[16]

Perhaps the most baffling principle of the Hungarian theory of socialism is labor value and the distribution of income. According to the ruling elite, the equalization of incomes is not only a matter of policy but a characteristic tendency that expresses itself in the lessening of income differences among the various social groups as well as between the rural and urban populations in Hungary. As part of the "socialist achievement," the equalization of incomes during the last twenty years has closed the gap between the highest and the lowest earnings from sixfold to fourfold.[17] However, it has also been realized that leveling of incomes is not an effective incentive for improving work performance—instead it has undermined worker morale. Hence it became apparent that the Marxist dictum—to each according to his production—should be the sole consideration if the goal of developed socialism is to create incentives for better and more efficient work. The result of the application of this formula, however, while leading to new incentives for better work habits, has also led to higher rewards and the accumulation of wealth and affluence, resulting in increased inequality. Does this mean, then, that the equalization process, inherent in the theory of socialism, has come to a halt or possibly is reversing itself? Or is the "socialist" principle of equality being reinterpreted or even replaced with new concepts that can be adjusted to the new "realities"? It appears that the answer to both questions is negative. The HSWP and its ruling elite are still committed to equality as a basic tenet of socialism; however, they are equally cognizant of present realities and thus are searching for solutions that will make them look credible in the eyes of both the members of the party and the highly motivated consumers in socialist Hungary. To reduce and properly regulate inequalities due to income differences within certain strata is, according to Valéria Benke, a task for social policy. Consequently the solution is "to strengthen the elements of interestedness to the detriment of forms of allotting," supplemented by a "social subsidy which takes into account, first of all, the number of dependents and the decisive influence on the situation of families."[18] All this, however, according to Benke, requires greater autonomy for the local councils and the implementation of socialist democracy. In any case, economic autonomy must also be strengthened because the real solution to the problem can only be a program of economic development.

Similar ideas were expressed by István Hetényi, minister of finance, when he cautioned that "with the increasing stress on efficiency in current economic thinking one can expect that some socialist tenets will continue to be ignored or reinterpreted. Supplying the population with more and better goods and services remains one of the basic targets of economic policy...."[19] The question arises whether or not increased differentiation of incomes and property ownership, brought about mainly through the encouragement of private enterprise, destroys the socialist means of ownership and hence reintroduces capitalism? According to Iván T. Berend, a prominent economist, the answer is no looking back into the past, Berend acknowledges that the opposite course—elimination of the differentiated market—certainly did not contribute to the strengthening of socialist values. On the contrary, the lack of goods led to corruption and to the defenselessness of consumers. The directed economy resulted in the wasting of materials and made bad quality the price for fulfilling the plan. This economic policy hurt basic social and human norms. Thus it was not so much the principles of socialism that were attacked by the economic reforms, which began in 1968, but the image of socialism that Hungary created. This image "did not adapt to changed circumstances adequately."[20] After quoting the appropriate passages from the *German Ideology* of Marx and Engels, Berend makes the following observations:

Thus we act according to the principles of socialism not by taking the course of penurious equalization but by keeping the development of an advanced state of productive forces by not allowing our economy to lag behind, and by creating the conditions for a new prosperity. Abstract principles and moral norms cannot be compared with reality. The socialist future can only be built upon the demands and conditions of reality.[21]

It would seem, therefore, that the stumbling block to the establishment of the limits of economic and political freedom within the framework of ideological constraints of Marxism-Leninism in Hungary are the perceptions and interpretations of "realities" as a guide to theory and practice. A good example of this dilemma facing Hungarian policymakers is the role of personal and private property in developed socialism. Both of these lead to ownership of the means of production by individuals rather than the state. Personal property includes objects belonging to a range of personal consumption and utilization such as a family house or a recreation home. Private property consists of entrepreneurial forms of production, such as restaurants, small farms, stores, artisans, and so forth. This ideological differentiation of the individual's property has given rise to an increasing number of contradictions both in practice and in legal regulations.[22] Private property encompasses a large group who contribute a large percentage to the national economy: approximately three-quarters of Hungarian families participate in these activities, and share in their income. In present-day Hungary, consumer goods, as typical objects of personal property, are derived to a considerable extent not from social industry but from various private enterprises. It is paradoxical, therefore, that both private and personal ownership are legally restricted—it doesn't make great legal or political sense. Eliminating this duality, according to Lajos Vekas, a prominent Hungarian jurist, would "remove uncertainty, and thus the property of individuals would be returned—without restrictions—to the mainstream of social production."[23] It should also be pointed out that the "second economy," a designation frequently used for means of production owned by individuals rather than the state, realizes successfully the Marxist principle of distribution according to work done, in the sense that in this sector performance does not adjust to the lowest achievable income, but rather an increase in income follows more work done. In the socialist sector, however, the differentiation of wages according to work done is present only in a limited way; and all this leads to indifference, withholding of performance, and low productivity.[24] Or, according to Valéria Benke, "Social equilibrium cannot be maintained by equalizing what should not be equalized. One must not equalize the situation of a well-managed business with that of a loss-making one, the position of a man who does good work with that of one who just works. This obstructs solutions to economic problems and diminishes the scale of value in people's eyes."[25]

The attitude toward work is not only a socialist value, as we have gleaned from the writings of Marxism-Leninism, but also a matter of economic and social justice inasmuch as it relates to such attitudinal questions as the relationship between individuals and groups and their achievement and social status. In other words, what are the mutually satisfying relationships between the various elements of society and society itself? The phenomena primarily manifest themselves in monetary terms, because it is basically the spirit of entrepreneurship that covertly moves every social system and every social group. It is not usually expressed in such blatant terms as "what do I have to offer this world and what do I get in return?" "What is my social status?" In Hungary today the key question is: How much direct or indirect recognition does the individual or group receive from society in exchange for their performance? This issue necessitates the creation of a system of measurement (not in a physical-chemical sense, but rather in a societal sense) and institutions that faithfully and justly evaluate what every individual is offering to society in physical and intellectual achievements. Although Soviet theoreticians experimented with different formulas, the measuring of human achievement remains an unsolved task in the socialist community. As a result there is still a low level of effectiveness in work performed and a relative retardation of economic efficiency in socialist countries. The reasoning by the members of socialist economies is very simplistic: everyone is supported by the marketplace. The results are obvious: everyone expects similar values in return for the value of his work. If, however, there is no method available to measure the value of work (performance), then a high degree of injustice will result. Hence it is not unusual to find Hungarians sitting in the neighborhood tavern talking about their work—comparing their working conditions, their performances, and their wages. Afterward they will walk away, saying "This is not right. "X" is not working harder, he is not smarter, and he is no more involved in his job than I am—how come he is getting paid some 2,000 forints more than I? This is not right!" As Hungarian citizens working in state enterprises realize more and more vividly that there are problems concerning the assessment of achievement, they increasingly want to partake of society's wealth without regard to their own participation in the work. Instead, they develop mediocrity in performance, which then results in mediocrity throughout society. Many workers in state enterprises feel that they are paid just for being there. Thus no one works very hard, no one works very slowly or very badly, there is simply a certain conformity, which, according to the ruling elite, goes against the basic principles of socialism. Although what makes today's socialist system in Hungary legitimate is that it is socioeconomically based on the principle of distribution in accordance with performance (achievement), the largest group in stratified Hungarian society asserts that today's Hungary does not guarantee that the members of this group can work efficiently and utilize their talents fully, mainly because the state is unable to acknowledge and compensate for their talents and their performance. This is especially true with the young intellectuals. Paradoxically, their talents and abilities are on a high level while their rewards are very low. Not surprising, their work performance often suffers. In spite of this, young intellectuals are still relatively optimistic and patient. The same can be said of most of the population, because they witness a certain development that, albeit slowly, has begun to take Hungary away from archaic reality toward modernization. They are confident that the ruling elite will be able to maneuver the economic mechanism in such a way that the three factors—ability, effective achievement, and compensation—will coincide with each other and will do so at a higher level. The present problem is *not* that the Hungarians work hard and receive little compensation for their work, but rather that they do not work hard and for that amount of work they receive very poor pay. This results in dissatisfaction prevailing throughout, from the low-paid beginners to the pensioners. The dissatisfied elements are not angered by the fact that a bricklayer or other craftsman earns ten times as much as they do, as long as they see that there is a certain degree of "business ethics" operating in society, and the consumer is not cheated. What angers them is the fact that their work is not properly compensated.

There are also contradictions of another, more sensitive sort. János Kádár and his colleagues are the only communist leaders in Eastern Europe who have admitted that a contradiction exists between the party's attempt "to retain a monopoly of power" and their wish for an economic system that functions effectively. They have concluded that the 8 percent of the population belonging to the HSWP cannot insist on controlling the rest of the country.[26] According to Janez Stanic, a prominent Yugoslav expert on Eastern Europe, the implementation of the Hungarian New Economic Mechanism had "quite logically" led to the admission that a reform of the political system was needed, since economic reforms could not be separated from political ones. As a result "these two kinds of reforms began overlapping in the early 1980s" when worldwide economic stagnation compelled East European leaders to rethink their own economic reforms.[27] According to Stanic, both Leonid Brezhnev and Yuri Andropov had approved of the reformist trends in Eastern European countries.

These findings by Stanic, however, are only partially true. In an address to the 13th HSWP Congress, on March 26, 1985, CPSU Politburo member and Central Committee Secretary Gregorii Romanov (who, by the way, was eased out in June 1985 from both positions by his rival Mikhail Gorbachev) failed formally to endorse Hungary's economic reform. Instead he called for closer economic and political ties with the

Soviet Union and the COMECON (or CMEA) countries and warned that closer economic ties with the West could be used to put pressure on communist states and interfere in their internal affairs.[28]

As far as "political pluralism" is concerned, that, too, was dispelled by György Aczél in his keynote address at the HSWP's national conference on January 12, 1983, when he rejected "those who wish to force on us— as a sort of formula for salvation—the ideas, structures, forms of the political pluralism of classical bourgeois societies which reached crisis point long ago."[29] However, Aczél and his colleagues left the door open by reasserting the party's commitment to "the growth of socialist democracy and its vitality" and the freedom of social criticism in the country: "We do not expect intellectual life and agitprop to provide a veneer that will cover up and hush up the contradictions of socialism: we need a critical analysis of past and present realities...."[30]

It should be obvious from the preceding pages that after the fiasco of the period of personality cult and the counterrevolution of 1956, the Hungarian elite had two options to follow: First, to restore and continue with the repressive mode of the dictatorship of the proletariat or, secondly, to introduce the rule of the so-called "collective leadership" and thus lead to gradual improvement of economic, social, and political conditions in the name of socialist construction in Hungary. For obvious reasons, the Kádár group (put in power by Moscow rather than Budapest) opted for the second course. Consequently, by 1968, after thorough preparations, the New Economic Mechanism (NEM) was introduced, bringing not only unprecedented economic improvements but also creating new demands for changes in the socialist development in Hungary. The aims of the engineers of this program gradually changed from seeking equalization to qualitative improvements in lifestyle in Hungary. The old socialist values of the right to security, work, culture, and peace, as well as to distribution according to work and to social allowances added to family incomes, have recently been amended by the new values of incentives and socialist democracy. The two are inseparable from each other "because the functions of socialist democracy include the recognition of individual and group interests, promoting their expression, the conciliations of interests and the forming of compromise so as to establish the cooperation required by common aims and tasks together with the right of collectives to reconcile their interests to the public interest."[31] Political authority in Hungary today is seeking a synthesis (or a compromise, but not in the Western sense) of activities whose purpose is to create an equilibrium (or reconciliation, through the workings of the HSWP) between self-contradictions and tensions prevailing in Hungarian society. The ruling elite, guaranteeing certain conditions for the people in the process of building developed socialism, finds itself in a dilemma of making good on some of the old values of socialist construction, such as to provide security and protection to work, when, as Valéria Benke writes, "... it is wrong to apply protection to a degree which has a consequence that we have protected bad products, unorganized work and poor management."[32]

The key questions yet to be answered are: Who creates the new system of values in the stage of building developed socialism? How many interests can exist in a "one class" socialist state and how should they be prioritized according to the teachings of Marxism-Leninism? And how to democratize power and enable citizens to share in it?" According to Kálmán Kulcsár, head of a coordinated research project in 1979 describing the types of lifestyle present in Hungary, the new system of values designed to cope with the existing contradictions should be produced by "society as a whole."[33] On the other hand, Valéria Benke assigns this task to the authoritative local and national policymakers. The problem is further compounded by the sheer fact that the distribution and execution of power rests solely in the hands of the members of the HSWP, although in theory "all power" has been in the hands of the "people" rather than in the hands of the "party."[34] For 8 percent of Hungary's population (the membership of the HSWP) to insist on controlling 92 percent is, according to Sándor Lakos, editor-in-chief of *Pártélet (Party Life)*, a detriment to the efficient functioning of the economic system in Hungary. What is needed, in Lakos' opinion, is for the party to continue to direct social developments but the party must become its own rival in the transmission of the work. Like Benke, Lakos recommends that "various governmental institutions should be encouraged and strengthened by the party to play an independent role." Since these institutions should represent the public views, their tasks should also be "to criticise the work of the party." Lakos is opposed to the creation of several parties. The most important thing to Lakos is that "different interests be properly represented through the entire political system when decisions are made."[35] A practical example of Lakos' proposals is the recent change in Hungary's electoral system referred to by László Hegedüs, secretary of the Hungarian People's Front, as a measure synonymous with the democratization process. At least two candidates for one seat must be permitted and the recall of deputies "who do not work well" is permissible. The aim, according to Hegedüs, is not only "to promote competition of views."[36] This kind of competition, as we have previously pointed out, is congruent with the basic ideas of socialism and has nothing in common with the bourgeois type of political pluralism because only interests "not opposed to socialism" are acceptable to the ruling elite. In this respect, the Hungarian parliament has failed to fulfill the role of a truly representative body. Since the overwhelming membership in the parliament consists of party members, it is doubtful that the interests of the constituencies are truly represented when these interests are quite often in conflict with the interests of the party. It is fair, therefore, to ask: Are the interests of the voters even voiced in the chambers of the Hungarian parliament? A similar concern, to permit the free expression and representation of organized groups in Hungary in order to strengthen and bring greater efficiency to economic reform was expressed by representatives of the labor unions. For example, Már- ton Búza, director of the Research Institute of Hungarian Labor Unions, claims "that instead of party transmission belts, the labor unions should become an equal partner of the state." This would presume closer con- sultation with labor union leaders and in all controversial matters the party would make final decisions. In other words, the party should retain its "leading role" but must abandon its "monopoly of power."[37]

SOCIALIST AUTHORITY

Neither Marx nor Lenin dealt explicitly with the subject of "author- ity."[38] Of course they were not sociologists or political scientists—they were revolutionaries; hence, their major concern was capitalist exploi- tation and their goal the destruction of the world capitalist system. Never- theless, there are some oblique references made by both to the concept of "authority," which in their articulation was frequently associated with such concepts as force, coercion, power, influence, leadership, subor- dination, sovereignty, and so on.

Marx distinguished between "sovereign political authority" under a bourgeois state, which could not under any circumstances be considered "rightful authority," and "enlightened order" that prevails in a "factory of the future" under the dictatorship of the proletariat, which is just and humane and, therefore, nontyrannical.[39] In other words, according to Marx, the state, which was the oppressive organ for maintaining the rule of one class over another (the bourgeoisie over the proletariat), entailed coercive power (authority) that after the world revolution would be eliminated along with the exploiting class (the bourgeoisie) and con- sequently replaced by an adminstrative organ of power (authority) that would be maintained by one friendly class, the proletariat. Hence, Marx's concept of authority (power) in the pre-revolutionary era is diametrically opposed to authority in the post-revolutionary period. When the capi- talists have disappeared, when there are no classes—when there is no distinction between the members of society as regards their relation to the social means of production—then both the state and political au- thority wither away. The same idea of withering away was expressed by Lenin. However, he went a little further to elaborate on the conditions that would follow after "the state ceases to exist." In Lenin's view

Only then will a truly complete democracy become possible . . . and only then will democracy begin to wither away, owing to the simple fact that, freed from capitalist slavery, from the untold horrors, savagery, absurdities and infamies of capitalist exploitation, people will gradually become accustomed to observing the elementary rules of social intercourse...they will become accustomed to observing them without force, without coercion, without subordination, *without the special apparatus* for coercion called the state.[40]

What Lenin is implying is that in this "process" of transition the people in socialist societies will develop a "habit of obedience" in a peaceful, voluntary fashion that will replace the authority of the state machinery. The ultimate stage of this developmental process is, according to Lenin, the withering away of complete democracy.[41]

Engels deviates from Marx's views, first by stating that a revolution represents "transfer of authority" and not its abolition; secondly, he argues, authority is not an absolute evil and by the same token autonomy is not an absolute good. "Authority and autonomy are relative things whose spheres vary with the various phases of the development of society."[42] Engels agreed with Marx that the political state, and with it political authority, will disappear as a result of the "coming social revolution," that is to say, "public functions need lose their potential character and be transferred into the simple administrations of watching over the true interests of society." But he was vehemently opposed to anti-authoritarian demands that the authoritative political state be abolished at one stroke, even before the social conditions that gave birth to it had been destroyed.

Lenin, like Engels, felt that authority was not an absolute evil and he considered the state, like Marx, "a machine for maintaining the rule of one class over another."[43] However, unlike Marx and Engels, Lenin justified the existence of the Soviet state (as a transitional state) with similar authority as was practiced under the previous bourgeois state. The only difference was in the class composition of society. Whereas in the bourgeois state the bourgeoisie (a minority group) was exercising coercive power against the proletariat (the majority), in the Soviet state, according to Lenin, the proletariat (the majority) was exercising coercive power against the bourgeoisie (the minority). However, once the bourgeoisie was eliminated, then the nature of authority—the coercive and dominant power of one class over another—would change automatically. There would be no need for coercion anymore; a voluntary habit of obedience to the symbols of the revolution would prevail in a society without exploitation. It is significant that Lenin conditioned the disappearance of political authority (equated with power and coercion) on the elimination of exploitation, not only in the Soviet state but "anywhere in the world"; only then "shall we consign this machine to the scrap heap. Then there will be no state and no exploitation."[44]

In the meantime, however, Lenin contends, "a special apparatus, a special machine for suppression, the 'state' is still necessary, but this is now a transitional state" compatible with the extension of democracy to such an overwhelming majority of the population that "the need for a special machine of suppression will begin to disappear."[45] Or as Engels wrote in his letter to August Bebel, "the proletariat needs the state not in the interests of freedom but in order to hold down its adversaries, and as soon as it becomes possible to speak of freedom the state as such ceases to exist." It would appear, therefore, that the key to understanding the concept of authority in Marxist-Leninist terms hinges upon the ability to define Marx's and Lenin's ideas of what in the contemporary world, specifically in Hungary, constitutes the presence of the exploiting bourgeois class, or, in Engels' word, "adversaries" to socialist society. Only then we shall be able to explain the phenomenon of the long-lasting transitional state in socialist societies. Even if we accept Lenin's qualification that the raison d'etre for the state machine is conditional on the elimination of exploitation "anywhere in the world," even then it is incumbent upon us to ask the question, what happened to Lenin's prognosis that the transitional state is compatible with the extension of democracy to such an overwhelming majority of the population that the need for a "special machine" (the transitional state) will begin to disappear? Whatever interpretations are used to find the correct answers to these questions, one thing is clear: Marx, Engels, and Lenin were in full agreement that the aim of the revolution (world or protracted) was in harmony with the *Communist Manifesto*'s call "to raise the proletariat to the position of the ruling class" and "to win the battle of democracy." Or, to put it in present-day language, the aim was to replace the old concept of authority with the new one, to abolish the so-called oppressive rule by the bourgeois class and replace it with full participation in decision making and the voluntary habit of obedience by the proletariat.[46]

In addition to "political participation," Lenin frequently used Engels' explanation of "democracy" as a method for freeing the proletariat during the socialist construction by referring to quotations from the 1891 Preface to Marx's *The Civil War in France.* "To develop democracy *to the utmost,* to find the *forms* for this development, to test them *by practice,* and so forth—all this is one of the component tasks of the struggle for social revolution."[47] Lenin was convinced that democracy will exert its influence on economic life as well and stimulate its transformation; in turn it would be influenced by economic development, and so on. This process he considered to be "the dialectics of living history." Therefore, one of the first tasks of proletarian democracy, according to Lenin, was "to cut bureaucracy down to the roots" and gradually to abolish it and thus to introduce "complete democracy" for the people. Because "under socialism," Lenin prophesied, *"all* will govern in turn and all will soon become accustomed to no one governing."[48] Bureaucracy to Lenin represented the oppressive "apparatus" serving the interests of the state. Hence, after winning political power, Lenin argued, the workers will smash this apparatus and establish a new one that will *not* be "bureaucratic." Lenin goes on to state that the destruction of the "bureaucratic apparatus" is possible because "socialism will shorten the working day, will raise the *people* to a new life, will create such conditions for the *majority* of the population as will enable *everybody*, without exception, to perform 'state functions,' and this will lead to the *complete withering away* of every form of state in general."[49]

Since our major focus is on socialist authority as practiced in contemporary socialist Hungary—in other words, authority in the post-revolutionary era—let us summarize the main ideas of Marx and Lenin with regard to their conceptualization of authority during this period. It seems that Marx and Lenin were in agreement (although they disagreed on the type of revolution—world vs. protracted) that immediately following the revolution, the dictatorship of the proletariat (which Lenin also referred to as the transitional state) would rule with similar coercive power (authority) as the previous capitalist state but for the sole purpose of getting rid of exploitation and hence eliminating the bourgeois class. They seem to have agreed that during this stage of socialist development the apparatus of bureaucracy would be smashed and replaced by the members of the proletariat, who would create a rule by "all" through the habit of obedience of the working class, in the process building communism and hence creating an environment where people would be accustomed to orderly behavior in a society where both the state and democracy would wither away. If this over-simplified formula of socialist development is, for the sake of argument, fairly accurate, then the ultimate question is, after the elimination of the bourgeois class in a state undergoing socialist construction, what kind and how much authority did Lenin perceive to exist, for how long, and exercised by whom? Was political authority in Lenin's view a phenomenon that would gradually regress in an evolutionary process—meaning total eclipse when exploitation ceased to exist anywhere in the world? Is the yardstick of this decline of political authority (in the contemporary socialist state) the gradual reduction and elimination of "bureaucracy"? Or should administrative power that exists today in socialist countries, specifically Hungary, be referred to as "nonbureaucratic"? Before we attempt to answer these questions, let us consider another caveat that might shed some light on the concept of socialist authority.

In the previous section of this chapter, "The Ideas of Marx and Lenin," we alluded to the fact that Lenin rejected Marx's idea of revolutionary spontaneity (based on political rather than economic conditions). The principal task for engineering such a revolution was assigned by Lenin to the communist party. Based on past revolutionary experience, Lenin insisted that the proletarian revolution required a well-disciplined and resolute leadership, a tightly-knit organization with thorough planning and hard work. This elitist organization would constitute the vanguard of the proletariat because, according to Lenin, the masses were not equipped to carry out successfully the tasks of the revolutionary struggle; they had to be led by a small group of professional revolutionaries—members of the communist party. The party was, in Lenin's view, the only instrument capable of bringing political consciousness as well as organization and mobilization to the proletariat.[50]Thus it is not surprising to learn that through his vanguard theory Lenin created a precedent for bestowing upon an elite—which was to rule the proletarian masses not only during but also after the revolution—the highest appurtenances of authority. However, as we have pointed out earlier in this chapter, there are several conflicting references (if not contradictions) by Lenin to this view. On several occasions Lenin made it clear that after the revolution, coercive power (authority) will be aimed only at the bourgeois minority class, and that after exploitation has been eliminated the period of socialist construction will begin, that is, rule by "all" and true democracy without the oppressive "bureaucratic apparatus." Could it be that Lenin (intentionally or by the fate of events in Bolshevik Russia) replaced the "bureaucratic apparatus" with the members of the communist party? If that were the case, however, would not the authority of the Bolsheviks have been limited to some sort of clerical position looking after the administrative chores of the transitional state—with insignificant powers? As we know from history, this was not the case. On the contrary, the Bolsheviks ruled ruthlessly while Lenin was in power and continued to do so long after Lenin's death. True, after February 1956, when Nikita Khrushchev started his campaign against the "personality cult" by disclosing Stalin's crimes, the Communist Party of the Soviet Union (CPSU) embarked on a road to restore the "Leninist" rule of collective leadership. Should this mean that since that time the correct interpretation of the role of the party in the affairs of management of the "state" is less authority, more participation by the masses, and greater democracy for "all"? Let us examine now the theoretical application of Marxist-Leninist authority in Hungary.

During the first period of the socialist development of Hungarian society, from WWII to 1956, known also as the era of the Rakosi personality cult, the political system of Hungary was party-centered. The party served to integrate society and controlled social policy. State organs were partly intertwined with party organizations, especially at the level of central authority. The traditional state representational organs were completely void of all self-governing local power functions. The lines of authority in the state were created and exercised within the party-centered political system; within the party itself authority was "centralized."

Every social problem, requirement, or tension found itself on the long, vertically-integrated hierarchy of authority, carrying the problem so high (because the subordinates were afraid to make a decision) that not only the options but also its reasons became incalculable for those affected by the decision. Issues were selected at random without demand or support for them, and the entire decision-making process allowed no feedback. The result was that instead of an economy achieving maximum efficiency and rationality, an economy developed of extremely poor efficiency perpetuating irrational motives, one that was wasteful and shortage ridden. Instead of firm political unity based on harmony and cooperation, political fear, in-fighting, terror within the party as well as without, and complete omission of democracy became characteristic.

Because political integration, dictated from the center by party bosses, replaced the economic conditions of production, creating a vast mountain of administrative tasks, a ballooning political/economic bureaucracy came into being to cope with this avalanche of paperwork. According to official figures, the administrative staff of the state increased by 164 percent from 1949 to 1954 and the economic administrative staff grew by 357 percent compared to 1938. This swollen bureaucracy, serving the interests of the monopolistic centers of authority, produced immense quantities of regulations, institutions, and edicts, stifling the creative capabilities of the individual in the process of social integration. Similar effects were felt by such organizations as the Patriotic People's Front, the trade unions, youth organizations, and so forth. The mechanism of vertical and horizontal organizational concentration reacted with an almost elemental force, and added further fuel to the centralization of authority. The revamping of organizations by making them impotent and at the same time linking them to the party-centered political system also resulted in their confusing the spheres of authority by allowing multiorganizational membership for individual leaders and by allowing committees to usurp all sorts of spheres of authority. Hierarchical relationships in this party-centered political system were based on personal dependence rather than institutionalized guidelines based on competence and law. This practice made relations of authority ill-defined, uncertain, and insecure, thus forcing participants of the political system to over-insure themselves by engaging in questionable practices for the sake of informal security.

A peculiar system of spoils in the division of spheres of authority ruled the country during this period of personality cult. This meant that a given person or organization did not have duties or authority as defined by law or organizational and operational regulations, but everybody had as many rights as he could grab, until his authority was challenged by others. A person's or organization's sphere of authority was often wider than the rules permitted, but just as often it was considerably narrower.

This situation contributed to great uncertainty and unpredictability in the system of authority, adding to growth in organizational conformity. Under such conditions it is relatively easy to understand why one of the most important elements of political life, *interests,* was simply omitted from Hungarian politics. Instead of a hegemonistic alliance, built on a wide social base, an extraordinarily unstable monopolistic power bloc came into being, based on nothing but the party apparatus (which had replaced the old bureaucratic apparatus). A single integration principle, a sole will guiding social policy was asserted—the will of an alienated political leadership lacking any democratic limitation, that believed itself to be omniscient and omnipotent. Consequently, as the post-1956 leaders of the HSWP acknowledged and proposed in their platform, Hungary experienced not only an economic and political crisis but the entire mechanism of authority and social integration was seriously damaged.[51]

What about the system of authority in Hungary after the 1956 dismantling of the cult of personality? How is "authority" perceived in the period of building "developed socialism"? What is the role of authority in "socialist democracy"?

Although a casual perusal of the post-1956 literature reveals that the greatest concern of the decision makers was economic development, far more important were the political issues relating to the system of authority; they were a prerequisite to the economic reforms that followed in the second half of the 1960s. After the catastrophe of 1956, the party leaders condemned the ill-conceived past practices of the personality cult and consequently reorganized the political mechanism of authority, the economic system, and the integration system of the entire society under the principle of centralized and unambiguous reforms and their total implementation. The party was now committed that these reforms should be started at the top, to be asserted centrally, and backed by the power of the party. The reforms, including the social policies, were to be total, encompassing every facet of social life; unambiguous, leaving no room for doubt; and systematic in implementation. The New Economic Mechanism became the centerpiece of the reforms but its success was very much dependent on political reform of the mechanism of authority.

There were two general trends changing the concept of authority, as can be seen at the level of structural analysis of social sub-systems. First was the gradual rationalization of the total process of social policymaking, calling for more and more expertise, recognition of legal, administrative, economic, and cultural values in Hungarian society. The second trend was democratization, which entailed the revamping of the power relationship of the party, which got underway after the first five years of consolidation. We should hasten to point out, however, that while these significant reforms in the structure and function of Hungarian society were taking place, at the same time a continuity in party policies was affecting three areas of social development: social ownership, economic planning, and eradication of antagonistic classes.

With the discontinuation of the monopolistic structure of political authority, the capacity for social development grew both quantitatively and qualitatively, allowing for the development of various political integration principles. While the communist political system still dominates, a qualitatively superior social unity and integration have been realized. Perhaps the most important change in the course of development of socialist democracy is the acceptance of the idea that on the macrosocial level, the integration of individual, group, and sectional interests generated in the economic system must be equally recognized in the sphere of political authority. In other words, the party leadership has legitimized interest articulation in the decision-making process. Currently, development of socialist democracy in Hungary is supposed to accommodate the articulation of conflicting interests not only in the economic but also in the political realms, thus creating a feedback effect in the political process. This linking of the economic and political systems is supposed to create an integrating mechanism in "developed socialism" in which the dominant authority continues to be the political power exercised by the party, but the social subsystems are able to influence the system through use of a mediation mechanism, namely, a more democratic arrangement of authority by the party. Thus it is appropriate to ask: In order to assure further growth of socialist democracy in Hungary, will the party, enacting its series of reforms, totally implement its social-democracy programs even if this means suppressing any anti-democratic political efforts? As we shall later illustrate, there are still quite a few remnants of anti-democratic forces present in the economic and political institutions of socialist development in Hungary. They appear primarily in the form of bureaucratic institutions and cumbersome organizations as well as the social-psychological residues of past conditioning factors. Many Hungarians still remember the omniscience and omnipotence of the party and their reflexes toward bureaucratic institutions are frequently triggered by stimuli from the past. The habits of democratic politics—in any nation—cannot be prescribed by theoretical formulas or imposed by edict; they have to be cultivated with great care and patience and practiced with sensitivity and understanding.

CONCLUSION

Although there is no clear-cut consensus on what constitutes socialist democracy in the present phase of "developed socialism" in Hungary, it is possible to hypothesize about some of the prerequisites to democratic reforms and the principles governing them, as seen by some of the more liberal members of the party leadership. According to Marxism-Leninism, they argue, democracy has no general concept; it has only a class content and, therefore, is not limited to the relationship of majority and minority. Consequently, democracy is present as long as the differences of interests (social, not economic) coming into being under socialist social relations can be expressed as political differences of opinion and as such can take part in the decision-making process. Socialist democracy in Hungary also presupposes the establishment of certain conditions and organizational patterns of behavior. The former includes political security and freedom of individuals and groups in their relations to each other and to the organizations of political authority, which must be guaranteed by a system of civil rights. Whereas the conditions of democracy are usually expressed by normative/legal institutions, the organizational pattern of behavior—which includes the formation of interests and their political articulation in the decision-making process—is derived from the constantly changing sociopolitical conditions of democracy. Hence development of democracy must guarantee the emergence of group interests, even if such interests are in conflict with the values already existing in society. The combination of the two—the normative conditions and the organizational system of democracy—presupposes the principles of one man/one vote and the rights of the minority to become a majority. According to this school of thought, the relationship and mutual system of guarantees of majority and minority embody the essence of democracy, that is, self-government based on political equality and freedom, a concept of authority respecting diversity, and the integration of society by consensus.

All of the above-mentioned principles and prerequisites to democratic reforms are based on the following assumptions of socialist development in Hungary. First, that class antagonism has ceased to exist; secondly, that social ownership is dominant, that economic planning prevails, and that Marxism-Leninism enjoys a dominant role in Hungarian society. The latter implies, as Aczél points out, "that there is—to use a fashionable expression—ideological pluralism beside the decisive role played by the Marxist ideology."[52]

In present-day Hungary we find that *all authority* is being exercised in the name of all the people. This claim is synonymous with the ideological tenets of Marxism-Leninism, according to which the socialist society of Hungary has only one economic class led by the members of the Hungarian Socialist Workers' Party. Since authority in this context is best defined as a manifestation of power (similar to Roberto Michels and Gaetano Mosca)[53] it makes very little difference whether the system of government is democratic or not, there is always a small group that performs all political functions, monopolizes power, and enjoys the advantages that power brings. According to Marxism-Leninism (as well as to Mosca again), authority, like power, is not something one is given by some law of nature or society; it is, like power, grasped and exercised by a consensual elite dedicated to upholding the principles of Marxist-Leninist ideology. Therefore the power to dispense and to exercise authority as well as to assume responsibility rests with a leadership group of the working class, namely the Hungarian Socialist Workers' Party. Since there is only one class interest in Hungarian society, theoretically there is no conflict between the ruling elite and the ruled masses.[54] That reasoning, however, does not imply that the existing social forces in socialist Hungarian society are in full compliance and agreement with the interests and policies of the ruling elite. As we have already noted, there are many and influential voices in the leadership position arguing for what we might conceptualize as "elitist pluralism," according to which all state power is based on the directing force of Marxism-Leninism—force consisting not only of the party but a multiplicity of social forces, organized in such a way as to avoid a position of absolute superiority by any one authority so that everybody can effectively control each other. Therefore the issue ever since the party took power has been and still is: how are authority and power distributed in Hungarian society?

As we have pointed out, until 1956 power and authority in Hungarian society was unsurped by a handful of party leaders who made themselves masters of the Hungarian body politic in the name of, but contrary to, the principles of Marxism-Leninism—under which the authority of the state was conferred upon all individuals. Their power rested on the worship of the personality cult of Mátyás Rakosi and company. As a result, bureaucratic authority, exercised throughout the state on all levels as well as in the political offices of the party, added convention and a legal seal to real power concentrated in the hands of Rakosi and his handpicked oligarchs. They personified the meaning of authority through the exercise of genuine dictatorial powers. Only after the reorganization of the party, especially the declaration of October 30, 1956, can one more clearly discern the different meanings of authority in Hungarian society.

Since neither Marx nor Lenin expressed extensive or coherent thoughts about the concept of "socialist authority" (and hence left no legacy for the contemporary disciples to follow), it may be appropriate to ask whether there is any similarity between the concept of socialist authority, as viewed by the present communist theoreticians in Hungary, and the concepts of authority developed by such thinkers as Mosca, Pareto, Michels, Weber, and a host of others? We have already alluded to Mosca's and Michels' views of authority as a phenomenon equated with power. The same view prevails among the Hungarian elite with one exception: several members of the liberal school of thought distinguish, as did Max Weber, authority from power, in that under authority "there is a certain minimum voluntary submission; thus an interest in obedience."[55] Therefore, authority implies that one person in Hungarian society controls another only to the extent that the one is able to persuade the other to change his mind. This group of liberal thinkers also believes that authority (existing as acceptance a priori of a directive) is present only to the extent that the belief system of Marxism-Leninism defines exercise of control as legitimate and establishes a political control mechanism (for mediation) that subjects all organized interests to the same rule.

At the present time there is little doubt that power and authority in Hungary rest solely with the party elite, and that authority, but not power, is entrusted by the party elite to various social groups in Hungarian society organized as "transmission belts" between the party elite and the masses. The party depends on mass support and therefore will formulate policies congruous with public demand even if this means at times that the party leadership must walk a tightrope. Therefore the intellectual tug-of-war that is currently taking place in socialist Hungary between the liberal and conservative thinkers is in reality a struggle for legitimation of authority; in other words, a battle of ideas over "socialist democracy" and the limits or boundaries of party authority over nonparty organizations in the decision-making process. This struggle should eventually resolve another issue, namely whether non party organizations can also exercise sanctions, which would automatically add to their authority/power over persons subject to these organizations. Hence what seems to be at stake is a redefinition of bureaucratic authority within the framework of the clearly-defined hierarchical roles played in Hungarian socialist society. When the process is completed, the relationship between the ruled and the rulers should be institutionalized, that is to say, duties and obligations should be specified, behavior toward institutions should be reasonably predictable, the character of communication should be unquestioned, and the maintenance of distance between those who command and argue and those who obey should become less pronounced. Some advocates of socialist democracy argue that only when the above political reforms are carried out, only then will it be realistic to speak of being "governed" rather than ruled under socialist authority in Hungary.

NOTES

1. The ideas of Marx and Lenin, summarized on the following pages, are based on the writings of Shlomo Avineri, *The Social and Political Thought of Karl Marx* (London: Cambridge University Press, 1968); Isaiah Berlin, *Karl Marx, His Life and Environment* (New York: Oxford University Press, 1959); Robert Conquest, *V.I. Lenin* (New York: Viking Press, 1972); Louis Fischer, *The Life of Lenin* (New York: Harper and Row, 1964); A. James Gregor, *A Survey of Marxism* (New

York: Random House, 1965); Sidney Hook, *Marx and the Marxists: The Ambiguous Legacy* (New York: D. Van Nostrand Co., 1955); György Lukács, *Lenin: A Study on the Unity of His Thought* (tr. from German by Nicholas Jacobs; London: N.L.B., 1970); David McLellan, *Karl Marx: His Life and Thought* (New York: Harper and Row, 1974); Alfred G. Mayer, *Leninism* (New York: Praeger, 1962); Mostafa Rejai, *Comparative Political Ideologies* (New York: St. Martin's Press, 1984); Adam Schaff, *Marxism and the Human Individual* (New York: McGraw-Hill, 1970); and Robert C. Tucker, *The Marxian Revolutionary Idea* (New York: W.W. Norton, 1969).

2. György Aczél, "The stages and crises of socialism," *The New Hungarian Quarterly* 23 (Autumn 1982); 10.

3. See "The changing image of socialism," *The New Hungarian Quarterly* 23, (Autumn 1982); 90.

4. György Aczél, "The challenge of our age and the response of socialism," *The New Hungarian Quarterly* 24 (Summer 1983); 26.

5. György Aczél, "A new system of values," *The New Hungarian Quarterly* 21 (Spring 1980); 11.

6. See Aczél, "The challenge of our age and the response of socialism," op. cit., 17.

7. Ibid., 16.

8. Ibid., 15–16.

9. Ibid., 18.

10. See, for example, Valéria Benke, "Social policy, reality, socialism," *Társadalmi Szemle* [Social Review] 2 (1982), summarized in "The changing image of socialism," op.cit., 90–93.

11. See Aczél, "The challenge of our age and the response of socialism," op. cit., 23.

12. Ibid., 24.

13. Ibid., 25.

14. Ibid.

15. It is interesting to note that the pre-1956 party slogan representing the concept of class struggle was: "He who is not with us is against us" (a paraphrase of the Bible, Matthew XII, 30).

16. See Aczél, "The challenge of our age and the response of socialism," op. cit., 28.

17. See "Hungarian society in the 1980s," *Magyar Nemzet* [The Hungarian Nation] (April 9, 1983).

18. See "The changing image of socialism," op. cit., 91.

19. See *Kisiparos Újság* [Artizan News] (November 19, 1983).

20. See "Catching up or falling behind? The lessons of a decade," *Magyar Nemzet* (December 24, 1983).

21. Ibid.

22. Lajos Vekas, "On questions of principles of individual property," *Jogtudományi Közlöny* [Proceedings of Legal Science] 5 (1982): 388–394.

23. Ibid.

24. Lajos Héthy, "The second economy, the small enterprise, and economic control," *Társadalomkutatás* [Social Research] 1 (1983); 29–43.

25. See Valéria Benke, op. cit., 92.

26. See Janez Stanic, "The Budapest style of pluralism," *Start* (Zagreb) (April 21, 1984).

27. Ibid.

28. See *Népszabadság* (March 27, 1985).

29. See Aczél, "The challenge of our age and the response of socialism," op. cit., 25

30. Ibid., 30.

31. See "The changing image of socialism," op. cit., 93.

32. Ibid.

33. See "Trends of development in the socialist way of life," *The New Hungarian Quarterly* 22 (Winter 1981); 122.

34. Stanic, *Start* (April 21, 1984).

35. See interview of Sándor Lakos in Ibid.

36. For further explanation of the electoral system and the freedom of the nominating process, see Chapter 2, "The Toilers' Share in Power," below.

37. See Stanic, *Start* (April 21, 1984).

38. Only Engels addressed the issue, though briefly, during the anti-Anarchist controversy when he examined the role of authoritarian discipline in economic production. See his "On Authority," in Robert C. Tucker, ed., *The Marx–Engels Reader* (New York: W.W. Norton, 1972), 662–65.

39. See Nicholas Lobkowicz, ed., *Marx and the Western World* (Notre Dame: University of Notre Dame Press, 1967), 127.

40. V.I. Lenin, *Collected Works*, Vol. 25 (Moscow: Foreign Languages Publishing House, 1960), 462.

41. Ibid., 463.

42. Robert C. Tucker, ed., *The Marx–Engels Reader* (2nd Edition, New York: W.W. Norton, 1978), 730–31.

43. Lenin, *Collected Works*, Vol. 29, p. 478.

44. Ibid., 488.

45. Lenin, op. cit., Vol. 25, p. 463.

46. Ibid., 460–61.

47. Ibid., 480.

48. Ibid., 481 and 488.

49. Ibid., 488–89.

50. For Lenin's concept of the party, see *What is to Be Done*, a pamphlet written in 1902, in *Collected Works*, Vol. 5, pp. 347–567.

51. For further details on the theory and practice of power mechanism under the Rakosi regime, see Mihály Bihari, "Political mechanism and socialist democracy," *The New Hungarian Quarterly* 24, (Winter 1982): 111–27.

52. See Aczél, "The challenge of our age and the response of socialism," op. cit., 26.

53. See the *Encyclopedia of the Social Sciences*, Vol. 2 (New York: MacMillan, 1930), 319; and Gaetano Mosca's *"Elementi"* in James H. Meisel, *The Myth of the Ruling Class: Gaetano Mosca and the "Elite"* (Ann Arbor: University of Michigan Press, 1958), 32–33.

54. This is particularly true in view of the application of what can be termed a typical Hungarian formula: The HSWP retains the elitist position of representing only 8 percent of the total population, while KISz (the Communist Youth

League) is a mass organization encompassing practically the entire youth population of Hungary.

55. See Robert E.L. Faris, ed., *Handbook of Modern Sociology* (Chicago: Rand McNally, 1964), 497.

2
The Rulers and the Ruled

It would be difficult to imagine the frank discussions presently taking place in Hungary—on such concepts and issues as socialist democracy, ideological pluralism, economic incentives, private property, election reforms, interest articulations, and so forth—were it not for the Hungarian Revolt of 1956 (officially referred to as the "Counterrevolution of 1956"). If not the most important turning point in the history of Hungary under communist rule, it certainly was a major one. The events of October not only ended the rule of the personality cult, but fundamentally changed the future economic and social structure and reestablished the authority of mass nonparty organizations through a policy of alliances (or national consensus). As György Aczél explained to Paul Lendvai, editor of *Europaeische Rundschau (European Review)*, in an interview in Vienna, "We had to reconsider the aim of socialist policy and the means of attaining it."[1] For the party to survive and regain credibility called for winning over the entire people, hopefully without bloodshed and suffering;[2] enlisting public opinion to help control persons and institutions vested with authority; making social life more democratic; establishing nondogmatic collective leadership; and, at the same time, maintaining close ties with the Warsaw Pact countries, especially the USSR. The major guidelines for achieving these objectives were accommodation of the party to specific Hungarian traditions and realities and attention to Lenin's warning that as long as there is a living society, there will exist contradictions—even under socialism. The naiveté (or the Soviet precedent) of the Hungarian dictators' thinking that they could impose a social structure free from interests and hence contradictions was both a costly lesson and an inducement for the succeeding ruling elite to rec-

ognize the indispensable role of organized masses in the socialist construction of Hungarian society. After a rude awakening, the party rulers
suddenly were forced to recognize diverse individual and group interests. Instead of alienating them, the party, through economic incentives,
mobilized mass support for improving the standard of living, and
through expanded grassroots participation in the decision-making process, the party began to build "socialist democracy." Many economic and
sociopolitical issues, however, remain unsolved.

As pointed out in the previous chapter, most members of the ruling
elite subscribe to the idea that true social representation of interests
should not and cannot depend on the existence of opposition parties or
an opposition press. However, there are others among the ruling elite
who seek some type of political mechanism that can guarantee the freedom of organized dissent through political articulation and provide a
mass media system accountable to the democratic public. There are, of
course, many other sensitive issues being aired among party leaders who,
in the final analysis, will eventually decide the limits of freedom and/or
restrictions in the relationship between the rulers and the ruled in Hungary. For the time being, however, one thing is clear: the 13th HSWP
Congress confirmed the *continuation* of Hungary's seventeen-year-old
economic reform as the only way to pull the country out of its current
economic and social difficulties. In other words, the Hungarian ruling
elite is committed to stay the course of economic and social reforms,
even at the risk of pitting the party's monopoly of power against much
desired economic efficiency. We can be assured, however, that at no time
will the same ruling elite jeopardize the party's leading role (control of
power) in the decision-making process by soliciting the input of mass
movements and agencies representing sectional interests. The latter include the trade unions, the Patriotic People's Front, the Communist
Youth League, the women's movement, various bodies representing cooperative and professional interests, and a host of associations and religious organizations. Their membership-at-large (as opposed to their
leadership) constitutes what may be generally referred to as the members
of Hungarian society ruled by the former—the party and government
elite(s).

The source of the "social contract" by which the rulers rule today can
be found in both the "liberation" (or as the critics view it, occupation)
of Hungary by the Soviet Army at the end of World War II and the
communist coup (with the aid of the Soviet Military Command in Budapest) in 1947.[3] Ever since that time the ruling elite—whether personality cult or collective leadership—has been fully committed to a socialist
system of government guided by policies based on the social ownership
of the means of production, a socialist planned economy, the power of
the working class, and the leading role of the Communist Party. These

principles, it would seem, are engraved in stone and thus are nonnegotiable. What was, and still is, left for negotiation and perhaps even compromise (an alien concept to Marxism-Leninism) is the way the ruled members of the society can make their contribution to the building of "developed socialism" in Hungary. In the final analysis, however, that too will be determined by the ruling elite and not by public opinion. Thus, while the party elite, ever since the tragic events of October 1956, is fully committed to permit democratic mass participation in the decision-making process at the lowest community level, it will not relinquish its dominant role of decision maker at the highest level of party and government organization.

THE PARTY AND STATE ELITE

The Hungarian Socialist Workers' Party (HSWP), like the other communist parties in the Soviet bloc, constitutionally and by custom is the most powerful organization in the state; it "embodies" the power of the Hungarian working class and feels "responsible" for the Hungarian people as a whole. The precedent set by the Soviet example since the Bolshevik revolution confers upon the party the highest authority of power and the responsibility for remolding society into a new form following the principles of socialism. This legacy is attributable, as we have pointed out in the previous chapter, to the Leninist theory of the "vanguard of the proletariat." It is different from Marx's ideas of the dictatorship of the proletariat. In this respect it would seem that the Hungarian party elite thinks of itself as being Marxist, but the model it follows is Leninist. Therefore it is not surprising that on the one hand, the Hungarian party leadership is toying with the idea of economic and social reforms, while on the other hand, it is resolutely trying to uphold the principles of Leninism. Of course there is a caveat in all this when it comes to application and interpretation of Marxist-Leninist ideology, which is like what Franz Kafka said about the truth: There is only one truth, but it lives, so its face changes in a lively manner. In a similar vein, János Kádár regards the party not as a ruling authority but as an organization in the service of the people.[4] Of course if 8 percent of the Hungarian population (the total party membership of 862,000) decides to have only 0.1 percent of the population (i.e., the party leadership) be the bona fide rulers of the country, then the party, by any standard (other than communist), is not an organization in the service of the people but is a ruling authority or dictatorship of the working class, which in turn is not fully represented. (In 1985, for example, the total percentage of foremen and workers in industry and agriculture who were members of the HSWP was only 48.6.[5]) By the same token, we may find it not surprising at all if "the people" would ask themselves the question, "When will we participate in this organization that is supposed to serve us and when will we have the right to decide what's best for us?" Incidentally, the disproportion of the percentage of communists within the population as a whole and the percentage of power that communists hold in their hands, which is rarely less than 100 percent, is something that troubles some members of the party elite. For example, the editor-in-chief of *Pártélet (Party Life)*, Sándor Lakos, not long ago pointed out that "the main political question has been how to democratize power and enable citizens to share in it." In theory, he went on to say, "all power has been in the hands of the people rather than in the hands of the party," but in reality the opposite is true.[6] How to democratize power, or how to create "party democracy," was the topic of a conference organized jointly by the Central Committee (CC) Department for Party and Mass Organizations and the Political Academy of the HSWP.[7] The message to the 300 higher party functionaries from the former Deputy General Secretary Károly Németh and from the head of the CC Department for Party and Mass Organizations István Petrovszki called for more genuine debate within the party and for increased participation by members in party work. To this end, Németh urged the creation of conditions under which party members could express their views without fear of "any detrimental circumstances," which implies that some members are indeed loath to air their views for fear of retaliation. Németh claimed that "the level of democracy in the party determines the degree of democracy" enjoyed by the state and society and in public life at large. "Socialist democracy," he asserted, "can only be realized if the individual institutions of the political system are able to express and formulate a variety of occupational, institutional, and local interests." Németh cautioned, however, that the state remains the only legitimate framework in which those interests may be asserted.

We have already alluded to the fact that the party and its ideology of Marxism-Leninism has changed its position from monopoly to hegemony within the framework of the Hungarian social system. Since the revolution of 1956, the party has initiated a new political forum, also know as ideological pluralism, according to which the existing differences in philosophical outlook must be mediated in order to achieve national unity in pursuance of the socialist objectives. As György Aczél clarified it: "The essence of socialist hegemony is to protect and strengthen the leading role of the socialist ideas while showing understanding for and convincing the other side."[8] Consequently, debates and dialogues between Marxists and non-Marxists, between socialists and nonsocialists, are part of the policy of "socialist hegemony"—debates that provide the party elite with valuable information about the nature and extent of grievances prevailing in Hungarian society. The rationale for such a mechanism is obvious when one considers such revealing facts as those contained in public opinion polls and in-depth studies of the Hungarian youth and student populations. For example, these surveys reveal that the great majority of young people have no political convictions; that they favor individualism and independence and reject collectivism imposed from above; that the drop in party membership among the younger generation is due to the dissatisfaction with specific party programs and to the deterioration in the standard of living.[9] It is important to point out, however, that this policy of socialist hegemony is limited only to those diverse views that show an appreciation for political loyalty to socialism. In other words, those intellectual-political opinions that are not anti-socialist ideologically and with which therefore the party strives for hegemony in its relations, or as the slogan by János Kádár so aptly put it, "He who is not against us is with us." Obviously, this practice does not include political dissidents who, in the opinion of party leaders, are maladjusted, untalented, mentally troubled, and/or disappointed people who never blame themselves but always society. Since, according to Aczél, "there is no opposition that has to be reckoned with in Hungary . . . there is no censorship in our country."[10] As a matter of fact, several party leaders boast that newspapers, journals, and other information media publish any "humanist view, no matter which part of the world it originated from, and even it it appears in a religious, bourgeois, or some other ideological guise . . . [because] we are tolerant in this respect."[11] However, one might also add a rhetorical question: Are those "humanist values" they publish not carefully selected from the world press to suit their major line of propaganda in vogue at a particular time and therefore the more critical they are of bourgeois policies the better? Consequently, the party elite's political tolerance is limited to criticism of method, priorities, and matters of detail —*not* the essence of socialism. The party representatives carry on a dialogue with those critics and even thank them for their useful observations and proposals. The revelation of hard facts by the Hungarian print and electronic media, which often are critical expressions of individuals but never of the system, should not be placed under a label of "freedom of information" in the tradition of Western journalism. No matter how embarrassing the criticism for the ruling elite, it must always exercise discretion to such a degree that it can claim "consensus" with the Hungarian people, acting together.

In theory the party elite promotes freedom of the press and tolerance of criticism; in practice, however, it is a different matter entirely. If an editor of a journal relies literally on the democratic rights decreed by the party or specified in the constitution, he will soon find himself in conflict with the everyday course of cultural policy, in other words the system, which tries to influence the press not by authoritative methods but by various psychological means. If an editor tries to escape these subtle and omnipresent pressures, he will immediately come into conflict with the formulators of cultural policy. Of course he cannot be charged with any breach of law, because he performed his official duties within the framework of such law. At the same time, however, his behavior cannot be tolerated either, because it would require a change in the unwritten rules of procedure. Therefore, should the editor flout the rules, he would automatically become the loser in a conflict of interests, unless his connections in the system of authority were exceptionally strong, which is doubtful. Consequently, very few editors in Hungary are willing to initiate conflictual situations. There are occasions, however, when some editors will try to do something innovative and so bold as to deviate from the rigid cultural policy in force; but as soon as they are chastised for this, they hastily retreat. In fact, there are certain editors who play this game of experimentation with new ideas on behalf of the establishment and not as part of the democratic forces in the country. Thus they fit perfectly into the scheme that in Hungary nothing is forbidden, as long as certain limits (the essence of socialism) are not exceeded. They appear to be brave enough to print innovative ideas because they have the support of the ruling elite. In this way experimentation can lead to changes in cultural policy, provided they prove to be improvements in the process of socialist construction.

While it is true that the party is a monolithic organization, practicing democratic centralism, it is also true that the party leadership—consisting of a dozen or so people in the Politburo and the Secretariat of the Central Committee, as well as a couple of dozen committees and committee teams (see Table 2.1)—is in the control of individuals, such as János Kádár and György Aczél, who represent the moderate position in the ideological field and the liberal or reformist views in the economic arena. Their working-class backgrounds, their persecution under the personality cult, and world public opinion are guarantees that the horror of 1956 will not recur. Both men are the senior members of the party elite and their long experience in party affairs makes them seasoned politicians who have a natural instinct for pursuing policies endorsed by a large subset of the Hungarian population. Kádár especially, whose title was changed during the 13th Party Congress from First Secretary to General Secretary,[12] is well liked by the multitude because he appears modest and because they believe that under the circumstances he is doing the best job anyone could do.

Even though the clear-cut division between reformers and anti-reformers no longer exists, there are differences among the various top party officials, as made evident by the reshuffle of the party leadership during the 13th Party Congress held in Budapest from March 25–29, 1985, and the meeting of the HSWP CC on June 23, 1987. In the Politburo, the Party Congress gave full endorsement to the reform movement by removing Valéria Benke, a former Stalinist, and Mihály Korom,

Table 2.1
Elite Positions in the Hungarian Socialist Workers' Party (HSWP)

POLITBURO

Members	János KÁDÁR	(74)
	György ACZÉL	(69)
	János BERECZ	(57)
	Judit CSEHÁK	(47)
	Sándor GÁSPÁR	(69)
	Károly GRÓSZ	(56)
	Ferenc HAVASI	(57)
	Csaba HÁMORI	(38)
	György LÁZÁR	(62)
	László MARÓTHY	(44)
	Károly NÉMETH	(64)
	Miklós ÓVÁRI	(61)
	István SZABÓ	(62)

CENTRAL COMMITTEE SECRETARIAT

General Secretary   János KÁDÁR

Deputy General Secretary   György LÁZÁR

Secretaries   János BERECZ
                                        György FEJTI
                                        János LUKÁCS
                                        Miklós NÉMETH
                                        Miklós ÓVÁRI
                                        Lénárd PÁL
                                        Mátyás SZŰRÖS

CENTRAL CONTROL COMMITTEE

Chairman   András GYENES

OTHER CC COMMITTEE CHAIRMEN

Agitprop   Gyula BERECZKY

Economic Policy   Miklós NÉMETH

Youth   János LUKÁCS

Cadre Policy   György LÁZÁR

CHAIRMEN OF CENTRAL COMMITTEE TEAMS

Cooperative Policy   István SZABÓ

Cultural Policy   Lénárd PÁL

Economic   Miklós NÉMETH

Party Building   János LUKÁCS

Table 2.1 (Continued)

CENTRAL COMMITTEE OFFICE

Head   Miklós ÓVÁRI

CENTRAL COMMITTEE DEPARTMENT HEADS

Agitation and Propaganda	Ernő LAKATOS
Economic Policy	László BALLAI
Public and General Administration	Péter VARGA
Foreign Affairs	Géza KÓTAI
Party and Mass Organizations	István PETROVSZKI
Party Management and Administration	László KARAKAS
Science, Education, and Culture	Katalin RADICS

CENTRAL PARTY INSTITUTION HEADS

Political College	József SZABÓ
Institute of Social Sciences	György ACZÉL
Institute of Party History	István HUSZÁR
Társadalmi Szemle	Valéria BENKE
Pártélet	Sándor LAKOS
Népszabadság	Gábor BORBÉLY

Source: *RFE Research* 11, No. 31 (August 1, 1986): 23–24 and *ibid.* 12, 28 (July 17, 1987), part 2, p. 23.

known as a hard-liner. It recognized the need to deal with the problems of the young and their growing ideological alienation by appointing Csaba Hámori, the young first secretary for the Communist Youth League since 1984, and the middle aged first secretary of the Budapest party committee, Károly Grósz. After the 13th Party Congress, under Kádár's leadership, the thirteen-member Politburo enjoyed an overwhelming majority favoring economic, social and political reforms. Those who did not always agree with the pro-reform policies of János Kádár included the long-time union leader Sándor Gáspár, a strong defender of workers' interests, and the pragmatist *Apparatchik*, Károly Grósz. At the same time, the removal from the Secretariat of the Central Committee of Kádár's long time associate, György Aczél, who now had to share the responsibility for cultural and ideological affairs with his successor, János Berecz—a former editor-in-chief of the party daily *Népszabadság* and a hardliner on reforms—signaled the beginning of a get-tough policy against dissidents and party dilettants.

Ever since the Party Congress in March 1985, however, the economic and social problems have intensified rather than diminished; so much so, that in June 1987 the Central Committee decided on a number of personnel changes at the party elite level, which included a new head of state and prime minister, thus casting a shadow over the future outcome of the projected reforms. Károly Grósz has taken over from György Lázár as chairman of the Council of Ministers (i.e., Prime Minister) who in turn replaced Károly Németh as deputy general secretary of the HSWP CC. The latter has replaced the retired Pál Losonczi as chairman of the Presidential Council (nominal head of state). Both Losonczi and István Sarlós, who has also retired, were replaced on the Politburo by János Berecz and Judit Csehák, a young country physician specializing in health and social welfare matters of the party. The Secretariat of the Central Committee, now managed by Kádár's old and trusted associate, György Lázár, underwent certain personnel changes that could for the time being place economic and social reforms in limbo. Ferenc Havasi, the staunch reformist, was replaced by a young technocrat and former economics professor, Miklós Németh, and István Horváth's responsibilities for organizational affairs were taken over by another young party activist and former professor of mechanical engineering, György Fejti. A third new member was added to the secretariat, János Lukács, who has specialized in organizational matters and is now head of the youth committee and party building. It is significant to note that these changes in the party hierarchy came not as a result of an intra-party struggle against the reformist policies of János Kádár, but as a consequence of the shortcomings in the implementation of the reformist policies since the early and mid-1980s. As a matter of custom, policies as such can never be wrong in a socialist system—only individuals can fail, especially those responsible for carrying them out. Thus, the new members of the party elite were handpicked by the old guard and then endorsed by the members of the Central Committee with the understanding that these changes were designed to strengthen the forces committed to economic reform, while stressing to a greater degree than before the necessity of political stability. As it now stands, expectations are that János Kádár will continue his expertise in the art of political balancing while cautiously preparing his own orderly succession. Under Kádár's guidance this group of collective leaders—young and old—will continue to rule, if not govern, the members of the Hungarian society in a nonobtrusive manner relying heavily on the men and women that were handpicked by them to head the complex, ever-bulging bureaucracy.

Hungary, like other socialist countries in the Warsaw Pact, is well known for its huge bureaucracies in charge of the administrative functions of the state. (See Table 2.2.) A foreign visitor from the West will soon discover that bureaucracy (and red tape) is everywhere. The same departments and functions recur in different organizations. The explanation frequently provided for this "albatross" is that following the "Liberation" (by the Soviet Army in 1945), the party considered it necessary to put into leading positions thousands of people who were assigned the task of building a new people's democracy. Consequently, a large number

Table 2.2
Party Representation in State and Government

PRESIDENTIAL COUNCIL (STATE)

Chairman (nominal head of state)	Károly NÉMETH	PB
Deputy Chairmen	Sándor GÁSPÁR	PB
	Rezső TRAUTMANN	
Secretary	Imre KATONA	CC
Members	Sándor BARCS	
	Tibor BÁRTHA	
	(Mrs.) Géza BÁNÁTI	
	Imre BÍRÓ	
	(Mrs.) Lajos DUSCHEK	
	János ELEKI	
	István GAJDÓCSI	
	Sándor HORVÁTH	
	János KÁDÁR	PB
	Gyula KÁLLAI	
	(Mrs.) Teréz Michelisz KRÉMER	
	Marin MANDITY	
	László NÁNÁSI	
	Károly NÉMETH	PB
	Géza SZÁLAI	
	János SZENTÁGOTHAI	
	Miklós VIDA	

COUNCIL OF MINISTERS (GOVERNMENT)

Prime Minister	Károly GRÓSZ	
Deputy Prime Ministers	Frigyes BERECZ	CC
	Judit CSEHÁK	PB
	István HORVÁTH	CC
	József MARJAI	CC
	László MARÓTHY	PB

Ministers

Agriculture and Food	Jenő VÁNCSA	CC
Culture and Education	Béla KÖPECZI	
Defense	Ferenc KÁRPÁTI	CC
Finance	Péter MEDGYESSY	CC
Foreign Affairs	Péter VÁRKONYI	CC
Foreign Trade	Péter VERESS	CC
Industry	László KAPOLYI	CC
Internal Affairs	János KAMARA	CC
Internal Trade	Zoltán JUHÁR	
Justice	Imre MARKOJA	
Public Construction and Urban Development	László SOMOGYI	
Public Health	László MEDVE	
Transportation	Lajos URBÁN	

Chairman (ministerial rank), National Planning Office	László MARÓTHY	PB
Central People's Control Commission	László BALLAI	CC

Table 2.2 (Continued)

MASS ORGANIZATIONS

Chief Secretary of the National Council	Tibor BARANYAI	CC
Chairman of the PPF	Gyula KÁLLAI	CC
Secretary of the PPF	Imre POZSGAI	CC
Chairman of the National Union of Cooperatives	István SZLAMENICKY	CC
Chairman of the National Union of the Agricultural Producers' Cooperatives	István SZABÓ	PB
Chairman of the National Assembly	István SARLÓS	PB
Chairman of the Constitutional Law Council	Mihály KOROM	CC

(Politburo: 18.4 percent; Central Committee: 34.7 percent; Total 53.1 percent)
Source: RFE Research 11, No. 31 (August 1, 1986): 24–25; and Magyar Hírek 40, No. 2 (January 24, 1987): 3; and Magyar Hírek, 40, 15 (July 24, 1987), p. 3.

of workers and peasants who had no previous experience and who lacked formal qualifications (many of whom in the meantime were handed diplomas without ever attending schools) were put in charge of a bureaucratic apparatus accountable for the implementation of the policies thrust upon them. Although in the meantime a new generation of bureaucrats came into being, most of the old ones continued to function in diverse positions in the various movements and agencies representing the sectional interests of the state.

Today the key positions of the huge state bureaucracy are in the hands of the Hungarian technocrats—a new breed of scientists and engineers who comprise the knowledge and skills of modern technology. They are responsible for developing new ideas and concepts for the continuation of socialist construction in Hungary. They are present at the highest political forums, in part as associates of scientific institutions and in part as research workers of party organizations or academic employees with party affiliation. In fact, in an oversimplified manner, they could be referred to as the men and women who constitute the "shadow government," the technocratic structure of authority. It should be noted, however, that until the mid-1960s, the relationship between these technocrats and the established political authority in Hungary was suspicion-ridden and inimical. Then an abrupt change took place: the experts were allowed to present their conceptions, to publish them in journals, and to debate them before scientific and intellectual fora. The party and government authorities did not identify with any of these new concepts and ideas until much later when the outcome of the debates had been crystallized. Many of these ideas became an integral part of the New Economic Mechanism (NEM), which was officially sponsored and launched by the party and government rulers in 1968. During this process several concessions were made by the originators of the economic reforms—

they consensually sacrificed portions of their theories and thus subjugated rational economic concepts to political ones, which they considered a palatable compromise. It is important to emphasize, however, that during the course of this process of making concessions or reaching a compromise, a commitment was made by the party elite that they would personally guarantee all-out support and continuation of the economic reform movement in exchange for the pledge by the technocratic bureaucracy that there would be no possibility or danger of usurping of power by them. This arrangement is also binding on the younger members of the party leadership who were elected or co-opted into the highest organs of the Central Committee of the HSWP. As a result, the percentage of the membership of the HSWP with university degrees increased from 10.8 percent in 1975 to 21.0 percent in 1985.[13] In this respect it is safe to argue that the highest authority of party and government faces a younger generation of technocrats, not as adversaries or rivals or even challengers of the former's authority, but as supporters, collaborators, and defenders of this authority as long as the policies of the reform movement are in force. Should there be any question as to the future possibility of a cleavage leading to a power struggle between the two groups, we may presume that the integration of the younger generation of technocrats into the party and government structure of authority is more likely to be the outcome.[14]

Furthermore, the organizational role of the technocratic bureaucracy in Hungary is quite different today from that of the top hierarchy of the bureaucratic apparatus prior to the NEM. (See Figure 2.1.) We have already pointed out that economic planning is one of the essential ingredients of socialism. Consistent with the reform movement in Hungary, during the 1970s economic planning was reorganized; it no longer deals exclusively with economics. It has been expanded to include demographic problems, changes in social structure, class differentiation, cultural issues, education, and health. Thus economic planning today is not solely concerned with matters of production and distribution; it also encompasses the area of social problems. As such it is linked to political processes through the politics of "planning the democratization of society," which means that the political leadership is gradually accepting the fact that Hungarian society has different organized groups with different interests and that a political decision is realistic only insofar as it takes into consideration some sort of synthesis of their interests. For the same reason, the programs included in the plans are realistic only inasmuch as they rest on some balance of these interests. For this reason, Hungary has reorganized the entire process of planning: today it can no longer be said that there is an expert bureaucracy whose job it is to formulate the plans expressing the optimum as seen by these so-called experts; rather there are hosts of representative organs for the different

Figure 2.1
The Hungarian System of Government

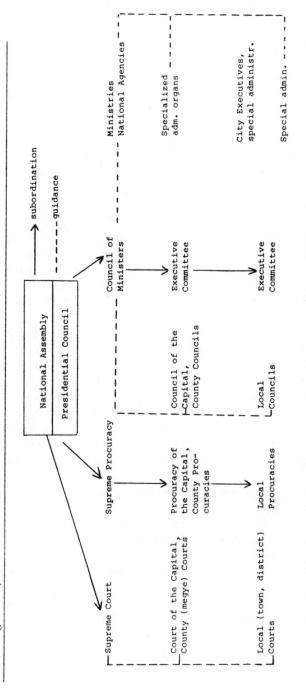

Source: Adapted from Hans-Georg Heinrich, *Hungary*, (London: Frances Pinter, 1986), 70.

interest groups who also have an input in the decision-making process when the authoritative policymakers must wrestle with such issues as those affecting the trade unions or the writers' associations, or the communist youth organizations, and those representing different sectional interests of the country. This way, in addition to economic rationale, decisions by the planners must include social, psychological, as well as political considerations. The proper mix of these ingredients should result in a balanced decision, which means that the "technocratic bureaucracy" must be open-minded, innovative, and dynamic. Consequently, their impact on the authoritative policymakers is also a positive one by requiring the political leaders to be pragmatists—motivated not by a common ideology but by a desire to weigh realistic situations. It would be fair to assume, therefore, that in theory it is the party elite that makes the decisions on key issues, but the de facto preparation of the data and input for these decisions is definitely in the hands of the technocrats, who in practice become part of the political structure. It is extremely rare to find a proposal originating from the technocratic bureaucracy—for example, the Planning Office or the Ministry of Foreign Trade or the Treasury—reaching the political leadership and being rejected in its entirety. Rather, it is more characteristic that such a proposal will be evaluated from a particular point of view, that of politics. However, the party elite is astute enough not to want to accept responsibility for a technological decision. At the same time, the technological bureaucracy is mature enough not to limit itself to its own special considerations, but tries to weigh the sociopolitical consequences in advance. As a matter of fact, we may assume that the technocrats are charged with the responsibility to prepare proposals that already encompass the sociopolitical ingredients. For example, a group of economists cannot make a blanket recommendation that the prices of goods and commodities be raised by 10 percent without considering the political acceptability of such a proposal.

Perhaps the most important change in the present-day operation of the reorganized Hungarian bureaucracy is what the renowned sociologist, Kálmán Kulcsár, called "the strengthening of the professional element, and an organizational 'channeling' of scientific knowledge into the decision-making process."[15] This observation by Kulcsár is particularly important when one considers the fact that Hungary spends the same proportion of its GNP on research and development as does the United States or the Federal Republic of Germany; however, in exploiting research results, Hungary figures at the bottom of the list in Europe. According to János Fekete, first deputy chairman of the National Bank of Hungary, there seems to be nothing wrong with the talent and competence of Hungary's 30,000 or so scientific researchers; the problem lies in the interface (the bureaucracy) between research and economy.[16]

Or, more specifically, according to Lénard Pál, Chairman of the Working Group on Educational Policy of the HSWP/CC and former secretary general of the Hungarian Academy of Sciences, the problem is with modernization of the planning, regulatory decision making, managing, training, institutional and organizational systems, and of the interest relations of society; in other words, the broad scope of Hungarian bureaucracy.[17] The social and economic problems that had accumulated by the end of the 1970s constitute a challenge that in turn demands social innovation. This challenge manifests itself in the exhaustion of the old bureaucratic means for solving the accumulated problems inherent in the former structure. Thus, hand-in-hand with building socialist democracy goes the streamlining of the bureaucratic apparatus and the demands for social reforms in Hungarian society.

THE TOILERS' SHARE IN POWER

In the foregoing section of this chapter our focus was on the rulers of Hungarian society, who in general terms make up about 8 percent of the population. In this section our concern will be with the ruled members of Hungarian society, comprising 92 percent of the population. Whereas the former are members of HSWP, most of the latter are members of different mass organizations such as the trade unions, the Patriotic People's Front, the Communist Youth League, the women's movement, cooperative and professional organizations, and various associations and religious groups. Strong party ties with these organizations are a prerequisite to the success of building socialist democracy in the country. For this reason, the guidelines for the 13th Party Congress urged party members to consult with noncommunists for a meeting of the minds and stressed the importance of the Party's ideological, political, and organizational unity; according to the guidelines, "the party must cultivate programs that have a mass appeal and reduce its preoccupation with bureaucratic or theoretical matters."[18] It also insisted on asserting the party's political guidance of the various mass organizations through party members who were also members of these organizations. Accordingly these guidelines were supposed to have been debated by party and other organizations with the objective of achieving a "national consensus."[19] Although there were debates of the guidelines by noncommunist mass organizations, these debates were limited in attendance and met with considerable skepticism on the part of the public. Not too many people who do not belong to the party really believe in the socialist democratization process. Many are of the opinion that the changes so far instituted by the ruling elite have been more cosmetic and less substance. Even at the meetings of the primary party organizations (there are approximately 25,000 of them), which were responsible for the preparation of the guidelines, a lack of vigor in participation and interest in the agenda was noticeable. One provincial journalist, for example, reported that many people were absent from the meetings because they were excused for being ill.[20] Another journalist listed among the topics discussed the price of tobacco, housing for Gypsies, and why the local gasoline station does not sell premium grade gasoline.[21] It would seem, therefore, that these days members of Hungarian society—regardless of whether they are rank-and-file members of the party—are far less interested in ideology and revolution than in prosaic problems that run close to home. What were the major changes contributing to socialist democracy and how do they affect the relations between the rulers and the ruled?

Probably the greatest achievement so far of the socialist democratization process was the enactment of the New Electoral Law in 1983, which went into force on June 8, 1985, when Hungary's local council and parliamentary elections were held. The preparation of this law involved citizens' participation in a three-week national debate of the draft proposal under the auspices of the National Council of the Patriotic People's Front (PPF).[22] The new law is grouped under four headings:

1. While individual electoral districts (constituencies) remain the basic framework for elections, at least 2 or more candidates must be nominated in each district for election to the National Assembly (parliament) and local councils (there is now a total of 59,270 council seats in Hungary).

2. In addition to the elected candidates, those who obtain at least 25 percent of the votes will become alternate deputies or council members. If a vacancy in their particular district occurs, they will automatically take over the vacant parliamentary or council seat, thus eliminating the need for by-elections.

3. For election to the National Assembly, prominent individuals (about 10 percent of the total number of deputies) were elected on a separate national list voted upon by all citizens eligible to vote. The candidates running on this national list were nominated by the PPF National Council on the basis of recommendations made by political and social bodies and special interest groups that are members of PPF. Thus the National Assembly, which had 352 seats, increased the number of deputies to 387, an increase of 35.

4. The interests of small localities joined together for administrative purposes under a common (or joint) council must be better represented in the work of the higher level councils; a self-governing local board was consequently established in each locality.

In accordance with Hungary's New Electoral Law, on April 15, 1985, local councils and other political, social, and corporate bodies of the Patriotic People's Front were instructed to begin organizing nominating meetings for the selection of candidates for local council and parliamentary seats. At these meetings, members of the electorate (about

7,500,000 Hungarian citizens, including 600,000 young "first-time" voters) were asked for the first time to put forward at least two nominees per constituency for each seat to be filled.[23] This meant that within one month, by May 15, the 352 parliamentary and the 1,571 local council constituencies had to nominate more than 700 candidate parliamentary deputies and more than 3,000 candidates for local councils.[24] Constituencies had the whole month to complete their nominations. Unlike local council constituencies, where there is one representative for every 600–1,000 people, the parliamentary constituencies, where one deputy represents about 30,000 people, had at least two nominating meetings. According to the law, every nomination made at the first nominating meeting had also to be submitted to a vote at subsequent meetings in the order they were originally introduced.[25] Eligible to participate in the nominating meetings were residents of the constituency and representatives of workers in enterprises, cooperatives, offices, and other institutions located in the district.[26] Nominations could be made by agencies of the PPF and other political, social, and corporate bodies,[27] as well as by any qualified voter present.

In an interview with the trade union daily *Népszava*,[28] Béla Molnár, secretary of the National Council of the PPF, was asked to explain how the PPF selected its nominees. Rejecting the commonly held view that these selections were made on the basis of "statistical considerations," Molnár insisted that the PPF's most important aim was to pick candidates "who enjoy the confidence of the people and who are suited to carrying out [the PPF's] policies." With the introduction of mandatory multiple candidacies, Molnár pointed out, special efforts had to be made to ensure that the nominees had "equal chances." Therefore, it was important to make certain that competing nominees had "approximately equal qualifications." Although, he admitted, there had been attempts in some districts to fix the election's outcome in advance, for example, by trying to get the chairman of the local council and a tractor driver on the same ballot, the PPF did not and would not allow such attempts to succeed. In order to guarantee the nominees an equal opportunity, the PPF would take great care to avoid situations in which young nominees would have to compete against old ones or men would have to run against women; in other words, situations in which people's prejudices were more likely to surface. In Molnár's view, it was similarly "natural" to avoid pairing clerics with party members.

Those receiving at least one-third of the votes cast by the registered voters present at the nominating meetings were accepted as official candidates for the local councils and the Hungarian National Assembly. As in pre-reform elections, however, nominations had to be made by "open vote," and the nominees, whether they were proposed by the PPF or from the floor, were obligated to make a written pledge to uphold the program of the PPF.[29] Had the participants been unable to find two qualified candidates by May 15, "the fate of the mandate" would have been decided by a special election. While it is true that nominees had to embrace the PPF's platform, the new electoral law allowed them at least in theory to prepare their own individual programs geared to the specific problems of their respective constituencies. Voters present at the nominating meetings were allowed to ask questions of the people recommended by the PPF and "could comment" on any individual program, expressing support for or objection to any parts of it. If a voter had a complaint or a recommendation about how a nominating meeting was conducted, he had recourse to contacting his local election presidium within three days of the meeting for a possible remedy.

With regard to pre-election campaigning, Béla Molnár claimed that some nominees had "yet to learn the moral rules of fair competition in public life." In the meantime, he said, it was up to the local PPF committees to prevent name-calling campaigns from ever materializing. On the other hand, he stressed, nominees were given "every assistance" in making their programs known, including publicity in the enterprise newsletter and even on cable television. The PPF, he added, did and would do again everything possible to ensure that the other nominee was given the same opportunity to present his views.

One of the more controversial features of the new law was the introduction of the so-called national list. The candidates placed by the PPF on this ballot ran unopposed and were "voted" upon in all 352 electoral districts. These "honorary" nominees, one provincial paper explained, are people "whose work and sphere of activity reached far beyond the boundaries of a given constituency."[30] On April 12, after months of vigorous propaganda, the PPF announced the names of these 35 "prominent" Hungarians against whom the weekly magazine *Magyarország*[31] claimed it would be hopeless for other candidates to run.[32] For the names of the "honorary" nominees, see Table 2.3.

One could ask the question: What made these 35 people so "special" that they were selected over arguably hundreds of other distinguished and qualified citizens? Did they really enjoy so much popularity in their respective constituencies that running against them would be merely an exercise in futility? A closer look at the composition of the list reveals that 23 of the 35 were current members of parliament and 21 of them had been serving for longer than one term. Of these 21 incumbents, 16 (76 percent) suffered a decline ranging from 0.1 percent to as high as 1 percent in popularity between 1975 and 1980, in terms of the number of votes cast against them. Only three incumbents gained popularity, and in the case of two (András Gyenes and István Sarlós) this may have been because they ran in different districts in the 1975 and 1980 elec-

Table 2.3

Composition of the National Nominating List According to Category of Representation

Category of Representation	Number of Nominees	% of the Total	Currently Not Deputy
Party (including mass organizations)	16[a]	45.7	3[e]
Clergy	6[b]	17.2	2[f]
Nationalities	4[c]	11.4	3[g]
Creative (academic, the arts, etc.)	5[d]	14.3	4[h]
Pensioners	4	11.4	0

[a] Fifteen CC members (including ten Politburo members) and the Chairman of the Central Control Committee. Of the newly elected Politburo, only Károly Grósz, László Maróthy, and György Aczél are not on the list.

[b] Including two Catholic, one Reformed, one Lutheran, and one Jewish representative.

[c] One Romanian, one Slovak, a Southern Slav, and a German.

[d] Three academicians, an actor, and a sculptor.

[e] Including recently elected Politburo member Csaba Hámori, PPF General Secretary Imre Pozsgay, and MNOT Chairwoman, Mrs. Lajos Duschek. (Note: István Szabó, who, like Hámori, was just recently elected to the Politburo, is already a member of parliament and hence would be up for re-election.)

[f] Jozsef Szakács and János Kiss.

[g] Mrs. Róbert Jakab, Marin Mandity, and György Mark.

[h] Only József Bognár is currently a member of parliament.

Source: *Magyar Nemzet*, April 12, 1985.

tions. The popularity index of two deputies (Kádár and Losonczi) remained unchanged.

Although at this point it is difficult to comment on the relative popularity of the nonincumbent candidates on the national list, one suspects, given their backgrounds, that it was only a secondary consideration in selecting them. Nine of the twelve are representatives of the clergy, the nationalities, and the creative fields (two, three, and four, respectively); and as such they seem to have been chosen with the intention of giving the list a more appealing "balance." It appears that the regime's effort to boost public interest in the "democratic process" through the nominating meetings met with mixed success. In constituencies where the outcome of the nominating process had been deemed to be a foregone conclusion, voter apathy remained high. *Magyar Hírlap (Hungarian Journal)*, for example, reported a nominating meeting for candidates to the local council at which only 28 of the almost 900 eligible voters showed up.[33] In other instances, according to reports, rooms were filled to capacity and the debates were spirited. The excitement and the unexpectedly strong showing by non-PPF people nominated from the floor in some districts could have initiated new questions about official tolerance in this matter. Of the first 362 nominating meetings for local council candidacies, for example, eleven of the people recommended by the PPF failed to get the one-third of the votes required to be nominated, and 40 people were chosen who were not on the PPF's "recommended list."[34] The two most interesting cases involving a bid for the nomination to the National Assembly are László Rajk, son of a former government minister executed in 1949 after a Stalinist show trial, but later rehabilitated, and the philosopher Gáspár Miklós Tamás, both prominent dissidents.

On April 18, 1985, the first of two required nomination meetings was held in the southern constituency of Budapest's fifth district. Much to the regime's surprise and embarrassment, the meetings did not follow the usual pattern of mock debates and prearranged outcomes. Rajk's supporters took advantage of Article 37, Section 2, of the electoral law, which stipulates that in addition to those nominated by the Patriotic People's Front, additional names may be put forward, and were able to muster the votes of about 40 percent of the 223 people present. This strong showing raised the hopes of many observers that the Hungarian regime might indeed be sincere in its alleged efforts to broaden democracy and that it might allow a token "outsider" to be "elected" to parliament.

These hopes, however, were soon to be shattered. The regime, clearly caught off guard by the first round of nominations, was determined to prevent similar surprises at the second meeting on April 22, 1985. Two hours before it was scheduled to begin, the hall was filled to capacity by communist activists, plainclothes men, and simple factory workers who were promised a day off in exchange for attending the meeting. Since they were there in the presence of their bosses, the voting by acclamation was a foregone conclusion. Needless to say, these "citizens" could not be swayed by Rajk's passionate speech, which touched on such controversial and timely issues as conscientious objection to armed military service, the environment, the fate of Hungarian minorities abroad, and other topics considered taboo for public discussion. Several of Rajk's supporters spoke ardently in his behalf, but many "concerned" voters made sarcastic comments and catcalls, creating a heated atmosphere that had long been absent from gatherings of this sort in Hungary. When the dust finally settled it was clear that Rajk's effort had not succeeded; with only 378 of the 1,388 votes cast on April 22 and 468 of 1,611 at the two meetings, he failed to get the necessary one-third to become a candidate.[35] Not surprised by this outcome, Rajk told foreign reporters that his intent had been to "test the system" and try to establish a precedent for the future. Despite the jeers and boos, he said he viewed his chance to address the voters as a "legal platform."[36]

At two similarly emotional meetings in the northern constituency of the fifth district, Rajk's fellow dissident, the philosopher Gáspár Miklós Tamás, was also proposed as a candidate.[37] Tamás, who is a former Rumanian citizen, failed to win the necessary support at the first meeting (he received only 47 of 310 ballots), but he had the chance to share the speaker's platform with one of the PPF's "prominent" nominees, Foreign Minister Dr. Péter Várkonyi, who reportedly appeared "distinctly annoyed" by what must have been an extremely uncomfortable situation as he was forced to listen to the dissident speak about the lot of the Hungarian minorities in Rumania and Slovakia and the potentially disastrous impact on the environment of the proposed Hungarian-Czechoslovak Gabčikovo-Nagymaros water project.

As many as 40 other individuals were taking advantage of the opportunity presented by the new law. They included such nondissident critics of the regime's policies as the economist Tamás Bauer and the engineer János Tóth, an outspoken critic of the Hungarian-Czechoslovak dam project. While their chances of success appeared slim, their efforts were important insofar as they provided indisputable proof of the desire among the electorate for an alternative. This has been corroborated by the results of other, less controversial local council and parliamentary nominating meetings, which have shown that people are not satisfied with the choices presented to them by the PPF; in many cases they have either rejected the PPF's candidates or added third or fourth candidates to the list. It must be remembered, however, that while the party could be embarrassed by a large number of the PPF's recommended nominees being turned down, in the long run it cannot lose. As the chairman of the Hungarian National Assembly István Sarlós warned, "only those people can become members of the National Assembly who are prepared to accept the PPF's election notice [its summarized program] and embrace the program, which reflects the goals of our party's 13th congress."[38]

It should also be pointed out that as an enforcer of the party's desires and a symbol of the regime's alliance policy, the PPF has played a pivotal role in preparing for and conducting the parliamentary and local elections, overseeing everything from the formulation of the candidates' compulsory "platform" on the basis of the party's policy, the organization of nominating meetings, and the selection of nominees, to the actual task of getting people out to vote.

According to official figures, about 1,500,000 citizens participated in the 42,500 local council and 719 parliamentary constituencies; 298 had double candidates, 50 had triple, and 4 had quadruple candidates. For the 42,500 local seats up for contention, 2,354 electoral districts nominated 3 candidates, 87 nominated 4; and the rest nominated 2.[39] Of the 152 people nominated from the floor for parliamentary deputy, 70 received the qualifying one-third of the total votes cast at two or more nominating meetings; 51 of them had been proposed in addition to the two nominees successfully put forward by the PPF. Of the 1,500,000 voters attending the meetings (20 percent of the country's 7,800,000 eligible voters), more than 150,000 asked to speak in support of proposed candidates.[40] When the nominating process was concluded with all the candidates safely within the fold of the PPF and potential "trouble makers" carefully weeded out, the basic outcome of the election had already been decided. According to the final count, the number of valid votes cast for parliamentary candidates was 6,716,387, or 94.6%. Of the total number of votes cast in the local council poll, 95.4%, or 6,797,822, were valid. With all the votes counted and the number of valid and invalid votes determined, the PPF daily *Magyar Nemzet* reported that 310 of the 352 contestable National Assembly seats had been filled and that 285 alternate deputies had been elected.[41] In 42 (12 percent) of the constituencies, however, neither candidate was able to muster the necessary percentage of the votes (more than 50 percent) and hence special runoff elections preceeded by new nomination meetings before June 22, 1985, had to be held in these constituencies. Similarly, special elections were also required in 849 (2 percent) of the 42,734 local council constituencies. Participation in the runoff elections was much lower than in the regular elections, which had a low turnout compared to the 1980 elections (94.6 percent vs. 99.2 percent). Only 83 percent of the eligible voters cast their votes for the 41 deputies and 41 alternates, and only 73.9 percent cast their votes for the 846 local council members and 783 alternates. Although 77 percent of the parliamentary seats were won by party members, slightly more than in 1980, there appears to be a noticeable decline in the number of professional party and state *apparatchiki* among them. For example, first secretary of the county party committee in *Veszprém* János Pap; long-time HSWP functionary István Szürdi; vice president of the National Council of the PPF, László Hegedüs; director of the

HSWP/CC's Institute of Party History István Huszár; former prime minister (1967–1975), Jenö Fock; former interior minister and ex-Politburo
member Béla Biszku; returned editor-in-chief of the PPF daily, Tibor
Pétkö; Secretary of the National Council of Trade Unions, Sándor Nagy;
First Secretary of the *Köszeg* HSWP committee, Ferenc Péterifi—and
others—failed to receive the 50 percent vote required for a seat in parliament.[42] As a result of upsets in the runoff elections, 20 candidates
were elected to parliament who were not nominated by the PPF, raising
the number of such members to 45. A look at the occupational make-
up of the members shows that they include more doctors (15), more
than twice as many agricultural producers' cooperative presidents (30),
and 25 percent more (about 100) technocrats (enterprise managers, engineers, technicians and so on).[43] Only three of the women candidates
competing against men in 42 parliamentary constituencies won, 27 lost,
and 12 failed to get more than 50 percent of the votes. It can be argued
that the electoral reform's original intent—to reduce the political and
ideological tension that has been aggravated by increasingly serious economic problems—has temporarily been carried out. If one adds up the
number of abstentions, the negative and invalid votes, and the votes cast
for the non-PPF candidates, one finds, however, that about 10 percent
of the population either considers the regime's policies unacceptable or
at least feels that there is a need for some kind of change. For the party
authorities the 1985 elections were a bold step toward more democracy.
Similar but more modest praises were echoed in both the Western media
and the Eastern bloc. A special correspondent, Jovan Pjević, for the
Yugoslav daily *Borba,* however, disagreed. According to Pjević, while
elements of the modified Hungarian electoral system were indeed "very
liberal," in practice the changes had essentially done nothing to alter
one-party rule in the country.[44]

Hand-in-hand with the new Electoral Law goes also the reorganization
and restructuring of the Hungarian local government system. As of
January 1, 1984, the country's districts *(járás)* ceased to exist as state
administrative units. Most of the district offices' authority was taken over
by the large borough *(község)* councils, which, like the town councils, were
placed under the authority of the counties. At the same time, the district
party committees were abolished, and their functions and spheres of
jurisdiction were transferred to the town and large borough party committees; the latter are now functioning under the direction of the county
party committees. The structure of the district courts, public prosecutor's
offices, police, people's control, and other state agencies were also adjusted to meet the new structural changes in local government. Similar
instructions were issued to the district mass organizations and public
movements to adjust their territorial agencies to the changes in public
administration and party structure.[45] These changes, plus the establish-

ment of local boards *(elöljárosság)* and the introduction of new settlement development policies, simplified administration by doing away with certain overlapping functions, which in turn significantly enhanced the role and importance of local council members. On the whole, with this reorganization, locally elected bodies were given a larger role, the standard of the work they perform has supposedly increased, and the publicity and social control of state activities has supposedly improved. According to Central Committee secretary and Politburo member Mihály Korom, the streamlining of the bureaucracy at the local level is not only an attempt to decentralize power, but also a fulfillment of a commitment by the party to implement the policies of socialist democracy. Eventually, Korom maintains, the country will move toward a "two-tiered public administration."[46] For the time being, however, Hungary has 19 counties, no districts, 97 towns (of which four—Budapest, Hajduböszörmény, Százhalombatta, and Turkeve—were omitted from being regional centers), and 43 large boroughs. The new regional centers consist of the remaining 93 existing towns and the 43 large boroughs, for a total of 136, instead of the previous 83 districts.

Another important change in the socialist democratization process occurred on April 17, 1984, when the Central Committee of the Hungarian Socialist Workers' Party (HSWP/CC) announced that in order to improve the system of economic management, the central direction of the state farms would be replaced in 1985 by self-governing bodies like those already adopted in agricultural cooperatives.[47] Many of the responsibilities that formerly fell to the state administration were transferred to the farms and their elected bodies. Hereafter, production plans, the use of profits, personnel matters, production methods, management, technical development, social policy, and the use of scientific research will be decided by the self-governing bodies. The Ministry of Agriculture and Food continues, however, to retain the right to create or dissolve farms, maintain legal control over the organizational and operational regulations of elected bodies, regulate agricultural markets, and exercise other administrative controls of an official character.[48]

In order to implement the decentralization process, the Ministry of Agriculture and Food began to make the necessary changes in the second half of 1984. Leaders of state farms and representatives of the party, labor unions, and the Communist Youth League (KISz) held a conference at which they coordinated their ideas about the new form of economic management and drew up regulations for the organization and operation of the new self-governing bodies and for the election of members to these groups.[49]

In compliance with an official statement following the conference, every state farm under the ministry's jurisdiction changed over to cooperative leadership in the first half of 1985; 96 of the 120 state farms are now directed by enterprise councils and 24 by delegate or membership meetings. An enterprise council usually consists of 25–40 members. Half of the members are elected by the farm workers from their own ranks; the other half are appointed by the branch leaders and the director of the farm. Each member of the delegate meetings represents about 10 percent of those working on the farm. On smaller farms, membership meetings are held with all of those working there participating. As of January 1, 1985, directors ceased to be appointed and are now elected by secret ballot by the enterprise councils or the delegate or membership meetings.

In order, however, to make a gradual changeover to the new system, new directors were not elected in most cases. Instead, self-governing bodies either confirmed the present directors in their positions for the next five years or replaced them forthwith.[50] By mid-March 1985, most of the incumbent directors had received the two-thirds majority necessary to stay for another five years. There have been several cases, however, of the director not being reelected, even though he was the only candidate.[51] In Heves County, for example, three former directors were not reelected by the enterprise council.[52] In such cases applications are taken for the vacant post. The procedure is similar when a director retires. Those nominated for enterprise councils or delegates' meetings were also rejected in some cases. On certain farms a candidate respected by his fellow workers defeated the candidate proposed by the nominating committee.[53] In the same Heves County, 13 of the 314 workers elected were not on the list compiled by the nominating committees.

The abolition of the National Center of State Farms was completed by June 30, 1985, and the creation of the self-governing bodies appears to make state farm management more independent and self-contained, but it was necessary, at the same time, for the Ministry of Agriculture and Food to set up an organization to ensure cooperation among the state farms. The National Association of State Farms was created in April 1985 to coordinate farm work and production. It does not, however, directly control the state farms. The new organization will also safeguard the farms' interests and organize services promoting production. Robert Burgert, a member of HSWP/CC and general manager of the Babolna Agricultural Complex, has been elected chairman of the association, and András Klenczner, the former general manager of the National Center of State Farms, its general manager.[54]

Another major change affecting the relationship between the rulers and the ruled in Hungarian society is the system of new types of management of Hungarian enterprises.[55] Prior to that change, however, the Hungarian authorities did some "housecleaning" of unprofitable enterprises.

On August 13, 1984, for example, Industry Minister László Kapolyi personally informed the 700 workers of the Budapest plant of the medium-sized Office Equipment and Fine Mechanics Enterprise (the Hungarian acronym for which is IGV) that on the basis of Finance Ministry law-decree No. 37/1978, the company was being liquidated because it was unprofitable. The next day the 500 workers of IGV's plant at Vásárosnamény were also told of the ministerial decisions. It was the first time in postwar Hungary that a state enterprise had been closed without a legal successor. The principal reason of IGV's liquidation was the fact that its economic operation could no longer be ensured. As a result of weak organization and management, the export-oriented IGV, which since the early 1970s manufactured cash registers and typewriters, could not tackle the new requirements brought about by the world economic recession.[56]

The decision to liquidate IGV was not a sudden one but the outcome of a painstaking process involving a number of state agencies. It was reached by the government's Economic Committee, which for the past two years had been scrutinizing IGV's woes. Also involved were the Planning Office, the Finance Ministry, and the National Material and Price Office, which all leaned toward liquidation without a legal successor, and the Industry and Foreign Trade Ministries, which favored elimination through a merger. The drawn-out debate was unable to produce a rational compromise until the Hungarian National Bank worked out a financial proposal. Of IGV's work force of over 700 in Budapest, about 650 were hired and retained by the Medicor Works, while the 500 workers of the other liquidated plant were retained to manufacture parts for Medicor.[57] Even so, there were rumblings from the workers and the trade union representatives about "misplaced humaneness" and indifference to workers' rights.

Toward the end of August 1984, Károly Demeter, general manager of the Tungsram Co., Ltd., revealed in a lengthy interview published in the party daily, Népszabadság[58] that in the past 18 months Tungsram's work force of 26,000 had been cut by 3,000 and that more personnel reductions were being planned. He gave as the main reasons the pressing need to make the enterprise more profitable and to modernize and improve its organization and management. The company was ranked 27th overall among Hungary's 2,676 enterprises and cooperatives, eighth according to labor force, seventh according to its nonruble account earnings.[59] Following a huge deficit in 1982, the State Planning Committee in 1983 worked out a financial plan to stabilize the enterprise by 1985. However, the problems of uneven production, below world level productivity, overcentralized management, and the lack of incentives continued to plague the enterprise. Thus the reorganization of planning and management, in which 80 percent of the top and mid-level managers were also dismissed, increased the autonomy as well as productivity of the enterprise. The most important thing, according to Demeter, was to make workers understand that these measures were being taken in their best interests so as to achieve more economical operations and provide better earning opportunities. Tungsram closed its krypton lamp plant in Miskolc (with 70 workers displaced), its Pécs plant (with 320 workers), and reduced its work force by an additional 1,200 by March 1985 in order to keep its operation stable and solvent.

The two examples of IGV and Tungsram provide a good idea of the difficulties encountered in the streamlining or closure of unprofitable enterprises, which is accompanied by the inevitable dismissal and re-taining of large numbers of workers. While the former aids the modernization process of the Hungarian economy, the latter contributes to tension between the pro-reformists and anti-reformists in Hungarian politics. According to Hungary's National Bank, "in 1984 at least 100 Hungarian enterprises were permanently insolvent." Enterprises and cooperatives lost 2,000 million forints ($40 million) in 1982 and 5,700 million ($114 million) in 1983, losses that were, for the most part, covered by the state budget.[60]

The need to eliminate redundant labor has long been recognized, but enterprises have been reluctant to take action in the form of layoffs, thus hindering the process of efficient labor regrouping. With the participation of the trade unions, the government passed a decree in May 1983 to alleviate the problem, essentially by subsidizing labor regrouping. However, according to the State Wage and Labor Office only a third of Hungary's enterprises have carried out labor regroupings, and this within their own gates in almost every case. As a result, the needed change in the structure of the labor force is not proceeding at an adequate pace, and labor shortages and surpluses still continue to exist side by side in Hungary.[61]

According to Albert Rácz, chairman of the State Wage and Labor Office, some 100,000 workers are holding redundant jobs in industry and must reckon with an "eventual change in their careers." This would mean temporary layoffs and retraining for different jobs, but no unemployment, Rácz pledged. At the same time, there were 90,000 jobs nationwide that needed to be filled, he stated.[62]

It is also worth noting that in the Tungsram and IGV cases, the trade unions appear to have accepted the rather painful decisions without any particular resistance. According to Tungsram labor union secretary János Góder, the union was doing its best to offer new jobs to those affected by the work force reduction, and one could not speak of layoffs except in the case of those workers for whom new jobs could not be found. According to Tungsram's party secretary Gábor Zentai, although "uncertainty" prevailed among enterprise workers, none of them should worry about unemployment.[63] Thus it is appropriate to ask whether the

IGV and Tungsram cases are a precedent for the 100 or so permanently insolvent enterprises, or are they only a window dressing used to appease the technocrats serving the party elite? Let us now examine the April 17, 1984, directive by the plenum of the HSWP/CC regarding the new types of enterprise management.

On January 1, 1985, Hungarian enterprises began a gradual change-over to a system of management based on a combination of collective and individual responsibilities. Apart from Yugoslavia (and now China), Hungary is the first country to introduce a system whereby workers' representatives can have a say in both the way the enterprise is run and, in some cases, in the appointment of its manager. Although the new system contains certain elements of democracy, the party will not, however, be losing much of its present control over economic management.

The relative democratization of the existing management structures is intended to implement the principles of Hungary's economic reform, first introduced in 1968. The first law that gave the workers the right to become involved in decision making was not passed until 1977,[64] but its implementation was so poor that it can be considered to have failed. Since the fate of the economic reform was often uncertain, because of both internal and external criticism of it, even a new law-decree passed in 1982, and similar in content to the 1977 decree, brought about little change to the existing structures.[65] The April 17, 1984, plenum of the HSWP/CC, however, finally came to grips with the issue. It strongly defended the economic reform and listed three types of management structures to be introduced in the different types of enterprises during the next two years.[66]

1. *Enterprises run by state administration or by managerial councils.* Enterprises providing community and public services and key companies classified as economically strategic will continue to be run directly by the state (ministries). These enterprises include those providing educational, military, cultural, and health services as well as public utilities such as transportation and the water supply. Although some of them will have a managerial council, to which some workers will belong, their function will be strictly limited by the supervising ministry. The top managers of these enterprises will be appointed (and dismissed if necessary) by the ministry. This essentially unchanged structure will apply to 20–25 percent of the enterprises, employing about 35 percent of the total work force.

2. *Enterprises run by an elected management.* Smaller enterprises with a work force of 300–500 people and with a fairly simple organizational structure will be allowed to elect their management directly or through their representatives. The work force can also make certain recommendations concerning the operation of the factory. It would, however, be

wrong to suppose that all persons applying for the managerial post would be automatically presented to the employees for consideration. When the ministry advertises a job opening, it not only sets high—sometimes too high—professional standards, but political standards as well. A prospective manager must have political schooling and documentary proof of political and moral reliability. This proof could be denied a candidate, for any number of reasons. If a close relative of a particular applicant, for example, had recently left Hungary illegally, the applicant might be denied the document certifying his political reliability and therefore be unable to become the head of an enterprise. Out of all those who apply for a post only a few will be presented to the workers for consideration. This procedure has been followed until now only by the cooperatives that had been showing definite advantages over large industrial enterprises for some time, precisely because their management was elected and therefore better qualified for the job, having a greater knowledge of the market.

3. *Enterprises run by enterprise councils.* Under this structure the state ministries will delegate some of their responsibilities to an enterprise council, half of which will consist of workers and the other half of the enterprise manager and his appointees. The party, the Communist Youth League, and the labor unions, will also "assist" in the decision making. "The object is to encourage the enterprises to take more responsibility for their actions."[67] The hope is that a bigger stake for workers in the enterprise's success will encourage better work performance. The new forms of management will not, however, change the basis for enterprise operations, which remains state ownership. The council will have the rights of an employer over the manager. It will not only elect the enterprise manager but will also have the right to remove him from his post. Thus, during the very first meetings of the new councils the present managers were voted out or had their positions endorsed. This has apparently caused such concern among enterprise managers that they are currently seeking to form an interest group under the auspices of the Patriotic People's Front to defend their own rights. Other managers "literally pleaded with the ministry to let them stay with the old system of state-managed employment."[68]

Interestingly enough, some workers interviewed about the new system had just the opposite fear. While the ministry could remove an incompetent manager without protracted deliberations, they feared that the council could drag out this procedure. They based their fear on the fact that only 50 percent of the council consists of workers; the rest of the members belong to the management. Should some of the workers be afraid of being openly critical of management, the council might never convince the majority of its members to remove the manager.

One worker mentioned, for example, that he himself, if he should run for the managerial job, would not like to be judged by his peers, since he did not believe that a worker is always competent to make such a judgment. Others were afraid that the same problem faced by shop stewards in presenting their arguments to the management might crop up for workers on the councils. Managers with professional and political training tend to have an upper hand over workers in formal debate, the latter naturally lacking the necessary experience and confidence to voice their views effectively.

Yet the ministries are optimistic that this joint responsibility will not increase the gap between workers and management but make them work together. They base their belief on the fact that since the closing down of unprofitable enterprises began, many firms fear this fate so much that the councils will do everything in their power to increase profitability. This in turn requires close cooperation between management and workers. Of course, if the workers on the council agree to unpopular measures that might be necessary for the enterprise's future, a gap may develop between them and the workers at large.

As mentioned before, the party, the Communist Youth League, and the unions will be present at the meetings and have the right to express their opinion on the matters under discussion. The party bodies will probably play a major role in selecting the few "appropriate" candidates from all the applicants for the managerial job. Thus, it is probably not the council itself that will have the major function in the selection. In an interview, one local party secretary defended very strongly the right of the party to take part in the decision-making process:

We are going to be present at all meetings of the council, and we are not going to be yes men. We have the right to express our opinion and, if the situation warrants it, will correct some of our decisions and will not remain silent. Of this you can be sure.[69]

Although this new law did not come into force until January 1, 1985, some enterprises were allowed to elect a manager by secret ballot before that date.

What, then, is the attitude of the trade unions toward the changes in the managerial system of enterprises, and how do they see their role in the decision-making process? Just a few months before the 13th Party Congress, the director of the Research Institute of the Hungarian Labor Unions, in an interview with a Yugoslav newspaper correspondent, insisted that Hungarian labor unions must become "an equal partner of the state."[70] At the congress, however, Hungary's uncontested labor boss for the past two decades, Sándor Gáspár, was more conciliatory on the issue. He recalled that the Hungarian labor union movement had "changed tracks" twice in the past 40 years: first in 1945, when it went beyond the narrow task of merely defending labor interests, and then again after the "counterrevolutionary events of 1956," when it became "independent" under the direction of HSWP. Since then, Gáspár claimed, labor unions had become an institutionalized component of policymaking and had been guided by Leninist principles. What was therefore needed today was not to change tracks again but to adjust to a new situation and search for new means and methods to carry out union tasks better. Unions had to take into account the new forms of enterprise management, the new regulatory systems, and the growth of enterprise independence and democracy. Gáspár said that under "socialist conditions" protection of the group's special interests had to be tied to that group's economic performance. He also said that the labor unions were seriously threatened by "bureaucratization," and he called for the urgent reestablishment of their character as a mass movement.

According to Gáspár, cooperation between the National Council of the Trade Unions (NCTU) and the government was both necessary and valuable and although the two sides shared common goals, they sometimes had different approaches and engaged in "sharp debates." The workers had been asking, Gáspár said, where the unions were when important decisions affecting them, such as price increases, were made. He answered that the unions had been present when the decisions were made and that the decisions had been arrived at on the basis of mutual concessions, meaning that a compromise had been reached, with compensatory wage increases having been granted. Thus, Gáspár claimed, not a single question affecting the workers' living and working conditions could be decided without consulting the unions. "It would be a big mistake," he said, to accept policy decisions passively and not fill the place reserved for the unions in the building of a "socialist society." The leading role of the party was not similar to papal infallibility, nor did it mean unending approval; the party looked upon the unions as a "policymaking force."[71]

In all, Gáspár came out strongly for union consultation, if not direct participation, in the formulation of major policy decisions; for new ways to improve union work; and for more, rather than less, government involvement in welfare policy matters. He firmly supported the party's economic policies and even accepted responsibility for the compromise reached between the NCTU and the pro-reformist ruling elite. The latter was considered a remarkable volta face for a man known to have been a long-time opponent of Hungary's economic reform. In this respect, János Kádár's strong influence on his fellow members of the Politburo proved to be working again at the right time and at the right place.

The final major change affecting the relationship between the rulers and the ruled in contemporary Hungarian society deals with law and order. Before we examine the two specific changes (the new Hungarian criminal code and the new Constitutional Law Council) it is necessary to point out Marx's view of society and law.

According to Marx, law as a special social phenomenon exists in society and is determined and influenced by other social factors; it is determined ultimately by economic life and is a part of the superstructure of society. Within the framework of the superstructure there are many social phenomena. Not only law, but also the state, politics, ideology, religion, morality, the arts, the sciences, and so on—they all are in correlation with one another. The superstructure is ultimately determined by the economy in the process of world history.[72] Consequently, law is not subordinated to the state because local rules are not made only by the activity of state organs. When the law regulates the social relations it also regulates the activity of the state organs and their connection with citizens. Even though the bureaucratic apparatus of the state is forced to follow the legal norms, law itself is not the base of the state because the activity of the state's bureaucracy is not only regulated by law but by moral, political, administrative, and technical norms as well. The rules of both the state and the law are first of all to protect the social order and the social relations of people; and to support the economic, political, and cultural life; and, of course, to serve the social powers within the society with regard to the interests of the ruling class. Thus, unlike in Western political cultures, there is no separation of state power and hence a division in jurisdictional organization.[73] Any changes, therefore, in the Hungarian judicial process must be viewed within the context of the Marxist-Leninist theory of justice.[74] The same holds true for the new Hungarian criminal code and the creation of a Constitutional Law Council (CLC).[75]

On December 22, 1983, the Hungarian National Assembly modified the constitution to provide for the creation of the CLC for the purpose of reviewing the constitutionality of legal provisions and legal directives.[76] In turn, Dr. Imre Markoja, minister of justice, submitted to the April 12, 1984, session of parliament a bill that regulates in detail the task and operation of this new body.

It became necessary to create the CLC because an increasing number of legal provisions and directives had been passed by a variety of government agencies without any central supervision. These provisions and directives presented several problems. They were not readily available to the public, their constitutionality was often questionable, and they often contradicted each other. In Hungary parliament is by no means the only lawmaker; agencies subordinate to the parliament often issue directives on their own initiative. Parliament, where the so-called elected representatives of the people are, meets for only six or seven days a year and passes only a few laws. The new CLC in Hungary is meant to monitor these extraparliamentary directives. However, because there is no separation of powers, the CLC cannot be compared with the United States Supreme Court. If there were such an independent judiciary, the party could not so easily violate the constitution whenever it served its interest. This is why the CLC is not an independent body but an organ of the National Assembly.

Some of the CLC's 11–17 members are elected from among members of the parliament, while others are public officials whose names are presented to the parliament by the Patriotic People's Front. There are also advisory members who are experts on law, an indication that some serious business might get done by the council. The Justice Minister, the Chairman of the Supreme Court, the Chairman of the People's Control Commission, and the Supreme Prosecutor are present at all CLC meetings.

Cases can be taken up either on the council's own initiative or as they are submitted by "authorized entities." "Authorized entities" include top-level state agencies, leaders of social organizations, leading corporate organizations, and the Budapest Municipal Council, as well as the county councils listed in the proposal. No religious bodies were listed, indicating that certain disputes will never appear on the council's agenda. Although it is not expressly forbidden for an individual to submit a dispute to the council, it is emphasized that this person will be referred to the organization most suited to represent his case.[77] This would make it virtually impossible for someone who objects to the military draft law, for example, to find an authorized organization to represent his case. This indirect representation will obviously lead to a filtering of suitable and unsuitable cases.

It is expected that the authorized entities will represent either their own viewpoints or those of their clients at the CLC meetings. In the ensuing debate the constitutionality of a directive (issued either by one of the authorized entities or by one of their clients who cannot argue his case directly) will be tested. This means that the constitution will be continually reinterpreted according to new developments in society. Should a directive be found unconstitutional by the council, it will first turn to the agency that issued the legal provision or legal directive. The council is authorized to suspend the regulation even before it has published its decision in a competent official paper. The implementation, however, of legal provisions issued by the National Assembly and the Presidential Council, and of directives and authoritative decisions of the Supreme Court, cannot be suspended. If a provision of the Presidential Council or the National Assembly should be thought unconstitutional, an opinion can be submitted by the Constitutional Law Council to the Presidential Council and the Chairman of the National Assembly which will forward the matter to the Presidential Council's and National Assembly's plenums. These bodies will make the final decision on constitutionality.

Despite the fact that individuals do not have direct access to the council, the Hungarian media praised it as a step toward democracy. Interestingly enough, criticism came from the party's official monthly, *Pártélet*, which expressed doubts about the usefulness of the CLC since it was not clear whether many organizations would refer to the council's authority. It is striking that the party should allow any criticism of the council, having supported its creation.

The enactment of the new Hungarian criminal code in 1979 (Law IV of 1978) is equally significant from its decision-making mechanism point of view and from its substance; for instance, it provides for sentence differentiation according to dangerousness; classifications of recidivists; use of fines as an increasingly popular penal measure (especially since economic conditions have improved in Hungary); use of probation and educational corrective labor as non-prison alternatives; recognition of the negative effects of imprisonment; and reliance on advances in medical science to treat alcohol problems and further differentiate among excusable mental conditions. In addition to refining the purpose of punishment to special and general deterrents, the penal code stresses education as the most effective means to its stated goal, while down-playing the factor or retribution.

Changing the Hungarian penal code was another example of fulfilling the promises of socialist democracy by the pro-reformists' movement. According to an American criminologist, Nancy Lisagor, interested in the revision process of the new penal code (she interviewed twenty-two individuals), her findings about the role of authority in the decision-making process are quite revealing.[78]

In the preparatory phase of the codification work, the Ministry of Justice commissioned about a dozen reports from research institutes and university faculty members working in their fields of expertise. In some cases the suggestion for the research originated with the researcher, usually through an informal contact with one of the authorities at the Ministry of Justice. According to Lisagor, policymaking of this magnitude started at the administrative section of the Central Committee where questions of state and law are dealt with. Its yearly program acted as a preparatory committee. This committee included ministers or deputy ministers and elaborated its program in terms of general guidelines, which were conceptualized in a political framework, not necessarily a legal or practical one relevant to what work you do. This ideological layer was crucial in determining the direction and extent to which further work in the area was needed. The guidelines were strictly worded opinions of the party itself, although they could have included diverse instructions on reason and motivation for change, direction of change, and actual changes that were needed. At this point the ideological statements and instructions went to the relevant Ministry of Justice, where the appropriate department appointed a committee to begin the work. The Codification Committee, chosen by the Ministry of Justice, was the state body that continued to interact with the party. The actual substantial decisions were made jointly in these two committees where most of the members belonged to the HSWP, in addition to also being members of a university, scientific academy, or governmental ministry.

Although the ideas originated in these two committees, they were often the "expected" ideas that were put forward since neither committee acted like a "brain trust." Some ideas, for example, were proposed by various research institutes, which were then discussed and considered by a commission before submitting them to the two committees. Thus it would seem that if research institutes take the initiative and act aggressively in suggesting relevant and important research topics, the party will stimulate actual academic and scientific work. Therefore in formal relations between institute directors and governmental ministers they can be an important factor in facilitating understanding and contact, although they are not decisive.

The Institute of Social Sciences is the research institute of the party itself. The new Director of this institute, György Aczél, is also a member of the Central Committee and the Politburo. A director of one of the Hungarian Academy of Science research institutes admitted that occasionally when they feel a positive outcome is very important, they forward their proposals or recommendations to the Institute of Social Sciences to be put forward by them. This kind of manipulation by the academic community indicates their full comprehension of where the power for decision making lies and how the game is played.

CIVIL OBEDIENCE

As noted above, changing the Hungarian penal code was motivated more by changes in ideology and less by a crime wave.[79] In relative terms, Hungary is a very stable society. With a few exceptions, the percentage of crimes per year and types of crime has remained virtually the same for the last 15 years. The homicide rate has remained around 200 per year over the past two decades. Crimes against property accounted for the majority of criminal offenses (150,000 cases in 1983 or 60 percent; the damage amounting to 400 million forint to individuals and 700 million forint to the public). There are about 600 cases of robbery each year; assaults constitute some 10 percent of the criminal cases; hooliganism makes up about 8 percent of the cases, while traffic offenses total 13 percent. On the average, about 14,000 driver's licences are taken away yearly. As for criminal cases, some 34 percent of the accused are repeat offenders. There are about 140 criminal cases per 10,000 residents. In 1983, there were 60,000 criminal cases; 160,000 family cases; 20,000 labor suits; 15,000 property cases, and a few thousand inheritance cases. Crime is increasing and becoming more serious only in traffic-related crimes, recidivist crimes, and juvenile crimes. During the same period, 80 percent of all sentences were accepted without recourse to appeal, and 6 percent of the cases were appealed and reappealed all the way to the Supreme Court. According to a public opinion poll, an overwhelming majority of respondents felt Hungarian courts were too lenient. In 1983, for example, half of the defendants received suspended sentences.[80]

The greatest concern of the legal authorities in Hungary during the past few years has been the rapid increase in the number of juvenile delinquents. In 1984, juvenile criminality was 10 percent higher than in 1983, and up 50 percent over 1980. It is predicted that juvenile delinquency will continue to rise at the same rate and that by 1992 about 10,000 young people will be sent to a correctional institution each year.[81]

Although many young people are involved "only" in stealing, violent crimes by juveniles were also on the rise. Robberies were up by 25.2 percent; aggravated assault and battery by 18.2 percent; gang rape by 17.5 percent; and drug abuse by 12.5 percent.[82] Indeed, 40 percent of all crimes in Hungary were committed by people under 24 years of age. These young people were born not only after 1945, but also after the so-called counterrevolution of 1956. These young people are the product of communism; many of the younger ones even have parents who were born under communism. Thus, the ruling elite can no longer blame this problem on bourgeois habits of obedience that were inherited from the past.

What are the leading causes of juvenile criminality? Although there is no consensus among the leading experts, most sociologists tend to believe that an accumulation of disadvantages, rather than one single factor, leads to criminality. This is probably why there is a disproportionately high number of Gypsy children among the juvenile delinquents in Hungary. In certain countries 80–90 percent of all thefts are committed by Gypsies.[83] The accumulation of disadvantages is not characteristic only of Gypsy children, and is not limited to economic factors. Many children come from broken homes or have alcoholic parents. Another major disadvantage is the fact that many parents are so busy making money in the second or third economy that they have almost no time for their children. Left to themselves, many children start drinking, find "bad company," and get involved in crime.

Another major reason for juvenile delinquency is the deterioration of their moral standards. As State Secretary for Justice Gyula Borics pointed out, the ease with which a crime can be committed should not be confused with the real reasons for the crime. Just because a child is left at home by himself does not, for example, mean that he must become involved in crime.[84] Yet only very few young people receive any moral instruction at all. Religion is no longer taught in schools, and attending church or professing religious faith is allowed only within limits. Poor discipline in the schools along with the inability of female teachers to assert a positive influence on young boys is a major contributing factor to the rise in juvenile delinquency. It should be noted that about 85 percent of the juvenile delinquents are boys.

The home, too, has lost much of its positive influence on the younger generation. Today, every third marriage ends in divorce, which is usually preceded by a period of infidelity on the part of one or both parents. Moreover, most Hungarian families are practically forced to become involved in the illegal economy in order to maintain their falling standard of living because the regulations are so contradictory that even to purchase basic goods one has to engage in bribes.[85] This illegal economy is already so widespread that it is practically impossible to take legal measures against it, since it would make criminals out of respectable people in high positions. Nevertheless, the children grow up knowing that in order to make ends meet one has to break the rules without being caught. It is only natural that children cannot differentiate between the rules that can be broken and those that cannot.

It is not known how many of the unwanted, so-called OTP children are among the criminals, but their number is presumably substantial. Since the National Savings Bank (OTP) gives parents buying a home a sizeable discount for every child, many have children as the only means of obtaining housing. Since a large share of these children end up in orphanages, the media became very critical about four or five years ago of the practice of treating children as commodities without giving them love or attention. Since the media are now silent on this topic, it can be assumed that they were centrally directed to refrain from dealing with this delicate subject. The problem of unwanted children remains, however, and orphanages and probably prisons are filled with them.

Orphanages occupy a special position in juvenile delinquency. In 1981, for example, there were 5,500 young people in orphanages in Budapest. During the year, 3,000 children escaped for varying lengths of time, and many were given shelter by adults who took advantage of them. The addresses of such adults circulate among the escapees from the state institutions. Although the youngsters are given shelter, they are expected to render certain services, especially sexual ones, to the "landlords"; girls are often forced into prostitution and give the money they earn to their "benefactor." Although the police know the addresses of many of the "landlords," it is hard to prove they have committed a crime. The young escapees are often introduced to crime by these landlords.[86]

The rate of recidivism is fairly high among the young people, about 25–30 percent. There are many reasons why children return to their criminal way of life. Many have no place to go after leaving prison. They are forced into the company of street people and led right back into criminal life. Once they are freed from prison, most of them have difficulty finding a respectable job, since only very few people are willing to hire a former criminal. Officials at a reformatory in Tököl, for example, have complained that many youngsters enter without much education and leave without having completed the eighth grade, which is necessary to continue education.[87] There are not enough professional social workers to take care of children after they leave prison. Many social workers are even afraid of visiting these young people because they live in an environment where there is animosity toward officials (for example, among the Gypsies), and it is not unusual for social workers to be chased away or beaten up.[88]

Since juvenile delinquency is closely related to other social problems, in the opinion of experts a solution can only be found if they are considered an interrelated entity. However, all indications show that this will not be the case in the near future.

At this juncture, it may be appropriate to ask what is the source of civil obedience in socialist Hungary? Why do people in socialist Hungary submit to the will of others, thereby empowering others? Do they do so because they anticipate some kind of reward for compliance or some deprivation for noncompliance, or because they have been socialized into the "habit of obedience," carrying its own justification? Under what kind of social contract does socialist Hungary function? Is it a contract of society, a contract of government, or what?

In the previous chapter we have stated the views of Marx and Lenin concerning the concepts of state and society. Therefore, it should be evident that the state, in the sense of a political community, and as an organized society, is not based on a social contract (as envisioned by philosophers such as Hobbes, Locke, and Rousseau) but on an economic class, called the proletariat, that has appointed a "fiduciary" or "trustee government" (the dictatorship of the proletariat) with which it makes no contract, but which governs the trust to rule until the elimination of the enemy bourgeois class when the state itself will wither away. During this interregnum the state is a legal association, constituted by the action of the members of the communist party (representing the working class of the society) in making a constitution and therein and thereby contracting themselves into a body politic. From this point of view we may speak of a "political contract," expressed in the Articles of the Hungarian Constitution. In this respect the party—that is, its leadership—is still a leviathan even when it is corporate. Therefore, it follows that control over individual attitudes is politicized and quite thorough. The suprem-

acy role of the party in the corporate state organization is clearly identifiable and well understood. Most organizational subordinates
emphasize the returns and play down the costs of obedience. Rather
than being considered coercive, the institutional chain of command is
defined as necessary and functional. Obedience in such cases is not felt
as a humiliation but as a constructive behavior of a person who is willing
to accept responsibilities. Such an attitude also serves as a rationalization
for life situations made more bearable for the individuals. This attitude
of obedience among subordinates in the organization of the socialist
state in Hungary becomes a social norm, acting both as an external and
internalized force for compliance upon the individual. The pressure to
obey comes not only from superiors but from the collectivity of subordinates. Indeed, the directives of superiors are often designed both to
police subordinates and to reward them for their efforts of self-policing.
The pressure for obedience, therefore, can be felt vertically from the
higher authority that controls performance, and horizontally from subordinates who, having internalized the meaning of obedience, are as
critical as the superiors. If the trend in the rise of juvenile delinquency
and the rapid decline in the belief system of Marxism-Leninism of the
Hungarian youth are symptomatic of the voluntary conformity with "the
habit of obedience" under socialist rules, then it would be difficult to
hypothesize that the greater the number of Hungarians born under
socialism and socialized into the "Marxist-Leninist habit of obedience,"
the greater acceptance of socialist values.

Another indication that civil obedience is not as voluntary as the ruling
elite would have us believe is the treatment of dissidents in Hungary.
As the arguments on ideological pluralism by György Aczél revealed,[89]
socialist democracy in Hungary does not permit articulation of organized
opposition (through a two-party or multi-party system); such a practice
would negate the Leninist concept of the vanguard of the proletariat
(rule by the party elite). Consequently, only constructive criticism is tolerated as previously explained under socialist democracy. Supporting
this contention is the suppression of Hungary's best known and most
successful *samizdat* (underground) journal, *Beszélö (The Talker)* in 1983
through a series of police raids, house searches, and confiscations, finally
culminating in the closing by the police of László Rajk's "samizdat boutique" in the center of Budapest. The journal ceased to exist until June
1984, when the ninth issue of *Beszélö* reappeared as an underground
publication. The most recent samizdat to appear in Hungary is *A Hírmondó (The Messenger)*, whose first issue came out in November 1983 and
which calls itself an "independent and uncensored publication" and dis-
closed as its objective the publishing of information that cannot appear
in the official Hungarian press. Several dissident publishers were subject
to police harrassment and persecution by the Hungarian authorities.

Some of the most notable cases include Gábor Demszky, György Krassó, Ferenc Köszeg, Sándor Csoóri, György Petri, Miklós Mészöly, Gáspár Nagy, Gábor Bouquet, Miklós Veress, Rezsö Forgács, and Ferenc Kulin.

In mid-September 1983, Deputy Minister of Culture Dezsö Tóth condemned the content and editorial policies of the controversial Hungarian monthly *Mozgó Világ (Moving World)* and announced the dismissal of its editor-in-chief, Ferenc Kulin. This administrative measure against a journal the younger generation had come to feel as representing its own views drew strong objections from young writers within the Hungarian Writers' Union and from students at Budapest's Lóránd Eötvös University, in the form of a protest resolution and the collecting of signatures in support of *Mozgó Világ's* ousted editor. The young writers' resolution was never reported by the Hungarian media but was sent abroad and broadcast by Radio Free Europe (RFE). At the end of October 1983, a stormy two-and-a-half hour debate between Tóth and some 800 university students was recorded by several participants and forwarded to RFE for broadcasting. While officials such as Tóth accused RFE of meddling in internal affairs, Hungarians interested in the free discussion of ideals rallied on the radio to publicize those issues (such as the controversy surrounding *Mozgó Világ*) that were either ignored or whitewashed by government officials.[90]

The case of Gábor Demszky, a prominent dissident publisher and sociologist who was brutally beaten by the police in early 1984, was a departure from the Hungarian authorities' practice of reserving violence for use against workers and other disadvantaged groups. When László Rajk's "samizdat boutique" was closed down, the police refrained from using physical violence against individual members of the democratic opposition. They only confiscated several thousand pages of samizdat material and issued warnings. Demszky's trial and sentencing to a six-month suspended prison sentence was the first case since the trial of Miklós Haraszti in October 1973 of a well-known member of the democratic opposition being brought before the court.

The increase in police harrassment is aimed at all segments of society exhibiting nonconformist behavior. As far as the democratic opposition is concerned, this harrassment manifests itself in the constant tailing of active members and the repeated stopping of their cars. Less active members of the opposition are warned in more subtle ways, including veiled threats to their jobs and career prospects if they remain active. The refusal to grant permission to travel abroad, the withdrawal of passports, and the offering of emigration papers to active dissidents are also common methods of intimidation. Further forms of police harrassment include house searches and large fines for unauthorized printing and for the possession and distribution of illegal publications.

In November 1984 a prominent dissident, the economist György

Krassó, was placed under surveillance. Krassó's appeal of January 3, 1985, to have the police surveillance lifted was rejected by the authorities. While under surveillance the police can enter his apartment at any time of the day or night. This, Krassó remarked to a Western reporter, was a grave violation of his personal rights, which should not be allowed without a court decision.[91] In his letter appealing the surveillance, which was published in *A Hírmondó,* Krassó pointed out that the alleged goal of his constant surveillance by the police was described by Hungarian law as "the prevention of crime and education to respect the laws and rules of socialist coexistence." As far as crime prevention was concerned Krassó mentioned the many futile attempts of the authorities to convict him on false charges by "falsifying police records and by pressuring witnesses to give false testimony." Krassó was acquitted every time by the court, since he had not committed a crime. In the fall of 1984, a new law-decree was issued that legitimized a number of police measures already widely in use that violate the basic rights of Hungarian citizens. According to the new law:

A policeman ... may inspect vehicles or parcels if he suspects that a crime or a breach of regulations has been committed. In the event of a breach or the endangerment of public security and order, the policeman may interrogate citizens to elicit information and facts.[92]

In practice this means that the police are free to rummage through people's bags and ask questions about personal belongings. Gábor Demszky was beaten by two policemen when he objected to their reading his private correspondence. The new law gives the police extensive rights to probe into the private life of a citizen by allowing them to search his personal effects. Identity checks on the street can now be combined with body searches and interrogations, in violation of civil rights laws that specify that witnesses other than representatives of the authorities must be present during house searches, seizures, and body searches. Thus the new law has given a great boost to state violations against the individual.

It is interesting to note that the great majority of people charged with "incitement" are of working-class origin. A study by a teacher at the Police Officers' College offers rare data showing that close to 60 percent of those convicted of "incitement and offenses against the public" in the last 10 years were workers.[93] "Incitement and offenses against the public" are discussed together, because the new penal code that became effective on June 1, 1979, recategorized a substantial share of the former "incitements" as "offenses against the public," most probably in order to reduce the statistics for "incitement" cases, which implies harsher offenses.

The crackdown on dissidents also included the Gypsies, Hungary's most disadvantaged group, who are often subject to police harrassment,[94] and the members of punk rock bands. In February 1984, for example, four Hungarian punk musicians, the Coitus Punk Group, were sentenced to two years in prison for singing songs attacking communism and the Soviet Union. Another more popular punk group, *Mosoly (Smile)* received a six-month jail sentence for calling for the extermination of the Gypsies. An appeal for genocide is apparently regarded as a lesser offense by the Hungarian authorities than anti-communist songs.

The increase in cultural repression was also manifested by the communist party's efforts to tighten its grip on the Hungarian Writers' Union. The HSWP forced Hungarian Writers' Union chairman, Miklós Duray, and Secretary-General Miklós Jovanovics to resign. Relations between the party and the union deteriorated in a power struggle, in which the party refused to grant the union the authority to implement necessary reforms. A well-known poet, Gáspár Nagy, was also forced to resign from the union under official pressure from the HSWP, which condemned him for writing a poem in honor of former Hungarian prime minister Imre Nagy for his role in the 1956 revolution. The party authorities also pressured the union to expel several unorthodox writers, among them the famous poet István Csoóri, who had signed a letter of condolence addressed to the Warsaw church where assassinated pro-Solidarity priest Jerzy Popieluszko once preached and which has a history of nonconformist activities. Incidentally, the Popieluszko case, as a political murder, is not without parallel in Hungary. In mid-1983 *Népszabadság* published an interview with Hungary's national chief of police Béla Borbarát following the mysterious deaths of Dr. János Elbert, a well-known literary historian and university professor, and his son. It was generally believed in intellectual circles in Budapest that Elbert, who was Yurii Andropov's interpreter when the late Soviet party and state leader was ambassador to Hungary, had wanted to have his memoirs published in the West German weekly *Der Spiegel*. Shortly after this became known, Elbert drowned in Lake Balaton near the city of Siófok. His body was found in shallow water near a pier. His sudden trip to the lake, which lies approximately 100 kilometers from Budapest, was inexplicable. His son, who openly told friends that he knew how to track down his father's murderers, was found drowned in the Danube a few days after his father's death. Upon learning the news of the double tragedy, Elbert's wife suffered a nervous breakdown and is still in a psychiatric clinic.

As allegations started to take shape in ever-widening circles that the Elberts had been killed on orders from the KGB, *Népszabadság* published an interview with Borbarát about the deaths of the Elbert family. He firmly denied any wrongdoing and said "things happen in life that, especially after the event, seem inexplicable to outside observers." He speculated that the reason for Elbert's unexpected visit to Siófok—instead of delivering a lecture at the university as he had always dutifully done—was his "sudden nostalgic attraction" for the city. Borbarát said that Elbert had "slipped on the stones" and fell as he was washing his face in the lake. Elbert's son, he went on, had had a history of suicide attempts.

The Hungarian writer and producer Rezsö Forgács also got a taste of the authorities' wrath when he was arrested during the summer of 1984 after his theater company, Kábel Színpad, had performed a stage reading of Ezra Pound's *Cantos,* which included mime scenes with naked women, in a Hungarian village in Tolna County. The production had already been staged nine times in Budapest theaters under official censorship and had received more than forty favorable reviews in the official press. After the village performance, Forgács, who is Jewish, was charged with pornography and with the spreading of fascist texts; the latter charge was later dropped. On February 13, 1985, Forgács was sentenced to seven months in jail for "public indecency" and the court also deprived him of his right to participate in public affairs for a period of two years. Ten days later Radio Budapest claimed that Forgács had a history of previous offenses and tried to discredit him by stating that although he claimed to be a writer he had no professional training. The radio also said that in the Budapest productions no naked women were shown. Even if this had been the case, however, nudity is nothing new on the Hungarian stage; some of the most successful theater productions have shown nudes.[95]

Although the Hungarian Young Writers' Union, of which Forgács is a member, voted to send letters of protest to Budapest's chief prosecutor and to the Minister of Culture, Forgács lost his appeal because the court rejected his argument that the production had already been legally performed and well received elsewhere in the country. The court refused to consider the reasoning that the words and stage movements were related or listen to any professional playwright suggesting that nudity was part of the play's poetry. The sentencing of Forgács, he said, apparently proves that the police are able to operate against anyone they want. It would seem that the Forgács case is an example of how the Hungarian authorities seek to nip nonconformist activity in the bud, even if this means disregarding evidence.

The recent harrassment of the opposition and the punitive measures against other manifestations of nonconformist activity leads one to believe that the Hungarian regime is determined to stifle activities that it regards as threatening to its control over society or offensive to the Soviet Union. Although the regime is now aided in its efforts by new legislation that extends police rights, it is clear that it has not succeeded in silencing the opposition. Hungary's carefully nurtured Western image as the "happiest barrack" in the Soviet camp can expect more severe blows as evidence accumulates that this barrack also has its off-limits areas, defined and enforced by the party and its agencies. To better understand the official limits of tolerance toward the plurality of opinion it is useful to read the party resolution of September 1984: "This plurality [of culture] serves the cause of progress only if...each workshop [of artists and newspaper staff] participates in the struggle to strengthen the position of Marxism."[96]

CONCLUSIONS

As pointed out in Chapter 1, socialist authority in Hungary is determined by the exercise of power, which in theory belongs to the working class but in practice is wielded by the party and bureaucratic elite(s) under conditions prescribed by the principles of Marxism-Leninism and Hungarian realities. This authority, which binds the Hungarian political process together, is composed of power to rule and the legitimacy of that power. It is the latter that gives the stamp of approval to the exercise of power, which is also a measuring device to establish the perimeters within which the rulers are able to obtain the agreement and cooperation of the ruled.

In socialist Hungary, before and after the revolution of 1956, power was held and is still held by one exclusive and homogeneous group: the party elite. However, there is a difference in style and distribution of political power before and after 1956. This change can be attributed to community goals, values, norms, external pressures, and above all tactics used by the ruling elite. At present, emphasis is more on a consensual rather than coercive style of power; it is more positive, by using incentives for innovation, rather than negative, as it was during the Rakosi era. In both empirical and normative terms, the present-day distribution of power depends more on the ability to influence or manipulate the ruled in Hungarian society—to change them, to win them over, and to persuade them that "socialist democracy" is the right way for them and for future generations. It is within this context that legitimacy is important to rulers because it implies a relationship, a judgment about their exercise of power and a reaction to it. Legitimacy in socialist Hungary is not a constant; it is a variable, testing the acceptance or rejection of the rulers' policies by the ruled. It is a phenomenon that turns power into authority, which presupposes increased participation by the toilers in the decision-making process and a greater commitment by the rulers to legal and constitutional processes of policy formation.

This idea was clearly stated by János Kádár at the autumn session of the National Assembly in September 1980, when he reiterated that "our most important method is persuasion, and not ordering people about.

Only in extraordinary historical situations the revolutionary forces of the nation must be ready to defend the cause of progress by force."[97] Kádár also stated that in Hungary there are no antagonistic or irreconcilable class conflicts or exploiting classes, and that the oppressive functions of the state "have faded and are about to disappear."[98]

While it is true that the party has changed considerably since 1956, the structure of political authority in Hungary today is still quite strong, especially if we consider the power the party wields in the decision making process. Although mass organizations and mass movements are considered essential for constructive work in building socialism in Hungary, it is well known that party members hold the most influential positions in these mass organizations and movements. Therefore to label these movements as "independent" is hyperbole. Of course, in moving downward and away from the core, this structure of authority is less centralized and more localized. For example, there are the administrative districts (the *megyek*) of the country, which have considerable local autonomy in economics. All power used to be concentrated at the top—at the National Planning Office, the Ministries, and the national trusts—with only a small amount of it trickling down to the productive enterprise. At present, there is real autonomy down to the level of enterprises, at least to the degree that the objective market-oriented circumstances have been incorporated into public thinking. In situations where the fluctuations of supply and demand make all decisions concerning one product, there is no longer any need for the National Planning Office or some other central organ to evaluate the factory's activities. Thus, it can be stated that the earlier archaic system is disappearing. The pyramid of authority is not as high as it used to be, its sides are "flattening," and more local power centers are in the making. There are accompanying differentiations in political and ideological thinking as well. However, there are still plenty of instances of outmoded thinking, but these are becoming less and less important.

Perhaps the reason for the slow progress in building "developed socialism" in Hungary is the fact that there are no good working models which the country could follow; therefore, Hungary is experimenting with rather than building a model. Furthermore, a model cannot be created in theory, only through practice, which presupposes that the authoritative members of the system always have a clear vision of what Hungarian society thinks and demands. The party, as we have pointed out, cannot exist without the people (meaning the support of the masses), for the very same reason that political authority in Hungary is meaningless without legitimacy. Hence, the party pursues a policy of alliances with the Hungarian working class and sections of society in mass organizations and mass movements. The aim and purpose of this policy is to mobilize mass support for constructive participation in building socialism through national consensus; to assure the success of this policy the party commands authoritative control vertically in all mass organizations, especially the trade unions, the Patriotic People's Front, and the Communist Youth League. A good example of how such a policy works is the framework for cooperation between the believers and the non-believers accorded by the PPF. At a meeting of the HSWP/CC in March 1981, János Kádár himself paid tribute to "the loyal behavior of churches and congregations and their readiness to undertake a positive role in public life."[99] Similarly Imre Pozsgay, general secretary of the PPF, at the 13th Party Congress attributed special significance to the fact that church—state relations had been placed on a constructive basis, which means that believers had not only acknowledged the existence of communism but had become active participants in its development. This cooperation had extended from common tasks in the peace movement to work in areas of social services through such activities as health care, alcoholism, divorce, abortion, and juvenile delinquency.[100]

Hand-in-hand with the party's alliance policy, the ruling elite instituted a series of changes in the organization and mode of operation of the Hungarian polity in order to make the concept of socialist democracy more appealing to the working masses of Hungarian society. They all contain the carrot-and-stick approach. The new Electoral Law of 1983, for example, makes it mandatory to have multiple candidates competing for office. However, it also calls for two nominating meetings which, as we have seen in the case of two dissidents, Rajk and Tamás, allowed the PPF to rig the nominations at the second meeting after it became known that at the first meeting the two dissidents had a good chance of winning nomination. Even though the new Electoral Law insists on multiple candidates, the results of the 1985 elections still show an uncontested control of parlimentary seats by all members of the party elite.

A similar vagueness exists in the pensioners' participation in the trade union organizations. In October 1985 the Presidium of the National Council of Hungarian Trade Unions (SzOT) established a Pensioner Work Committee to examine retired people's financial, medical, and social situation. This committee can give opinions and make suggestions on issues related to pensioners but can make no decisions. In February 1986, *Magyar Nemzet* reported that "organizational conditions" had been created for pensioners to participate in making decisions related to themselves in trade union organizations and the work place.[101] Although the paper called this a step toward "representing the interests of pensioners," it failed to elaborate on how, if at all, pensioners' representatives could actually influence decision making.

In the field of economics, the decentralization of agriculture in 1984 through establishment of new self-governing bodies and the abolition of the National Center of state farms in 1985 was followed by the creation of new types of management for Hungarian enterprises, also in 1985. Skillful attempts were made by the ruling elite to gain increased worker participation in the decision-making process for the purpose of creating greater incentives in work ethics while at the same time share in the responsibility of modernization of Hungarian industry. It is much easier to explain the folding of an unprofitable enterprise by reaching such a decision through the participation of the workers than to leave it entirely up to the management to make these unpopular decisions. This is a particularly sensitive area for the ruling elite to tackle, since the proletariat in Hungary functions under the premise of guaranteed job security. Parenthetically, it should be pointed out that officially there is no unemployment in Hungary because Marxism-Leninism requires that everyone must work. Consequently every mature person in Hungary must carry a workbook. When such a person becomes employed, the workbook is stamped on the ledger as "entering work"; similarly when that person leaves the work force, the workbook is stamped on the ledger as "having left work." After three months without a stamp on the ledger showing that the person is employed, such an individual can be apprehended as a vagrant or a burden to society. Incidentally, if the regime wants to find cause for persecuting any member of Hungarian society, it can "arrange" for citizens to become unemployed so that they can be harrassed. Many dissidents find themselves in such a situation.

While the ruling elite is boasting about the freedom of the press and tolerance of criticism, only constructive criticism is permitted. The two taboos, the party and the USSR, can never be wrong and must never be criticized. Only within the framework of self-criticism can the two subjects be questioned but then again, only by the members of the ruling elite and within their secret meetings.

NOTES

1. See "György Aczél answers questions on Hungarian society," *The New Hungarian Quarterly* 22, (Summer 1981); 129.

2. For the persecution of Hungarians accused of "counterrevolution" after October 1956, see Jenö Fónay, *Megtorlás* [Revenge] (Zürich: Svájci Magyar Irodalmi és Képzömüvészeti Kör, 1983).

3. See Hugh Seton-Watson, *The East European Revolution* (New York: Praeger, 1961); Ferenc Erdei et al., eds., *Information Hungary* (New York: Pergamon Press, 1968), 289–98; Stephen D. Kertesz, "The methods of communist conquest: Hungary 1944–47, "*World Politics* 3 (October 1950); 20–54; and Peter A. Toma and Ivan Volgyes, *Politics in Hungary* (San Francisco: W.H. Freeman, 1977), 3–11.

4. See "György Aczél answers questions on Hungarian society," op. cit., 138; and János Kádár, "The basis of consensus," *The New Hungarian Quarterly* 23 (Summer 1982); 7–9.

5. See *A Magyar Szocialista Munkáspárt Központi Bizotságának elözetes jelentése a XIII Kongreszus Küldötteinek* [Preliminary Report of the HSWP/CC to the Delegates of the 13th Congress] (Budapest, 1985).

6. See Janez Stanic, *Start* (April 21, 1984); for further explanation of "sharing in power by citizens," see above in Chapter 2: "The Toilers' Share in Power" and "Civil Obedience."

7. *Népszabadság* (November 22, 1985). Most of these ideas were first tested in the CPSU ideological monthly *Kommunist,* probably for endorsement. See his "V interesakh postroeniya razvitogo sotsialisticheskogo obschestva" [In the Interest of Building the Development of Socialist Community], *Kommunist* 10 (July 1985); 70–81.

8. See "György Aczél answers questions on Hungarian society," op. cit., 135.

9. See Ágnes Dus, ed., *A magyar ifjúság a 80 években* [Hungarian Youth in the 1980s] (Budapest: Kossuth Könyvkiadó, 1984); András Knopp and Katalin Radics, "Concerning the situation in young intellectuals," *Társadalmi Szemle* (July-August 1984): 52–68; István Harcas, "Concerning the living standard of young workers," ibid., 78–88.

10. See "György Aczél answers questions on Hungarian society," op. cit., 135.

11. Ibid., 136. For a more detailed discussion of the media in Hungary, see Chapter 6.

12. Apparently during the Congress, in a secret meeting, Kádár was given the option to become chairman of the Presidential Council (nominal head of state) to replace the old and ailing Pál Losonczi, which he rejected with the stipulation that he would either retire or continue in the same position. The former alternative was vetoed by the CPSU because it would have set a dangerous precedent; thus as a compromise he was promoted to the present status so that his deputy could assume greater responsibilities.

13. See *A Magyar Szocialista Munkáspárt Központi Bizotságának elözetés jelentése a XIII Kongreszus Kuldötteinek* [Preliminary Report of the HSWP/CC to the Delegates of the 13th Congress] (Budapest, 1985).

14. Cf. Rezsö Nyers, "The efficiency of the intellectual resource," *The New Hungarian Quarterly* 23 (Autumn 1982): 36–44.

15. *A mai magyar társadalom* [Contemporary Hungarian Society] (Budapest: Kossuth Könyvkiadó, 1980), 291.

16. See "Innovation—From words to reforms," *The New Hungarian Quarterly,* 23 (Summer 1982); 109.

17. See "Introduction" to *Magyar Tudomány* [Hungarian Sciences], as quoted in ibid., 110.

18. *Népszabadság* (December 1, 1984).

19. See *Magyar Nemzet* (December 2, 1984).

20. See *Hajdu-Bihari Napló* [Hajdu-Bihari Daily] (November 21, 1984).

21. Ibid. (November 10, 1984).

22. For the articles and sections of the law, see *Nagyar Közlöny* [Hungarian Journal] (December 27, 1983).

23. Article 8, Section 1.

24. See *Népszabadság* (April 15, 1985).

25. Ibid. (April 16, 1985).

26. Article 8, Section 2.

27. Article 37, Section 2.

28. April 15, 1985.

29. See Article 40, Section 1, and Article 45, Section 2.

30. *Kelet Magyarország* [East Hungary] (March 23, 1985).

31. *Magyarország* [Hungary] (March 10, 1985).

32. *Magyar Nemzet* (April 12, 1985).

33. April 18, 1985.

34. See "Hungarian situation report No. 6", *Radio Free Europe Research* (May 16, 1985), 11.

35. See *The Times* [London] (April 24, 1985).

36. Reuter (April 23, 1985).

37. See *Neue Zürcher Zeitung* (April 24, 1985).

38. Ibid., and Radio Budapest (April 15, 1985, 6:30 p.m.).

39. See *Heti Világgazdaság* [World Economic Weekly] (May 25, 1985) and *Népszabadság* (May 16 and 25, 1985).

40. *Népszava* (May 16, 1985).

41. *Magyar Nemzet* (June 10, 1985).

42. *Népszabadság* (June 10, 1985) and *Magyar Hírlap* (June 24, 1985).

43. *Magyar Nemzet* (June 10 and 11, 1985).

44. *Borba* (Belgrade) (July 6–7, 1985).

45. See *Népszabadság* (October 14, 1983).

46. See *Pártélet* [Party Life] (April 1983): 3–10.

47. Ibid. (May 1984). Hungary's total agricultural area is 6,582,400 hectares. Of this, 1,000,800 hectares (15.4 percent) belong to the state section (state farms, agricultural combines, and experimental and model farms for scientific research), while 4,650,600 hectares (70.2 percent) belong to the agricultural cooperatives. Specialized cooperatives, farming partly on a cooperative and partly on an individual basis, occupy 155,400 hectares (2.4 percent), and small farms—that is, all private plots, private garden plots, ancillary farms, and private farms—occupy 775,600 hectares (12 percent). There are 129 state farms, 1,347 agricultural cooperatives and cooperative associations, and 62 specialized cooperatives; *Statisztikai Évkönyv 1982* [1982 Statistical Yearbook] (Budapest: Magyar Központi Statisztikai Hivatal, 1983). More than 2,200,000 families are engaged in small-scale agricultural production. See *Magyar Nemzet* (May 19, 1984).

48. See *Álami Gazdaságok* [State Farms] (November/December 1984).

49. See *Heves Megyei Népujság* [Heves County People's News] (March 13, 1985).

50. See *Népszbadság* (March 13, 1985).

51. See *Békes Megyei Népujság* [Békés County People's News] (April 6, 1985).

52. See *Heves Megyei Népujság* (April 6, 1985).

53. See *Népszava* [The People's Voice] (March 22, 1985).

54. Radio Budapest (April 24, 1985, 6:30 p.m.).

55. See Law-Decree No. 33/1984 in *Magyar Közlöny* 46 (October 10, 1984).

56. See Katalin Bossányi, "Why has the IGV been liquidated?" *Népszabadság* (August 14, 1984).

57. See *Kelet Magyarország* (September 2, 1984).

58. August 25, 1984.

59. See *Heti Világgazdaság* [World Economic Weekly] (December 24, 1983).

60. Ibid. (September 8, 1984).

61. See *Népszabadság* (August 26, 1984).

62. Ibid. (September 8, 1984).

63. *Népszava* (September 1984).

64. Law VI, 1977, in *Magyar Közlöny* 98 (December 27, 1977).

65. Law-Decree No. 1048/1982 in ibid. (December 15, 1982).

66. See László Bállai, "The development of enterprise management," *Pártélet* (October 1984): 15–21.

67. See *Daily News* (Budapest) (October 18, 1984).

68. See *Heti Világgazdaság* (January 12, 1985).

69. See *Kelet Magyarország* (December 24, 1984).

70. See Stanic, *Start* (April 21, 1984).

71. See *Népszabadság* (March 27, 1985).

72. See Mihály Samu, "The correlation of society and law from the aspect of Marxist viewpoint," *Archiv für Rechts- und Soczialphilosophie* [Archives for Law and Social Philosophy] 67 (1981): 112.

73. Ibid., 119; see also Csaba Varga, *A jog helye Lukács György világképében* [The Place of Law in Gyorgy Lukacs's Thought] (Budapest: Magvetö, 1981).

74. Samu, op. cit., 112.

75. Mihály Samu, *Hatalom és állam* [Power and State] (Budapest: Közgazdaságli és Jogi Könyvkiadó, 1982).

76. See *Magyar Hírlap* (April 13, 1984).

77. See Dr. Peter Schmidt, "The direction in which the political system develops," *Pártélet* (February 1984): 25–26.

78. See Nancy Lisagor, "The new Hungarian criminal code," *The New Hungarian Quarterly* 23 (Autumn 1982); 157–162.

79. See Attila Rácz, *Courts and Tribunals* (Budapest: Akadémiai Kiadó, 1980).

80. See the television program "Hatvanhat" [Sixty-six] (October 1984). The "66" program is a monthly telecast on a selected topic with questions from the audience, a cross-section of the Hungarian public, and an expert responding to the question. The expert on this particular program was Dr. Imre Markoja, president of the Supreme Court and presently minister of Justice.

81. See *Népszava* (November 10, 1984).

82. See MTI, *Daily News* (February 20, 1985).

83. See Anikó Soltész, "Whose sin is it?" *Ifjúsági Szemle* [Youth Review] (July–September 1984); 49–56.

84. See *Magyar Hírlap* (February 6, 1985).

85. See *Magyar Nemzet* (March 9, 1985).

86. See Radio Budapest (March 12, 1983, 1:00 p.m.), as reported in "Hungarian situation report No. 4," *Radio Free Europe Research* (April 6, 1985): 33–36.

87. Ibid. (June 22, 1984, 6:30 p.m.).

88. See *Ifjúsági Szemle* (July–September 1984).

89. See Chapter 1, above.

90. For details see "Tightening or consistency?" *Élet és Irodalom* [Life and Literature] (September 23, 1983); *Neue Zürcher Zeitung* (October 27, 1982); *Ma-*

gyar Hírlap (November 1, 1983) and István Lázár, "What's moving?" *Új Tükör* [New Mirror] (December 4 and 11, 1983).

91. See BBC Current Affairs Research and Information Section, *Caris Report* 6 (1985).

92. See *Magyar Közlöny* (November 21, 1984) (Law-Decree 48/1948, Paragraph 2).

93. See Lajos Kovács, "Causes of administrative and public violations as reflected in an empirical study," *Magyar Jog* [Hungarian Law] (February 1984): 122–140.

94. Their present population is approximately one-half million or about 5 percent of the country's total population. The Politburo of the HSWP/CC passed a resolution in 1961 stating that Gypsies are not an ethnic minority—they possess neither a common living area nor a uniform culture. The Hungarian Academy of Sciences estimates that 39 percent of all Gypsies are illiterate, in contrast to the estimated 1.5 percent of Hungarians who fall into the same category.

95. See *Heti Világgazdaság* (November 12, 1983).

96. See *Társadalmi Szemle* (October 1984): 17.

97. See his "The basis of consensus," op. cit., 7.

98. Ibid., 8.

99. Ibid., 17.

100. See *Magyar Nemzet* (March 28, 1985). For further details on this issue, see Chapter 5, "From Traditionalism to Nihilism: The Transformation of the Family and Religion as Institutions."

101. *Magyar Nemzet* (February 26, 1986).

PART II
WHO GETS WHAT, FOR WHAT?

3
Finding Loopholes in the Bureaucratic Red Tape

Officially, Hungary has two economies: the first comprising the state enterprises and the cooperative sector of the economy; the second including small-scale farming, private workshops, retail trading, and regular and occasional work done on the black market—all influenced by the marketplace. In 1980 the Political Committee of the Hungarian Socialist Workers Party (HSWP) declared that the second economy conducted useful activity, and consequently it should not be restricted but should be integrated into the organization of the socialist economy. In accordance with the principle of distribution according to work done, performance in the second economy is adjusted to the highest rather than the lowest achievable income. In the first economy—the socialist sector—the differentiation of wages according to work done is limited, which leads to indifference, withholding of performance, and low productivity.[1]

Unofficially there is also a "third economy," which encompasses such activities as manipulating enterprise materials for profit, renting of property, and deriving income by violating customs regulations or through tax evasion. The hidden or unregistered income derived from the third economy, according to a study by the Economic Research Institute, was estimated at about 100,000 million forints a year, or approximately 20 percent of the total income of the Hungarian population.[2] According to this study, first there are those to whom moonlighting brings an estimated 12,000 million forints annually. The second category consists of "income correctives" such as more or less voluntary tips and gratuities. Hungarians give between 10,000 and 12,000 million forints in tips a year. Every third person gives a gratuity of 150 forints for doctors, and approximately half of those receiving hospital care give 1,000 forints.[3] Bribes, charging high prices, and giving short weights also serve as a means of "correcting" income, but they are also, of course, forced on the population. The third type of unregistered income is related to illegal activities such as fraud, theft, and misappropriation of funds.

According to the official press, there are three main reasons for the flourishing third economy: the shortage of goods and specialists; inflation, which makes supplementary income necessary; and the fact that many firms have a monopoly of certain goods and services. The former head of the HSWP/CC Social Sciences Institute, István Huszár, pointed out that the dynamic improvement in Hungarian living standards slowed to a halt in 1984, which resulted in the intensification of social conflicts.[4] Many families were no longer able to maintain their standard of living with regular work, so 75 percent of all families found secondary sources of income. The poorest 12–15 percent of the population was hardest hit by the deterioration of economic conditions.

Because of the economic and political changes instituted in Hungary recently, the social structure has become more differentiated. The impact of the first, second, and third economies on Hungarian society has resulted in the creation of various interest groups, for example, industry and agriculture in the first economy, and a total of eleven interest groups in the second and third economies: the managers, the professionals, the skilled worker elite, the semi-skilled professional stratum, the non-manual and manual workers in the tertiary services sector, those who live primarily on income derived from the second economy, those industrial workers in towns whose skills cannot be utilized in the second economy, unskilled workers, the stratum working in agriculture, clerical workers, and various deprived groups such as the Gypsies, those living in worker hostels and factory settlements, and those living in backward villages (each of these subgroups numbers approximately 200,000). To this must be added an approximately equal number of families who are in a deprived situation through some individual handicap (sickness, old age, large number of children, deviation).[5]

While denouncing the materialism and egotism of Hungarian citizens at regular intervals, the ruling elite knows quite well that under the present economic circumstances economic manipulation is a way of survival for many people. As János Marón, a member of the Presidium of the PPF warned, the roots of the third economy are very deep and there are "few people in the country who do not participate in the third economy one way or another."[6] The atmosphere of constant economic manipulation induced sociologists to study the "new Hungarian culture" and the "new type of personality." Miklós Hernádi, for example, recently wrote a book in which he examines the two phenomena.[7] In it he describes Mr. Kovács, a person who indulges in such petit-bourgeois sins as individualism, materialism, egotism, and corruption. Public places are crowded with people like Mr. Kovács who are convinced that one can buy anything and anyone with money. Hernádi finds that Mr. Kovács' need to get the best of everything is legitimate; it is only the means by which he expresses this need that are "inhuman." There is a prevalent notion in Hungarian society that if one wants to get the best, "a sunny table in an outdoor restaurant, good fabrics at a store, or tasty meat at the butcher's, one has to pay extra money."[8] Mr. Kovács has allies in this "inhumanity"; the waiter leads someone who does not look like a good tipper to a bad table; the salesman offers fabrics of inferior quality to those who do not have Mr. Kovács' gentlemanly appearance. Mr. Kovács is in a position to get the best goods, because others get inferior products. Hernádi is not overly concerned with this problem because he feels that Mr. Kovács and his allies have "only the future to fear, the abundance of goods, and the real quality of citizens."

Hernádi's observations are fully corroborated by the author's observations and interviews with Hungarian citizens representing a cross-section of Hungarian society. The case studies that follow this and the following chapters were written with only a minimal amount of editing in order to capture the style and tone of the interviews. However, it should be emphasized that while the names and locations are fictitious, the cases cited are typical situations based on real facts.

MONEY HAS NO SMELL

The Hungarian ruling elite exercises complete control over every citizen and noncitizen in the country. There are four main types of control:

1. Every citizen over the age of 14 has a personal identity booklet *(Személyi igazolvány)*, which contains the most important personal data, address, place of employment, education, marital status, and so on. Any change in these vital statistics must be reported at the local council within 48 hours. The individual turns in a completed form, and the officials enter the data in the identity booklet and also in a central registry. In order to facilitate a computerized registry, everyone receives a serial number. The first digit is 1 if the person is a man, 2 if a woman (or if neither... Hungarian laws do not take that into consideration); after this follows a 4–digit personal number. So someone having the number 24 511 250 863 is a woman, born on November 25, 1945, who has personal identity number 0863. With this system, everyone can be immediately identified. Every official piece of paper must bear the person's number.

2. If a foreigner visits the country, he must report his/her place of stay within 72 hours. If staying in a hotel or in an IBUSz room (a private room that is rented to tourists under state authority), then the hotel clerk or the owner of the room registers the guest automatically, often without

the knowledge of the individual. If one stays with friends or relatives, one must register in person. In accordance with good Hungarian custom, the forms (priced at 1 forint!) are not available at the police, where one has to register. As a result, the foreign visitor has to spend his scarce time locating a tobacconist's shop or a post office where such forms are sold, and such places are usually not open in the early morning. After this is accomplished, one spends about 2 minutes filling out the form and another 2 minutes at the police station. The individual's visa form is stamped and this proves that he is registered. When he leaves the country, this stamp is checked at the border or the airport.

3. Every worker also has a workbook *(Munkakönyv)*, which, in addition to the personal data, contains all information concerning the individual's work relationships (changes of jobs, disciplinary actions, etc.). Thus, when one starts at a new job, his previous life is immediately visible, and references can be requested from previous employers. Many people lose this book when it is convenient, and obtain a new one at a new place of employment (a bottle of cognac is the usual price for this). The new book will contain only positive references, and the individual is "clean."

4. According to the new law concerning passports, there is now only one type of passport in effect for all Hungarians. Before there used to be one for socialist and one for capitalist countries, in addition to one which was issued to those traveling on official business. Hungarians can travel to socialist countries as often as they want, without limitations, and they can obtain as much currency for those countries as they want. To the West, in accordance with the new laws, they can only travel once a year if they travel on private business. This is simple on paper, but it is much more complicated in practice. A few examples will illustrate this point.

Mr. Kovács has not traveled to the West this year yet, but last year—having purchased the hard currency he is eligible to obtain once every three years—he visited Greece. Thus, this year he cannot purchase any hard currency from the Hungarian National Bank (Magyar Nemzeti Bank). And since he does not have any hard currency, he cannot get a passport. But of course Mr. Kovács knows the applicable loophole *(Kiskapu)*. There are actually several solutions. Let us say our friend wants to go to Austria. He needs hard currency. He can buy that on the well-established black market. (Everyone knows someone who has friends or relatives abroad: When they come to visit they do not use the official places to exchange their money to forints, but sell the dollars to their friends, for 25–50 percent more than the official rate.) A Hungarian citizen is not allowed to have more than 50 dollars in his possession. Thus Kovács must legalize his dollars. He has a distant relative in Sweden, who is now asked to write a formal (fake) letter of invitation, indicating that all expenses relating to the trip will be covered. He can make such promises because in the meantime, the aforementioned foreign visitor has transferred a certain sum to his account. Thus, in accordance with the letter of invitation, Kovács has the necessary hard currency and he will be issued a passport. Of course he will not travel to Sweden, but the transfer of money from Sweden to Austria is a simple banking matter. Kovács could even avoid this extra hassle if he were not afraid of the customs officials at the Hungarian border. He could simply smuggle out the purchased dollars; in that case, the letter of invitation would simply serve to facilitate the issuance of a passport.

Then there is Zsuzsi, who works for a foreign trade firm. She has no financial worries because she comes from a wealthy family (her father is a private craftsman working with plastics, so they have so much money that they do not know what to do with it). Thus, when she travels abroad, she does not purchase the usual "stuff" (nylon stockings, etc.) with her saved-up money, but rather puts it upon her return into a legal dollar account (the so-called "BC account"). The Hungarian National Bank gives her an official paper that she has her own hard currency, so the Ministry of Internal Affairs routinely gives her a passport. Last year, for example, Zsuzsi went to Spain. Of course there is only so much hard currency one can save from per diem allotments, but Zsuzsi is smart enough to find a loophole here, too. She knew that she would need about 400 dollars for the trip to Spain, so she purchased that amount on the flourishing black market. Then she took her own 400 dollars from the bank, went to Spain, and spent it. After her return, she went to the bank and redeposited the money, saying that she did not spend it. On her next trip, she can use the same trick, and this way always have hard currency available. Now of course, the people working at the bank are not idiots; they know that she must have spent some money in Spain, but no one is asking any questions. They do not even care if Zsuzsi's money "comes back" in different hard currency, even in currency from countries she never visited. The main thing is that the hard currency should remain within the borders. When Zsuzsi told me of this trick, she added that "money—especially hard currency—has no smell." She also said that people who have a certain amount of hard currency are considered "reliable," and the authorities are more forgiving with them than with others. No one really knows what is the principle behind this "I-see-nothing" attitude, but this is not important as long as the arrangement is advantageous. Besides Zsuzsi, her relatives are also enjoying this "arrangement"; with her permission, they can also take advantage of her supply of hard currency.

Zsuzsi's friend—a university teacher—uses an even more refined "arrangement." He stays away from the black market, because if he were caught, it would mean the end of his career. On the other hand, he can easily obtain hard currency once he is outside the borders; not only because he has a relative in England, but also because he made many friends who visit Hungary regularly. They stay at his friend's home, and he escorts them on their shopping trips. Not only does he help them as an interpreter, but he also pays for their purchases. At home, they settle accounts in hard currency. Of course, he does not receive the money on the spot, but "launders" the money by placing it in a BC account. The purpose of this service offered by the Hungarian National Bank is to make it possible for Hungarian citizens to keep hard currency in a semi-official manner. These accounts pay no interest (this is one aspect of the state's business!), but once the citizen has a valid passport in his hands, he can pick up as much of this hard currency as he wants, and he can take this out of the country without any risk. Money held in this account, however, is not good enough to justify a request for a passport (that is why it is called "semi-official"). But the money held in this account can be made "wholly official" by taking it out of the country, and, upon returning, putting it back into the "official" hard currency account. A BC account can be initiated two ways. From abroad, anyone (friend, colleague, relative) can send a check, indicating that the money is for the purpose of starting a BC account. Thus, if one has any "black" currency in his possession, he can give it to someone and ask him to "launder" it by starting a BC account. The parents of Zsuzsi's friend make a yearly trip to the West by using his accounts. They base their passport request on his official account, but they use the money that is in his BC account; this way his official account is never reduced. Thus, it is sufficient to have about 500–600 dollars in this official manner; after this, one does not have to worry about traveling for several years. By the way, if one's relatives are in Hungary, they can—after documenting their relationship to the citizen—personally open a BC account.

Above is a description of how one can make a private trip to the West once a year, and how one can obtain the required hard currency for such a trip. Obviously one has to be clever enough to accomplish this. But a good Hungarian goes further. The above example applies only to trips for private purposes. An even better deal would be to make it appear that one's private trip is actually an official trip. This is more difficult, but not impossible.

Péter Nagy works at a research institute; he is a section chief, and a recognized authority in his field. Other than chasing skirts, he likes to travel, possibly even more than to chase women. And he travels to the West four to five times a year. How? He "organizes" trips for himself, using his official prestige. Today's Hungary is very tight with hard currency, so getting any of it from the state is nearly impossible. Thus, Peter obtains hard currency using one of the methods described above. He also knows one to two years in advance all the conferences to be held in his field. Then he chooses one of the conferences to be held in a city he would like to visit, and finds a buddy or colleague who lives abroad and who is willing to write a letter of invitation stating that the organizers will cover the expenses of the trip. If the colleague living abroad is influential enough, he can actually arrange that the expenses are covered; if not, no problem: Peter goes abroad using one of the above described methods. The invitation is good not only for securing a passport, but also for obtaining so many days of vacation with pay from his institute. Thus, he travels several times a year, without using up any of his vacation time. Of course, this method also has one minor limitation: One is tied to the dates, places, and topics of conferences. But a good Hungarian usually finds a way to overcome such a small obstacle.

Another academician, András, is frequently invited to give lectures. This means that he is invited anywhere, anytime, without regard to conferences and themes. For this, he needs a letter of invitation, indicating the topic(s) of lecture(s) and also the fact that the host covers his expenses. If the host only covers the expenses of maintenance abroad, then András can receive some travel monies from his institution. What this means is that, using this method, he could travel on university time, using the state's money to cover some of his expenses.

With such travel opportunities at hand, who can say that Hungary is not a free country? One merely has to find the ways and means of this freedom. Sometimes one needs a magnifying glass, because the loopholes are very small, yet a great number of people fit through them. There are, of course, risks involved in such travel. The authorities, for example, could inquire, how did the traveler live while abroad if he brings back *all* his money? But a smart person can always think of something. For example, there are relatives and friends living abroad who are given as the source of money gifts. If anyone doubts it, there is no way of checking on it. The relative living abroad is smart enough to corroborate such statements.

In most cases, Hungarians do not travel abroad merely because of the beauty of the scenery. Another important consideration is the fact that there are many goods abroad that can be inexpensively purchased and profitably resold in Hungary. The most sought-after of these items are fashion items, cosmetic articles, and technological equipment. For example, using January 1984 prices as a reference point, a small personal computer (such as the Texas Instruments 99/4A) could be purchased in Western Europe for U.S.$150–200, which, even if we take blackmarket rates, equals less than 10,000 forints. If someone brings this into Hungary, the customs agents will estimate it to be worth 80,000 forints and demand that he pay 40 percent of this amount (32,000 forints) as import tax. In Hungary, there is such demand for a machine like this that the state-operated chain of stores selling used technological articles will gladly purchase it for 80,000 forints. What is the balance? 10,000 (price) plus 32,000 (customs duty) plus 2,000 (tip to the clerk at the used-article store to facilitate matters), equalling 44,000 forints expense against 80,000 forints income. Pure profit thus totals 36,000 forints. The situation is similar with other technological items such as video equipment. Even if one makes only one such purchase on each trip abroad, a profit of 36,000 forints per trip is attractive. In the case of computers, "Uncle State" caught on and now there are permits and additional taxes involved. They killed that business, but there is always something else instead. The process is endless, as long as there are such acute shortages of advanced technology items in Hungary. These shortages are the cause of such artificially high prices. This kind of "import" cannot be stopped by administrative regulations. There are two main reasons for this. On the one hand, even the highly reliable "comrades" need these items, so a strict administrative order would hurt them, too. At the same time, the state virtually relies on this "private import" to make up for the shortcomings of state-managed imports, which are caused by a short supply of hard currency.

The painful side of these procedures is the relatively high percentage demanded by the state as customs duty, which can be considered as "income tax" paid by the "importers." Of course, loopholes can be found here, too. If a citizen spends a longer time abroad, the laws provide for various duty concessions for him. The base amount is 6,000 forints; everyone can bring in goods to this value, even if they have stayed abroad for only one day. For every additional month the citizen spends abroad, this limit is raised by 10,000 forints. (Of course, the customs agents always consider the domestic price, which is often artificially inflated.) After spending a full year abroad, one can bring in *everything* duty-free, although still with the requirement to pay taxes. This gives everyone a great idea. It is obvious that a person who spends one year abroad does not *need* everything. A few months before his time abroad is up, this person finds out how many good friends he has at home. He starts getting request after request for various items, from friends . . . and friends of friends. Of course he can only bring in as many items as would be normal to have in one household. So he figures out what he needs, and starts filling the orders. He brings everything in duty-free, and sells it to his friends for hard currency. Sometimes, special favors are more valuable than hard currency. He places the money he earns on the deals in his hard currency account, claiming it represents what he saved during his stay abroad. One enterprising individual, a scientist, spent one year in England. Upon his return, he sold the items he bought for steep Hungarian prices and had a villa built in one of the most desirable locations in Budapest, on the side of Gellért Hill. All this out of one year's savings!

Everyone is happy except the state, which loses its "cut," but everyone looks at this as "taking back one's share" from the state.

There is another method of avoiding high duties. The rate is usually based on the domestic value, except in the case of items from the West German Quelle department store; in this case the duty is based on a compromise figure. The resulting rate, especially in the case of mechanical items, is ridiculously low.

Working abroad, due to the difference in pay scales, is such an advantage that it could never be matched by earnings at home. As a result everyone who can tries to obtain an assignment abroad. Of course, this is not easy and there are people who dedicate their entire activity to this goal. This practice is particularly prevalent in research institutions or universities. One characteristic method is getting a foreigner involved in a research program that is already under way. After a few "jointly written" articles appear (to which the foreign scientist may only contribute his name), the next logical step is an invitation to work abroad. In part this is to "repay" the Hungarian colleague's kindness, and in part it is designed to make permanent a relationship in which one partner works and the other shares the glory. In addition, this also means that foreign institutions obtain relatively cheap talent.

BUT MONEY TALKS

In Hungary, the Constitution guarantees the right of health care for every citizen. This is a beautiful principle, but it does not always work that way.

Every residence falls under the care of a district physician (körzeti orvos) to whom the resident must go for health care. There is no choice given here; your treating physician will be determined by your residence. This physician will make all basic examinations, and if one is ill, he has to be called. If further examinations are necessary, the patient must be sent to specialists or clinics; this is also arranged by the district doctor. He also puts the patient on sick-leave. During illness, one receives "maintenance money," which is 70 percent of one's salary if one is at home, but only 50 percent if one is at the hospital. The above format is simple, but there are several "twists" to it. In principle, the district physician must make house calls, but sometimes he does not do so. The child of Mr. Kovács becomes feverish. Kovács calls the doctor, who says that he is busy, he can only come the next morning. At this Kovács tells the doctor to consider the child a private patient. Ten minutes later the physician is on the scene, and his fee is 200 forints.

In the hope of obtaining better health care, patients give their doctors "gratitude money" (hálapénz). Taking the designation literally, this would be a reward for extra quality work, paid out of gratitude, but in fact it has become generally expected—indeed, demanded. One of the preconditions of treatment somewhat above the standard level is gratitude money paid "in advance." Mr. Kovács' friend, also a university professor, has a secretary whose husband spent two months in the hospital. This professor was opposed in principle to paying gratitude money, so he did not pay—at least not to the physician. After two months he paid it to someone else—for the man's funeral. The husband did not receive treatment that was above average, and the "average" treatment was not enough for recovery, or even survival.

The district physician also prescribes medicine, and there is room for maneuvering here, too. Drugs sold without prescription are generally difficult to find. Due to the occasional shortage, people sometimes hoard them, in order to ensure their own supply when the need arises. Thus a great number of basic medications—for example, oral contraceptives—completely disappear from the shelves. Could this be one of the covert methods of influencing population growth, instead of a simple shortage? Medicines are generally very cheap. If one has a prescription, one generally pays only 15 percent of the total price. This includes even imported medications.

The situation is similar with hospital care. There is much manipulation, starting with the obtaining of a hospital bed, all the way to release from the hospital. There is a general shortage of space in the hospitals, and this becomes even more acute during the summer months. The reason is quite simple: "Comrade Big" decides to take a long vacation here or abroad, and for the duration, places his aged parents into a hospital, ostensibly for the purpose of a "complete physical." In certain hospitals the beds have a "fixed" price. For example, Mr. Kovács' neighbor took his wife (to give birth) to a Kispest (southern district of Budapest) hospital, rather than to one in his neighborhood. He was expected to pay 5,000 forints to the head physician. Since these are considered questions of life and death, everyone is willing to make sacrifices in order to receive good care, in a good institution, and to be under the care of competent personnel.

Even in Hungary, an illness can bring on financial ruin. We must figure not only the gratitude money and the loss of much of one's income, but the complete loss of any earnings "on the side," which are often much more than one's official income. For example, a university instructor officially earns 7,200 forints, but on the side he is able to pick up another 11,000 forints. His wife (a teacher at another university) also makes 11,000 forints in "extras." In the case of illness, the National Health Board (*Szocialis Társadalombiztosító Központ* or SzTK) makes up for none of the unreported income.

Dental care is also a worry for Hungarians. If one goes to the "state"

(SzTK) dentist, one has no choice in the matter of who treats him or her and how. Treatment is not always proper. The dentist tries to get rid of the patient as fast as possible. Thus, often he pulls teeth that could have been saved. As a result, everyone who can goes to a private (*magán szektor*) or Maszek dentist, which is not cheap. A simple handshake is 200, a filling 650–700, extraction 400 forints. In the case of more complicated treatment, such as a root canal job, the expenses may reach into the thousands. A good set of dentures starts at 5–6 thousand forints. Almost everyone goes to a private dentist, but only if it is an absolute must. As a result, there are a great number of people with bad teeth, because people start going to the dentist only when their teeth hurt, and at such times the disease is already in an advanced state.

Let us look at the same question from the point of view of the physicians. No matter what his position, the salary of a doctor is ridiculously low: 5–7 thousand forints plus a certain amount of extra for night and weekend duties. Without "gratitude money," the doctor could not support his family. Thus he is forced to rely on the gratitude money and/ or to pursue a simultaneous private practice. In a portion of his dwelling, he maintains a small clinic, with the most crucial equipment. If a patient comes, the basic fee (the handshake) starts at 200 forints. The better physicians may ask for as much as 1,000 forints per visit. In addition, of course, there are fees for special medicines, injections, prescriptions, special examinations. In the vast majority of cases, there is a great difference between how the doctor treats the patient in an "official" as opposed to a "private" capacity. In the latter case, one may see personal caring, humane treatment, and maximum effort.

There is a great solidarity among physicians. This does not mean that they never make statements against each other, but that in conflict situations they support one another—right or wrong. For example, the father of Kovács' friend was hit by a car when he rode his motorcycle. The car failed to respect his right-of-way. After two weeks stay in the hospital, he died of his injuries. Since the driver of the car was a physician, his colleagues in the hospital tried to "help him" by stating acute hernia as the cause of death. Thus the guilty driver escaped the usual 2–2 1/2-year prison sentence, and got off with a light fine. Kovács' friend appealed the judgment. At the second trial, the driver was again judged not guilty, because the subpoenaed physician-expert, standing up for the profession, concurred with the opinion of the other colleagues. Afterward the driver told Kovács' friend (in private, of course, without witnesses) that he should quit wasting his time and money on appeals, because there was no physician who would go against the word of a colleague.

A mathematician at a university in Budapest was involved in another piquant affair. His childhood friend, a lawyer, asked him to testify before the court. The story is very revealing; therefore, it should be cited in full.

There was a nurse, Kati, who worked in one of the Budapest hospitals. For nurses, the supreme achievement is to land a physician for a husband. This brings improvement in both material and social prestige. Earlier, Kati worked in a hospital in the countryside. Her boss was married with several children, and 30 years her senior. Kati initiated an affair with him, but he rejected the offer. Thus, she had to leave the small hospital, and so she moved to Budapest. At her new place of employment there were six physicians in the ward where she worked. Five of them were married, and one, Laci, was single. Not only was his salary excellent, because he had a well paying private practice, but he was also expecting a sizeable inheritance from his old parents. Being familiar with the behavior of nurses, Laci did not initiate any sexual contact with any of the nurses, including Kati. As things happened, however, Kati became pregnant. True, she lived with a low-ranking, poorly paid young man, but the other doctors in the ward (according to the lawyer, all five of them) also had sexual contact with her. Kati gave birth, and now the story begins in earnest. Instead of naming the young man with whom she lived as the father, she became greedy. She looked for a better (wealthier) candidate. The other five doctors also thought that Laci "has nothing to lose," thus he should be named as the father. There was only one problem: Laci had nothing to do with Kati sexually. No problem: Kati was able to describe Laci's apartment. Since she was never really there, her testimony failed under cross-examination. There were also "witnesses" to the fact that Laci made advances toward Kati. For example, during a social gathering he had patted her derriere. Since one cannot possibly conceive from such an innocuous gesture and since this was part of a game, this also failed to convince the court. One of the five married doctors left the hospital, and he then testified on Laci's behalf. Every normal person would think that the case was over— but no. In Hungary, a blood test was ordered to determine the possibility of fatherhood. In the case of Laci, the test showed that there was a 97.5 percent chance that he could be the father. This was where the mathematician came into the picture. Laci's lawyer asked him to look over the test material. There were several problems. One of them was that the statistics were based on a Bavarian region in West Germany. It is well known that the frequency of blood groups is different in Hungary, thus the same testing material should not be used without making some adjustments. At the same time, the introduction of the testing equipment into Hungary was good business for someone, and one of the involved persons was highly placed in the Ministry of Health. A critique of the testing procedure was not in his interest, and this became evident during the trial. Every one of the physician witnesses testified against the mathematician, but they failed to come up with convincing arguments. Their final argument was: this is not a mathematical but a medical problem. Thus the decision was left up to the expert from the Ministry of Health, who just happened to be the man involved with importing of the testing apparatus. There was never any doubt about the decision. Laci lost his case, and he is now paying a monthly sum in child support without ever having once been Kati's lover. As for the mathematician, he started having difficulties at his place of work. By now he probably has had to change jobs. There is no proof that his newly arising problems have anything to do with his testifying in court, but there is suspicion. The court even found it insignificant that the original results of the blood test had subsequent corrections on them, and did not think it was necessary to repeat the test.

So much for the mathematician's story. There is another aspect of health care which should be mentioned: the GyES *(Gyermekgondozási segély*, or aid to care for children).

Any woman giving birth to a child in Hungary receives a four-month leave (with full pay).[9] After this, until the child is three years old, she stays on GyES status. This means that she can stay home with the child, she receives a significant stipend every month, and her job will be available when she wants to return to work. Of course, she can change her mind and go back to work earlier. This is the bright side of GyES. There is also a darker side, however.

Let us consider the situation of the factory or office where she works. A young woman is trained to do a job, and then she disappears for three years. Someone can be hired to replace her, but for the next three years this is an uncertain position, since the young mother can come back any time. As a result, there is a reluctance to hire young married women, especially in a position that requires serious training. A professor in Miskole is in serious trouble because two of the computer operators at his department are on GyES, and he cannot hire anyone to replace them. Thus work is going much slower, and he is harrassed because of this.

There are other aspects of GyES. In Hungary, if someone builds a dwelling, he receives 40,000 forints from the state per child. If the wife is home on GyES, she is also considered a child, and the 40,000 forints is due her. Many women go on GyES at the beginning of the construction, but as soon as the bank loan is arranged (as soon as the 40,000 is approved) she goes back to work.

The women who stay home on GyES fall behind on many accounts— because they get out of practice at work, but also because they become alienated from their husbands. No matter how cute the child is, staying home with it can become very boring. A wife is also a human being, so in the case of most married women this is the period when they start becoming unfaithful to their husbands. It is a time when they have the time, they have the place, and there are plenty of partners. Women on GyES are ideal catches for men, because there is no worry about having to marry them. Even married men favor "arrangements" of this kind. The women on GyES can be visited during the day, and conferences and business trips can be used as excuses. For example, among the men mentioned as "six partners" in the next section, "Building Your Own Home With State Money," every one of the men had some experience with young wives on GyES. The men considered them grateful partners, enjoying the break in the dull routine of the day. An interesting episode describing this "arrangement" appeared on state television. In a country town, the young wives on GyES organized a callgirl network. For months, business was good. There were waiters in nearby espressos who recommended the ladies to customers. The apartments were empty because they took care of each other's kids while Mommy was busy. One of the husbands was given the name of the espresso by a friend. He visited the place, where he was given his own address, with his own wife waiting. The police ended the entire network.

Apropos of prostitution (further details on the subject are presented in Chapter 5, under "Sex Within and Outside the Family"): On paper it is illegal in Hungary. In reality, there are a great many prostitutes in Budapest. They can be picked up on the street or in various places of entertainment. Rákóczi Square in the VIIIth district is one such place. The ladies must be approached, the price (200–1,500 forints) must be agreed upon, after which one goes to the lady's apartment. One significant activity is renting rooms for this purpose *(kégliztetés)*. Most of the ladies' problems with the law arise from the fact that they do not pay taxes on their earnings. But since there are no medical checks, there are also problems with veneral disease, especially syphillis. One or two shots takes care of the disease, but the state tries to prevent its spread by insisting that every patient report his/her sexual partners during the past period, who in turn are called in for checking. One can imagine what the effect of a letter from the "VD clinic" could be if a cheating husband's wife opens it up. The situation is similar with women picked up in bars. After one or two drinks one can leave with the lady. The use of various precautions is recommended. The price in this case is somewhat higher; in some cases only hard currency is expected: 100–200 Deutschmark is a good average. The cost of medical treatment should also be calculated into that figure.

In Hungary abortion is legal for anyone, as long as it is done through official channels. The woman must go before a so-called AB Committee, where they take her personal data, they issue a permit, and—for a fee of some 700 forints—the abortion is performed at a specified institution. Since Hungary is a small country and everything becomes commonly known soon enough, the woman may worry that her abortion will be talked about. Thus, privately arranged abortions are also a flourishing business. They are performed in private apartments, for as little as 4–5 thousand forints, and a woman only has to remain there about 1–2 hours. For this, of course, one needs recommendations. For example, when a university faculty member got one of his students pregnant, he had to solve the problem quickly. He turned to one of his former girl-friends for advice, and she recommended one of the best-known private gynecologists in Budapest. The operation was performed the very same night in the doctor's apartment. The same woman had had several previous abortions. When she became pregnant the last time, she was issued the usual pregnancy record book, in which the data of the present and previous pregnancies are inserted. In order to maintain confidentiality, she was issued *two* of these booklets; one for her doctor, containing all information, and another one for her family, in which the previous abortions were omitted.

BUILDING YOUR OWN HOUSE WITH STATE MONEY

A Hungarian, especially if he is young, has considerable trouble finding a place to live.[10] Most often, young people live with their parents for a while, and they try to obtain a place of residence from that assured basis. If, in the meantime, the parents die, the problem is automatically solved, whether the apartment in question is owned by the parents or owned by the district council.

Tanácsi (council-owned) rental units are owned by the state. The state is required to take care of the necessary repairs and renovations. For this service, as well as for the right to inhabit the dwelling unit, the resident pays a monthly rent. Years ago, this rent used to be very low, even for a low wage earner. For example, the three-room apartment of a five member family used to be 250–300 forints (approximately U.S.$8–10), which was approximately 10 percent of the average wage rate then. If the renter dies, then a member of the family, a relative, or any other dependent who "officially" resided with him (meaning, that he was registered at that address) could inherit the right to dwell in that unit as a renter. Thus, one of the practical methods of obtaining a dwelling is to become a co-resident in one of the units. This can be accomplished in several ways. If one is a dependent or a close relative, then the process is a natural one. In many families, exactly for this reason, the grandchild is registered at the address of his grandparents, even though he continues to live with his parents. From time to time he appears at the dwelling of his grandparents, and at such times he turns to the neighbors and the concierge with small requests and questions, in order to make his presence noticed by as many people as possible. One may also register at an address by paying for the privilege. For a certain monthly payment the subtenant may live in one of the rooms, and he can also use the kitchen and the amenities. Such registration is usually referred to as "temporary," meaning that the primary tenant can have the subtenant removed, even if this takes a lengthy and torturous process. (In Hungary, no one can be simply put out on the street; in order to force someone to leave a dwelling, he must be provided with at least a sublease opportunity.) If the primary tenant dies, and the subtenant can document his claim to an apartment *of that size* (which is determined by a number of factors), then the apartment is usually registered in his name, and his worries are over.

A frequent method of obtaining a council-owned apartment is the signing of a contract to take care of the primary tenant. Referred to as *eltartási szerzódes,* such a contract is usually made with elderly primary tenants; they allow another, usually younger person or couple to move into one of their rooms (as in the cases of subleasing), in exchange for which the other is required to pay and to take care of the elderly party. The contract is made in writing and is approved by the district council. Subsequently the council regularly checks whether the caretaking duties are fulfilled. The relationship is one of being at the mercy of another person. The elderly party must be aware of the fact that the dwelling situation of the other party is only solved after his death. It is not known whether or not the other party had ever engaged in urging such a death, but the situation is a source of much excitement, irritation, impatience, and fighting. As a result, vulnerability may become mutually felt. On the one hand, every function of the person being cared for (including even the biological functions) depends on the contracted party, while on the other hand the younger people are obliged by their contract to "serve" the other(s). Often the mere performance of these duties is exceedingly difficult. If the caretakers are working, they can't be at home. In this case they either hire someone to take care of their elderly partner, or attempt to have him hospitalized. Thus either the money paid to "nurses," or money paid to doctors (who arrange the hospitalization), and to hospital personnel, constitutes an extra financial burden. The elderly partner, if he feels neglected, can turn to the district council with his complaints; if the complaints appear well based, the contract is declared invalid. Everyone signing such a contract is afraid of this, because obviously all of the money and time invested previously is simply lost. The reader not thoroughly knowledgeable of Hungarian conditions may say, "Why the long torture? Why not simply sign a contract with someone who is very old or very sick, someone who will pass away soon?" There is a rub. The relationship must be maintained for at least six months in order for the surviving partner to inherit the apartment. In a valid case, he will be eligible to claim the apartment, even if the deceased person has relatives, because the right of residency/inhabitation is not subject to simple inheritance laws. Whoever wants to continue residing in the dwelling unit must be a registered resident there *at the time of the deceased's death.* A friend of Mr. Kovács obtained an apartment through this type of "caretaking" contract. An old lady, living by herself, asked 40,000 forints just for signing the contract. (This amount is often equal to the yearly wage of a young person.) Kovács' friend also paid 1,500 forints each month, and cooked, cleaned, and did the laundry for the lady besides. In fact, it was the life of a servant. Everything turned out relatively well, because the old lady only lived for three years. Now, let's figure. The apartment cost the friend 94,000 forints and three years of servant-like existence. More precisely, he obtained the right to live in the rental unit for this, paying a monthly rent. He did not obtain any real property, because this apartment cannot be sold, and he will not get his money back. When he becomes old, the entire process will be repeated.

These types of "caretaking" contracts are on the increase in Hungary. Part of the reason is that the shortage of dwelling units is not reduced; another factor is that retirement incomes do not keep up with inflation and price increases. The physical survival of many elderly persons can only be assured by obtaining external support, one form of which is the contract outlined above.

The apartments owned by individuals are referred to as "keepers" (öröklakás), and their owners do not pay rent. Whether one builds a dwelling unit or buys one, he can receive a bank loan to help him. While he is repaying this loan, his unit is tax exempt; afterward he must pay taxes on the unit. Thus there is a monthly payment involved in this case, as well; add to this the down payment, which is at least 50 percent of the total price. Nowadays, one square meter of dwelling space costs between 10,000 and 25,000 forints, depending on the quality, age, modernity, and location of the unit. One subject interviewed, paid 10,300 forints per square meter of his recently-built apartment. One year later, he was offered 18,000 for the same unit, an 80 percent increase in value. This is not primarily a question of inflation; it is simply derived from the fact that an apartment, ready to be occupied, is much more valuable than a half-finished unit, which, due to unforeseen problems, may never be ready for occupancy. A finished apartment may be purchased from the state, through the National Savings Bank (OTP), or the district councils. In the case of units marketed through the OTP, auctions are held; whoever can put down the highest down payment will receive the unit. If several people offer the same amount, the question is decided by "pull"; a phone call from high places can decide everything.

The district councils distribute another type of unit, called "cooperative" *(szövetkezeti)* apartments. These are significantly cheaper than the "keepers"; one can move into them by making a much lower down payment. The balance can be paid in monthly installments, during the next 20–30 years.

The regular rental apartments are also assigned by the district councils. Here, an interesting question arises: What decides who gets what kind of apartment? A request form must be filled out for every unit owned by the district council. Besides the usual data, these forms contain information concerning the wealth of the petitioner (he must indicate whether he has a car, a weekend house, etc.). He must also indicate the amount of his monthly income, how many people would be residing with him, and who they are, where he is presently residing, under what circumstances, and so on. Based on these data, the district council decides what type and size of dwelling unit the petitioner is entitled to and places him on a ranked list of other petitioners. The individual's place on the list is determined by computers, based on an established point system. At the beginning of each year they decide how many people they can satisfy, based on available apartments; usually, very few. A young couple and their three children lived in a 1 1/2-room, 52 square meter apartment. Both he and his wife were scientific researchers, but they could not work in that apartment. They requested another one, with just one additional room. They even agreed to give their small flat (owned by them!) to the state, in exchange for the right to move into a larger *rental* unit. When the husband visited the district council, the person in charge of his case told him that there would not be a need for an apartment change because by the time the case was taken care of, the couple's two-year-old son would be a married man himself. Of course this is an exaggeration, but it reflects the present dwelling situation realistically. This was the impetus for the young researcher to start building his own house.

Another method of obtaining an apartment is simply to appropriate one. Let's look at a concrete case. Let's say Kovács is a young man, he is just married, and they have no apartment. But they have found out (since it is a small country there are few secrets) that the apartment of one of their relatives is located in the spot where the state is planning to build a large apartment unit, or due to the condition of their relative's dwelling, the district council has decided to demolish the entire building. They quickly move in with the relatives, paying them for this privilege, and wait. When the date of demolition arrives, the council is obliged to find an apartment for them immediately. On top of that, the state pays them for the apartment and the real estate appropriated. The amount is decided rather subjectively by the committee sent out. Recently there was a lawsuit in Budapest, in which it was proven that the committee in question readily declared a higher value on an apartment in exchange for a bribe. In this particular case, the committee estimated the value of the unit to be 50,000 forints higher in exchange for a 10,000 forints bribe. This is called clean business; the committee is happy and the former tenant is too. Of course it should not be forgotten that 50,000 forints were earmarked to provide new apartments for the people. But this would only help someone else, so why should they worry?

Recently it has been made possible for a non-Hungarian citizen to own a dwelling unit in Hungary. For example, retirees of Hungarian descent frequently like to move back "home." Generally speaking, this is not entirely because of the nostalgic sentiments of the individual; "filthy lucre" often plays a part in this decision. For instance, while a $500/month retirement check in the United States does not even provide the minimum standard of living, in Hungary, even according to the official exchange rate, it amounts to 20,000 forints. Such an amount can provide even luxury items and travel expenses. After all, an 8,000 forint monthly salary is considered high. If the individual desiring to relocate to Hungary is able to pay for an apartment in U.S. dollars, he enjoys a certain advantage; he is guaranteed to walk away with the auctioned apartment.

As mentioned earlier, most people obtain a dwelling unit by building one.[11] Let us examine the procedure involved, based on the experience of one of the subjects interviewed. János tried to solve his problems through the district council, and he even advertised in the papers. (The dailies accept private ads.) János indicated the size of his present apartment, along with his desire for a larger one. A great number of people called him, but they could not agree on a deal. Many of the callers were not interested in this particular exchange offer, but were seeking similar arrangements themselves; thus, they were inquiring about the prevailing prices and possibilities. Altogether there were three serious callers, all of them elderly people who lived alone in a large, council-owned apartment. In the event of their deaths, these apartments could not be inherited by their relatives. János' apartment was at an excellent location; it was even equipped with a telephone. However, it was on the fourth floor and there was no elevator. This scared off the elderly people. There was no other course for him but to build.

For days, János buried himself in the papers' classified ads, where lawyers and law firms announce the organization of collectives for the purpose of joint building. The basic condition is that on a given lot there is a possibility to have a certain type of dwelling unit. Only the clients are missing. One of the ads attracted János, and he looked up the given address, where he was received by an elegant, wealthy-looking lawyer. He immediately showed several designs to János, along with a description of the lot, illustrated with maps. János selected a design for a unit containing 6 apartments, which appeared well located. The lawyer informed him of the projected costs, and this also appeared favorable. As it turned out later, the projected costs were surpassed by more than 60 percent. The next day, János spoke with a former classmate of his, who was personally acquainted with the lawyer. Based on the principle that "it makes a lot of difference who your neighbors are," the classmate called up the lawyer, asking him to inform János concerning every new potential partner, and asking him not to sign a contract with anyone without János' consent. According to the contract, the lawyer promised to take care of all legal problems arising during the construction, while making absolutely no guarantees concerning any financial arrangement. In order to become a "partner," one was required to put up 235,000 forints; this amount was to cover the legal expenses, the cost of officially registering the property, the cost of design, and the expenses of the so-called technical inspector. At the same time, the six partners also concluded a contract with each other. Aside from the usual legal mumbo-jumbo, these contracts contain one important clause; namely, that if any one of the partners were unable to pay during the construction, the others would have the right to sell his share to someone else. This was important because inability to pay would present a difficult dilemma for the others. They could either stop the construction and wait for an improvement in their partner's finances, or they could loan the necessary amount to their partner. Meanwhile, however, prices could rise, the partners would continue to live in unpleasant conditions, and they could lose some of their skilled contractors, whom they came to know. A loan to the partner could also be a problem. The cost of the house could increase by, say, 50,000 forints if that is how much they loaned to the partner. He could sell his share to someone else, at a price reflecting the increased value. The others could take him to court, and may get their money back, but at a rate of only a few hundred forints per month, at a very low interest. (It should be pointed out that interest rates are very low in Hungary: 2–3 or 5 percent, according to the agreement.)

After about eight months, a six-person group was formed which seemed acceptable. "Acceptability" meant that all members appeared able to make all payments for the duration of the construction. This was the team: one university professor, one physician, two private entrepreneurs (one vegetable seller, one cosmetician), a computer expert who frequently traveled abroad, and a friend of a friend who often visited the West, since his wife was in foreign trade. The university professor appeared to be the lowest paid, but because he was in a fortunate specialty, he was able to earn quite a bit doing consultations. First, they signed the contract with each other; then they made the required down payment and purchased the lot. According to the former owner of the lot and the lawyer, the lot was connected with gas, electric, and water lines, and it had sewers. However the contract, drafted by the partners' lawyer, stated that the lot "can be equipped with utilities." The partners, none of them being lawyers, did not notice this small difference in wording. Numerous problems arose from this later; let's take them in order.

The lot was not, in fact, connected to the sewage system. True, the municipal sewage plant gave permission to have the lot connected to their sewage line, but this was not so simple. The house was built on a slope, located lower than the sewage line on the street. Pumping could solve this problem, but in case of power failure (which occurs frequently) the sewage would flood the house. The unbelievably high expenses are something else again. Thus, János visited the office involved, told the official that the "permitted solution" was not feasible, and, expressing his gratitude in advance (in a case like this, this means the offer of a certain sum of money), he requested an alternative solution. After giving it some thought, and after some discussion concerning the amount of money involved, a new permit was issued, at a cost of 5,000 forints. A connection to the lower sewage line was now permitted. Fortunately, another group was building on the next lot. Since they had similar problems, they decided to tie into the sewage line built by the partners, thus sharing the expenses. As a result, the 5,000 forints turned out to be an excellent investment. Of course, since János had no receipt for this sum (bribe), he had difficulty being reimbursed by his partners. They agreed, verbally, that in all similar cases in the future, the person making the "payment" should describe it in writing to the others, and they would immediately reimburse him. In this instance, János received his money. He was only sorry that he did not claim a higher amount, say, 8,000 forints; his partners would have believed him. (Let us stop for a moment and consider the question of confidence among the partners. János and the other partners were guided by the basic principle; have a clean conscience and no cheating, because as soon as someone cheats, they believed, the circle of confidence is broken and no one will trust anyone else ever again.)

The group had permission from the electric company to hook up to an existing electric power line. However, two problems arose. One, the permit was "in principle" only, alloting such a low amount of energy that it would not even power one automatic washing machine. The more serious problem was that the electric company did not recognize the permit as valid; they had no copy of it on file, and the person signing it had left for the West six months previously. Thus the permission had to be applied for again. It was obtained relatively inexpensively, for two bottles of French cognac. The new permit still only allowed for the same low amount of electricity. Only later, after the completion of the house, was the necessary amount of electricity permitted.

The water line extended to the lot, so there was no problem with that. A new type of gas line ("city gas") was laid on the street, but it ended some 100–150 meters from the house. The group faced a dilemma: they could bring the gas line up to their house, but, in accordance with prevailing regulations, they were obliged to install a line to which the next house could also be connected—free, of course. Thus it was in everyone's interest *not to* initiate the gas line construction, but to wait for someone else. As usual in cases like this, János initiated a discussion with all interested parties. They agreed to install the line at shared expense, sharing the cost in accordance with the number of apartments involved. The three houses altogether had 28 units; János' group paid 6/28 of the total cost.

Obtaining the permits, organizing, and putting together the basic material conditions took seven months. In addition, it took 6 months to organize the group, and one month to take care of legal details; in other words, a total of over one whole year.

Now the group could begin the actual construction. Since none of them were trained builders they had to find a contractor. According to the lawyer, a six-unit house is too small for a nationalized state firm, but too large for a private entrepreneur. Thus, there was no legal way to obtain a contractor. The group had to use the characteristic Hungarian loophole. The lawyer recommended that they use the "do-it-yourself" method. On paper the group purchases all the materials and they build the house themselves. Due to the skill requirements, they employed tradesman for the more delicate tasks, and the entire construction was under the supervision of a "technical inspector." A member of the group (the computer specialist) had an acquaintance who was willing to be the inspector, for a monthly fee of 2,500 forints. For this amount he met with the group and visited the site once a week and signed every purchase order.

Personal contacts are important in the building trade also. Without contracts, it is difficult (if not impossible) to obtain materials. The lawyer recommended an old friend of his as a person who was able to solve problems. This man was a private entrepreneur who asked for payment in cash; this way there was no record of money changing hands, and thus no taxes. As each stage of the construction came up (foundation, structure, etc.), he made a preliminary bid, which included the procurement of materials and the subcontracting of the work. (He added a 3 percent surcharge for the purchase of materials.) If he were to hire the masons and other skilled workers officially, he would have had to pay taxes. In order to avoid this, he made sure that (on paper) the hiring was done by the group of builders. Payment, of course, was done through the private entrepreneur. He always signed the purchase orders, and these were always accepted by the OTP as legal. The strange thing here is that these kinds of bills were accepted without any contract, guarantees, or tax papers.

As the construction proceeded, every member of the group ran out of money. More and more often, they decided to work on the house themselves instead of having to pay more. They performed the tasks of bricklayers, ditch-diggers, and so on. Everything would have been all right if there had been sufficient supervision, but during this period, the inspector was otherwise occupied. Certain tasks had to be done twice, or repaired later. For example, the unevenness of the walls had to be corrected by applying thicker layers of plastering. In the purchasing of materials, they continued to pay the extra amounts ("gratitude money"). When the house was 40 percent ready, they were qualified to ask for a bank loan. After application, a committee came out from the OTP and decided that the house was not quite ready enough for a loan. Since the loans were desperately needed, the bank told the builders they could obtain loans if they showed a sufficient bank balance by presenting their bank deposit books. Of course, if they had had money in the bank they would not have needed loans. A variant of the Hungarian loophole worked in this case, too. The partners borrowed their friends' bank books, which are nameless and their identity cannot be determined, even by computers. Thus proving that they did not need the loans, they were granted the loans. At the time the OTP usually loaned 340,000 forints at the annual interest rate of 2 percent. On top of this, one could also receive loans from the firm he worked for in the amount of 50–150 thousand forints. The amount could be higher if one's spouse also worked. In some cases, one could amass loans amounting to 200–300 thousand forints. Loans like these are free of interest, and the company one borrows from even pays the cost of handling the money.

One member of the group, the husband of the export/import agent, did not take advantage of this type of a loan. He wanted to change jobs in the near future, and a loan like that would have tied him down for several years. Instead, he went to the director of the company and made this "generous" offer: He would not ask for a loan (money for this purpose is always scarce!) if the company would allow him to use certain pieces of equipment at institutional rates (i.e., very cheaply). The director immediately agreed. The builder achieved a double gain; he acquired certain needed equipment for the construction at a very low rate, and also left himself free to change jobs. Two months after the completion of the house, he became a private entrepreneur, an auto-parts dealer in one of the busiest parts of the city.

After granting the loans, the OTP regularly paid all bills signed by the "private helper" or by any of the private tradesmen working on the house. The equipment borrowed from the company significantly lowered expenses, as their usage fee was deducted from the other bills. After a while, however, the partners got the notion that the inspector was favoring his own pocketbook when filling out the bills. Their suspicions became stronger upon hearing one of the bricklayers mention the fact that he had met the inspector at the home of one of the private entrepreneurs, where he went to have the bills filled out. This may not have been significant, but the difference between the acceptable level of costs for each phase of work and those actually charged was steadily increasing with time. (What should be added here is that there are regulations controlling the price each private tradesman can ask. However, since these are unrealistically low, and nobody would do the work for them, "private arrangements" are made, in accordance with the quality expected.) On this particular construction, the actual price was nearly always close to the maximum level usually accepted. The building partners could not prove anything, but they fired the inspector anyway and hired another one. After the completion of the house, the tradesman told János, while drinking, that there was indeed some hanky-panky between him and the inspector. They each would cite a figure; if the two figures agreed they wrote it down. If there was a difference, they always wrote down the higher one, and they split the difference between themselves. Everything, of course, was without paper, receipt, or records. Everyone benefited except the six partners.

The house was built in three years. If we take the first meeting with the lawyer as the starting point, then it took four and a half years to build it. This is quite a long time, but compared to the promises received at the district council, quite short.

Finally, the residents could move into their new homes. Each week they met to take care of the expenses. Everything appeared in order, but it was not.

While the construction was still proceeding, they could not break down every item of expense exactly. For example, it was impossible to keep a record on how many bricks were required for each dwelling unit, and so forth, let alone the shared areas, such as the stairwells. Thus, the partners agreed that the final breakdown of costs would be made on the basis of apartment sizes. This brought newer problems. Due to the imprecision of the construction, each apartment became considerably larger than planned. (János, for example, gained 8 square meters). This meant the ratios also changed. There were also various modifications in the original plans. Who benefited, for example, from a wall that was not built? Similar situations arose in connection with units where more expensive details were added, such as thicker insulation. The distribution of extra expenses created new legal problems, as did the fact that the recording of the house had to be officially changed, due to changes in the sizes of the units. Private agreements are not always sufficient, because the "selling" of any real estate or portion thereof is accompanied by a 17 percent transfer fee, based on the real estate's value. What or who could determine the value of a few square meters?

The lawyer who organized the entire affair had already been paid, and he now refused to have anything to do with it. The partners could not agree; the only solution was to take the case to the courts. No decision has yet been rendered. The offshoot of the story: Relations between the partners are ruined. For decades they will live with neighbors who are "related" to them through law suits. And all this is on account of a house that they jointly acquired after four and a half years of hard, tension-packed effort. Additional results of the affair: One of the partners is getting divorced; another one has filed for divorce.

Even though the above story does not reflect only joy and optimism, the people involved can consider themselves lucky. They have accomplished their aim. Another friend of János' undertook a similar project eight years ago. Construction was not started yet when the tradesman took off with their money. He is now in prison, but the money has not been recovered. The 250,000 forints usually required to get in on a project like this is the equivalent of five years' wages, based on average Hungarian earnings.

CONCLUSIONS

The evidence is overwhelming that the present level of socialist development in Hungary does not provide for the society as a whole a standard of living that is commensurate with a model promoted by the Hungarian ruling elite and the Hungarian mass media. There is a wide gap between theory and practice. Hungary still suffers from a limited industrial capacity, an economy of shortages, underdeveloped infrastructure, and so on; these weaknesses also exert a negative influence on the way of life of the Hungarian citizens.

In this context the housing problem is probably the most serious one concerning the future lifestyle. The quantity of existing dwellings throughout the country is insufficient and the quality is rapidly deteriorating. While it is true that between 1960 and 1978 the number of persons inhabiting 100 dwellings has decreased from 349 to 288, and the number of persons per hundred rooms has decreased from 236 to 149, the housing issue was and still is a great social problem in Hungary. In 1977, for example, there were 396,282 applications for housing, but only 50,746 were allotted.[12]

It is difficult to lead a socialist, or for that matter a normal, life in overcrowded conditions with more than two generations living together and in the absence of elementary civilized conditions. These conditions hamper complex personality growth; they may entail consequences in which the primary relationships important for society (marriage, parent and child) may weaken and provide favorable breeding grounds for antisocial influences. Approximately 30 percent of the adult population in Hungary is not adequately housed—mostly the young. Even the most optimistic young couples spend many years with their parents before they can acquire an apartment of their own. Thus a period in the lives of almost all of them is ruined by the lack of adequate housing. (The seriousness of this issue is also discussed in Chapter 5, under "Problems with the Socialist Egalitarian Model.")

The housing situation exerts another negative influence on the lifestyle of many Hungarians due to the methods of acquiring a dwelling. Under the present rules, only the lowest income groups can hope for a council-owned apartment, but there are not many such apartments, far fewer than qualified applicants. Considering that more people are entitled to apartments than the existing number available, and that they sometimes have to wait for very long periods, a large portion of the population are compelled to resort to private building, availing themselves of different forms of state support. The consequences of this are more "outside" work (often during working hours), corruption, the extortion of tips, and extra reward money. Stopping these practices seems impossible, all the more since extra work is justified not only by individual needs, but also by the different phenomena produced by the economy of short-ages—so that in a certain sense, the subjective and "objective" needs meet. This is a considerable source of extra tips and bribes.

Such undertakings as the construction of private homes may establish habits that will survive long after housing has been obtained. It is not surprising to find, therefore, that these negative habits have already become acquired characteristics of the young people and that they will be transmitted to the next generation. Another consequence is that the hopelessness of young couples of ever getting a home of their own can lure them into irresponsible ways—finding any means to achieve their objectives. All of this may give rise to a new personal or public ethic that is contrary to the socialist values and morality projected by the ruling elite. On second thought, there is no need to dramatize the situation or exaggerate the problem of corruption in Hungary due to lack of housing, when in the USSR (the model of socialist development), with fewer incentives for private housing, corruption, according to Gerald Mars, is as high as 25 percent of personal disposable incomes; in Italy, 33 percent of GNP; in England 5–7 percent; and in the U.S. approximately 10 percent.[13]

It is said that the Eskimos have several dozen words for snow, perhaps because there is so much of it where they live. Could it be that the Hungarian range of synonyms describing corruption is thriving for the same reason? Dr. Elemér Hankiss, a well known sociologist and a member of the Hungarian Academy of Sciences, raised this question and listed more than a dozen words in the Hungarian language for gratuities, from petty tips to major bribes.[14] The most controversial form of gratuity is the one given doctors. In the private sector between 1972 and 1982 the growth of gratuities in the medical profession was second only to that of those of stone masons.[15] During those ten years, "fees" for various operations increased by 500 percent, reaching an average of four and even five digits in the case of heart surgery. The motives for paying this extra money are, according to the study, not the most cited ones, such as gratitude, consideration for doctors' low salaries, a desire to get better treatment, or just mere custom, but the fact that medical services are free. It is well established that if something is free, the demand for it becomes endless. Surveys have shown that Hungarian citizens visit their doctors much more frequently than necessary, and particularly attentive medical care consequently becomes less common. Thus when it is available it must be especially honored with a gratuity.[16] On the other side, some doctors accept money from a patient since otherwise the patient believes that his special illness or condition is hopeless. Besides, extra incomes have become legal in practically every sphere of social production. Bribery is widespread in the social services, in the wholesale and retail trade, and in every other area where goods and articles in short supply are purchased. In 1983 the party daily *Népszabadság* took a firm stand against the deteriorating conditions caused by corruption. The article urged the authorities to act "before something that is not yet common but is spreading becomes universal, and unlawfulness becomes legal."[17]

Ever since 1975, when free medical care in Hungary was made available by law to every citizen, the health service has been overburdened to an extraordinary degree and the quality of the service has deteriorated. The average number of patients per general practitioner is about 2,500, but consultations average 30,000 a year. The number of properly equipped hospital and outpatient clinics is inadequate. Consequently, the overburdened doctor, who lacks the time and equipment to examine the patient properly, shifts the responsibility for a diagnosis to others, referring the patient to the next grades, which leads to overburdening of these as well. The number of patients seen by the whole of the health system grows year by year (outpatient services altogether average 15 visits a year per capita), and efficiency declines throughout.

At this point the spontaneous selective mechanism of the social hierarchy comes into play. Those who have better connections or more money want to ensure better quality medical services. Since tensions and dissatisfaction increase on both sides (doctors are dissatisfied as well as patients), there are pressures to reduce the extent of demand. It becomes obvious that the better-off enjoy more (in quantity as well as quality) health service. Consequently, there are rumblings in Hungary (especially among low income groups) that free medical services should be available only to those who cannot pay. This new socialist ethic, however, is a clear contradiction of the earlier unambiguous socialist goal of equality. Is it possible that under socialist democracy this issue, as well as many others, will eventually be resolved according to Hungarian realism?

NOTES

1. See Lajos Héthy, "A 'második gazdaság,' a kisvállalkozás és a gazdaságirányítós" [The 'second economy,' the small enterprise, and economic control] *Társadalomkutatás* [Social Research] 1 (1983): 29–43. See also Tamás Bauer, "A második gazdasági reform és a tulajdonviszonyok: Szempontok az új gazdasági mechanizmus továbbtejlesztéséhez" [The second economic reform and ownership relations: Some considerations for the further development of the NEM] *Mozgó Vilaǵ* [Moving World] 8 (November 1982): 17–42.

2. See *Magyar Hírlap* (February 22, 1985). For purposes of better understanding the monetary value of the Hungarian currency, which is not convertible, the 1987 dollar/forints exchange rate was 1:50.

3. See *Népszava* (February 25, 1985).

4. "The transformation of social structure," *Valóság* (February 1985). Huszár, who now is head of the HSWP/CC Institute of Party History, has been replaced by György Aczél.

5. See Tamás Kolosi, "A strukturális viszonyok korvonalai" [Outlines of structural conditions] *Valóság* 11 (1982): 1–17.

6 See *Magyar Hírlap* (February 21, 1985).

7. Miklós Hernádi, *Olyan, Amilyen?* [Should We Accept It As It Is?] (Budapest: Kozmosz, 1984).

8. Ibid., 76–86.

9. For further details on financial allowance, extra time off and other benefits to working mothers giving birth to children, see András Klinger, "Population policy in Hungary: Scope and limits," *New Hungarian Quarterly,* 23 (Summer 1982): 115–25. See also Chapter 5, under "Problems with the Socialist Egalitarian Model."

10. For a lively but thorough discussion of one Hungarian's personal account about the trials and tribulations of coping with bureaucratic red tape, corruption, and "wheeling-dealing" when building your own dwelling, see Janós Kenedi, *Do It Yourself: Hungary's Hidden Economy* (London: Pluto Press, 1981).

11. See Zsuzsanna Székely, "Building a house" in Gusztáv Hegyesi, ed., *Író Szemmel* [With the Eyes of the Writer] (Budapest: Kossuth Kiadó, 1982), 30–42.

12. See Kálmán Kulcsár, "Trends of development in the socialist way of life," *The New Hungarian Quarterly,* 22 (Winter 1982): 132.

13. See Gerald Mars, *Cheats At Work* (London: George Allen and Unwin, 1982), 10–16.

14. See Elemér Hankiss, "Variations on corruption—One of the most dangerous forms of enviromental pollution," *Valóság* (June 1983): 56.

15. See Mária Petschnig, "On medical gratitudes—Not on an ethical basis," *Váloság* (November 1983): 47–55.

16. See *Népszava* (December 10, 1983).

17. See Jenö Szántó, "Something must be done," *Népszabadság* (September 14, 1983).

4
It's Who You Know, Not What You Know

There is an ongoing debate in Hungary about the growing differentiation of incomes and the accumulation of wealth in certain segments of society. There seems to be two main reasons for this concern in Hungary's "socialist" society. One is that with the stagnation and decline of living standards for the majority of the people, public resentment toward the conspicuously rich has become more common. The other reason is that the "new phenomenon" of isolated wealth needs some explanation, since it is not compatible with the slogans of equality the Hungarians became accustomed to hearing from their ruling elite for the past 40 years.

According to a public opinion survey conducted in 1982, the great majority of the Hungarian public (95 percent) believed that there were wealthy people in Hungary and 84 percent acknowledged the existence of the poor.[1] Compared with figures in 1973, when 20 percent of the public claimed that there were no poor or rich segments, this indicates a greater recognition of financial inequality.

The change in people's perceptions was also clear in an article in the party daily, *Népszabadság*.[2] Referring to various sociological surveys, the articles pointed out that there had been an increase in the disparities in the living standards of people who had started with similar qualifications and had achieved the same financial status several years ago. According to the article, social differences existed within the traditional segments of society but could not be described by the conventional tools of class analysis. Most inequalities were not inherited but were "the results of today's social processes and of individual and family efforts." People who acquired their wealth illegally "through superficial work, cunning, and even through corruption" were singled out as responsible for the "dis-locations of our [Hungarian] value system."

In an interview with a provincial daily, County Assistant State Pros-ecutor Dr. Irme M. Tóth found that "an unjustifiably strong desire for wealth has emerged in the last couple of years."[3] He pointed out that although materialism was contrary to socialist values, more and more people resort to circumventing the law to augment their income by taking on private work. Tóth, however, failed to mention the most important reason for the emergence of private work. Most families work in the second economy (i.e., take on a private, second job) not to accumulate wealth, but more importantly to complement their low incomes. On the one hand, the state guarantees employment, but it cannot guarantee wages sufficient to satisfy many human needs. This is why employed people work as much as they are paid for—sometimes more, sometimes less—which continually creates labor force shortages, and, at the same time, makes it possible for people to find additional well paid jobs. They do this in a quiet and assured way, because no one is dismissed so long as everything is politically correct. In Hungary, "private work" in state enterprises has been legalized, thus enabling people to use enterprise machines and, by producing additional products, to make twice as much money as during their normal work.[4]

Who are the very rich Hungarians? In 1984, the literary and political weekly *Élet es Iradalom*[5] dealt with the rich in Hungary in several articles. An article by György Andai described 13 people who belonged to the very rich, "having 5 or 6, even 10 to 12 times the average monthly income." Most people Andai reported about worked; some owed their wealth to their inventiveness and resourcefulness, others to family wealth. They came from a variety of professions (doctors, artisans, law-yers, economists, and roofers, for example) and had a standard of living far above average. Andai, like Tóth, put most of the blame on people who acquired their wealth illegally through corruption and speculation induced by the prevailing liberal economic atmosphere in the country.

In reaction to Andai's article Katalin Mogyoró, who conducted a so-ciological survey about the rich in Budapest, remarked that Andai had given the false impression that "the more liberal economic atmosphere of the past decade has produced a group of parasites [the rich] who threaten socialism."[6] Referring to her sociological survey, she pointed out that the rich in Hungary belonged to the so-called "poor-rich" in comparison with wealthy people in the West.[7] The wealthy she inter-viewed "would not even be considered upper-middle-class in capitalist countries." While a family in Hungary who owned a five- or six-room house was considered wealthy, in Austria or even in the socialist GDR this corresponded to the needs of an average family. In capitalist coun-tries even skilled workers were able to buy the most fashionable cars.

The highest incomes in Hungary could not compare with those in the West, since graduated taxation did not allow a monthly income to reach more than 30–40 thousand forints. Mogyoró concluded that it was "not a good approach to fight against the wealthy as a group just to uncover the criminals and tax evaders among them."[8] Based on past experience the decrease in the gap between the highest and lowest earnings was a double-edged sword. On the one hand the equalization of incomes had been praised as "socialist achievement"; on the other hand, the leveling of income proved to be an ineffective incentive to improve working performance because it undermined worker morale. As pointed out in Chapter 1, the Hungarian ideologues thus came to the conclusion that payment according to the amount of work accomplished should be the sole consideration if the goal is to create incentives for better and more efficient work. Of course, such suggestions raise suspicions that the "socialist" principle of equality is being reinterpreted or even replaced with new concepts that can be adjusted to the new realities.

DOES IT PAY TO WORK?

In accordance with the principles of Marxism-Leninism, the Constitution guarantees every citizen the right to work (employment). This means that whatever the cost, the government will assure full employment. This guarantee of job security by the state has been seriously questioned by responsible members of the present ruling elite. Some of them are convinced that such a guarantee is inconsistent with Marx's teaching of labor value and the expectations of socialist democracy.[9]

The employee is not afraid of losing his job; whatever he does he can't be fired, not even if he is not needed. In other words, he must be employed, even if he is useless. And as long as he is employed, he must be given work, even if it is make-work. Of course, seeing this, the other employees ask themselves, "Why should I work hard?" Thus, work ethic and morale suffer. In a nutshell, this is the crux of state employment.

In addition to state jobs, there are also independent and semi-independent employees who build their own socialism. Let's look at this first from the side of the employee. For any young person—16 years of age or older—there are only two options open: to go to work or to continue in school. It is compulsory for every child to attend eight grades of elementary school. After that, one is either employed as an unskilled worker, or continues studying in the trade schools or high schools. After two years of trade school one is employed in one's chosen trade. After one completes 4 years of technical high school or "gymnasium" (humanities high school), one either goes to work or continues studying. One can become a technician, or one can apply to a university for admission. Whatever one studies, however long, eventually he will have to take a job.

It is said that when one is young, one is enthusiastic, one wants to save the world. Entering the workplace with such grandiose plans, one's enthusiasm lasts until one receives the first few slaps. In every workplace there is a clique of "know-nothings" endowed with authority and maintaining a defensive alliance with each other; their work motto is, "Everything is OK as is." They view anyone who wants to change things as the enemy. When such a person is "tagged," the clique will begin to harrass him. As the saying goes, "the horse that pulls the hardest will be loaded down the most." The youngster will be loaded down, and not always with meaningful work. He will be asked to administer and account for a number of tasks. He will be asked to take on extra work, participate in political activities, and by the time he notices it, he will realize that he does not have enough time and energy to do his assigned job, while the number of loafers whose work he is doing is steadily growing. At this juncture, the gung-ho worker usually does one of two things: He either continues working hard, often crippling himself—the growing number of heart complaints and attacks attests to this—or else he joins the ranks of the loafers. At times, the clique of loafers becomes an organized association, with parties taking place during working hours. One of the subjects interviewed, a university instructor, went through such a process. Not only did he teach more, he also performed many research and administrative tasks for the others who performed various party functions, thus earning extra income for them. This is how it worked. The functionaries of the party, KISz, and the union took on fewer or no hours of classroom instruction, claiming that they were performing "societal work." Of course, in return for this "societal work"—which is supposedly voluntary and free—they always received various remunerations (bonuses, awards, extra vacations) whereas those who performed less public jobs did not receive any. Most of "societal work" and the many meetings that go with it take place during working hours; it is easier to talk away the hours during party meetings than to perform concrete work. These "societal work" colleagues were always so involved that the young instructor not only had to substitute for them in their classrooms, but often in their office and consultation hours as well. At the universities, extra income is earned by performing so-called "extra research" work, which is managed in the following manner. An institution or enterprise enters into a contractual agreement with a university department, with the purpose of completing research on a specified topic, for a specified amount of money. Upon submission of the final report, the contractee pays the predetermined amount, of which 70 percent goes to the Ministry and the bureaucracy of the university, and the rest may be distributed among those who performed the work. In reality, about half of this amount goes to the functionaries of the department, and the rest to those who did the actual work.

Some cases are even more outrageous. Another ambitious young university instructor, Pali, was introduced to a relatively well-to-do firm, in order to agree on a research project. The project was unusual, and its success was less than certain, so they agreed to begin the work without contract and to formalize the affair when success was more certain. This way, Pali spent one or two days weekly working on the project, without any remuneration. There was progress made, and they worked out a new method. It was time to sign a formal contract. Pali reported his results to the department, enumerating the achievements and describing the new methods. For several weeks, he did not hear anything further, nor did the department chairman provide him with any information. Finally, Pali looked up the man he had originally had contact with, who told him that the enterprise had signed a contract with his department. When Pali returned to the department, he was shocked to learn that his name was not on the contract; the contract money had already been picked up and distributed among the other department members. In other words, he had been tricked. What can one do in a case like that? Nothing. Everyone is completely at the mercy of the department chairman. He is also a dean of the school, and the most powerful man around; he frequently drinks with the union steward; thus, they are good friends. Pali could not turn to the party, either, because for years they had been trying to recruit him, and for years he had been evading them. He could not even complain about the matter to his colleagues, because everything depended upon the goodwill of the department chairman (pay increases, extra work, travel, etc.). A few tens of thousands forints were not worth cutting one's chances forever. So Pali remained silent, fuming to himself. Later he tried to become one of the "select ones." He did some favors for one of them, and as a result, he was invited to one of the evening "discussions," which was also connected to a birthday celebration. Everyone arrived bringing a bottle of brandy, so Pali knew there was going to be some serious drinking. One of the computer operator "girls," dressed rather skimpily, jumped up on the table, whereupon everyone started grabbing her. There was more continued drinking. Pali could not drink on account of his gallbladder problem; he tried to nurse one glass throughout the night. The department chairman discovered this and yelled at him, saying he always knew Pali was a coward, but did not think that he was even afraid to drink. After this, of course, Pali's career in that department was in doubt. Two years later, he left the university, hoping to join a smaller agricultural university. The prestige was lower than at the other university, but the pay was higher and there seemed to be less harrassment.

The change of workplace took the following course. The opening position, with promise of advancement, was advertised in the appropriate trade journal; Pali submitted his application, which was acted upon favorably, and therefore the potential new employer requested Pali's release from his old employer. At this juncture, however, complications arose. There was a man working in the department where Pali applied who also happened to be the executive secretary of the university (serving the Rector)—on a half-time basis. At the same time there was a "comrade" at the Ministry of whom everyone was tired; thus they got rid of him by making him the executive secretary of the university—full-time. The previous part-time secretary had to be compensated for the loss of his status, so they made him the chairman of the department. Now Pali faced a difficult choice: should he, as an internationally recognized expert in his field, become a faculty member under the chairmanship of an ignoramus, or should he reconsider his application and remain in his old post? Since everyone at his old place already knew that he was leaving, the latter solution would have meant problems. So he decided to take the new position. And that is when the problems really started.

The chairman, being a former Ministry bureaucrat and entirely ignorant of the department's subject matter, was unable to manage the department members and accomplish any work. Thus Pali was named to be his assistant chairman. This was a most thankless job, because if things went well, then it was to the merit of the chairman; if not, then the assistant was not doing his work well. The mistakes of many years had to be corrected quickly. The assistant chairman—who did not have any real power—distributed the work projects and talked them over with colleagues, but the actual chairman vetoed these decisions without talking them over with the assistant, and even declared that the assistant was only performing his own work and that the distributed tasks lacked professional validity. After many years, this resulted in Pali becoming an introvert; now he always works by himself, he never includes any of his colleagues in any of his contracts. The chairman could not interfere in matters of professional work, because he had no expertise. Instead, he came up with various regulations of his own. Everyone had to be in the department between 8:00 and 4:30; the department's phone line could not be used, and incoming calls on the line were forbidden. Since he could not offer instruction in the subject matter of the department, he taught courses in specifically concocted, useless subjects. For years the students protested against the mindless classwork they had to endure, to no avail. Pali, seeing that he could not count on any professional aid or even understanding within the department, decided to work just hard enough to maintain the minimum level required and to keep his real scientific activities separate from the department. In fact, Pali developed a double identity: one was connected with his always-defensive bureaucratic life at the university, and the other with his successes at home and abroad. Pali came to hate his place of work more and more. His co-workers at the university became very jealous of him, and as a result they tried to do anything in their power to make his life unpleasant. On one point they succeeded. Since his university was called "agrarian," they were able to claim that his work was not relevant to the work of the school. He was not recognized and it was forbidden to cite from his writings in the publications of the university. As is the case for any professional in Hungary, they prepared a qualification report on him, too. In this, there were excerpts that bordered on slander: "He likes to use colleagues for private purposes"; "his relationship with superiors is bad"; "there are objections to his work methods"; and "his work is not within the profile of the university." Some of these statements had some truth in them, but the report was silent on the process behind the facts, which made an idealistic man turn away from his professional place of employment. Then one day Pali was surprised to learn that the chairman would be transferred to another department and that he would be appointed as the new chairman—for the usual one-year trial period. His assistant, however, was picked from another department. (She was, however, the wife of a party functionary, thus a reliable, stable person.) Before the change took place, the former chairman talked to every member of the department, warning them that the change could present a danger to them because the new chairman was going to come up with unrealistic demands. (He meant that under the new chairman scientific activities would take priority.) Everyone panicked, and they started to take precautions, not professional ones, but political ones. Everyone immediately took on various assignments, becoming KISz secretaries, vacation stewards for the union, members of the women's committee, and similar political positions. By the time Pali took over as chairman, nearly every member of the department had become "untouchable." Not only could he not fire them, but also if work was not getting done, he could not blame them for it. For example, an exam had to be prepared on short notice and of course it was not ready in time. When Pali raised the issue to those responsible, the answer was that they had an important party mission to accomplish and had no time for the exam. Pali emphasized the priority of professional responsibility, for which he was denounced by the school's party secretary because he did not appreciate the importance of political work.

Another example: The researchers of the department are worse off than the instructors because they have to be at work all day (7:45 to 4:45), and only have one month vacation instead of the usual two. There was an "untouchable" person in the department employed as a researcher. The poor soul was half blind, he could barely see the blackboard—so he was completely unsuitable for teaching. His father, however, was the chief of the control department in the Ministry, which was a powerful position. During the yearly inspection of the books, Pali was told by the dean of the school to reclassify the person in question as an instructor. Pali expressed his reluctance, at which he was told that certain "social organizations" originated the request. He went back to the department and called together the so-called "Big Four," consisting of the secretaries of the party cell, the KISz organization, and the union, and himself. Pali outlined the situation and the instructions he received. Since the representatives of every "social organization" were present, and they knew nothing of the whole affair, Pali was mystified. Then he asked the researcher in question "whose idea the transfer was." It turned out that in the course of the inspection, the Ministry had found some discrepancy, and the researcher's promotion was the price for keeping the matter quiet. The man's father and the university comptroller had already made the deal; the chairman merely had to initiate the action. After this, Pali went to the president of the university. This meeting took only one minute. Pali was given an order to implement the reclassification at once. Demoralized, Pali returned to the department and told the entire story to the "Big Four." A week later he was summoned to the office of the school's party secretary, who told him that it was a tactical mistake to execute the promotion with the knowledge of the public. For them, it would have been preferable if Pali quietly went along with the instructions. Not only would they have achieved the promotion of an insider, but they would have lowered Pali's prestige. Every member of the department would have thought Pali was a tyrant who acted without asking anyone's opinion. One way or the other, Pali would have been the loser. Meanwhile, Pali began working on a dissertation toward the highest scientific degree in Hungary (Doctor of Sciences, or *Tudományok doktora*). His topic was approved by the Academy. At that time, Pali's appointment as chairman was to be made permanent. The dean talked with Pali and after going into great detail in connection with the previously mentioned cases, the dean told Pali that the leadership was not sure that Pali would make a good leader, so they decided to give Pali another year of trial assignment, after which his appointment would be considered again.

In the entire history of Hungarian universities, there has not been a similar case yet. This uniquely negative step shook Pali's position, not only at the university, but in his public and professional life as well. Pali's staff saw that he had become timid, regardless of the merit of his judgments. A chain reaction started: more and more of his department members used political excuses to avoid work. This proved harmful not only to Pali, but also to the university. But in truth, who really cared about that? The shared goal of those above and those below was simply to get out of as much work as possible. In order for them to become successful, they first had to break-in the chairman, so that he would not make a fuss. They succeeded fully. During the additional year of probation, Pali had a limited course of action. He became very quiet; he did not care about the interests of the university, he behaved like one of the boys, and he tried to realize himself through extracurricular channels. As an alternative, Pali could have refused to accept the chairmanship, in which case he would likely find another ignoramus as his boss and the entire torture would start all over again. He could always transfer to another university, but that would simply mean "jumping from the frying pan into the fire." The circumstances would not change greatly. Pali chose the first alternative. Since that time he has had no problem around the university. Pali's former department chairman continually tries to make trouble for him, but since he is cautious, these attempts fail. Thus, on the surface, everything is fine around the university, but Pali became a bitter man. Of late he even has heart complaints. It appears that in Hungary one cannot even go mad without penalty! Pali looks for success on two fronts: professional and financial. Let's start with the first one.

In cooperation with other serious-minded colleagues in Hungary and abroad, Pali continues his professional "hobby." The number of his scientific books and articles is growing by leaps and bounds—and gaining international recognition. It appears that in the near future Pali will be awarded the highest professional degree in Hungary. He regularly gives lectures at home, and is often invited to participate in conferences. Pali is one of the consultants to an international project, and in this capacity he travels abroad frequently. Because of his scholarly achievements, it is almost certain that Pali will be made permanent chairman soon.

Financially, Pali is also well off. He takes on fewer "extra research" assignments at the university because the 30 percent Pali would receive is not much. Other projects pay better. For example, an agricultural coop wanted to set up a complete computer system. Pali, whose expertise is actually physics, but who is equally at home with cybernetics, and the leadership of the coop made a deal for 800,000 forints (about U.S.$16,000). The deal still did not materialize, because a private firm undercut the price by half; in their case, the overhead is only 10 percent instead of 70 percent as charged by the university. This is the price one must pay for bureaucratic red tape. Even though they have better experts, Pali and his department cannot compete with private firms; they are crippled by regulations. Since he cannot count on receiving many extra research assignments, Pali joins a semi-private collective. He knows many people, and this way he can obtain many assignments for this group. If he does not do any work on the project, he receives 10 percent of the profits. In this capacity he earns about twice as much as his yearly salary at the university. Also, there is no jealousy involved in this work. Neither the chairman nor the members of the department know that Pali is doing this, because this type of work does not require prior agreement by the authorities—as long as he can do his job at his primary post. Pali also prepares software programs and sells them. Nowadays anyone in state employment—if he can—considers his daytime job secondary and does the absolute minimum required of him. Emphasis is placed on work performed for the so-called enterprise work associations (*gazdasági' munkaközösség*, or GMK), the civil legal associations (*polgári jogi társaság*, or PJT), the various cooperatives (*szövetkezetek*), and so forth. Naturally one could take full-time employment with these, just as one could open a private store. However most people are wary of this, because they are afraid that at some undefined future occasion this could be considered as turning one's back on the public sector. The most certain course, therefore, is to take a public job where one does not have to work very hard and to make the real money on the side, after regular working hours.

Many Hungarians believe that the solution is to take a job abroad. There is an old saying: "If you are looking for a way out of your financial problems, head for Hegyeshalom [the crossing point between Hungary and Austria]." Twenty percent of whatever one earns abroad must be exchanged for forints, and one has to pay retirement contributions in hard currency. These are the only two reservations—the rest of the money is free; as a matter of fact, one can keep 40 percent of it in hard currency. Pali also used this opportunity several times. For years he worked with two colleagues, one of whom lived in Budapest and the other in the United States. Pali was more successful than the other Hungarian. He was well-liked for his organization and scholarly performance. The other Hungarian (Pali's friend) was less successful; he used the results of joint research as his own, and committed similar blunders. This, however, did not bother Pali, because he considered the entire matter primarily as a money-making scheme—his professional interests focused on other activities.

Problems developed later when the other Hungarian, Bela, got into trouble in Hungary. He was caught several times mishandling his company's funds. When he was forced to look for a new job (which he easily found), Bela started blaming Pali for his misfortunes. News of this reached the United States, too, and the result was that Pali was hindered in his further visits to a particular U.S. university where Bela had friends. Pali no doubt will find other opportunities, but this is an interesting and typical case in which Hungarian methods were used to harm a Hungarian competitor abroad. By the way, soon afterward the same U.S. university invited one of Bela's close friends to be a visiting professor.

Pali's work ethic and struggle for survival in the academic life is typical rather than an exception; the same kind of struggle goes on every day, everywhere else in Hungary. The situation is not likely to change as long as enthusiasm and devotion are less valued than opportunism. Sooner or later, most Hungarian experts will seek work at some research institute located somewhere abroad. During the process of competition for good jobs abroad, however, many people are being thrown to the wolves; those who survive soon come to recognize where the new opportunities lie. After all, they are products of a system where "fair play" has an entirely different meaning than the one used in the West. This point can be further illustrated by a closer scrutiny of academic life in Hungary.

DOES IT PAY TO STUDY?

To get into a university, everyone must take oral and written entrance examinations. Admission is dependent on the points earned during those exams, combined with the points brought from high school. It is possible to increase one's chances of being admitted by raising one's test scores or by earning favorable treatment at the final interview.

An applicant's original score is based on the grade average at his high school; in other words, the same achievement will earn better grades at a weaker school. Thus the solution is to enroll your child in a mediocre high school and hire a private tutor. This way, the child will learn what he has to and his grades will look good, too. The private tutor should be carefully chosen. It is not advisable to hire the child's own teacher; this could result in scandal. The teacher could recommend a friend of his, and this is ideal. ("I teach your stupid pupil, and you teach my idiot; we'll both make money.") At the high school level, the going rate for tutors is 150 forints per hour. This means that by teaching one hour per day, one can earn the equivalent of the average Hungarian salary.

The score on the written exam can be "improved" in two ways: one way is by guile during the exam, the other way is after the exam. For example, a young instructor, Rudi, proctored during the entrance exam. One of the girls became ill, and she was brought a glass of water from the neighboring dean's office. The water came on a tray, accompanied by a paper napkin that contained the solution to three of the most difficult problems on the test. Subsequently it came to light that the young lady was the niece of the staff member who brought the water, and that one of his colleagues also participated in the action; he "decorated" the napkin. Since everyone's identification card is checked at an exam, it is dangerous to try to have someone substitute. False identification and falsification of exams can be punished by a prison term; therefore it is doubtful that anyone would make such attempts. Another example involved a boy with a huge bandage around his face—the pretense was that he had a bad toothache or the like. It turned out that he had a walkie-talkie hidden in the bandage and communicated the problems and solutions through it. The windows were open, there was enough noise so that his discreet voice could not be heard. Students can also cooperate. For example, they may ask to go to the bathroom, where solutions can be hidden in various places and thus passed on.

Scores can subsequently be improved either at the grading, or during the oral exam. Since the exam papers are marked by code names, they must be identifiable by the "friendly grader." This can be prearranged; certain marks may be used, or a certain answer can be started with a certain phrase, and so on. In this case the grader "improves" the exam, adding enough to make it look good or simply grading leniently. Prior to the oral exam, the committee members are required to review the written exam. At this time, a friendly remark can make the difference.

The best opportunity for "arrangements" is the oral examination. It may be sufficient to know one member of the committee; he can help by asking the appropriate questions, or by making small helpful remarks. It has also occurred that the student "accidentally" wound up before the teacher who had been his private tutor for years. The teacher in this instance actually mentioned in the dean's office that he would like to see Mr. X. in his exam.

Based on the scores, a so-called "summit committee" makes the final decision. The process is on two levels. First, the Ministry of Education designates a certain score, below which everyone must be rejected. Consequently, the offsprings of "decorated" persons, who have performed special service for the country, are admitted before anyone else. If one has a friend on this committee, he can recommend admission on the basis of one with "special talent" (who only failed the exam because of nervousness), or "special need" (aged parents). Some suitable excuse can be found for nearly everyone. A recommendation like this will receive immediate support. After all, next year someone else may have a protégé, and then he would need the support.

Well-connected teachers employ a combination of the above methods. For example, they do not ask exorbitant prices for private tutoring, but make an agreement that after successful admission exams, they will receive a larger sum. Since the teacher is often a faculty member at the university where the new student will attend, it is advisable to add a little bonus to this amount; after all, there will be exams and term papers during the coming years, and help is always welcome.

And help is forthcoming, too. According to Rudi, one out of every three or four students has someone who "speaks up for them." In common practice, it is not practical to fail the favored students of a colleague. When it comes time to take the make-up exams, he will have another professor, anyway, and he will probably pass him.

There are many ways of finding a patron; some of the most popular ones are the following. In the case of a pretty young lady, everyone thinks of the same thing: "She will occasionally be 'nice' to one of the faculty members, and she will get her diploma." Or one can hire a private teacher and pay him. Or one can promise other advantages. This is usually prevalent in the evening (continuing education) courses where the students are often successful men in good positions. Their goodwill may come in handy sometime in the future. Rudi's senior colleague, for example, maintains contact with some of his former pupils; among them are managers of department stores, hotel managers, or high-ranking bureaucrats. They can be helpful. Thus, many faculty members soon acquire a number of acquaintances in high places.

While help can be extended during exams, several teachers prefer to write diploma-theses for students as a way of earning extra money. The going rate is 15,000 forints, and in the case of Ph.D. dissertations it is 20–50 thousand forints. Of course the student must memorize the entire text because on the final examination they could pose questions on any portions thereof. This method is especially widespread on the doctoral level, since in these instances one does not have to attend classes, only turn in a dissertation and undergo a comprehensive examination. One can find a friend among the members of the examining committee, and some of the details can be discussed with him. During the building of the house described elsewhere, Rudi's friend wrote a chapter of specialized text for someone; in payment for this, he received the use of the person's weekend house by Lake Balaton for a week, and 80 square meters of parquet flooring for the home he was building at a 75 percent discount. This amounted to a saving of some 30,000 forints, and he spent no more than one afternoon on the writing of the chapter—a fantastic hourly wage! This was a neat business; it did not cost the other person anything either. He simply purchased the parquet in his own name at a wholesale price. The only loser was the state, but this is not something to take into consideration. (As the slogan has been modified: "The country is mine, I will take my share of it now!")

In Hungary, one usually attends university for five years; after that the student receives a diploma that is roughly equivalent to the American Master's degree. The doctoral dissertation is simply handed in, without any prerequisites of class attendance. In addition to the Ph.D. granted by the universities, the Hungarian Academy of Sciences also grants two academic ranks: that of "candidate" and that of "Doctor of Sciences."

A candidatorial dissertation may also be presented without any class attendance, but this method is risky because in this instance no one will be interested in granting the individual the passing judgment. After the completion of the dissertation and the passing of several tests, the defense of such a dissertation is public. Another method is to take on a three-year process of postgraduate state scholarship or candidacy (aspirantura). During this period, the aspirant receives the equivalent of his previous salary while working under the supervision of one of the powers-that-be. Distinguished scholars take on the supervision of an aspirant in the hope of remuneration; after passing all exams, they usually receive 10,000 forints, and after the granting of the degree, another 10,000 forints. Since they are interested in having their protégé's degree granted, there is a joke about it:

The rabbit is defending his dissertation about the skinning of animals. The fox stands up and criticizes the rabbit's method, claiming that his own skin could not be removed that way. The rabbit calls the fox out into the corridor, and reappears within 5 minutes, dragging the fox's pelt. Now the wolf rises and sharply criticizes the rabbit's dissertation. He is also invited to go outside; after 10 minutes, the rabbit brings in the wolf's skin. At the same time a lion sticks his head in the door and asks, "Anyone else would like to question my student's method?"

One can obtain a candidate degree abroad as well, if one finds a scholar abroad who is willing to serve as his supervisor. Since nearly everyone likes to visit Hungary, people gladly take on the supervision of a Hungarian aspirant, in the hope that later they will be invited to Hungary. Of course, this is equally true in the case of domestic *aspirantura* as well. The first step toward obtaining the degree of Doctor of Sciences is the submission of an autobiography, a list of publications, and "proof of being cited" (*idézettségi lista*). After this, the Academy decides whether the person is in principle worthy of the degree or not. If one is rejected at this stage, he has lost for good. If he is favorably judged, then he can turn in practically anything; his degree is essentially guaranteed.

At universities, these degrees are important, because one's position is closely tied to them. The lowest rank is the *gyakornok* (lecturer), which is held for one or two years after the completion of classwork. After this period, one can become a *tanársegéd* (instructor). Next, after obtaining one's doctorate (U.S. equivalent of a masters plus an extra dissertation), one becomes an *adjunktus* (assistant professor). Each stage is defined by contracts, usually made for 3–5 years, after which one may, in principle, be dismissed. In practice, however, this is rare, because in 3–5 years one surrounds himself by "protectors," or takes on a number of political/ social functions. The candidate degree is required in order to become a *docens* (instructor), and in order to become an *egyetemi tanár* (university professor) one usually has to be a Doctor of Sciences. These positions are usually for life; one can hold them essentially forever.

Higher ranks or scientific qualifications command more money, but they also ensure more power. A department chairman is at least a *docens,* and higher qualifications will ensure that one becomes a member of scientific or academic committees. These are riven by in-fighting: various communities of interest fight against each other. Every clique wants to glorify its own protégés, since their appointment to some committee strengthens the entire group's influence. Consequently, the same cliques usually try to cut each others' throats. For example, the candidacy dissertation of a certain interviewee was "tabled" for an entire year. Their method was simple: they sent the dissertation to each one of their members. Each of them sat on it for two months, before announcing that they were not interested in serving on the evaluation committee. After every member had his turn, the dissertation had to be turned over to another committee, which caused a delay of another two months before the defense was successful. Since that time the candidate became a department chairman, and his dissertation for Doctor of Sciences is now under evaluation. Nowadays, however, he works closely together with a member of the Hungarian Cabinet, a person who is too high in the ranks of authority to have "his rabbit" harmed. There is an old saying in Budapest: "Everyone's worth is equal to the sum of his friends' worth!"

THE PROTECTORS OF WORK ETHIC

Survival and success of any employee in Hungary depends not so much on the person's skill and professional performance, but his connections. As we have noticed from the above examples, everyone in Hungary needs protection. One can even generalize that the weaker or more ambitious a person is, the greater the need for protection. Thus, an opportunist will always seek the most effective protection. The source of such protection can be found in three organizations: the party, the Communist Youth League, and the trade unions.

The trade unions are present at every workplace. The committee of the local union is involved in every aspect of the workplace. In every smaller unit (shop, university department, bureaucratic section, etc.), there is a union steward (*bizalmi*). The stewards have quite a bit of power, but more on this later. The average union member seldom hears of his union. Every payday his membership dues are deducted from his salary (this amounts to anywhere from 30 to 200 forints per month). The union also distributes the annual allocations to the factory/institute vacation place. This is how it works. The possibilities are listed and posted; every member signs up, indicating his preferences, and then the whole thing is turned over to a central bureaucracy. The allocations are made on the basis of the material wealth, social conditions, and previous record of the individuals. There are few opportunities and many applicants. Aladár, for example, has been working for *20 years* and during this time he was provided a free vacation at his workplace's resort *twice*. He works at a research institute that has 500 employees; every year, some 25–30 of them are eligible to vacation at the institute's resort. Simple statistics tell us that this means one vacation per person every 20 years. Needless to say, the average union member at most workplaces hears nothing more of his union.

The steward is "democratically" elected at regular intervals. This is the way this works. At a meeting, the union leaders state their opinion concerning who should be nominated. The potential nominees are praised to heaven, and afterward, the members present are asked to make nominations from the floor. Generally there are no such nominations, for a simple reason. Let us put ourselves in the position of the average worker. In the opinion of the head "honcho," so-and-so is the best man for the job of steward. In this situation, it would be controversial to stand up and propose someone else's name instead. The leaders will not be happy to see someone disagreeing with them, and, if their nominee wins, the new steward will remember those who tried to oppose his election. This, of course, could have a number of negative consequences, because the steward has considerable influence. To be sure, he is usually quite tame in his relationship with the leaders (he wants to be renominated), but his opinion is asked on a number of matters. These include, among others: pay raises, bonuses, promotions, extra vacations, trips abroad, and so on. If written permissions are required, his signature must appear next to that of the person's direct supervisor. When it comes to vacation allocations, for example, the steward's opinion is decisive. What this means also is that every steward faces a dilemma. If he consistently behaves as the "bosses' man," his co-workers may turn on him and make his life miserable. On the other hand, if he opposes the leaders every time his conscience dictates, his career may be ruined by the leaders. So the best course for him to follow is one of moderation: give everyone a little bit.

The union local's committee not only deals with some of the touchy local questions, but also becomes involved in all other problems of the enterprise: wages, working conditions, social circumstances, and so forth. In approaching these problems, the committee works in close cooperation with the enterprise's party committee. It should be pointed out, however, that on major issues the decisions are made by the so-called "Big Four," consisting of the enterprise's leader, the party secretary, the head union steward, and the representative of KISz (*Kommunista Ifjúság Szövetsége*, or Communist Youth League). The latter is actually a branch of the party dealing with youth. Unlike the HSWP, the KISz is a mass organization; nearly every young person belongs to it. They generally join during their first year after finishing the eighth grade. In high schools, for example, each class forms a basic unit of the KISz; the members of the class elect their own leaders, who are responsible for directing all "KISz-work." This consists of academic competitions, political, trade, and cultural lectures, and debates. They also organize trips to theaters and movies, while the sport commissar encourages athletic competition. For example, each class may have its own soccer team, and the school will have its own also. Since there are no other organizations to which the young can belong, the KISz is expected to protect the interests of youth in every field. In most schools, one notices an interesting contradiction: the best students tend to be "passive," while the enthusiastic organizers in KISz have weak, if not disastrous, academic records. Thus, in a number of KISz organizations a conflict develops between the outstanding students and the organization's leaders. For example, when Mr. Kovács' son, Peter, attended the university, his "People's Republic" scholarship grant was vetoed by the KISz. The leaders of the KISz admitted that Peter was a good student, but since he never participated in their activities, he was considered unfit for the honor. Of course, the most active KISz members could not get the scholarship either, because their achievements were poor.

When the news of the recent events in Poland reached Hungary, there were some young people who tried to form a politics-free youth organization, on the model of the Polish Solidarity. They called this budding organization the FISz (*Független Ifjúság Szövetsége,* or Independent Youth League), but it never gained wide support, because it never produced a program that made sense. Every proposal they came up with already appeared among the aims and goals of the KISz. Thus they found it impossible to attract crowds. Moreover, they would have never been granted permission by the authorities to operate as a legitimate mass organization. One of the major tasks of the KISz is to recruit suitable members for the party and thus to make it look "younger." After some deliberations, the leaders of the local KISz unit determine which of their members would be suitable for party membership. The next step involves consultations with one of the older party members. After this the list of new candidates is finalized, and the party bureaucracy takes over.

At this juncture it might be appropriate to ask, what are the reasons a Hungarian citizen may have for joining the Hungarian Socialist Worker's Party (HSWP)? Let us consider some concrete examples. A good friend of Mr. Kovács, Jóska Kiss, is a member of the party leadership at one of the universities, and he is also responsible for the recruitment of new members. To begin his work, he must find out who the potential candidates are. Since he does not know everyone at the university, he must talk to the several other functionaries attached to the various departments. After they give him tips, he makes up a list and talks with each of the candidates. In most cases, this is merely an informal talk, wherein he describes to them the conditions and process of admittance. In other cases, his persuasion is called upon, in that he should try to influence the potential candidates to take an active interest in membership. Some of the reasons he may cite are:

- If the potential candidate is a student, it may be pointed out that in order to be considered for membership he must prove himself. During the university years, the student has already exhibited the proper traits through his KISz work. If he does not join the party before he leaves the university, he has to start with a blank record at his place of work. In such cases, it may take several years before he can even be considered for membership. While he is still at the university, he can join and become one of the "chosen few" without much effort.

- If the candidate is career-oriented, he can be convinced through this. He will be told that at the various party forums he can work with his supervisors hand-in-hand, as an equal partner. If he achieves a position where he is entrusted with a special party function, he can even become more powerful than his supervisors at the workplace. It might also be mentioned that in considering promotions and appointments, the opinion of the party is always asked, and in cases like that, his work within the party organization could mean a lot. Another factor is that party members can develop good personal contact with leaders.

- In the case of dissatisfied, critical persons, the task of convincing is not difficult, either. It can be pointed out that, as a nonmember, his word will count for very little, and he won't be able to bring about changes; in most cases he won't even be noticed. Criticism coming from outside the party ranks is usually dismissed as irrelevant bellyaching. Comments and criticism coming from party members, however, is taken as well-meaning, constructive criticism. If they are voiced before a party forum, the leaders must listen to it and answer. Thus any kind of problem and contradiction can be brought up within the party ranks. Certain cases can be pointed out, where the party secretary raised the issue with the leadership and the problem was immediately looked into.

- Some people join simply because they are looking for someone to share their lives. These are lonely people, whose personal lives are unsuccessful. They want to belong somewhere. In their case, the community character of the party can be stressed.

- Many people inherit their Marxist worldview from their families. They join the party out of inner compulsion and conviction. The usual procedure with these types of people is to praise them, tell them that people like them made the party as great as it is today, the vanguard of the working class, and so on.

- There are those who are looking for a sense of being protected and that is why they want to join. They seldom admit this openly, but if the tendency becomes obvious, then the tactic is to stress the strength and educational influence of the party. Candidates of this stripe must be assured that "in our ranks" (inside the party) everyone can freely express his/her opinion; no one can be harmed because he/she expressed a view with decent, honorable intentions.

After the candidate has committed himself to join, the process starts. First, the local party cell discusses his request to be admitted to the ranks. Anyone who reaches this stage usually receives total and unanimous support. Two old members must sponsor the admission request. They must have known the candidate for years, and must be willing to give a written opinion concerning him. If the candidate is a KISz member, then the local KISz organization may be one of the sponsors. If this is the case, then a special KISz meeting must be convened and the proceedings must be presented in writing.

After this, the candidate fills out the admission form, affixes his photograph to it, and receives the party's "Organizational Rules" from one of the older members, so that he can read it. The autobiographical section of the admission form must contain the statement that the candidate has read the Rules, and accepts them as binding for himself. This, in fact, is a promise to obey party discipline. In addition to several formalities, the Rules also state that a member must subject himself to the will of the majority and that after voting he will not express contrary or critical opinion, even informally. This is where the poor candidate is caught. He can express his opinion once, but if that goes against the official line, or even if it does not agree with the official line completely, it will be voted down by the machine. After that, the member must keep his mouth firmly shut.

Now the leadership of the party local will call in the candidate. This is a formality, and he will receive unanimous support. The next meeting of the local will actually accept the new member. The "apparatchik" responsible for recruitment usually announces the candidate, who then tells his life story, and the sponsors will read their sponsoring statements. A few of the colleagues will praise the candidate, and voting follows. The candidate is usually accepted without opposition. Now he is inside the "charmed circle."

The average party member usually only notices that he is a member on paydays, when they deduct his membership fee (ca. 200–400 forints) from his salary. Of course there are regular meetings, which are announced and scheduled at the start of each year. Even the themes of the meetings are pretty much fixed. Time permitting, other topics can be raised by those present. One of the important tasks of the locals is the preparation of "reports on the public mood." Every local has one member assigned to the task of preparing a monthly report. He talks with every party member as well as with some of the more prominent nonmembers and collects the problems that occupy people's attention. These could be big issues, such as the situation after Andropov's death, or smaller ones, such as the dirty plates in the factory's cafeteria. The questions are jotted down without names, so we are not talking about "spies" or informers. During the next membership meeting, the leaders of the institution/factory/whatever answer the questions that relate to conditions within their authority. If a great number of local questions arise, the theme of the meeting can even be changed. The "report on the public mood" is received by the Executive Committee of the local cell. They discuss it, and forward its most important points to the party organ of the district or the city. In turn, the latter will forward such a report higher up in the party organization until it reaches the central leadership. Thus the top party leaders are able to form a picture about the mood of the citizens. Of course, it is debatable whether such distantly-removed or strongly-revised reports reflect the real, or a spurious, state of affairs in Hungarian society. Obviously no city, district, or whatever, wishes to appear to have more "problems" than the others, because the local party leaders could be held responsible for such conditions.

The membership meetings discuss a great many things. Here, for example, is the agenda from one of the recent meetings Jóska Kiss attended:

- discussion of the work plan of the local cell;
- lecture on the state of Hungarian economy;
- the experiences of party-building;
- the progress of scientific research at the university;
- the activities of the university's armed militia unit;
- the role of the Youth Parliament within institutional democracy;
- the activities of the KISz local;
- the activities of youth in public life;
- the issues of peace struggle and international thaw.

Every topic is presented by a lecturer, announced in advance. After the 30–60 minute lecture, a question-and-answer period follows. Regardless of the topic, usually the same 8–10 people get up to talk. The important thing is not what one says, the main thing is simply to get up and speak. The chronic commentators are the butt of jokes. There is a sign-up sheet circulating during the meetings, so it is advisable to be present. The leadership of the party locals is elected for five years. The elections are similar to those for union officials. The leadership and the Executive Committee of the local cell are very important. Their opinions are sought out before any important decisions are made by the institution/factory/whatever. The party locals' opinions on issues concerning the workers' welfare are particularly important. They also approve or disapprove requests for travel abroad. Thus, in fact, everyone needs the support and sympathy of the party local. The party local is very well informed about all affairs of the institution. For example, at a typical meeting the leaders of the cell at the university might discuss the following: the receiving of the new freshman class; public works undertaken by students; responses to the tasks of the local; the social circumstances of youth; the initiation and maintenance of political education; the modernization of teaching; the status of party propaganda; the dissemination of recent decisions by the Central Committee; and academic promotions. The same leaders also often receive information not available to the average citizen. For example, they are told about problems of foreign and domestic policy; and sometimes they find out about price rises in advance. The aim in these cases is to create a well-informed group of cadres, who can influence public mood in the direction the ruling elite would prefer.

WHAT MONEY CAN BUY

In Hungary, as in other East European countries, there are relatively few supermarkets. Thus, shopping is done in several smaller specialized stores, taking a great amount of time. If we add the fact that often certain items are simply not to be found, then the shopping situation becomes even more complex. During the last two or three years the government tried to help the situation by allowing private stores to operate. This, however, complicated matters by creating new conditions that at times are in sharp contrast with the principles of Marxism-Leninism. It is not surprising, therefore, to hear the facetious remark that "everyone is building his own socialism."

Let's start with everyday shopping. If one does not reside near one of the large shopping centers (e.g., Skála, Flórian, Sugár, etc.) then shopping could turn out to be an excruciating experience. Let's consider that most of the women finish working between 4:00 and 4:30 p.m. (it is very rare for men to do grocery shopping). After that, they pick up the child(ren) at the school or at the daycare center and go shopping, often with a small child on their arms. Since everyone shops at the same time, there are crowds. Often one has to stand in line just to obtain a shopping basket or to get inside the store. In the crowded store, the people are nervous; they must watch their children too, because if they knock something off the shelves it has to be paid for. To add to the nervousness, one must stand in another line if one wants to exchange bottles or if one wants to purchase meat. These are usually not pre-packaged, but have to be individually weighed and wrapped. If the "gentle customer" wants to be (God forbid!) choosy—let's say she does not wish to purchase the fat parts of the meat—she will incur not only the wrath of the clerk, but also that of the people standing behind her in the line. Of course there is another line at the checkout counter. If the checkout clerk should shortchange the customer and she complains about this, she is again likely to be yelled at by the others. And, of course, she would have to return to the same store to face the same clerks and the same fellow-shoppers the next time.

The above only begins to depict the problems. Since fruits, vegetables, and freshly cut meat can only be purchased at specially marked stores, the above scenes may be repeated. Hungarian shoppers usually require fresh food items daily: milk, bread, and so on. Thus the "pleasures" of shopping occur daily.

For larger shopping, on weekends, for example, it is more practical to visit one of the shopping centers, where one can acquire the items more easily and in a more civilized atmosphere. Many people prefer the large market-centers (*vásárcsarnok*), where the various agricultural co-operatives have their own booths and sell fresh produce.

Hungarians can't complain about the availability of food; basically they can purchase anything. The shopper, accustomed to Western standards, can only complain about the slowness of service and the uncomfortable conditions. In the area of manufactured consumer goods, the situation is entirely different. Not only is it difficult to obtain building materials without "gratitude money" (as discussed in Chapter 3), but there are "unobtainable items" (*hiánycikkek*) in almost every area of existence. They can range from the rubber gaskets for espresso coffee brewers through clothes items to auto parts; almost anything. And this is where there is room for "private business."

In the summer of 1985, Mr. Kovács' friend, a retired mining engineer, needed a right rear fender for his "Zhiguli" car. He spent three whole days visiting almost every auto-parts store in the country, but he could not find the item. After this, he stumbled into a "private" store in Budapest, where he immediately found the fender. Of course, the price was 30 percent higher than the state store's "theoretical" price. ("Theoretical" since the item did not exist.) Several other friends of Mr. Kovács had similar experiences when they tried to find such items as Bosch spark plugs or locks for "Trabant" cars. For a long time, Mr. Kovács thought that the private stores had their own network for procurement and their own import contacts. He was very much mistaken.

In the description of building a house (in Chapter 3), we referred to one of János' partners who used his employer's machinery (very cheaply!) for private purposes. After completing the construction, he and a friend opened a private auto-parts store. Within six months, János' former partner traded his old car for a brand-new Zhiguli, completely refurnished his home, and even purchased paintings from famous artists. He gave the impression that his monthly income was equivalent to at least U.S. $1,000. When János discreetly questioned his former partner about this, for weeks he would evade the questions; but after a while he revealed something that was a complete shock to János, but nothing more than a common occurrence to János' former partner and entrepreneurs like him. The revelation to János entailed a detailed description of his former partner's personal connections with acquaintances, not actual work. What this amounts to in reality is that private stores obtain most of their merchandise from the same state-owned stores from which the average citizen would like to purchase them. In other words, as soon as a shipment of "interesting" stuff arrives in the state-owned stores, the "agents" of the private stores immediately snap it up. Ten percent of the bill is usually given to the sales clerk, so they benefit as well. After this, the citizen can look for the goods in vain; the goods have been transferred to the private stores, where they are sold for about 30 percent more. This price difference is considered "honest and respectable." Of course, the 30 percent profit can be considered fantastic in Hungarian eyes. Much of this would be taken away by the progressive taxes, but there is a way to get around this too. According to regulations, every item found in the store must be covered by a piece of paper, proving its origin, its price, and so forth. If the owner has papers covering 10 batteries, then he can only have 10 batteries in the store; but he can have God-knows-how-many elsewhere. Every morning he takes only as many items to the store as he can safely keep there. Thus, he can sell several hundred items, and still the governmental authorities would only know of a few, for tax purposes. The "auxiliary storage" can be anything: a garage, a weekend house, or a friend's home. The important thing is that the tax authorities should not find out.

Of course, there are other affairs as well that can be taken care of on a "who-knows-who" basis. As mentioned earlier, certain items cannot be found even in the private stores; and quite often these items are absolutely necessary for, let's say, someone's car. The average citizen cannot obtain these even from private stores because they are reserved for certain friends or comrades, who can do important favors in addition to paying the high prices. For example, they can make arrangements for the use of the sidewalk (as parking space or unloading zone), or they can cover up certain shortages arising from spot-checks, or they can arrange the purchase of state-owned real estate at low prices, and so on. Thus the owners of private stores are not only well-off financially, but also occupy a certain privileged position in society, based on the principle of "you scratch my back, and I scratch yours."

A valid question arises: if these phenomena are so repulsive, why are they tolerated by the majority of the population; why don't they boycott these stores? Since these practices are permitted by the state, they cannot be opposed by organized action. If someone tries to fight the practices as a lone wolf, he will simply deprive himself of certain consumer articles. Thus, because of a well-established norm, the population is at the mercy of the situation. Incidentally, the case of the auto-parts store owner is typical; similar situations prevail in the areas of both manufactured and agricultural goods.

Earlier, we referred to a private vegetable seller. Officially he can't be called a private entrepreneur, because he manages the store of an agricultural collective. Since the state stores don't always have fresh goods, and often run out of things, most people readily "make the sacrifice" and make their purchases at the private or semi-private stores. In reality, however, this willingness constitutes a limitation that for the vegetable seller represents an opportunity. Every morning, the vegetable seller and his friends make the rounds of markets and purchase fresh goods from the producers at the lower "producers" price. This is then sold together with the merchandise obtained through official channels. The considerable profit does not appear on any records, so it is tax-free. Since the vegetable seller is also part of the "protected circle," it is not likely that his earnings would be seriously investigated.

Incidentally, if the authorities should like to question the high income of the Hungarian entrepreneurs, it is conceivable that an investigation could be initiated by individuals in high positions who are unreachable by the network of mutual protection. There are, however, measures that can be taken to prevent this from happening. Private businessmen usually complain about the bad business situation and put their money into gold, collectibles, or hard currency, where it is less visible. As mentioned in Chapter 3, if they have relatives in the West, they can forward the illegally purchased hard currency to a "cousin" who can re-deposit it in the Hungarian National Bank in a so-called "BC account," in the name of the Hungarian relative. This money then can be spent on any trips abroad. The leftover amount can be re-deposited, and any newly acquired amount can be put into this account. The above mentioned vegetable seller, for example, purchased 8,000 U.S. dollars a few years ago. This is too large an amount to be placed into a BC account, so he asked his wife's younger brother living in West Germany to buy a Volkswagen Golf in exchange. Everything went well, but now they are getting a divorce. In the proceedings, the woman insists that the car is hers, because it was given to her by her brother. The husband can do nothing, no matter how furious he is, because if he revealed the existence of illegally obtained dollars, he could go to jail. The wife was similarly "smart" when it came to the jewelry and cash hidden in the apartment; they "disappeared," and the husband can't even mention them, because they were illegally obtained. Since these constitute about two-thirds of the family's wealth, the courts can only dispose of the remaining one-third. What can the unfortunate, deprived husband do? He can be furious and he can beat up the wife, but that would only jeopardize his situation.

Waiting in lines and not finding items one needs is, indeed, an excruciating experience for the average Hungarian shopper. However, queuing up for items and then discovering that overnight they increased in price by 30 percent is, to say the least, exasperating. As far as prices go, they are rising in Hungary, too. Price rises can be accomplished in two ways: one is the official, pre-announced method; the other one is the concealed, unannounced price increase. One of the largest price increases of the first type was implemented on July 23, 1978; at that time the price of everything, from food to construction materials, went up. This increase was pre-announced—not to everyone, of course, but at least to the workers who were party members. The party organized meetings at every job site with this purpose in mind. Notifying party members of price increases not only ensures that they are able to stock up before the prices go up; it also means that they can influence their social environment in a positive manner by isolating the would-be complainers. In spite of such preventive measures, however, there were plenty of complainers. For example in the district of Csepel—also known as "Red Csepel" because it has the largest concentration of industrial workers in Hungary—someone placed a slice of bread and lard (a traditional poor-man's food) in the hand of the Lenin statue, with a sign: "This is not what you promised us!" There were also talks of work slowdowns. Naturally, there was no mention of any of this on the radio or television broadcasts. Such pre-announced price increases occur about 2–3 times each year. They are announced only to party members, but their news soon spreads all over the country and people buy up everything. There is a joke addressing this issue:

Comrade Gorbachev asks Comrade Kádár, "How come the Hungarians do not seem to complain too much about increasing prices?" Kádár tells the Soviet leader that in Hungary there is an old Mr. Kóhn, who is always told about the price increases well in advance. He therefore makes up various jokes about the higher prices, which quickly spread all over the country and people laugh about it; so that by the time the increases go into effect, no one seems to care much about them. Gorbachev "borrows" old Mr. Kóhn. Back at the Kremlin, Gorbachev tells the old man that he will have the same task in the USSR (to make people laugh), except for the fact that in the Soviet Union, prices never rise and everyone is happy. Answers Mr. Kóhn: "I thought I was the one telling the jokes."

Then there are also the "concealed" price increases. The price of an article may simply go up without announcement. The price tag may even continue to show the old price; the customer finds out about the increase at the checkout counter. Even more frequent are the price increases introduced by the private merchants (*magán szektor* or *maszek*). They generally sell everything for 25–30 percent more than the state stores. The trouble is, the state stores tend to run out of merchandise. If one wants to purchase a popular "missing" item, one may buy it at a private store, for a much higher price, or by exchanging for it a "favor." The previously mentioned half-owner of the private auto-parts store, for example, has one set of rear quarter panels for the Lada 120 model, which is one of the "shortage" items. He is saving it for the time when he needs a great favor from someone. The familiar situation prevails again. One must be content to do without certain articles unless one has personal acquaintances or connections. And there are plenty of "shortage" articles. It is particularly aggravating that expensive pieces of equipment often remain idle because of missing items that cost only pennies. As a consequence, many auto repair shops do not even take on work until the required parts are obtained. If the part is unobtainable, the car may stand around for 6–10 months.

There is, of course, a group of privileged people who have the necessary connections, who are members of better circles, who can be corrupted, and who in turn themselves are ready to corrupt others. They can "arrange" nearly everything; they can buy anything they wish. They are both financially and materially better off than the rest of society. The "privileged" may belong to one or more of the following categories:

- they may be active in one or another type of private undertaking—they may operate a private store, or provide services on a private basis;
- they may be working in jobs that provide them with opportunities to receive tips and other types of gratuities (waiters, car repairmen, etc.);
- in addition to their state employment, they may be partners in enterprise work associations *(gazdasági' munkaközösség,* or GMK) and thus perform extra work, after hours, using the state enterprise's equipment and space, for wages negotiated separately, or in "civil legal fiscal associations" *(polgári iogi társaság,* or PJT) performing white-collar work.

Those failing in the latter categories receive their minuscule paychecks from the state in exchange for unhurried work and earn multiples of that amount during the subsequent hours. There are a great many people, of course, who do not have the opportunity to operate in such rackets. Most of the factory workers (i.e., the members of the "ruling class") must do without such lucrative choices. They face a daily struggle, because their wages, rising at the rate of 2–3 percent annually, can hardly match the 10–15 percent or higher rate of inflation. (Officially, of course, the rate of inflation in Hungary is never higher than 81/2 percent!)

Opposed to the "privileged" is a social class, becoming more and more populous, that lives in relative penury; and this causes a certain amount of social tension. The majority of workers on fixed income constitute the consumers for the subsidized food and clothing items. They eat without variety, exist in a rather unhealthy manner, and all the while they encounter the villas and weekend houses of the others. As one consequence, nearly everyone tries to go after "earning on the side." As the saying goes: "If you work, you don't have time to make money!" This applies, of course, to work performed for the state, particularly in positions of responsibility. For example, the young university teacher we mentioned above receives 500 forints, on top of his monthly 6,900 forints, for being chairman of the department. For work performed on a "private" basis, however, he could earn as much as 12–15 thousand forints more a month. His earnings are limited only by the threat of taxation.

From the previous discussion, the question immediately arises: who is the idiot who remains a worker for the state—who is reluctant to become part of the private sector? Well, there are those who do not have this choice; then there are those who are too timid or unwilling to face the risks involved; and finally there are those people who have no confidence in the permanence of Hungary's liberal approach to the issue of private enterprise. It is a widely-held view, especially among intellectuals, that "going private" is a clear indication of one's opposition to the system, and that therefore should the present liberal phase come to an end, such behavior could present certain difficulties for the individual. Thus there are a great many people who don't want to become private entrepreneurs themselves, but who at the same time are green with envy at the sight of the *maszek*'s wealth. As the old Hungarian saying goes, "It is easier to mouth off than to get down to hard work." In Hungary today, there is not even an attempt to create equality between individuals. The period of socialist equality is long gone, and Hungary best exemplifies this within the Soviet bloc. People will never work well without receiving at least the hope of opportunities for bettering themselves. And, of course, as soon as these opportunities are present, the better, more aggressive, more fortunate, and more talented individuals will leave the rest of the pack behind. The law of natural selection works on the financial level, too. Anyone who falls behind, falls behind radically. True, the prices of staples are low, but anything outside that range is very expensive. For example, the price of gasoline is 20 forints/liter, which equals 80 forints or U.S. $1.80/gallon. If one takes hourly wages into account, the disparity is much greater. Thus, the maintenance of even a slightly higher-than-average standard of living is impossible on a state salary. The trend in the distribution of wealth and income in Hungary does not appear very promising. There is an economic stratum of society (ca. 30 percent) that is becoming steadily poorer; another 30–40 percent that maintains its standard of living; and finally about 30–40 percent of the population, whose life is becoming steadily better. Consequently, the gap between the two extremes is constantly widening. Obviously this trend cannot continue for long, under the conditions of socialism. "Where do we go from here?" is the daily topic of conversation in Hungary; it appears that everyone is intently watching developments. What will happen? In the opinion of most mature Hungarians, the answer is simple: whatever Hungary's "Big Brother" will suggest and whatever Kádár's successor (with the blessings of the CPSU) will decide. And, of course, this is no reason for great hope, in the long run. As a consequence, a number of

Hungarians are maintaining good contacts with the West, not only because in the event of deteriorating conditions this would provide an escape route for them, but also because working for the West is a lucrative and permitted activity.

The least profitable manner in which work for the West can be undertaken is by working for a company that performs work for foreign enterprises. In such an event all workers receive the target premium in order to induce them toward effectiveness and quality.

A more lucrative way is to be sent abroad by one's firm to perform some task for the contracting partner. In situations like this, one receives the base pay in forints, and a per diem in foreign, usually hard, currency. One can visit home on weekends, and depending on one's length of stay abroad, one receives a certain amount of duty-free status. The basic amount is 6,000 forints, and each additional month's stay means an additional 10,000 forints. If one stays abroad longer than one year, one may bring in just about anything, except a car, free of duty obligations.

An even better situation is to go abroad after landing a contract to do so. In this case, one pays taxes on one's gross pay, and 20 percent of the remainder must be sent back to Hungary to be received in forints. The Social Security contribution (ca. U.S. $40.00) must be paid without reimbursement; but the rest of one's earnings is free of any obligation. Generally, the state does not even bother to collect taxes. There is, for example, an agreement between the United States and Hungary concerning taxes. In the case of certain types of employment, the Hungarian working in the United States does not pay any taxes. Unless someone turns him in, he doesn't pay any taxes in Hungary either. Thus he can bring in his money or the goods he purchased, duty-free. And, of course, we have already discussed the advantages of having dollars in bank accounts.

There are "dollar shops" in Hungary, selling items that are difficult or impossible to obtain elsewhere (drinks, tobacco products, cosmetic articles, clothing items, electrical items, etc.). Foreign visitors may use these stores without limitation, while a Hungarian can only use them if he has dollars *not in excess* of 50 U.S. dollars. Here, the role of the black market dollar, or dollars received from relatives or friends, comes into play. Frequently these friends or relatives living in the West make the first payment on the purchase of a new car for their Hungarian protégé. The most fashionable East Bloc model at this time is the Soviet Lada 1200. Its price is 140,000 forints (ca. U.S. $3,300.00), half of which must be paid in advance. In spite of this, there are long "waiting lists" for this car; often the waiting period is 6 years. However, if the payment is made from abroad in "hard" currency, delivery is made within one month. There are no questions asked in cases like this; the main thing is that the state treasury receives the dollars.

There are also stores for diplomatic personnel. They are for foreign diplomats and those Hungarians who can prove the immaculate pedigree of their dollars. The prices in these stores are considerably lower than in the regular dollar stores. Any Hungarian having an account at one of these stores can wield great influence because of his access to Western goods whose potential power for influence is great. Access to these stores is another sign of privilege in Hungary.

CONCLUSIONS

In the spring of 1983 the Hungarian Television Science Club organized a debate about Hungarian society in the 1980s.[10] The reaction of the viewers was that "money reigns in Hungary." In other words, unlike in the Soviet Union, in Hungary financial wealth can guarantee access to roomy apartments, vital medicines, stylish clothes, automobiles, pleasant vacation resorts, travel abroad, and social status. These and other elements of comfort are usually made available by the state authorities to high level party and state bureaucrats, managers of state and cooperative factories and farms, scientific institutes, and military leaders; or they can be obtained through friends and connections; or they can be brought back from the West by those whose jobs authorize such travel; or they can be acquired by people making money in the second and third economies. Money per se, unless it is convertible foreign currency, is not the objective of the Hungarian citizen; it is what money can buy that matters. Therefore, most Hungarians prefer to exchange their money for assets that have international value. Regardless of what the scriptures of Marxism-Leninism state, success in Hungary is measured in terms of a materially comfortable and cultured life. After all, the party and bureaucratic elite set the standard for such aspiration. It means positioning onself strategically rather than just accruing income. The Hungarian game is not of monopoly, but of chess, and those who play with chicanery and boldness live well. Those who are honest and timid will belong to the masses, who just eke out a living. It is not surprising, therefore, that Hungarians from an early age are being taught hypocrisy at home and in schools, because survival beginning with adolescent life requires the mastery of "artful behavior." Moreover, what is right or wrong, good or bad, depends on one's perception and values. Hence, cheating, corruption, deceit, concealment, favoritism, bribery, and other practices considered by the Hungarian authorities illegal, are not a new phenomenon; it can be argued that they are a by-product of the existing economic system in Hungary. As Miklós Hernádi observed,[11] those who participate in the black market have only the future to fear—the abundance of goods and the real quality of citizens. The assumption is that with increased liberalization of the economic system and the implementation of socialist democracy, these social ills will gradually disappear. Besides, sociologists, anthropologists, and historians, who dealt with this subject, are fully aware that these ills are not exceptional but endemic; that they are not marginal but integral to the organization and rewards of work—that they are a phenomenon of human nature.

In dealing with the "villains," the government has recently instituted several measures; however, the gap between the very rich and very poor has been widening rather than narrowing. For example, regulations that restrict the ownership of private property aim at preventing the accumulation of wealth and at warding off speculation. Most people, however, are successful at finding loopholes for investing their money. Many people feel that regulations governing the acquisition of property do not eliminate the social resentment resulting from the differentiation of income, because such resentment is simply channeled toward other manifestations of wealth.[12] Two recent regulations on private property reflect efforts at combating corruption but also reveal how ineffective some measures are. The first restricts selling cars that are less than three years old on auto markets. Salesmen, however, have already found a way to circumvevnt the regulation by giving the buyer "operation rights" over the car instead of "ownership rights."[13] The other decree forbids any middleman in the sale of vegetables. Its enforcement is proving to be extremely difficult, since speculators are unwilling to give up their lucrative "jobs."[14]

A modified income tax law that took effect in 1984 provides further incentives to artisans and private entrepreneurs. Under the previous system, artisans and private retailers with an income of more than 200,000 forints had to pay a tax rate of 75 percent on the excess; as a result, a considerable number of them closed their shops for several months, saying it was not worthwhile working because of the corresponding increase in taxes. With the new tax law, the highest tax rate is 65 percent and only applies to that portion of individual incomes exceeding 600,000 forints. Before, artisans had to pay considerably higher taxes than professional workers (writers, artists, and other self-employed professionals). The new law creates uniform tax rates; it does not differentiate between the type of work and takes only the amount of income into account.[15]

The number of shops selling Western luxury goods, for which Hungarian buyers pay in forints instead of the Western currency demanded in similar shops in neighboring socialist countries, has risen considerably in the last few years. The popularity and success of these shops indicate that some segments of Hungarian society are immune to the country's economic crisis. Obviously these shops are meeting the growing demands of a segment of society that can afford a substantially higher standard of living than that of the average Hungarian. According to official figures, the average wage in Hungary in 1984 was 4,800 forints per month.[16] Individuals earning ten times the official wage amounted to about 5 percent of the economically active people. On the other hand, 28.2 percent of the Hungarian population in 1983 had an income below the accepted minimum (or poverty level), even though the minimum is no more than 2,500 forints per month. While the rich include lawyers, engineers, writers, party apparatchiks, top-level bureaucrats, house painters, collective farmers, electricians, business contractors, doctors, boutique owners, small manufacturers, building contractors, prostitutes, and a host of individuals specializing in goods or skills that are in short supply, the poor consist of retirees, single parents, petty bureaucrats, unskilled white-collar workers (mostly women), young teachers with families, and many people without apartments living in sublet rooms, and those unable to cope with their lives such as alcoholics, compulsive gamblers, bagwomen, and young people living on the street.[17]

The problem is not so much the inequality and the differentiation in income. That different performances are given different rewards is in itself no violation of socialist ethics. Indeed, the standard of living in Hungary—in most cases higher than any of the surrounding CMEA member states—is the overall reward for these individual differences and makes such differences palatable. The problem lies in the fact that such differences are so vividly and dramatically manifested against a background of failed communist utopia. The contrast between the occupants of villas with two-car garages, Mercedes, the dachas with swimming pools—and the overcrowded workers' hostels—is too great for the lower economic strata to accept the nouveau riche class emerging in socialist Hungary as equals. According to the semiofficial government daily, *Magyar Hírlap*, it is the conspicuousness of wealth that has resulted in the "antirich" mood prevailing in Hungary.[18] According to Hungarian authorities, however, the problem does not lie in "settling accounts" with the rich, as long as the source of their wealth is legal, but rather in the creation of adequate welfare and financial security for all. In the final analysis, only the improvement of economic conditions for everyone can eliminate social tensions. Since higher incomes were the natural result of a more liberal and efficient economy, they must be accepted and "peacefully tolerated" because, according to the authorities, those who are fighting against the growing differentiation of enterprise or individual incomes are also working against themselves in the long run. The only solution to the present tensions, the authorities argue, is the strengthening of the market mechanism and the creation of equal opportunity for producers, salesmen, and consumers, despite the fact that there are people who blame the reforms for their economic difficulties. Many Hungarian workers feel threatened by the more liberal activity of the market mechanism and fear for their jobs and position in society when faced with new challenges created by the implementation of the principles of socialist democracy. Whether or not the much needed "national consensus"—a prerequisite for building developed socialism in Hungary—can be maintained in the face of growing protests against the wealthy will very much depend on the ability of the ruling elite to deal equitably with the centrifugal and centripetal forces of Hungarian society. On the one hand it will be necessary to continue with the liberalization policies of the market mechanism, and on the other, to provide more satisfactory solutions to the rising costs of commodities and the lowering of the standard of living of the masses.

Opinion polls of the last few years have reflected growing discontent among the Hungarian public about the economic situation. According to Katalin Farkas and Judit Pataki, the authors of a study in the journal of the Institute for Mass Communications, *Jel-Kép [Symbol]*, many concepts and norms of "developed socialism" that had been instilled into the public's mind have proven illusory. Promises of an automatic rise in living standards, steady growth in the economy, stable prices, and the absence of inflation have not been kept. As a result, the public's "economic mood" has become more and more pessimistic. The year 1979 was the most pessimistic year, with the price increases affecting the basic living standards of the population and sending the public's mood sharply downward. There was a period of renewed pessimism from the beginning of 1982. According to the authors, causes of this pessimism were to be found in rent increases, in increases of the price of transportation, reductions in the scope and amount of travel discounts, and supply problems developing from the restriction of imports in 1982.[19] Similar findings were reported by the director of research at the Theoretical Research Institute of the Trade Unions, József Balogh, when he spoke on Radio Budapest on April 11, 1984, about a study he conducted from 1979 to 1984 that measured changes in social contentment. While in 1976, 92 percent of the people interviewed expected an improvement in their living standards, in 1979, after price increases, this percentage plummeted to only 14 percent; in 1981 to 9 percent; and at the beginning of 1984 to a mere 4 percent. Lack of economic organization, reduction in labor productivity, unutilized industrial capacity, and a lack of democracy were additional sources of discontent. However, another source on a par with price increases was the complaint that people received the same amount or even less for more work. All of the above-mentioned sources of discontent were a logical cause for many Hungarians to enter the second and third economies.

NOTES

1. Lajos Géza Nagy, " 'Poor' and 'Rich,' " *Jel-Kép* [Symbol] (January 1984).
2. September 18, 1984.

3. See *Észak-Magyarország* [Northern Hungary] (August 19, 1984).

4. See Slavoljub Djukić, "Enigmatic sources of income," *Politika* (Belgrade) (December 11, 1983).

5. July 13 and 20, 1984.

6. Ibid. (September 7, 1984).

7. See *Mozgó Világ* (January/February 1984), 34–42.

8. *Élet és Irodalom* (September 7, 1984).

9. See Chapter 1, pp. 18–25.

10. See "Hungarian society in the 1980s," *Magyar Hírlap* (April 9, 1983).

11. Hernádi, *Olyan, Amilyen?* [Should We Accept It as It Is?] (Budapest: Kozmosz, 1984), 76–86.

12. See *Magyar Nemzet* (June 9, 1984).

13. See *Magyar Hírlap*, (September 4, 1984).

14. See *Népszava* (September 4, 1984).

15. See *Heti Világgazdaság* (November 19, 1983).

16. See *Magyar Statisztikai Zsebkönyv, 1984* [1984 Hungarian Statistical Pocketbook]; and *Heti Világgazdaság* (November 19, 1983).

17. See Szikra Katalin Falusné, "A vagyonosodásról" [On the accumulation of wealth], *Közgazdasági Szemle* [Economic Review] 11 (1982); 1314–30.

18. September 15, 1984.

19. See Katalin Farkas and Judit Pataki, "The balance of eight years," *Jel-Kép* 1 (1984): 117–119.

PART III
THE HEDONISM OF
AUTHORITY

5
From Traditionalism to Nihilism: The Transformation of the Family and Religion as Institutions

Recent studies by prominent economists, sociologists, even psychologists, dealt with thought-provoking questions concerning the stability of Hungarian society. For example Elemér Hankiss, a distinguished sociologist, in the literary monthly *Valóság*,[1] alleged that the rapidly changing nature of current society was responsible for much of the confusion among the population. Nobody knew, according to Hankiss, how long a certain measure would remain valid; what applied one day would no longer be in force the next. Similarly, historical events were subject to such radical changes of interpretation that people had lost all awareness of their historical roots and national identity. Lifestyles had changed overnight for members of the rural population who were forced to take jobs in the cities; the result was a disorienting psychological shock. Or, while the worker was expected to follow certain rules of a centrally planned economy during the day, in the evenings he had to adjust to the semi-market economy of his second job. Double standards and chaotic conditions were to blame for the mental confusion of the individual, who in this way was denied respect for his history, his culture, his traditions, and even himself.

What Elemér Hankiss was able to state freely in an official publication, an equally able scholar and critic, István Csurka, could express only unofficially during a secret meeting held in mid-June 1985 near Budapest with representatives of Hungary's main opposition groups.[2] Csurka blamed the Hungarian authorities, whose policies were responsible for the deterioration of the country's cultural and moral fabric. According to Csurka, Hungarian society has succumbed to a compromise by the Kádár regime, which had promised more tolerable and more humane life to all those who were willing to forgive and forget. Many had taken up the offer, and as a result "entire generations have been raised by parents who have stubbornly refused to talk." An entirely new system had been erected on principles of reticence. Nihilism had become the main undercurrent of Hungarian life, according to Csurka. The emigration waves, the catastrophic demographic situation, rampant alcoholism, the high suicide rate, and the general lack of interest in the Hungarian identity could all be traced to this source. The "nihilists" of contemporary Hungary had been numbed into believing that nothing they could do was of any use and this was an attitude that socialist authority in Hungary had found fairly easy to exploit and to manipulate.

As to the causes that had lead to the development of this quasiculture in Hungary, Csurka offered two major developments. First had been the divesting of Hungarian society of its peasant-centered character. In other words, as a result of industrialization and urbanization, which was an unavoidable trend of development in Hungary, a cultural vacuum was created that had not been filled by anything new. On the contrary, those joining the agricultural cooperatives had not taken their traditional values with them, and those migrating to the cities had soon lost their cultural identity and pride as they were absorbed into the dark masses under the neon lights.

A second factor responsible for the weakening of the social fabric of the country Csurka attributes to the impact of communist rule on the family and religion as institutions. Csurka does not blame the communist system alone for the disintegration of these traditional social units; as a matter of fact, the entire industrial world had been affected by this development. In the case of Hungary, however, urbanization and technological development went hand-in-hand with the period of socialist transformation during which "the impact of Hungarian nihilism was the strongest." The aim to create the "new socialist person" also involved the breakup of the family with traditional values. What are the fundamental changes in the family structure? What is the meaning of the socialist egalitarian model? What are the successes and failures of the Hungarian population policy? How do Hungarians see themselves in the present phase of "developed socialism"?

CHANGES IN THE FAMILY STRUCTURE

Hungarian ideologues start with the assumption, derived from Engels, that in societies based on private property the unequal participation in the social division of labor determines conditions within the family. Therefore, in the monogamous family that developed with private property, men attained domination and women became slaves. This difference between the sexes determined the functioning of the family even where there were no open clashes between husband and wife. The women submitted and did not rebel against male supremacy. Even if the wife contributed with her work to the family income, this was only in the form of auxiliary work (e.g., in the families of peasants, shop-keepers, etc.); or she complemented her husband's earnings (e.g., taking in washing or cleaning other households). In other words, the husband was the breadwinner and, therefore, he played the dominant role in the family. Hence, in ideological terms the family type characterized by role division is identified as an "asymmetrical family" (typical in capitalist societies). The other type, which Marxist-Leninist ideologues identify as an egalitarian socialist model, where the ruling principle is identical roles for both sexes, is called the "symmetrical family." The main character-istics of the latter are two instead of one breadwinners and egalitarian division of family tasks (e.g., shopping, household chores, bringing up the children, etc.). The emphasis in the symmetrical model of the family structure is on the socialist equality of sexes, that is, a "unisex" approach to family roles. However, because of the declining trend in population since the early 1950s and its impact on the stability of Hungarian society, there is an inherent contradiction between desired socialist goals and population policy aims. In several instances in the past when the clash between the two interests became a matter of exercising priorities, pop-ulation policy prevailed over socialist policy. The socialist ideal for the Hungarian family structure is still "to develop methods which would help women with several children to bridge the gap in their careers, and to strengthen the unisex pattern of husband–wife relationship within the family."[3] In practice, however, it very seldom works that way. Today in Hungary over 90 percent of all women engaged to be married hold down jobs and most of those who do not, find themselves in training for a job. Therefore, young people who marry nowadays consider it natural that the wife should be a wage earner—after all, this is what they have seen in their own family. Furthermore the schools prepare them for it and the system demands it of them. Most young people think that, beyond jointly providing for the family, they will also share chores and ensure each other equal rights and opportunities for preserving their relationship to develop their personalities in keeping with their incli-nations. According to various surveys, the symmetrical relationship be-tween husband and wife does not last very long. The deviation from the symmetrical model usually begins with the birth of the first child. Labor and nursing rests entirely with the mother; they are not shared, and together they occupy all her time. While the new mother is on childcare allowance, the father has to take on some extra work outside regular working hours to compensate for the difference between the wife's for-mer earnings and the childcare allowance. Consequently his share of the household chores will diminish and hers will increase. Furthermore, because of the time away from her job the woman's career is interrupted whereas the husband's advances both in status and income. A woman returning to her job after several years' absence must not only make up for arrears but with a child in kindergarten she must stay at home and look after it from time to time. As the gap widens in their incomes, she will be a second-string breadwinner and therefore she is looked on as somebody on whom one cannot fully depend. Thus there are two consequences that follow: first, the attitude toward family expansion becomes negative, and second, the symmetrical model of a modern family structure based on a unisex approach to family roles gradually diminishes. Hence the authorities in socialist Hungary face a dilemma whether to promote the socialist value system described in the symmetrical model of the family structure or to deviate from it by promoting a population policy with large families, even if it means a return to the asymmetrical model in the family structure. Of course the problem is more complex than it appears on the surface.

PROBLEMS WITH THE SOCIALIST EGALITARIAN MODEL

Hungary was on the losing side in both world wars. The Peace Treaty of Trianon in 1920 reduced the area and the population of the country by approximately two-thirds, and over 3 million ethnic Hungarians became overnight citizens of foreign countries. (Today Hungarian minorities living in neighboring countries number about 4 million). About 5 percent of the population perished in World War II. Another major loss of population (about 250,000) occurred during and after the October 1956 Revolution. Today there are about 4,715,000 (or 40 percent) people of Hungarian origin living outside Hungary.[4]

In 1980 the Hungarian population numbered 10,715,000. Population density was 300 inhabitants per square mile. There were 192 children to 100 families. According to demographic calculations the loss of population by the year 2000 can be anywhere between 20 to 400 thousand. The future outlook is not very encouraging; some Hungarian writers (e.g., Gyula Illyés) have been haunted by the idea of the death of the nation. The reasons for the declining population are many; some are of sociopolitical nature, others encompass economic, cultural, and psychological explanations. During the early 1950s, for example, legalized injustices and forced industrialization caused greater change to the social structure within a few years than the preceding 100 years had done. Even during the period of economic and political stability of recent years, the suicide rate and alcoholism have been alarmingly high. In addition to alcoholism and suicide, other factors contributing to the declining trend are given by the experts as the catastrophic housing situation, fewer marriages, a high divorce rate, the changed position of women in society, increasing economic difficulties, the stagnant living standard, stillbirths, more frequent abortions, a low fertility rate, an imbalance in the age structure, and the breakup of the traditional family unit.

After the end of WWII, the usual baby boom that follows wars lasted about 4 years. Then, after 1951, the birth rate began to decline and fell below 20 per 1,000 inhabitants again in 1952. (See Table 5.1.) The Rákosi regime responded with a population policy imposing heavy penalties on doctors and patients for abortions. The gist of the population policy was to force people to bring more children into this world than they actually desired. The Ratkó Law (prohibiting abortion) was actually effective for only one year, 1954, when there were 23 live births recorded per 1,000 inhabitants. By 1956, the live births fell to 19.5 per 1,000—a considerable drop—and therefore in June 1956 the Ratkó Law was repealed and abortions were made readily available. The trend of a declining birthrate continued with a few exceptions in 1968, 1973, and 1975. Thus the Hungarian authorities considered demographic changes in the country a very serious problem requiring a long-term population policy with linkages to social and economic policies.

The first comprehensive population policy was introduced in 1973 with changes and amendments regarding implementation added almost every year. The features of this policy include such things as financial assistance, extra time off, accommodation preference, a network of creches and nursery schools, health services, and so on.

There is no family allowance paid for the birth of the first child; for the second child the current allowance is 2,500 forints. The allowance has increased 4 times since 1974—partly because of inflation. The allowance paid for the third child is nearly twice as much as that paid for the second child.

A working mother giving birth receives 20 weeks of maternity leave with full pay. After that she receives a childcare allowance to rear her child at home until it is 3 years old. The social insurance organization pays about 25–40 percent of the national average monthly earnings to the mother. The amount of the allowance varies according to the number of children in the family (800 forints for the first, 900 for the second, 1,000 for the third and subsequent children). It is interesting to note that while the population trend is declining, the recipients of childcare allowance have increased by about 35 percent since 1973.

In accordance with the population policy, the working mother is entitled to one day per month without pay, two paid days of additional leave if she has one child under 14, and 5 or 9 days to mothers of 2 or 3-or-more children under 14 years of age, respectively. They are also allowed sick benefits for the nursing of a sick child (up to 60 days maximum for children under 3 years and 30 days for children between 3

Table 5.1
Annual Live Births in Hungary 1920–1983

Year	Live Births	Per 1,000 Inhabitants
1920	249,458	31.4
1930	219,784	25.4
1941	177,047	19.9
1946	169,120	18.7
1947	187,316	20.6
1948	191,907	21.0
1952	185,820	19.6
1953	206,926	21.6
1954	223,347	23.0
1956	192,810	19.5
1957	167,202	17.0
1960	146,461	14.7
1962	130,053	12.9
1968	154,419	15.1
1970	151,819	14.7
1971	150,640	14.5
1973	156,224	15.0
1975	194,240	18.4
1976	185,405	17.5
1980	148,673	13.9
1981	142,890	13.3
1982	133,559	12.5
1983	127,553	11.9
1984	124,934	11.7

Source: *Statisztikai Évkönyv, 1967–1984* [Statistical Yearbook] (Budapest: Central Statistical Office, 1976 to 1984); *Statisztikai Havi Közlemények 1985* [Statistical Reports].

and 6 years old). The daily average number of women on sick pay for this reason increased from 13,000 to 21,000 between 1973 and 1979, which means that about 0.5 percent of the workers were absent on an average day by virtue of this benefit.[5]

In spite of all the financial assistance and childcare benefits, according to László Cseh-Szombathy, the head of the Institute of Sociology of the Hungarian Academy of Sciences, "social allowances cover only 15 to 20 percent of the cost of supporting a child in Hungary today; thus the per capita income of the family dwindles with the birth of each child."[6] It is questionable, therefore, whether or not the financial benefits serve as an incentive to encourage an increased birthrate. Cseh-Szombathy is also of the opinion that other material incentives would be relatively futile because the girls reaching childbearing age in 1985 and later were born in the 1960s, when the birthrate was very low. Therefore no essential change can take place in the population numbers even if intentions to have children should suddenly change.

As a result of the 1973 population policy, the network of childcare establishments (creches and nursery schools) increased by almost 35 percent to exceed 65 thousand by 1985. In spite of this, "creche overcrowding is a perennial problem: an average of 127 children are enrolled to fill each 100 vacancies, but the average utilization of the capacity is still only 86 percent."[7] A similar trend applies to nursery schools. The capacity was 364,000 at the end of 1979, about 110,000 more than in 1973. "In spite of this large increase, several tens of thousands of applying children could still not be accepted, owing to the increase in the number of nursery age. The nurseries are also overcrowded: an average of 126 children are enrolled for each 100 of the vacancies."[8] Therefore, working mothers with nursery- and creche-age children have no choice but to stay at home and take care of their young ones.

Adequate housing is perhaps the first prerequisite for family growth. Preference to large families was promoted by the accommodation measures passed at the end of 1980 in accordance with the population policy. Young people are given help with home purchase loans as well as the allocation of council homes. Assisting families with 3 or more children resulted in reallocation of 25,000 large families between 1974 and 1979, but 12,000 families remained on the waiting list because there were no accommodations for them.[9]

Although the housing situation shows an improvement—142 inhabitants per 100 rooms in 1983, compared with 265 in 1949—the situation is still desperate. In 1984, a little more than 50 percent of apartments in Hungary were fully equipped with modern conveniences; only about 14 percent had central heating and close to 50 percent had no toilets. About 40 percent of the family feuds that lead to breakup are caused by unsolved housing problems. In 1984, 52 percent of all married couples in Budapest were living with their parents, compared with 13 percent a generation ago; and only 11 percent of all young couples had a local council apartment, compared with 42 percent a generation ago.[10] A 1982 survey shows that only 19 percent of young married couples started their married life in their own home and most of them (70 percent) acquired their own home only by the sixth year of their marriage.[11] According to demographer András Klinger, "The divorce rate is twice as high with those [married couples] who have no home of their own."[12]

In 1985, Zsolt Oszlányi, deputy head of the department dealing with housing at the National Planning Bureau, wrote: "The housing situation is worse than before, indeed even hopeless. Essentially nothing has improved."[13] Thus the Seventh Five-Year Plan (1986–1990) included the provision of new forms of advance savings plans for young couples who wished to build or buy apartments. Similar plans were introduced in 1971 with, unfortunately, strange consequences. Young couples who pledged to have two children had 30,000 forints per child, that is, 60,000 forints in all, taken off their repayments to the National Savings Bank on any loans they had taken out to set up house. Recently, however, gynecologists found an increasing number of women in Hungary suffering from imaginary pregnancies. The symptoms were those of a real pregnancy; however, examinations proved that nothing else but imagination created the baby. "In nearly every case all young mothers were married, lived in local council or in their own apartments and all received an official allowance of 60,000 forint."[14]

By 1990, 56,000 new apartments are to be made available in Budapest, yet these will not be sufficient to house the 66,000 families on the current waiting list, not to mention the additional 35,000 new applicants for housing expected over the next five years. The waiting period for two-children families may be as long as four years and for childless couples at least ten years from the date of application. Although in June 1985 the daily of the Patriotic People's Front, *Magyar Nemzet,* stated that apartment sharing no longer existed in Hungary, in reality there were 9,642 apartments with co-tenants. Hungary's high divorce rate and the dire housing situation have created a new type of sharing. Often after a divorce the two parties will remain in the same apartment with their new spouses and children.[15] Annual vital statistics reveal that during the second half of the 1970s the frequency of first marriages declined somewhat and the average age increased a little (to 24.2 years for men and 21.2 years for women in 1979). The number of remarriages by divorced people declined considerably, and the number of births to unmarried mothers rose somewhat (in 1975, 5.6 percent of all newborns, and in 1980, 8.2 percent, were the children of unmarried mothers). The ratio of those entering into their first marriage at various ages shows the number of men born after 1950 declining steadily. In the case of women the drop is smaller but also noticeable. Thus when they reach their fiftieth birthday, 19 percent of men and 9 percent of women will still be single.[16]

Demographic factors also played an important role in the rise of the number of births to unmarried women. These are primarily, marriage at a later age, and secondly, the higher frequency of divorce and fewer remarriages. Unmarried mothers, are, according to these findings, most frequently young single girls and divorced women over 40. It is interesting to note that there is a close correlation between unmarried mothers and low educational achievements.[17]

The number of marriages in general is on the decline in Hungary; between 1971 and 1981 the figure had dropped by 22,000 (see Fig. 5.1).

Figure 5.1
Marriages and Divorces in Hungary

Year	Marriages	Divorces
1948	9.0%	0.6%
1960	10.7%	1.2%
1970	8.9%	1.7%
1982	7.1%	2.7%

Source: Ötlet, [Idea] (October 13, 1983).

Divorce on the other hand is increasing by leaps and bounds; for example, in 1978, out of 100 marriages 35 would end in divorce.[18] In 1982 divorce was at its highest rate since the end of the last century: 28,857, or 12,000 more than in 1960. According to another demographer, B. András Bálint, there are twice as many divorces in the cities as in villages. This indicates that relationships are more permanent in the provinces; or to put it differently, religious/moral considerations are deeper in the rural areas, where the restraining force of the community is also stronger.[19] Needless to say, with the transformation of the family structure the divorce rate in Hungary has increased steadily.

Changes in the moral code and in social habits are also a cause of the decline in the number of marriages. Greater permissiveness, increased financial independence of women, and the perception that marriage is not the only way for the majority of women to gain security are all contributing factors to the decline in the number of marriages. In Hungary it is easy to marry and also easy to get a divorce. There is also a lack of marriage counseling service to reconcile partners before the breakup of the family.

The family gets little help from the outside when it comes to learning how to handle conflicts. What they have seen in the family of their parents is in most cases inadequate, because the prior generation followed the customs of an earlier asymmetrical model of family structure, with greater sex differentiation. Schools do not, in general, offer courses in family behavior. Furthermore there are only a limited number of people qualified to counsel couples in family disputes. Professional advice is only available if one or the other member of the family has symptoms of serious psychological disturbances and seeks medical advice.

Since the repeal of the Ratkó Law (prohibiting abortion) in 1956, Hungary has learned from experience that fertility cannot be legislated;

Table 5.2
Live Births per 1,000 Women Aged 15–49

Year	Live Births
1921	116.8
1930–1931	88.0
1940–1941	71.3
1948–1949	75.7
1959–1960	59.7
1969–1970	57.2
1975	72.8
1976	69.9
1977	67.3
1978	64.1
1979	61.5
1980	57.6
1981	55.7
1982	52.2

Source: *Statisztikai Évkönyv, 1982* [Statistical Yearbook] (Budapest: Central Statistical Office, 1982).

therefore very limited health information services, as well as medical practice, on family planning through effective contraception has been introduced. While the number of abortions used to be much higher than live births, since 1974 this has been reversed. (See Table 5.2.) Parallel with this trend, the number of women using oral contraceptives has strongly increased: as many as 680,000 women used this method in 1980, two-and-a-half times as many as in 1973. In other words, about 27 percent of women aged 17–49 relied on oral contraceptives. Among married women the ratio was even higher: 60 percent used modern contraceptive methods.[20]

According to public opinion polls conducted in 1974 by the Central Statistical Office on the issue of using modern or traditional methods of birth control, two-thirds of the people interviewed accepted the modern concept, while 43 percent of them indicated disagreement with the traditional view.[21] A strong correlation existed between the followers of both conservative and modern views and their religious attitudes. The proportion of conservative and modern views was 72 to 28 percent among religious people, while this was the reverse in the other groups, with 38 percent following the conservative, and 62 percent the modern view. (The correlation coefficient for attitude with piety: $+0.62$ for conservatives, -0.21 for moderns).[22] Thus it appears that the Roman Catholic Church in Hungary and the socialist authorities see eye-to-eye on official population policy; they both seek higher fertility and lower birth control.

The low fertility rate has also been influenced by an overall aging of the population. From the end of the last century to 1980 the proportion of older people (those over 60) grew from 7.5 to 17.1 percent of the population, resulting in approximately 2 percent fall in the fertility rate. According to projected data, the proportion of older people will increase to 19 percent by the year 2000. While the proportion of 70–79-year olds has grown from 2 to 6.5 percent and that of the 60–69-year olds from 5 to 9 percent, the most spectacular rise has been among the 80-year olds, with a seven-fold growth since 1900. In 1984 only 50 percent of the older people were in the 60–69-year-old group, 38 percent of them were 70–79-year olds, and 12 percent were 80 years or older.[23] The consequences for today, and for the future, are an imbalance in the population profile and problems such as rising medical costs, shortages of hospital beds, pension payments and so on.

In 1981 a total of 2.1 million pensioners lived in Hungary, 19.4 percent of the total population. In 1984 the number of pensioners rose to 2,215,300, or 20.7 percent of the population.[24] It is estimated that the number of pensioners will be closer to 2.5 million in 1990, almost 25 percent of the total population. (Since the introduction of the pension system in 1952, women become eligible for old-age pension at 55, and men at the age of 60. People doing heavy manual work, however, become eligible even earlier. If one wishes to continue working, and this is acceptable to the employer, retirement can be and often is, postponed.) The costs of social care for people past retirement age absorbed 8.5 percent of the budget and 5.4 percent of the national income in 1970, and 13.9 percent and 10.3 percent, respectively, in 1980. As a rule, pensions are very low, particularly to those who retired before 1980. The average monthly pension was 2,300 forints in 1980, which was only 58 percent of the average wage. In 1984 it was less than 3,000 forints per month, received by 70 percent of the country's pensioners; however, 48 percent received less than 2,500 forints.[25] Since then there have been several cost-of-living increases which, unfortunately, have not kept up with the spiraling inflationary trend in Hungary. (The pension paid is

33 percent of final earnings after 10 years of work, 63 percent after 25 years, and 75 percent—the maximum—after 42 years of employment.) Only those holding certain high decorations are entitled to retire with full pay.[26] Because of the substandard income of the pensioners, many depend on support from their children or a second income usually derived from part-time employment. In 1979, for example, about 406,000 pensioners carried on gainful occupations. Working pensioners supplemented their pensions with wages earned in the amount of about 1,200 forints per month, which was more than 50 percent of the average pension. Nearly half of the pensioners employed belonged to the 60–69 age group, which means that nearly 30 percent of the pensioners between 60–69 years of age, and about 12 percent of those of 70 and older worked part-time.[27] The worst part of it is that those who retired earlier, and therefore received lower pensions, as a rule, have practically no opportunity to supplement their income because they are too old and feeble.

During the period of the asymmetrical model of family structure, older people on pension played a significant role in the rearing and supervision of young children in the family. Married children of older parents on pension (in most cases father only) considered it to be their responsibility to look after their aging, and in some cases ailing, parents. The family unit consisted of a close-knit relationship of members caring for each other and their relatives regardless of whether or not they lived in the same household. The symmetrical model of the family structure has changed all this. The two-breadwinner parents have no time (and in many cases no inclination) to take care of their young ones, or for that matter, to look after their aging and ailing parents if they don't live in the same household, or to ask their parents on pension to take care of their siblings because, as pensioners, both are probably on inadequate income and are therefore engaged in part-time work and have no time for the grandchildren. In other words, it is a vicious circle: one problem leads to another with the result that the transformed family unit is not functioning as well as planned by the state authorities or as anticipated by young couples at the time of marriage. The same problem prevails within the multi-generational family unit where couples with young children live in the same household with one or the other's in-laws. Taking care of grandchildren or taking care of the older parents and taking part in household chores are no longer opportunities for helping one another, but because of the necessity to be breadwinners (full-time or part-time), the family relationships contain the seeds of conflict rather than harmony. In 1983, two or more adult generations lived together in one-fifth of Hungarian households, with their adult children. The necessity of living in the same household is due principally to the housing shortage. Young couples able to start their married life in their own home are exceptions. Their most typical accommodation is a room in the home of either in-laws. This, of course, leads to a situation in which the parents, who accepted their son- or daughter-in-law into their own home want to lead their lives according to their own wishes. Consequently the young couple feels a loss of independence, and very often clashes in attitudes develop.

Even though the living together of different generations is not free of conflict, the situation of the aged who live alone is even more grave. About 15 percent of those over retirement age have no relatives and more than one-fifth of pensioners live alone; most of them are women.[28] The aged men rely first of all on their wives, who are usually younger— wives of 62 percent of men 75 and older are still alive while only 16 percent of women of similar age can still rely on their husbands.[29] One of the more urgent problems in Hungary—the nursing of old and ill people—is due to the fact that families are unable to carry out the traditional function of care. The large number of females employed outside the home is responsible for this problem. The proportion of working women among females of working age exceeded 70 percent in the early 1980s. The burden of home nursing, therefore, falls increasingly on those past working age. About 35,000 people were attended by social workers in the early 1980s. This amounts to 25 percent of the number of over 75-year olds living alone and 60 percent of the number of those 80 and older. Those two figures indicate that the network of social workers leaves much to be desired. The demand for social and public health services, for example, is about 3 times as great among the aged as among young people. In 1983, for example, about 16,000 did this kind of work; however, 14,600 of them were "voluntary" workers, probably getting some kind of compensation. Similar problems exist with day centers for the aged. Although they have increased from 75 in 1968 to 835 in 1983, these centers are far too few to accommodate the present needs in Hungary.[30]

An interesting phenomenon is the transformation of the family structure in the countryside. The village population has grown older because of the migration of young people to the cities. Consequently older people left to themselves in the villages can count on little help in coping with everyday problems. "The constant withering away of the territorial organizations and service network of villages with a declining population adds to the difficulties of the aged."[31] This metamorphosis of the village population is even more serious if one considers the fact that the small farmers were the backbone of the traditional Hungarian culture, which is now in disarray.

The decline in the birthrate, due to a variety of causes that had a culminating effect in the change of the family structure, is only one side of the demographic problem that Hungary has to face. The other side, causing the same effect, is the high mortality rate, which is rising at an unprecedented pace. Between 1960 and 1983 the mortality rate rose from 10 per 1,000 to 13.9 per 1,000 inhabitants. The group mostly affected is the male population between 30 and 57 years old. Although the major causes of death in that group are alcoholism and suicide, natural causes of death have also risen.

Alcohol in Hungary means an escape from the hardships of daily life, a release from frustrations and emotional stress accumulated on the job or in the home environment. There are approximately 250,000 alcoholics in the country and about another 1,000,000 Hungarians have drinking problems. The problem has even spread to young mothers on maternity leave. Boredom is certainly one cause of excessive drinking, and nowadays young mothers will often gather in groups to drink. The groups with regular drinking habits are, according to Rudolf Andorka, skilled workers and young urban professionals with a rural background.[32] Hungarian sociologists consider alcoholism to be a social rather than a health problem.[33] People drink, they say, either to celebrate or to relieve social tension. Twelve-hour work days, chronic housing problems, the fear of being rejected in old age, and so on, are all contributory factors. If alcoholism is a way of showing defiance or resignation, then the permissiveness of the population is understandable.

Alcoholism is a very costly affair; this is probably the reason why the government is so anxious to curb it. Table 5.3 shows the estimated cost in 1982, which was three times as much as was spent on higher education during the same year.

Although alcoholism seems to be more of a social problem, the state authorities treat it as a health problem. However the state health sector only has facilities to treat eight percent of alcoholics and only one in forty actually succeed in abstaining.[34] It is not surprising, therefore, that the regime is trying to unload the burden onto the various churches who will accept the responsibility for the treatment of alcoholics.

In an attempt to curb the rapid rise of alcoholism in Hungary the National Assembly and Price Office, on April 21, 1986, raised the prices of alcohol beverages by 14.1 percent. Hard liquor prices were raised in 1973, 1978, 1979, and 1981; yet alcoholism in Hungary continued to increase. Between 1960 and 1983 the amount of hard spirits consumed increased by 343 percent.[35] In 1986 Hungarian per capita annual consumption of alcohol stood at 11.7 liters, of which hard liquor accounts for 4.8 liters (second highest in the world). Another 1.5–2.00 liters of illegally produced alcohol should be added to this figure.[36] The general consensus in Hungary is that the latest price increase might deter some young people from buying hard liquor but it will be of no use to the one-half million addicts who need expert medical attention. The price increase is likely to cause even more problems in the family life of the

Table 5.3
Suicides

Country	Per 100,000 Persons (Latest Available Figures)
Hungary	45.6
Denmark	30.0
Austria	27.6
FRG	21.7
France	19.6
Japan	17.1
Poland	12.7
USA	11.5
Australia	11.0
England	8.9
Italy	6.4
Israel	6.0
Ireland	5.7
Spain	4.1
Greece	3.3

Source: *U.S. News and World Report* (April 2, 1984).

addicts, since the average family already spends every year more than one month's wages on alcohol. An estimated 36 out of every 100 forints on food in the average family goes to alcohol, and the equivalent of 6.6 percent of Hungary's Domestic Net Material Product is spent on alcohol—as much as the state spends on education and culture. State revenues from the sale of and taxes on alcohol amounted to 52 billion forints in 1985.[37] Furthermore, alcohol is the reason most frequently cited in divorce courts for the breakdown of marriages.[38] (See Table 5.4.)

Suicides, too, are taking a serious toll in Hungary. There were 4,880, or 45.6 percent per 100,000 inhabitants, in 1981.[39] This number does not include the attempted suicides, which are estimated to be almost three times higher. Hungary has the highest suicide rate in the world.[40] The main reasons for suicides are, according to Hungarian experts, alcoholism, mental illness, the increasing proportion of old people, the impersonal nature of urban life, stress, and the decline of religion. (See Table 5.5.)

In addition to the increasing mortality figures derived from suicide and alcoholism, the relevant disease categories contributing to mortality in Hungary are typical for any industrialized country. For example, in 1984 circulatory diseases caused 78,233 deaths; cancer 28,685; cirrhosis 3,451; and accidents 12,559.[41]

Table 5.4
Estimated Value of Economic Damage Caused by Alcoholism in 1982
(1 billion = 1,000 million)

Reason	Billion Forint
Losses in production and sick pay	7.5 - 8.0
Medical treatment	2.9 - 3.2
Industrial and traffic accidents	3.1 - 3.3
Criminality	0.5 - 0.6
Total	14.5 -15.1

Source: Ágnes Dus, ed., *Társadalma beilleszkedési zavarok Magyarországon* [Problems of Social Adjustment in Hungary] (Budapest: Kossuth Könyvkiádo, 1986), 53.

Regardless of the high mortality rate and the low fertility rate and their causes, most researchers examining the stability of Hungarian culture and society blame the various problems arising from the dislocation of the family life. The family has lost its cohesion and its protective role. Similarly, men and women who live alone are more vulnerable than those who can share their joys and worries with a partner. The problem, according to a number of sociologists (e.g., Dr. Gábor Hegyesi), is not so much the declining population of Hungary but the socioeconomic and cultural conditions that have created a state of uncertainty, indifference, and decline of traditional values that provided nourishment for optimism and stability in the past. According to the Hungarian psychiatric association (which, by the way, was not founded until 1980), every second Hungarian suffers from some form of neurosis. This was revealed in the political and economic weekly of the Communist Youth League, *Ötlet [Idea]*.[42] The periodical blamed this high incidence of neuroses on the ever-increasing number of hours worked by the average worker. According to a survey conducted by *Ötlet*, about 15 percent of the population takes sedatives on the job in order to cope with stress. About 50 percent of workers have difficulty falling asleep at night because of problems encountered on the job; the same number of interviewees had jittery stomachs because of nervous tension and 31 percent of them suffer from regular migraine headaches. Of those questioned, 45 percent had 2 or more of the above symptoms. Similar findings were

Table 5.5
Suicides in Hungary 1921–1982

Year	Number of Suicides (yearly average)	Suicides per 100,000 People
1921–25	2,289	28.0
1931–35	2,910	32.9
1945	3,006	33.3
1946	2,144	23.8
1948	2,178	23.8
1950	2,074	22.2
1952	2,407	25.3
1953	1,999	20.8
1954	1,772	17.7
1955	2,015	20.5
1956	1,923	19.4
1958	2,312	23.4
1960	2,592	26.0
1962	2,532	25.2
1963	2,720	27.0
1964	2,903	28.7
1965	3,020	29.8
1967	3,150	30.8
1968	3,457	33.7
1970	3,582	34.6
1971	3,697	35.7
1972	3,851	37.0
1973	3,854	36.8
1974	4,307	41.1
1975	4,020	38.1
1976	4,304	40.6
1977	4,390	41.2
1978	4,525	42.3
1979	4,770*	44.9
1980	4,809*	45.2*
1981	4,880*	45.6*
1982	4,569*	43.5*
1984	4,764	44.7

Statistical Yearbook 1981, 1982, 1984.
Source: Mihály Gergely, *Röpírat az Öngyilkosságról* [Leaflet on Suicide] (Budapest: Medicina, 1981), 14, 58, 122.

reached by the National Insurance Company of Hungary. Of course neuroses, according to several psychologists and sociologists, are not only job-related problems. The rapidly changing nature of current society is held much to blame. The disruption of the population's sense of its past and its national identity, rapid changes in lifestyles, double standards in the economy, and similar factors have given rise to a shapeless and confused society.

SEX WITHIN AND OUTSIDE THE FAMILY

Since women in Hungary usually work about 8–8 1/2 hours a day, most children quite early wind up in preschool institutions; nursery up to the age of 3, kindergarten after that. Many plants or institutions have their own kindergartens, which makes it convenient to deliver the child there. In these daycare centers, boys and girls soon get used to each other's company, which has advantages as well as drawbacks. One great advantage is that the difference between the sexes becomes accepted as natural, even in the case of children where there are no siblings of the other sex. An early curiosity among children concerns who has or does not have something "between the legs." Children quite early become enlightened about the details of childbirth and learn some of the more vulgar expressions. The early, exaggerated information, however, often results in problems (e.g., when four-year-old girls, living in overcrowded apartments, play a game called "stick-it-in" with five-year-old neighbor boys). Thus, the interest in the opposite sex begins long before it has any biological meaning.

At age six, the children begin school. At first there is a degree of rivalry between the boys and the girls, in studying and in sports as well. But by the age of 12–13, more serious activity begins. Some of the examples are provided by parents and some by television or the movies, which are full of kissing and bedroom scenes, along with rather explicit language. In more affluent families, children may have access (when the parents are at work) to pornographic movies, which were smuggled into Hungary and are very popular VCR entertainment. Girls and boys both try to demonstrate that they are "grown up" by trying to imitate these scenes. At first they only kiss, but soon they also initiate sexual activities. A female elementary school teacher told the following story at a teacher's conference. As part of her duties, she was responsible for the "protection of youth." In grades 7 and 8, there was at least one pregnancy each year. The problem was that neither the teacher nor the majority of the kids noticed the pregnancies. It came to light only when the pregnant girls became ill, or when a sharp-eyed gym teacher noticed it. In the case of the latter, it was often too late. The situation is the same with the boys. The kids are generally poorly informed about sexual functions. Many of them have never heard about contraceptives, and because of fear of their parents they would not have any available anyway. So, in the cases of "getting acquainted" at age 13–14, the outcome is often pregnancy. Of course, boys' friends consider this kind of sexual contact as a valuable experience, as a "good deal." They are often quite envious of each other for it. For example, a university student ran into a 17-year-old girl at a party. She behaved like a worldly woman, and they wound up in his room. When he noticed that she was still a virgin, she simply told him that she was "embarrassed that nobody wanted her yet."

According to a saying in Budapest, there are three things necessary for good sexual contact: "Someone to do it with, something to do it with, and somewhere to do it." When one is young, there is seldom a problem with the first two requirements. But there is often a problem with the "where?" During school years, there is not much of a problem; the parents are seldom home before 5 or 6 p.m., while school lets out at 2 or 3 p.m. There is a 3-hour hiatus. Sometimes as many couples go up to an apartment as it has rooms. If there is a sibling, he or she can be part of the activities, or else he or she can be sent away, perhaps to a movie. If the family has a weekend house and uses it over the weekends, the apartment becomes available for a few days. Parties are frequent meeting places—they are unsupervised and often end in lovemaking.

Teenage girls are desirable for older men, not only because of their youth and beauty, but because they are not demanding. A dinner or a small gift will get results. The age of consent is 14; below that, it is rape, regardless of consent. Men often check the girl's ID card before they take her up to their rooms. There is a Hungarian anecdote about it. Question: "When does a Budapest girl go to bed?" Answer, "At 8, because by 10 she has to be home." The girls are naive, it is easy to gain their confidence. The "father-complex" often contributes to their naivete; the girls seldom notice that the men only look for a quick bed-partner.

After finishing high school, the young person no longer has the free time to "fool around." If the youngster continues his education, the pattern of behavior remains the same. But if he or she takes a job, the chances for daytime sex are radically reduced. Because of lack of time and space, many young people seek a way out through early marriage. In such cases, the differentiation between love and desire is obscured. Of course they can't escape entirely from their parents, but now they can do anything they want in their own room; they have a license to do it. Due to a lack of emotional contact, the result is often alienation, which is exacerbated by the cohabitation with one partner's in-laws. As pointed out above, family fights are a common occurrence in such intergenerational living situations. One typical young couple interviewed in Budapest lived with the husband's in-laws for two-and-a-half years in a small, 3-room apartment. During that time the son-in-law was subjected to unusual stress in an explosive living situation that led to daily conflicts with the in-laws. Here are some examples of incidents that occurred in that family:

1. In order to acquire more money (for the purchase of their own apartment), the husband took on more and more work. He would come home around 9:00 in the evening. The in-laws could not pass this up without making nasty, ill-intentioned remarks.

2. Frequently the mother-in-law would enter the young couple's room, because she explained, some of her stuff was stored there. Most of the time this was not a great problem, but in the evening or in the middle of the night, this often interrupted private activities. When the children asked her to leave at times like this, she would cry for hours about the lack of love.

3. The mother-in-law would behave the same way in the bathroom/toilet, regardless of what one might be doing in there.

4. The son-in-law was a record collector. On Sunday mornings he would stay home to listen to his records, instead of going to church with the rest of the family. This used to earn him regular abuse, and when the in-laws and wife arrived home, the mother-in-law would immediately turn off his stereo.

5. Other members of the in-law family made every effort to make the son-in-law look bad.

As in other cultures, mothers-in-law are frequently subject to ridicule. In Hungary there is an abundance of jokes about the mother-in-law:

"Why do they bury mothers-in-law with their heads downward?"
Answer: "So they will scratch their way out the wrong way."

"Why do they place Alka-Seltzer in the mother-in-law's coffin?"
Answer: "So the worms won't get an upset stomach."

An old woman is hanging out the window of an 8th story apartment, and a man is hammering away at her grappling fingers with a hammer.
A passer-by: "What are you doing to that poor old lady?"
The man: "She is not an old lady; she is my mother-in-law!"
Passer-by: "Look how stubbornly the old bitch is hanging on!"

Aron is working in the forest, when they bring him the news that his mother-in-law has died. He continues to work. Later, his father comes out and asks him why he did not come running in when he heard the news. Aron's answer: "Work before pleasure!"

One major cause for the alienation between young marrieds is their forced coexistence with their elders. There are other reasons as well, for example, overwork. On simple salaries, they can just get by. If they can't save money, they can't think about an apartment of their own. So they accept extra work, which in turn brings on nervousness, tenseness, and irritability. This goes on for years, to each other's detriment. Often, they divorce after they have obtained an apartment of their own.

The young wife takes care of the house and raises the child or children. As a result, she falls behind her husband in intellectual development. The "primitive" woman becomes embarrassing in front of "elegant" company. After a while, the husband tries to get rid of her.

If the woman stays home to raise the child (the State provides a three-year paid period for her to do this), then she looks forward to years of boredom. Often the only way out of this is the "friend of the family," who visits her during the day.

Men may work far away from home, even abroad, leaving the wives behind. During the week, many of these lonely and bored wives are regularly visited by a "friend," after children are put to bed.

Due to a variety of reasons, divorce is often the only answer. This has different implications for men and for women.

The woman—especially if there is a child—is materially secure. She will get the apartment, and if it can't be divided, the husband will be asked to move out. They don't put him out on the street, but offer him the choice of at least three subleases. He has to take one of them, regardless of the price. After this, the rent for the sublease combined with the child support (20 percent of his salary for one child, 40 percent for two children, and 50 percent for three or more) will take most of his money. He can forget about saving up enough money for another apartment. Of course, he can always marry another woman with an apartment of her own. But this can turn out to be simply a case of "from one bad marriage into another."

In divorces, if the apartment is owned by the couple, its value will be split. If it is a rented unit, the woman stays and the husband can take half of the remaining assets. Everything is more complicated if the unit is big enough so that it can be co-inhabited by both of them. A series of actions begins, as each tries to get rid of the other. In the case of the vegetable seller, this is what happened. The court gave both daughters to the mother. The only chance he had was to morally ruin the woman, so he could prove that she was not fit to raise the children. He paid one of his virile and good looking acquaintances (unknown to his former wife) a handsome amount to seduce her. The woman's confidence was easily gained, and one evening (after announcing that he was going to be out of town) the husband was able to surprise his wife in an act of infidelity, in the company of witnesses, and so on. The following day he asked the court to change its verdict and to take the children away from the "immoral" woman. Meanwhile, the woman had her own tricks going. Knowing that the man was quick to anger, she provoked a violent fight, which ended in a heavy slap by the husband. She ran out of the house, yelling for help and claiming that the "beast" wanted to kill her. The next day she also sued him, for battery, and demanded that he be removed from the premises. It seems impossible to get rid of a former, undesirable mate peacefully. The situation can become unbearable, resulting in silent bitterness, dirty tricks played on each other, and occasionally attempted murder or even murder.

The child can become an instrument for harassment or blackmail. The courts decide precisely the frequency of visits, but it is common to hear of denial of visits, or the forced extra visits.

A few years ago, an interesting case made the headlines. A stranger (claiming to be the mother's sister) took a 3-year-old girl from a kindergarten. The police investigated for weeks, and the picture of the child was shown on TV. The culprit: A divorced woman whose daughter had been legally removed from her because of the mother's past as a prostitute. She went to a small village, mended her ways, and her new friends started suggesting to her that she could get her child back if she went to the courts. She was too lazy to do this, and she could not find the child, who was with the child's father. So, in order to prove her moral worth and courage, she stole someone else's child and presented it as her own. It did not occur to her that television viewers in the village would recognize the child and report her to the police. Furthermore, kidnapping a child is impractical because any new inhabitant must have an ID and must be reported to the district council.

A soured marriage does not have to end in divorce. Why should one have to pay, if in the end the two still have to live under the same roof? Of course, the two partners may stay together for other reasons as well, for the sake of the children, for example. In cases like this, pleasant, peaceful coexistence can develop, even in the sharing of finances. Both partners confine their sexual activities to outside the family unit, and they simply do not discuss this. In the case of a family with three children, husband and wife have their fun together (movies, theatre, concerts), and on occasion they even have sex, although this is rare. They realize that if one of them became emotionally involved with an outsider that could present problems. Three years ago, a husband almost filed for divorce; he had met a younger but extremely crafty student. He fell in love. She was too eager and pushed for divorce too soon and too hard. He was strong enough to break up with the young lady. In a situation like this, the biggest problem is that of "Where?" One can't bring the other person home, after all. Borrowing an apartment from a friend is the usual solution. The "tryst" hotels have not caught on in Hungary yet, and the legitimate hotels are expensive. On the other hand, one can always borrow the place of a friend for 2–3 hours, in exchange for the promise of a half bottle of booze. If one has a nice office, one does not even have to go this far, or if one owns a car, one can always use the mountain greenery for romantic purposes.

Sex for money is something else. This came to light during a 1985 court case in Szeged, Hungary. On June 7, 1985, the Csongrád County Court in Szeged sentenced Kálmán Rácz, a 29-year-old former waiter, to three years and four months in prison and his accomplices from 5 months to 3 years, as well as a fine totaling one million forints, on charges of procuring and currency offenses.[43] The trial created a sensation in Hungary, so much so that a women's weekly, *Nök Lapja [Women's Paper]*, devoted two extensive articles in consecutive issues to the trial, including an analysis of Rácz's personality based on an interview conducted in the prison where he was detained.[44] The fascination was also justified on ideological grounds. After all, prostitution is not supposed to exist in communist countries. (See Chapter 3, under "But Money Talks.") A generation ago the Hungarian authorities claimed that it was only in a socialist society that prostitution could be eliminated, since "socialism" assured the full equality of women.[45]

Prostitution is officially banned in communist countries. After the transfer of power in 1949–1950, all licensed brothels were closed in Hungary. Prostitutes were "re-trained" for other professions—many of them became taxi drivers and at times remembered how to make use of the oldest profession in the world, if and when the opportunity was favorable. Thus "socialism" did not fully conquer the oldest profession. From time to time the press reported the discovery of prostitution rings or the arrest of those violating the socialist moral code. The number of women arrested for prostitution was always very small, however (e.g., only 127 in 1983). The reason is that prostitutes can avoid criminal prosecution for prostitution by obtaining a work permit for some other kind of work; the result is that "prostitution" convictions are often subsumed under convictions for loitering. Whether it is loitering or prostitution, in 1981 a television program on crime, "The Blue Light," openly admitted that "even the socialist way of life is unable to stop gainful carnal pleasure, that is, prostitution."[46] Thus in October 1984, the Presidential Council introduced tougher penalties for vagrancy and related crimes, prostitution among them. These measures were taken when it became clear that many people in Hungary were earning large sums of money that were never reported to the tax authorities. A "lady of the night" interviewed in "The Blue Light" program admitted to a yearly income of 1,500,000 forints, or more than 5,000 forints per day—the average monthly wage in Hungary.[47]

In fact, it was this kind of income that was reported by the 15 "Cuki cuties," all dolled up in the latest fashions, ostentatiously displaying their gold and jewelry in the Csongrád County courtroom when they went on trial with their "Godfather," Kálmán Rácz and his accomplices. The charges against them: running and participating in a callgirl racket for foreign truck drivers, currency violations, and receiving stolen goods.[48]

It seems that until Christmas 1984 the Cuki Expresso bar, located outside Szeged near a highway frequently used by foreign truck drivers, was doing all sorts of business: a snack bar, a currency exchange, and a "comfort station" (i.e., a brothel) for foreign truck drivers. The people who frequented Cuki were not only truck drivers but all kinds of vagrants, homosexuals, and many women between 15 to 38 years of age. One could buy almost anything there, from blue jeans to American cigarettes and black market items as well as foreign currency. The most sought after clientele were foreign truck drivers from the West with hard currency. Kálmán Rácz had managed the Cuki Expresso Bar since October 1981 and by summer 1983 he added prostitution to his business. He rented several apartments in Szeged where he would keep his "Cuki's girls" for his favorite customers. As leader and chief pimp, he also employed shuttle service drivers from the bar to the apartments. Most of the customers paid in foreign currency and the prices averaged DM 30–100/U.S.$10–20/500–1,000 Austrian shillings. As business improved, prices went up. All in all the Cuki Expresso Bar became a multimillion-forints operation. Kálmán Rácz and his male accomplices were arrested in late December 1984 and the "Cuki cuties" were arraigned shortly thereafter.[49] They were sentenced to serve 5–14 months.[50]

While the "girls" maintained that they were forced into it, according to Rácz, none of the girls had been forced into prostitution. "It was not necessity that drove them to this life—only their greed for money." However, it was also money that motivated the authorities to seek retribution for lost revenues.

HOW MUCH UNTO CAESAR AND HOW MUCH UNTO GOD

Churches in Hungary today are at the mercy of the state, not only politically but also financially. By 1950, all church property had been confiscated and all religious orders disbanded, with some minor exceptions in the field of education. During that year Hungary's Roman Catholic Primate, József Cardinal Mindszenty, was sentenced to life in prison and his staunch followers subjected to persecution, repression, police raids, terrorism, and mental anguish. After the forced disintegration of organized religion in Hungary, in 1950 the Rákosi dictatorship decided to rebuild the churches in Hungary in the image of the revolution and thus the state agreed to give financial support for a period of 18 years with the anticipation that the churches would either succumb to the new order or else be eliminated. On April 26, 1984, the chairman of the State Office for Church Affairs [SOCA] and state secretary, Imre Miklós, stated that the state has continued to provide financial aid to the churches since January 1, 1969, "because it was needed and also because of the existing good state relations."[51] According to Miklós, state aid to priests amounted to about 74 million forints a year and state aid to religious schools was 4 million forints. In addition, churches receive some 30 percent of the sum allocated in the state budget for the maintenance of historical buildings, since they own about one third of them. Incidentally, the so-called church-owned historical buildings are houses of worship and museums that represent national assets rather than private ownership. The only additional income the churches receive is from the believers' donations and financial aid from abroad in the amount of about 1.5–2 million dollars a year. However, even with the additional aid from abroad, according to Miklós, religious organizations in Hungary have become completely dependent on the communist state, in spite of the often proclaimed principle of the separation of church and state. Constitutionally, all churches and religious organizations are equal. There are twenty altogether: the Catholic, Reformed and Lutheran Churches, the Israelite Religion Association, thirteen denominations united in the Hungarian Council of Free Churches, the Greek Orthodox and the Hungarian Unitarian churches, plus the Hungarian Buddhist Mission. Relations between the state and the country's so-called "free" denominations—there are 13 of them—are conducted in the spirit of the agreement signed with the other churches.

The most significant among these agreements was the one signed between Hungary and the Vatican on September 15, 1964, "which has led to the essential securing and consolidation of the church's domestic situation,"[52] or more appropriately to a concordat allowing the state to dictate its terms. Or, as Party Leader János Kádár put it in February 1976, "The churches, without exception, are loyal to our system and accept socialism as the country's goal and program . . . this compromise promoted rather than harmed a cause of the revolution . . . this is not an ideological concession but political cooperation carried out in the interest of set political goals. . . . "[53] In other words, the Hungarian authorities were not about to promote a real rival of both religiousness and the churches. Instead they created a new concept of relationship between party and nonparty members and among workers, peasants, and intellectuals called "HSWP's policy of alliance." It was therefore no fluke when First Secretary János Kádár remarked to the 13th HSWP Congress in 1985 that the settled relations between church and state were a good example of the party's successful alliance policy.

In the 1964 document three points were agreed upon between the Vatican and the Hungarian government. First, certain episcopal appointments were accepted by both sides. Secondly, the oath of allegiance to the constitution and the laws of Hungary, which had to be taken by certain people holding church offices, was to be considered binding by the church, but only insofar as those laws did not contradict the principles of the Christian faith. Thirdly, the Hungarian Papal Institute in Rome was to be administered by priests acceptable to the Hungarian government. In return the government guaranteed that the Papel Institute's activities would not be disrupted and that every year each Hungarian diocese would be allowed to send a young priest there. These three points of agreement constituted a major breakthrough for the Holy See, establishing contacts with a socialist country in the Soviet bloc. The 1964 agreement opened a new phase of dialogue between two opposing belief systems. Today, as in 1964, the Vatican view is based on the assumption that Marxism-Leninism and the Catholic faith are irreconcilable, that the Marxist-Leninist authorities are wrong when they restrict human freedoms, especially religious freedoms, and that criticism therefore of Marxism-Leninism is not only justified but necessary. The Vatican also believes, however, that dialogue with Marxist-Leninist authorities is imperative in order to improve the situation of Catholics in those countries and thereby enhance civil liberties in socialist societies. The Vatican is cognizant of the fact that dialogue with Marxist-Leninist authorities is a two-way street requiring cooperation from the latter. Therefore, the sharp confrontations between state and church have gradually been supplanted by a modus vivendi based on mutual compromises and concessions. From the Marxist-Leninist point of view, however, a dialogue with the churches—including the Roman Catholic Church—is cooperation with them but only insofar as this cooperation does not jeopardize the leading role of the party in Hungarian life and society. As pointed out in Chapter 2, especially in the "Conclusions," the "alliance" (or sometimes called "hegemony" policy) is an outgrowth of the concept of socialist development motivated by highly practical considerations such as winning the support of the broad strata of organized Hungarian society toward "national unity" and the building of socialism. In other words, the party rulers, in order to accomplish their objectives of building socialism in Hungary, established a partnership relationship with organized groups, according to which the party assumed full power and responsibility for the state's affairs. As State Secretary Imre Miklós pointed out, while a given church represents its own followers, the state (i.e., the ruling elite of the party) represents the interests of all Hungarian citizens. The power of the state is in the hands of the party, just as the church has power over the soul, and neither power should be abused.[54] Politics aside, most church leaders in Hungary believe that there are sufficient common objectives to warrant a dialogue between church and state despite the criticism from some quarters claiming that the Hungarian religious leaders are too accommodating. József Cserháti, Bishop of Pécs and secretary of the Bench of Catholic Bishops, for example, defined the common objectives of church and state as "the creation of a new humanism that emphasizes the interests of the community, a broader democracy that stresses the priority of the individual and the promotion of a stronger social bond that could be called socialist democracy but that we define primarily as a more humane democracy."[55]

The chief and most influential advocate of peaceful coexistence between church and state was the late László Cardinal Lékai, the Roman Catholic Primate of Hungary from 1976 to 1986. To him, the most important thing for Hungarian Catholics was to be loyal citizens of their country and at the same time to search for God with the help of the church.[56] With the apparent approval of the Vatican, Lékai followed a policy of "small steps," aimed at reconciling differences and improving relations between church and state. His policy of "small steps" followed the road of "quiet, peaceful dialogue," which he argued was fully supported by the Vatican because it had been initiated by the Holy See and had produced good results.[57]

Similar views were expressed by non-Catholics in the other churches' hierarchies. For example, the president of the Lutheran World Federation, Bishop Zoltán Káldy, is of the opinion that the primary role of the church in society is to serve in cooperation with the system rather than to criticize state policy. Just as Lékai did, Káldy occupies a seat in the Hungarian Parliament and frequently expresses views on foreign policy that are very similar to those of the Soviet Union. What Káldy describes as "theology of service," others have referred to as "political collaboration."[58]

Another example of Marxist-Christian dialogue is the international conference that took place in Budapest at the end of February 1984. It was attended by 60 Marxist and Christian philosophers and theologians from 15 countries. The outcome of the conference was a proclamation specifying that the guidelines for Marxist-Christian dialogue must be based on "respect for each other's viewpoint" and a "better atmosphere for the solution of current conflicts and common human problems."[59]

Reflecting on the history of church/state relationship in the Soviet Union, one might ask why does the party need the churches? Why to solicit the cooperation of church organizations and why should the communist authorities in Hungary provide legitimacy and fora to religious leaders when they themselves are wedded to the idea of atheism and anti-religious propaganda? The answer to these questions lies in the peculiarity of the Hungarian road to socialism. As alluded to in Chapter 1, under "Hungarian Theory of Socialism," after 1956 the party leaders recognized the mistakes of the Rákosi era and to correct the situation pledged themselves to extend "democracy" to the broad masses of workers, peasants, and other social strata under the umbrella of the "united front." They recognized that socialism cannot be the cause of the members of HSWP alone. Socialist democracy, they argued, requires a comprehensive exchange of views and participation in society-framing action by working masses, public opinion, party and nonparty members as well as believers and nonbelievers (atheists).[60] This thesis became even more acute after the new Hungarian reforms were set in motion in 1968. The party and state authorities depended on the support of the broad strata to make the new economic policy work. The New Economic Mechanism [NEM], as it was called, had its ups and downs. Since the end of the 1970s mounting economic and social problems have threatened the political stability painstakingly achieved by the Kádár leadership in the aftermath of Hungary's traumatic national crisis of October 1956. In the 1980s the party alone can no longer cope with the many aspects of a growing social malaise that could lead to general destabilization. With national unity endangered, the Hungarian authorities had no alternative but to turn to the churches for support. As we pointed out earlier in this chapter there are several problem areas of common interest between church and state. They include such social problems as the mounting rates of abortion, suicide, alcoholism, juvenile delinquency, prostitution, and criminality, a decrease in the country's birthrate, and the fragmentation of family life. In 1984, for example, there were between 50 to 60 church-run charitable institutions in the country. Despite disagreement between state and church over such issues as the opening times of churches, religious education, the shortage of clergymen and how to make up for it, the institution of compulsory education, the abolition of denominational equality, and others, progress was slow but nevertheless forthcoming. In 1984, for instance, the government agreed to the establishment of a women's religious order, a longstanding Catholic church request. Since 1982 it is possible to hold religious classes in parish halls, whenever existing church buildings prove inadequate. Another breakthrough is the growing involvement of lay persons, who, after studying theology, can now teach catechism and perform other tasks. Church members have also been given a new opportunity to function as social workers. For years the clergy has aided the old, the sick, and the mentally retarded in homes and healthcare centers. Thus, where the socialist planners and ideologues have failed, the churches are now being given an opportunity to join the common rescue operation. The first priority of the Kádár regime during the present period of turbulent economic and social problems is to maintain and strengthen "national unity," even if it means more concessions to religious organizations.

As for other achievements, on the occasion of the tenth anniversary of his appointment as archbishop of Esztergom, Lékai listed among the "fruits of mutual goodwill" the setting up of a three-year correspondence course in theology for some 450 laymen a year at the Catholic Theological Academy of Budapest; the establishment of a house for spiritual exercises for Roman Catholics at Leányfalu (near Budapest) and the Hungarian chapel in St. Peter's Basilica in Rome; the growth of Catholic book publishing (in 1984, for example, a total of 98 religious works were published, including hymn books, catechisms, the Bible, and religious belleslettres); the construction of new churches and religious buildings (according to State Secretary Miklós, a total of 628 churches have been built in Hungary since 1945); and the increasing participation of the church in the care of the elderly, sick, and handicapped.[61] The most recent progress characterizing church/state relations, agreed on in March 1986, was the expansion of a new female religious order to run social and charity services and the increasing role of specially trained laymen who are allowed to perform certain rites and functions to alleviate the worsening shortage of priests. The religious order, which was formally founded in 1985, has no connection with any preexisting religious order. It brings together women, who as nuns, provide social and charity services. It is called the Sisters of Our Lady of Hungary.[62] The operation of this order started in Budapest and will eventually be expanded throughout Hungary. It is important to note that before the new group was founded the four existing religious orders in Hungary were limited to teaching only.

The Hungarian authorities and episcopate also reached an agreement on the creation of the corps of lay cooperators. The latter may be men or women, married or single, and they may serve full-time or part-time on either a temporary or permanent basis. Most of the cooperators at present are graduates of the adult theology courses the late Cardinal Lékai initiated a few years ago. The bishops choose the cooperators but the government authorities reserve the right to reject the choice. Only permanent full-time cooperators need swear allegiance to the state, as priests must. Because they are not ordained, they cannot sacramentally consecrate the Eucharist or impart the sacrament of confirmation or holy orders. Although unable to celebrate Mass, they can substitute for a priest in many ways that make them unique within the Catholic church.

On the negative side, the churches—especially the Roman Catholic Church—face many problems and criticisms. Among the many criticisms that have been leveled against the late Cardinal Lékai and his bishops is the charge that they have gone too far on the path of compromise with the promoters of atheism, thus allegedly "letting religion be ground down" in Hungary.[63] Mostly because of distrust, many believers have turned away from organized religion and gone so far as to form their own basic communities. Thousands of small prayer and meditation groups have sprung up since the mid-1970s, each usually with a small number of members, many of them young people and intellectuals. Some basic communities, especially those grouped around Father György Bulányi, a Piarist priest, have criticized the Catholic church "authorities" for their ready acquiescence in the state control of the church. In March 1982 the Conference of the Council of Bishops accused Father Bulányi and his followers of spreading mistaken teachings about the faith and of wanting to introduce a new church discipline. In June 1982 Father Bulányi was suspended. Under the instructions from state authorities to "create order" in its own ranks, the church hierarchy transferred young priests sympathetic to dissidents to other parishes. They were also condemned for having advocated pacifist views and for having encouraged conscientious objection to military service. Again at the state authorities' urging, Cardinal Lékai openly rejected such views and disciplined several priests who supported them. It is interesting to note that Hungary's Christian denominations do not forbid military service in principle, except for the Nazarenes, who cannot take up arms and who, on the basis of an accord with the state, serve for a shorter time and without carrying arms. While ten to twelve Nazarenes a year are able to serve without bearing arms, between 100 and 150 conscientious objectors in Hungary are serving from 30 to 36 months for refusing to bear arms.

The basic communities have also come into conflict with the church hierarchy over matters of doctrine. They have accused the church of having compromised too much with the communist authorities and, therefore, call for a return to a more fundamentalistic form of religion. The response of the church hierarchy was expressed by Cardinal Lékai in 1983.[64] According to Lékai, the basic communities were like "wild offshoots," originating from neither the roots nor the stem of the church. The church was trying to cut them back "carefully and with love" so that they would not harm the discipline and unity of the Hungarian church. The basic communities, however, were opposed to any pruning and, therefore, continued in their struggle against the Marxist-accommodating church hierarchy. So much so that in an interview in 1984, State Secretary Imre Miklós stated that the most important objective in the development of church/state relations was the strengthening of national unity through the consolidation of the "political alliance of peoples with different ideologies" and the increasing participation of religious believers in public affairs.[65] Miklós' concern was fully justified in view of the fact that the overwhelming majority of youth has rejected the official Marxist-Leninist ideology, although some of them pay mandatory lip-service to it in order to ensure their own well-being, and many of them opted to follow religion. The question is, whose religion? The churches, the Catholic church in particular, are worried about this trend because they are unable—unlike in Poland—to attract young men to the priesthood. The main concern of both church and state is the widespread alienation felt by many young people who seek a solution in the basic communities instead of either the Communist Youth League (KISz) or the organized church.[66]

Aging and the steady decrease in the number of Hungarian clergymen make it increasingly difficult for the churches to provide communities with religious services. About 60 percent of Hungary's population of over 10 million belong to the Catholic faith, at least in name. The rest are either atheists or belong to several smaller religious orders among which the Reformed (Calvinist) and Lutheran churches are the largest. About 4 percent of Hungarian citizens are Lutherans. The Catholics are grouped in eleven dioceses with 2,228 parishes. In 1986 there were only 2,600 priests and 250 monks and nuns, compared with 3,583 and 11,538, respectively, in 1950. More than half of the bishops heading Hungary's eleven dioceses are in their 70s and several of them in poor health. On July 8, 1986, Archbishop László Paskai, aged 59, was elected as the new chairman of the Bench of Hungarian Catholic Bishops to replace László Cardinal Lékai, who passed away on June 30, 1986, at the age of 76. Paskai is expected to follow Lékai's policy of "small steps" in both church and social affairs.[67] If one accepts the opinions expressed by a sample of people on a television program called "66," then the continuity of the policy of coexistence between church and state is the only course for the future. On April 26, 1984, a 60–minute television interview of the Chairman of SOCA, Imre Miklós, with a participating audience (with the aid of electronic buttons) of 66 people, gave responses to a host of probing questions by the producer of the program, János Bán, as well as the invited members of the audience. At the start of the program 65 of the 66 audience members agreed that today's Hungarian society could only be built collectively by believers and nonbelievers. Similarly 41 members felt that improvement was needed with regard to church/state relations; 22 felt they were good and 3 that they were bad. The audience was also optimistic about ongoing negotiations between state and church: 60 members felt that most issues under debate could be solved, 4 felt that there were significant differences, and 2 that the issues could not be resolved. On the question whether believers and Marxists should be tolerant of and cooperate with each other, 57 audience members said yes, 4 disagreed, and 5 had no opinion. It is interesting to note that among the 66 people in the audience, 8 were clergymen.[68]

CONCLUSIONS

The growing social malaise and the lack of confidence in the future is best reflected by the continuing demographic fall, the rising crime rate among the youth, the high level of alcohol consumption and of suicides, the large number of divorces, and the fragmentation of the family. There seems to be an inherent contradiction in the Hungarian social policy that, on the one hand, calls for social progress through tranquil functioning of the family unit, and on the other, the recognition that the symmetrical family unit no longer meets some of the needs of both society and individuals. The need to hold two or more jobs to make ends meet has resulted in rising mental confusion of the individual, who is searching for an identity based on cultural and socioeconomic stability. The authorities are no longer trying to hide the facts about these ills but find it difficult to make up for decades of neglect in such areas as health services, social benefits, housing, the training of young people, the caring for the aged, and other problems.

In a survey conducted by the Mass Communications Research Center in Budapest in December 1984, 45 percent of a sample group of 1,200 people said that the last five years in Hungary had been characterized by worries and problems.[69] The most vital problem mentioned was, as in other surveys, housing, which was cited by every second person (48 percent). Equal weight (41 percent) was given to the improvement of the situation of pensioners; improvement of health services was mentioned by 33 percent and the betterment of the situation of young people by 32 percent of the respondents. By January 21, 1986, when these and other issues were aired on Radio Budapest between the popular writer Bulcsú Bertha and Mihály Kupa, a head of department in the Ministry of Finance,[70] it was evident that the worries and problems in Hungary had increased rather than decreased. Responding to Bertha's suggestion that some of the money allocated to various social programs be used to increase wages, Kupa asserted that financially the country was already "standing on the edge of a cliff." Certain basic entitlement programs had to be maintained, pensions had to be paid and adjusted, and prices had to be kept down. This was costing more and more money. At the same time, he explained, the economy had continued to fail to generate enough funds to keep up with the growing cost of these programs. It did not help that the subsistence level had risen to around 3,200 forints (a very high figure when one considers that in 1984 70 percent of the country's 2,215,300 pensioners made up 20.7 percent of the population[71] and were receiving less than 3,000 forints per month), which was considerably higher than previous estimates.

The lack of central resources, however, was not the only or even the main reason for the widening gulf between the rich and the poor. Much more serious reasons were the social injustices that were permitted to regenerate themselves. Communism, with its promise of "complete equality," Kupa added, was a "distant thing." Although differences in character, talent, flexibility, personal initiative, and so on played a role, social origin still remained a decisive factor in determining who would and who would not succeed in Hungary today. While Kupa admitted the existence of enormous inequalities in the country, he argued that, in order to promote economic development, talent and performance had to be rewarded. The problem was more with illegal and dishonest income and less with private initiative. Kupa also warned that should economic fairness and justice fail in the future, the government would be forced to rely more heavily on "disciplinary measures" and perhaps even "reintroduce a kind of egalitarian system" that would only hinder economic development.

In other words, while on the surface the main worries and problems appear to be strictly economic in nature (e.g., the polarization between the new rich and the poor), the deeper causes of inequality in present-day Hungary are social in manifestation, stemming from a basic change in the family structure. There seems to be a cause—effect relationship between the newly emerging unisex family with two breadwinners and the aspirations of both coequal members for affluence and a childless, free-of-responsibility modern life. Therefore, the demographic worries in Hungary are fully justified. If the projection that the population of Hungary will have fallen by 350,000 by the turn of the century is right, the proportion of the largely unproductive people will grow and man-power will fall. If the national political boundaries become more open, a massive immigration into Hungary may occur, which would create problems of assimilation. There are those in Hungary today who look upon population growth as a moral question. To them, economic considerations are secondary; childless couples or parents with a single child are individualist egotists, and indifferent to the national interest. On the opposite side of the spectrum are those Hungarians who condemn the above views and who argue that more children are born when the economic conditions of the families are improving. Yet according to a popular writer and literary historian, Dömökös Varga, "The more children there are in a family the lower its standard of living."[72] Of course, the size of the family depends on many other phenomena, including the instability of the institution of marriage, the high divorce rate, abortion, alcoholism, and suicide—all are symptomatic of the social disintegration of traditional values at the center of which stood the asymmetrical family unit. The inner nucleus of that organization was held together by a set of norms that were deeply rooted in religious faith.

Today that faith in some cases has been replaced by a new materialism. While Marxism-Leninism provides the official foundation for this materialism, private initiative and private enterprise encouraged by the economic reform since 1968 attract a large segment of the society toward materialism, and the compromised churches and religious associations are no barrier to the motivation for material rewards sought by the multitudes. As a matter of fact, the religious organizations signed an agreement pledging loyalty and support to the state, which in turn gives them the legitimacy to function as defenders of the soul. But Hungarians who have staunchly retained their faith prefer to organize their own small, independent prayer groups, known as basic communities, rather than submit to the official hierarchy of the churches, who advocate co-existence and cooperation between believers and Marxist-Leninist atheists. The most impressive phenomenon today is the resurgence of religiousness, perhaps as a result of official persecution or as a reaction against the new materialism. This resurgence of religious belief had spread to all social strata and age groups. According to Miklós Tomka of the Mass Communications Institute of Hungarian Radio, the enduring appeal of Christian values is the chief reason for the reassertion of religious belief among Hungarians.[73] This finding, of course, contradicts the allegations made by the official press that the trend in the rise of religiousness in Hungary is a product of economic difficulties and social problems. Tomka's survey indicates that even though as many as 79–82 percent of all believers have for years stopped actively practicing their religion, their faith has remained unshaken and in many cases has perhaps been strengthened by trying times. The chairman of SOCA, Imre Miklós, himself admitted that the communists were to blame for this situation because atheistic Marxist-Leninist ideology had been unable to provide a compelling alternative.[74] In its efforts to change the attitude of the young Hungarians who have become disenchanted and cynical amid the current difficult situation in their country, the state authorities have reluctantly concluded that they need the support of the churches not only for maintaining national unity but also to carry out the much needed social and charity services among the old, the sick, and the mentally retarded in homes, hospitals, and healthcare centers. What better way to find a solution to some of the national social ills than to dump them into the lap of the churches. As a result, the churches—especially the Roman Catholic Church—have a basis for seeking a greater and more active role within the framework of Hungary's present society and political culture. There is, however, a caveat to this: the compromise is between two unequal partners. On the one hand, the state authorities have almost total control over society and can break the compromise with the religious organizations if they feel their authority seriously threatened. On the other hand, the religious organizations try to expand the limits of religion's social role without evoking the wrath of the political authorities. Priests, for example, must accept the dictatorial demands of their church leaders and of the State Office for Church Affairs. Those who refuse to comply, like Father György Bulányi, are likely to be disciplined by their bishops, most of whom believe in small gains won at the expense of relinquishing a degree of control over church life. In this respect one can argue the Hungarian Catholic Church occupies a special position within the Soviet bloc.

NOTES

1. Elemér Hankiss, "Felületes társadalom?" [Sloppy society?] *Valóság* (February 1986): 37–47.

2. See "A Monori Tanácskozás 14–16 Junius 1985" [The Monor Meeting 14–16 June 1985] (Budapest: Mimeographed Report, September 1985).

3. László Cseh-Szombathy, "The family, its members and society," *The New Hungarian Quarterly* 22 (Summer 1981): 57.

4. See Nagy Kázmér, *Elveszett alkotmány: A hidegháború és a magyar politikai emigráció 1945–1975* [The Lost Constitution: The Cold War and the Hungarian Political Emigration, 1945–1975] (London: Gondolat Kiadó, 1982).

5. See András Klinger, "Population policy in Hungary: Scope and limits," *The New Hungarian Quarterly* 23 (Summer 1982): 122.

6. See Éva Árokszállasi's interview with László Cseh-Szombathy, "Kis család, nagy család" [Small family, large family], *Magyar Hírek* [Hungarian News] 34 (May 9, 1986): 29.

7. András Klinger, op. cit., 122.

8. Ibid., 123.

9. Ibid., 123.

10. See Hungarian Situation Report #10, *Radio Free Europe Research* (July 11, 1983), item 6.

11. Klinger, op. cit., 123.

12. Ibid.

13. Zsolt Oszlányi, "Mai lakáshelyzet Magyarországon" [The Housing Situation in Hungary Today], *Társadalmi Szemle* (June 1985): 142–47.

14. See Péter Kertész, "Fordulópont" [Turning Point], *Magyar Nemzet* (December 7, 1983).

15. *Magyar Nemzet* (June 28, 1985).

16. See Magda Czernák, "Születési kohorzok elsö házasságköteseinek alakulása Magyarországon a második világháború után" [First marriages in Hungary after the Second World War in terms of both cohorts], *Demográfia* 4 (1982): 429–64.

17. See Árpád Mészáros and István Monigl, "A házasságon kívüli születések és ezek demográfiai összefüggesei" [Birth to unmarried mothers and their relationship to other demographic factors], *Demográfia* 2–3 (1982); 209–24.

18. Cseh-Szombathy, "The family, its members, and society," op. cit., 60.

19. B. András Bálint, "Népmozgalmi statisztika" [Demographic statistics], *Heti Világgazdaság*, (March 31, 1984).

20. Klinger, op. cit., 124.

21. Edit S. Molnár, "Birth control, abortion and public opinion," *The New Hungarian Quarterly* 23 (Summer 1982); 128.

22. Ibid.

23. See R.R. "Az idös lakósság problémai" [Problems of the older population], *Magyar Tudomány* (March 1984): 234–37.

24. *Statisztikai Évkönyv 1984* [1984 Statistical Yearbook] (Budapest: Central Statistical Office, 1985).

25. *Statisztikai Havi Közlemények* 2–3 (1985).

26. See Gábor Papp, "The aged in Hungary," *The New Hungarian Quarterly* 24 (Spring 1983); 130–39.

27. Papp, ibid., 133.

28. Ibid., 134.

29. Ibid.

30. See Éva Árokszállási's interview with Zsuzsa Ferge, "Túl a hatvanon" [Past sixty], *Magyar Hírek* 34 (April 25, 1986); 12–13.

31. Papp, op. cit., 136.

32. Rudolf Andorka, "Alkoholizmus és társadalom" [Alcoholism and society] *Népszabadság* (May 14, 1985).

33. *Magyarország,* (April 30, 1986).

34. *Magyar Hírlap* (March 27, 1986).

35. *Esti Hírlap* [Evening News] (March 26, 1986).

36. Rudolf Andorka, "Alkoholizmus a mai Magyar társadalomba" [Alcoholism in today's Hungarian society] *Pártélet* [Party Life] (May 1986): 29–33.

37. *Magyar Hírlap* (March 29, 1986).

38. *Magyarország* (April 30, 1986).

39. Mihály Gergély, *Röpírat az öngyilkosságról* [Leaflet on Suicide] (Budapest: Medicina, 1981), 14, 58, and 122.

40. See *U.S. News and World Report* (April 2, 1984).

41. *Statisztikai Zsebkönyv* [Statistical Pocketbook] (Budapest: Central Statistical Office, 1984).

42. *Ötlet* (April 24, 1986).

43. *Népszabadság* (June 8, 1985).

44. *Nök Lapja* (April 13 and 20, 1986).

45. *Új Magyar Lexikon* [New Hungarian Dictionary] (1961).

46. *Magyar Nemzet* (September 30, 1981).

47. Ibid.

48. *Népszabadság* (June 8, 1985).

49. *Délmagyarország* (January 14, 1985).

50. *Népszabadság* (June 8, 1985).

51. See *Magyar Nemzet* (April 29, 1984).

52. See Bishop Jozsef Cserhati's article in the Catholic magazine *Vigilia* (September 1984): 641–53.

53. Quoted by Imre Miklós in *Magyar Nemzet* (May 6, 1984).

54. See Foreign Broadcast Information Service, *Daily Report, Eastern Europe* (April 26, 1984): F2–F14.

55. *Vigilia* (September 1984): 641–50.

56. See *Magyar Hírek* (April 13, 1974) and *Magyar Hírlap* (February 15, 1976).

57. See his interview in the Italian Catholic journal *Il Regno* as reported in *Frankfurter Allegemeine Zeitung* (January 30, 1986).

58. See *Napról Napra,* [Day to Day] (July 26, 28, and 31, 1984).

59. *Reformátusok Lapja* (March 25, 1984).

60. See György Aczél, "The challenge of our age and the response of socialism," op. cit., 25.

61. See *Új Ember* (March 2, 1986).

62. Ibid. (April 6, 1986).

63. See Richard Bassett's summary of criticism in *The Spectator* (July 20, 1985).

64. *Budapest Rundschau* [Budapest Review] (December 27, 1983).

65. "Expanding possibilities for cooperation," *Magyar Hírlap* (January 14, 1984).

66. See James M. Markham, "Signs of religious revival in Eastern churches," *The New York Times* (January 23, 1984).

67. See *Népszabadság* (July 9, 1986) and *Frankfurter Allgemeine Zeitung* (July 9, 1986).

68. See Foreign Broadcasting Information Service, op. cit. (April 26, 1984): F2–F14.

69. Endre Hánn and Lázár Guy, "Az ötéves mérleg" [The balance of five years] *Jel-Kép* [Symbol] 3 (1985).

70. See Hungarian Situation Report No. 3, *Radio Free Europe Research*, (February 25, 1986), item 2.

71. *Statisztikai Évkönyv, 1984* [1984 Statistical Yearbook] (Budapest: Central Statistical Office, 1985).

72. See Domokos Varga's articles in issues 41 and 42 of *Élet és Irodalom* [Life and Literature], referred to in *New Hungarian Quarterly* 23 (Summer 1982): 125.

73. See Miklós Tomka, "Vallásszerep a társulatunkban" [The Role of religion in our society], *Kritika* (January 1985): 4–5.

74. See his interview in *Magyar Hírlap* (January 14, 1984).

6
Mass Media and Quality of Life

Ever since 1968, when the party authorities introduced the economic reforms, the party has become socially conscious, and as a result it has embraced many traditional values and patterns of Hungarian culture under the umbrella of national unity and the alliance policy. This new blend of Hungarian socialism runs throughout the social fabric and aspires to the goals of improved socioeconomic conditions and political tolerance that can provide the greatest good for the greatest number. As sociologist Elemér Hankiss put it, "Today, 'the other society' tries to integrate the different cultural, religious, political, and social tendencies by accepting and consciously preserving their specific [traditional] properties."[1] It is not surprising therefore that in December 1984 respondents to the public opinion poll conducted by the Mass Communications Research Center considered the country's economic situation, living standards, and their own financial situation the most important, and ideology, the reform of the educational system, and democracy at the workplace the least important issues.[2] According to many observers, Hungary, after the initial success of economic reforms, has become a consumer-oriented society. Yugoslav journalist Drago Buvać, writing in the Zagreb daily, *Vjesnik,* aptly posed the question: "Will Hungary break through the barriers of the existing system in terms of its economic and political structure by continuing with the unfinished reforms, or will Kádár's policy definitely collapse?" Buvać encouraged Hungary to resist pressure from both the East and the West and to continue with the reforms.[3] The Hungarian experiment has been carefully studied and copied by the Chinese[4] and of late Soviet experts have expressed an interest in the Hungarian method of agricultural production.

To a tourist from anywhere in the West, traveling through the Soviet bloc, Hungary is the place of relaxation and enjoyment. If one wants, for example, "Levis" blue jeans, one can find them in the several shops or in the large "Skála" department store that has stacks of them, at reasonable prices and payable in forints, not dollars. If one desires the latest in men's and women's fashions, one can find them in any of the stores on Vörösmarty Square. The restaurants are filled with well-dressed, laughing customers, and on weekend nights the streets are alive with the strains of gypsy violins and "Saturday Night Fever." On a sunny weekend the roads from Budapest are clogged with Hungarians heading for their weekend houses at Lake Balaton. Hungarians know how to enjoy the "good life." There are no lines of forlorn shoppers at Budapest's steel-and-glass vásárcsarnok food market. The stalls are overflowing with meat, milk, eggs, and fruit.

True, there are quite a few millionaires in Hungary; but there are even more Hungarians who just eke out a living. There are economic incentives for making money and that keeps most Hungarians hustling. Yet the gap between the haves and the have-nots is widening and that in itself is cause for concern among the policymakers. The party and government authorities seek solutions based on the formula of keeping the economic incentives alive while at the same time implementing laws of social and economic justice through taxation and social enhancement measures as well as leisure time. All this is freely and accurately reported in the Hungarian news media. As a matter of fact, the party and state authorities, who control the media, take credit for the achievements and proudly acknowledge Hungary as an economic showcase in the Soviet bloc.

The printed and electronic media in Hungary are a party enterprise. All the mass media belong to or are controlled by the HSWP. The sanctioned auxiliary organizations belonging to the alliance of the united front—the Patriotic Peoples Front, the trade unions, the Communist Youth League, the National Council of Hungarian Women, the churches, and other associations—publish newspapers and magazines, but their content is strictly controlled by the party. Alternative sources of information are usually suppressed by official propaganda campaigns, although a limited quantity of some Western newspapers and magazines is available, mostly at hotels frequented by international tourists. For all practical purposes the party exercises a monopoly over dissemination of information in the country. Personal analysis based on an individual's intellect and acumen, if different from the official line, is not tolerated. The truth is a matter of party pronouncement through the usual mass media channels, which are controlled by the party organs. Hence the printed and electronic media actually operate as party spokesmen, jointly presenting the "facts" as perceived by the party, suppressing dissenting facts and opinions, fabricating evidence whenever necessary, and in general, doing everything to facilitate the implementation of party goals. The party regards Hungarian journalists and radio and television personalities as an indispensable vehicle for creating the legitimacy of the ruling elite.

Ever since the party committed itself to the building of democratic socialism in the country, its official policy toward dissent has included a measure of tolerance toward dialogue to prevent pent-up emotions from becoming explosive. Within this framework the party authorities have allowed church-sponsored newspapers, which are strictly controlled by the official censorship. Therefore it is safe to generalize that the mass media in Hungary are an exception to the rigid and heavily censored news media typical throughout the Soviet bloc countries. Even so, the Hungarian mass media are at the opposite extreme from the Western media. For example, the Hungarian press is not concerned with the two major functions of the Western press: information and entertainment. Truth in Hungary is not found out by debate, research, trial and error, experience, exchange of information, analysis, and documentation, but by the decisions of the censors whose task it is to facilitate the implementation of party interests and goals. The need to promote the party's interests determines the content of the Hungarian newspapers. They cannot include material that is not sound from a Marxist-Leninist point of view, and does not echo the party line. However in this regard, too, Hungary is an exception rather than the rule of the Soviet bloc example. Because party policies support economic and social reform in the country, the press reflects that interest in its communications to the readers. According to a regional paper for Veszprém, Napló [Daily], 20 percent of the material it carries comes from the Hungarian Telegraph Agency (MTI) and some 20 percent from Centropress (an information pool of the Hungarian newspapers). About 10 percent of the newspaper space is devoted to advertisement, and 15 percent is allocated to contributions and articles by nonstaff members. Consequently only 35 percent remains for the newspaper staff.[5] In other words, the controls established by the party are less rigid than in many other countries within the Soviet bloc. Nevertheless, the controls are there; both the party and government have their agencies for censorship. The party sets the guidelines, which are passed down by the Central Committee's Agitprop Department to the lowest party organizations and to the editors-in-chief of the media. The government's top control agency is the Information Bureau of the Council of Ministers, currently headed by Rezsö Bányász. The editors are carefully selected and always well informed about the proper treatment of important topics and where silence is advised. Noncompliance can cost an editor his job. An example of the consequences of disobedience was the case of the monthly, Mozgó Világ (World of Motion), whose

Editor in Chief Ferenc Kulin was removed in September 1983 for his alleged "systematic defiance" of party guidelines. The periodical's entire editorial board resigned in sympathy with him; the new board that took over in January 1984 did not deviate from "acceptable" journalism and therefore continues to function "normally." (For details, see Chapter 2 under "Civil Obedience.")

THE PRESS, RADIO, TV, AND THE VCR

It would not be too farfetched to argue that the printed media in Hungary are the fairest of all their counterparts in the Soviet bloc. In spite of such a liberal generalization, however, even in Hungary there are two "taboos" that cannot be discussed, debated, or written about: the leading role of the party, and the friendship and loyalty to the USSR as the leader of the socialist camp.

The three major dailies are the *Népszabadság [People's Freedom]*, the *Magyar Nemzet [Hungarian Nation]*, and the *Népszava [People's Voice]*. The first one is the official organ of the HSWP, the second one of the PPF, and the third one of the trade unions. In addition, there are numerous weeklies and monthlies. Although their content is basically the same, the styles of the three newspapers differ somewhat. The *Népszabadság* is closest to the target set by the party line, the *Népszava* is intermediate in its approach, and the *Magyar Nemzet* is the most liberal of the three. Some Hungarians even refer to the latter as an "opposition paper," which is of course an exaggeration. The first two to three pages of this paper discuss foreign news; pages 3 and 4 talk about economics and cultural life in Hungary; after this there is a page of less significant news combined with gossip, items of interest, and obituaries; and finally there is a sports page. Thus, almost everyone starts reading the *Magyar Nemzet* from the back. As the Budapest saying goes: "We start looking it over as we do a well-built woman—from the rear."

The commentaries and news covering events in foreign countries are generally similar to those of the other socialist countries. Frequently the more sophisticated Hungarians refer to the coverage of news from the West as carbon copies of the Soviet party organ, *Pravda*. There is an old Budapest adage: "*Pravda* costs five kopeks [about 1 forint], while the Budapest dailies cost about 2 forints. Why?" Answer: "Someone has to pay for the translation."

Events abroad are usually viewed through the required ideological prism but information on these events is generally realistic. Sometimes there are even dissenting views concerning some of the events in Western Europe, such as in the case of the cancellation of the September 1984 visit of Erich Honecker (General Secretary of the Socialist Unity Party) to West Germany, but such critical opinions are rarely voiced. If a news

item could prove to be embarrassing (e.g., spying, the expulsion of diplomats, Polish events), then the Hungarian press simply does not mention
it. If an announcement appears to be too demagogic, they print it under
the designation: "As reported by TASS." And there are usually no comments on these; everyone interprets it in his or her own way because
the Hungarian press simply refuses to give an editorial opinion unless
the party considers it an unusual case. Concerning this practice, there
is another Budapest joke: "How did fairy tales begin in the old days?"
Answer: "Once upon a time. And now?" Answer: "As reported by TASS.
How did fairy tales end in the old days?" Answer: "If you don't believe
it, look it up yourself! And now?" Answer: "If you don't believe it, *they*
will look *you* up!"

A good example of this kind of reporting was the Soviets' shooting
down of the South Korean passenger plane on September 1, 1983. News
was gradually reported in this manner: On the first day ("as reported
by TASS"), the three major Hungarian newspapers wrote about a certain
real object that penetrated and left the airspace of the USSR. After this,
similar announcements appeared daily but the fact that the plane was
shot down was announced only on the fourth or fifth day, after the
Soviet admission. Even on the first day, Hungarians reading between
the lines suspected that something ugly must have happened, but they
were uncertain whether or not the domestic press was uninformed or
did not want to write about it. Thus, the designation: "As reported by
TASS." Incidentally, shortly after the truth became known (mostly from
news reports disseminated by Radio Free Europe, Voice of America, the
BBC, or television news from Vienna and Yugoslavia), Budapest was
teaming with cynical jokes about the incident: On a plane the flight
attendant asked a passenger, "What would you like with your coffee?"
Answer: "Saccharin but not *Sachalin*." Or "Why do Koreans prefer to
wear tight shirts?" Answer: "Because Russians are likely to fire at loose
shirts!" (In Hungarian, "loose" is pronounced "boe" and shirt "ing";
together: "Boeing.") An even more sagacious joke goes like this: Two
Soviet fighter pilots chatting: "Look, is that a passenger liner?" The
other: "You hit it right on the head!"

A more recent example of the suppression of information was the
reporting of the accident at the Chernobyl nuclear power plant on April
28, 1986. That evening, Radio Budapest had a four-sentence announcement—as reported by TASS—about an accident at Chernobyl due to a
defect. On the following day the trade union daily *Népszava* noted that
no details were known about the causes of the accident, the nature of
the damage to the reactor, the number of victims, or the extent of the
damage. The coverage increased in length starting on May 2, after radioactivity was reported to have reached Hungary on the nights of May
1 and 2; however, the reports insisted that everything was normal and

that there was no danger of radioactivity in the country. Yet several days later the media announced that radioactivity had been decreasing and was reaching the normal level. This prompted the TV comedian József Árkus as well as the public at large to ask: "If radioactivity did not increase in Hungary, what then had to decrease?"

Coverage was increased again on May 4 when the Soviets gradually began to provide more information about the accident. About one-third of the reporting was domestic in origin. One quarter was based on TASS and Soviet newspapers, including statements by various Soviet officials. Another quarter consisted of reports about Eastern Europe, most of it coming from Poland, then Czechoslovakia, the German Democratic Republic, and finally Rumania and Bulgaria. The remainder was derived from Western sources. The coverage consisted strictly of news items, without any editorial comment. The Hungarian media never raised any serious questions about the accident or attempted to comment on it. On the contrary on May 7, 1986, the party daily *Népszabadság* published the first editorial about Chernobyl, basically repeating the Soviet accusations that the United States and some unnamed NATO countries wanted to raise Chernobyl to the level of an international crisis and were making unfounded statements for propaganda purposes in order to divert international attention from the U.S. aggression against Libya, the nuclear tests in Nevada, and the "Star Wars" missile defense program. The editorial also charged that the United States had not provided any information for three weeks about the accident in 1979 at Three Mile Island in Pennsylvania.

Because of the slowness in providing information to the public at large, many Hungarians were in a panic about possible radiation contamination of food and water as well as radiation fallout. It took a concerted effort on the part of the media, especially radio broadcasts, to make the findings of the National Joliot-Curie Radiation Biology and Radiation Health Research Institute known to the general public: that there was no immediate danger from radiation fallout and that it was unjustified and potentially harmful to take iodine tablets unless prescribed by a physician. Although Hungarian foreign trade officials reacted indignantly to the EEC's ban until the end of May on the importation of fresh meat, livestock, vegetables, and other foodstuffs from Eastern Europe, on May 22, 1986, the Hungarian government announced that it would pay compensation to its vegetable producers and traders for some of the losses they had incurred as a result of the Chernobyl accident.[6] The compensation for the total losses of Hungary's agricultural sector as a result of Chernobyl were estimated between 300 to 400 million forints, or about U.S.$8 million. According to the Ministry of Agriculture and Food, the turnover of Hungary's vegetable market fell by some 30 percent in the first half of May 1986, affecting 15–20 thousand tons of produce.[7] Although the Soviet government provided a one-time payment of 200 rubles to families relocated from the Chernobyl area, Hungary was the only Soviet-bloc country that provided compensation to their farmers for the loss of contaminated foodstuffs.

Here again jokes abound about the coverage of the Chernobyl nuclear accident. For example: "What lowers radioactivity the most?" Answer: "TASS." Or "What does the physician in Kiev tell his patients who need radiation therapy?" Answer: "Go outside into the backyard." Or, referring to the success of the soccer team from Kiev, question: "Why did the Dynamo team play so well in the finals of the European Cup?" Answer: "They were running on nuclear energy and had two German guest players, Geiger and Mueller." If a news item could prove to be embarrassing (e.g., Soviets caught spying, expulsion of Soviet diplomats, Solidarity demonstrations in Poland, etc.), then the Hungarian press simply does not mention it. The possible wisdom in this policy is to prevent the potential Hungarian readers from making accusations of printing obvious lies in the Hungarian papers.

The average Hungarian usually informs himself this way: in the morning he reads the papers, in the evening he watches TV news, and then combines what he heard and saw with what Radio Free Europe (or some other Western Hungarian-language radio station) says. Whatever is announced as fact at home, he believes. Whatever is announced as "reported by TASS," he half believes. Whatever is not mentioned in the socialist press, and the Western sources talk about, he believes according to his temperament and his political background. According to many sober Hungarians, it is harmful to remain silent on certain events, because this way Western propaganda does not have an effective counter. It would be simpler to write about everything, in a proper manner. Instead, on some occasions even the Hungarian papers engage in disinformation. A good example was the coverage of the controversy over the installation of the Pershing II and the Cruise Missiles in Western Europe as a response to the Soviet-based SS-20s targeted on Western Europe. The Hungarian press never mentioned the fact that the NATO decision of December 1979 gave the Soviet Union a five-year lead time within which to negotiate an agreement with the United States on the dismantling of some of the SS-20s, as a compromise to stop deployment of the Pershing IIs and Cruise Missiles. When the deployment began, and the Soviet delegation walked out of the negotiations in Geneva on November 23, 1984, the Hungarian press claimed that the negotiations broke down because of the U.S. deployment of missiles in Western Europe. As far as factual reporting is concerned, the news item, reporting the events, was not a lie, but the context within which it was reported was an act of disinformation. Many wise Hungarians are quite aware of and cautious about the nuances and oblique references used in the socialist press. They are reminded of this cleverness in the reporting of a car race, which supposedly happened in East Berlin: Only two cars take part in the race: a Mercedes and an East German Trabant (a small car with a four-cylinder engine and molded plywood body; the socialist Volkswagen). Naturally the Mercedes wins. The results are reported in the socialist press: "Fantastic international car race! Our Trabant finished in second place! The Mercedes ended up in next to last place!" Obviously, there are no lies in this story; everything depends on the way the story is presented.

Although there are guidelines—emanating from the top of the party machine to the lowest levels of the party headquarters—spelling out what can or cannot be printed, the reporters themselves are sensitive enough to know the boundaries within which they can exercise their freedom of expression. On March 20, 1986, the National Assembly passed a new press law, which defines the rights and duties of journalists and the right of the public to fast and timely information. The new law prevents journalists from passing on information that "would hurt the constitutional order of the People's Republic and its international interests ... and public morals."[8] Just about any piece of critical writing could be rejected on one of these grounds. As a matter of fact, János Berecz, HSWP secretary and former chairman of the Agitprop Committee, went so far as to state that none of the country's "socialist achievements" or its "national historical or moral values" could be questioned under the "pretext" of freedom of the press.[9] The new law seems to provide greater freedom for the press inasmuch as it defines the right of citizens to information and requires all government officials, state and economic organizations, and social bodies to respond to requests for information from reporters, thus enabling more coverage of sensitive subjects in the media. According to the new press law, the journalists will have to submit a copy of their report for review to the persons they interview and the latter cannot prevent its publication unless their remarks have been altered. According to the semiofficial daily *Magyar Hírlap*, some journalists fear that the new press law represents a "tightening" of the controls over the printed media in Hungary.[10] It appears that the new law restricts journalists from prying into certain areas, such as writings critical of certain periods of party history, or the treatment of the Hungarian ethnic minority abroad, and it further restricts the government permission for publishing, which is directed against the opposition, since the 1983 press law did not entirely eliminate samizdat periodicals. Several samizdat publications have appeared in Hungary in recent years; for example, *Beszélő [The Talker], A Hírmondó [The Messenger], Tájekoztató [The Signpost]*, and a few lesser known typewritten or mimeographed publications. The writers of these and other underground newspapers include a mix of political

critics and opponents of the Kádár regime, exponents of the peace movements, as well as the basic church committees. In September 1983 a law
was passed, aimed at the dissidents, making it illegal to publish and dis-
seminate information without government approval. Violators were subjected to punishment by heavy fines and jail terms. There were many
incidents involving police harassment of dissidents, house searches for illegal literature, including the closing down of László Rajk's samizdat boutique in May 1983. The 1986 press law does, in fact, provide a firmer basis
for cracking down on unauthorized samizdat publications.

One of the aims of the 1986 press law was to enable journalists to pay
closer attention to the enormous inequalities that exist in the country as
a result of social and economic injustices caused by illegal and dishonest
income. Indications for this are the heavy penalties imposed on individuals hindering journalists in the lawful practice of their profession, which
includes such things as refusing to give information to the press by any
responsible citizens in the country, even ministers, managers, directors,
and the entire establishment of the movers and shakers of the NEM.
Whereas in the past the fashionable topic for newspaper coverage was
the international situation, now the emphasis is on the domestic scene
covering economic and social problems. The 1986 press law is part of
an overall policy dealing with the expanding social and economic problems; during the fall of 1984, for example, the "Economic Police" were
created, with the mission of investigating financial crimes and misde-
meanors. In the area of fruit-and-vegetable merchandising they performed diligently and offered the following, not exactly uplifting,
picture: Between the producer and the final seller there are a great
number of middlemen, who never see the merchandise, but who still
take their percentages. A few of them were arrested in a spectacular
manner and sentenced to prison. Of course, the new Economic Police
could not eliminate shortages derived from the basic contradiction of
forced production and product distribution. In other words, they are
working on the symptoms, but they are unable to deal with the core of
the problem—an economy based on shortages. That, however, is a
deeper problem—symptomatic of the system, and as such it is a taboo
that cannot be discussed or written about. The situation is similar in the
area of auto-parts supply, or any other consumer field that is plagued
by shortages. The private entrepreneur (maszek) can be sent to jail, or
be ruined through taxation, but that will not solve the problem. Hence
the Hungarian journalist writing about economic crimes—due to illegal
profiteering—has a thankless job to report about the symptoms but not
the problem, because to write about the taboos could under the new
press law send the journalist to prison. Here again the wisdom of Hungarian humor is very revealing: "How did the people march in the May

Day celebration in Budapest?" Answer: "In 2 lines. Line one, the unsatisfied people with the political police behind them. Line two, the satisfied people with the economic police behind them."

If a Hungarian reader wants to find out more than the official line has to offer on a daily basis, he or she will turn to a popular weekly, called *Magyarország [Hungary]*. At times it deals with delicate topics, those that no other publication covers. In addition, it contains commentaries on domestic and foreign policy alike, a column on economics, an excerpt from the press abroad; it is a high-quality publication. The topics from a sample issue (October 21, 1986) include: Kádár's visit to Paris; relationship between West Germany and the People's Republic of China, in connection with Chancellor Kohl's visit; meeting of West European ministers of defense; the bombing attempt in Brighton, U.K.; the Japanese economic miracle; the economic situation in the USSR; the Yugoslav economy; the dialogue between the state and church in Poland; the anti-Mafia agreement between the United States and Italy; Austrian economic worries; women criminals; two articles on fine arts; one article each on flower gardening, health, and food preservatives; one article about the first days after the liberation ("Szeged 1944"). In addition, the middle of the weekly contains about six pages of selections from the press abroad (e.g., remembering the Moro affair; U.S. presidential elections; interview with Woody Allen, etc.). As noted, the topics are many and varied. Of course, there are tendentious aspects also. There is too much coverage about the economic problems of other countries. The reason? The editors of the weekly want to impress the Hungarian reader that the economic conditions abroad are no better than in Hungary. Several "delicate" themes are also covered; they are either taken straight out of Western publications or else a staff member writes a commentary about them. In the first case, the choice of source, and in the second the skill of the commentator, assures the proper amount of partnership so that there is no deviation from the guidelines or the taboos.

Perhaps the least expensive and, therefore, the most popular form of entertainment today in Hungary is television. Surveys carried out by Hungary's Mass Communication Institute indicate that Hungary has become a television-watching country on a massive scale. According to an announcement by Radio Budapest,[11] 95 percent of the population living in households has a television set, predominately black and white (compared with 98 percent for Britain and 97 percent for the F.R.G.). For several years Hungarian viewers have been watching television for an average of 140 minutes a day, compared with 113 minutes in Austria, for example. The rising cost of movie tickets, soccer games, concerts, restaurant meals, and so forth, has contributed to making television watching Hungary's most popular way of spending free time, the surveys revealed. Although currently there are no television programs on Mondays, that may change in the near future because of the growing foreign competition. As for the radio, according to the same surveys, Hungarians spend an average of 118 minutes a day listening to radio broadcasts.

The organization of broadcast media is entirely different from that in the United States. There are three radio stations and two TV channels in Hungary. None of them are specialized, as in the United States, into "Country," "Rock," and so on. Every station has a variety of programs. Only Radio 3 emphasizes music, but even there one can find news, radio-plays, and cultural programs. Television programming is done regularly from mid-afternoon until late at night. Channel One sometimes has programs in the mornings, with the exception of Mondays. The programs are structured somewhat like the Public Broadcasting System in the United States. Prime-time begins at 8 p.m. In a sample week (October 22–28, 1984), the viewing included the following programs: The Onedin Family (British); Hungarian globetrotters; Soccer matches; Isaac Stern concert; documentary about the 1934 regicide in Marseilles; documentary about an actress; live broadcast of a play; entertainment variety; TV-play on a historical theme; and a show of Frances Gall, singer; in other words, a limited selection of a short variety. Evening news is at 7:30 p.m., and there is a shorter newsbreak later, too. Sunday evening a more comprehensive program called "The Week" sums up the events. That week in October 1984, there were, in addition: one economics lecture (25 minutes); two political reports; one commentary on military policies; and one economic broadcast. The total time of these programs was less than the time spent on soccer, hockey, and other sports. Although there is not a great amount of direct political programming on the air, there are well-edited and skillfully presented programs that have political significance. For example, a children's movie for TV presentation, shown on a Sunday morning, dealt with a historical theme dating back to the feudal times in which "the good guys," meaning the poor, abused, and exploited servants and landless peasants took matters into their own hands and through a violent rebellion against "the bad guys," meaning the nobility and the priests, took possession of the estate, freed the jailed serfs, and distributed the land and wealth among themselves. Of course, most of these programs are not spontaneous; they are carefully planned and skillfully put together to convey a message to the viewers. Thus there are many people who don't watch such programs. They just switch to the other channel—not unlike the subject of another Hungarian pearl of wisdom: "Ivan Ivanovich, Moscow steelworker, watches one of Brezhnev's 4-hour-long speeches. About halfway through, he switches to the other channel, where he sees a policeman, complete with rubber truncheon, who asks him: 'Why aren't you watching Comrade Brezhnev?' "

Some Hungarians with a good roof-antenna and a good geographic location (near the Western border) can receive more than the two domestic TV channels. Even in Budapest, one can watch one Austrian, two Yugoslav, two Czechoslovak, and one Soviet channels. (The last one comes through the relay station at the Mátyásföld Soviet base.) The most significant breakthrough in TV communication is the one between Hungary and Austria. The link with Austria, by Western satellite via cable since the end of 1985, means that about 100,000 Hungarian households are hooked to the satellite-produced 3-SAT program jointly produced by Austria's ORF, West Germany's ZDF, and the Swiss television station SRG.[12] The television links with the West clearly represent an attempt by Hungary to achieve trans-border media cooperation in accordance with the Basket Three civil rights provisions of the 1975 Helsinki Final Act.

A similar agreement was reached between Austria and Hungary on the establishment of a joint German-language radio station called "Rádió Danubius."[13] The new station is located at Kábhegy, in the Lake Balaton area, some 90 kilometers southwest of Budapest, which every year attracts about 4,500,000 German-speaking tourists from Austria, the F.R.G., Switzerland, and the G.D.R.[14] The station began its broadcast in May 1986, with a 12–hour program every day; ORF contributes the speakers, moderators, musical materials, and advertisements and the Hungarian radio service provides the news program. The aim is for the radio station to be self-supporting through advertising; Hungary expects to earn 20 million Austrian schillings a month in this manner.[15] It would appear that the communication links with the West also helped the Hungarian authorities to tackle a sensitive ideological issue, that is, how to dispense with jamming. As János Berecz (who in March 1985 replaced György Aczél as CC Secretary in charge of agitation and propaganda) put it, "To forbid reception would be senseless, since it would be very difficult to endorse the prohibition and it would also be contrary to our concept of [democratic socialism]."[16]

Video viewing and taping is the latest fad in Hungary, especially among the nouveau riche. At the beginning of 1985, it was estimated that there were about 20,000 video cassette recorders; by the end of the year their number was expected to increase to over 100,000.[17] The combined price of a television and a video cassette recorder is around 100,000 forints, and the price of a domestically manufactured video recorder is an exorbitant 42,000 forints, higher than the average worldmarket price. While in the F.R.G., for example, the cost of a new recorder equals the price of 100 movie theater tickets, in Hungary it is the equivalent of 7,000. Furthermore, the price of a movie theater ticket in Hungary, about 11 forints, can hardly be compared with the 80–150 forints one must pay for the privilege of renting a video cassette.[18] Because of the shortages of quality video hardware and video cassettes, Hungary is facing a booming video blackmarket, confusion over copyright laws, a gap in the regime's system of proprietary controls over the media, and, consequently, a massive influx of (from the authorities' point of view) undesirable ideological influences. The discovery of this new, exciting form of entertainment by private enthusiasts and blackmarket operators (capitalizing on the huge discrepancy between supply and demand) turned the home video revolution into an unprecedented bonanza. In a country where the average monthly wage is below 5,000 forints, successful blackmarket entrepreneurs can earn as much as 70,000 forints a month. The reason for their success is the apparently insatiable appetite of Hungary's new video buffs for such taboo themes as religion, anti-Soviet sentiments, sex, and violence—something that neither MOKEP (Enterprise for the Distribution of Motion Pictures) nor Videóteka (Central Video Library) can provide.[19] Tapes dealing with these topics are illegally smuggled into the country, duplicated, and sold at high prices. In addition to private collectors, even privately operated bars, restaurants, and discotheques have been buying and showing such tapes to "drum up business." Members of a disc- and video-jockey ring arrested in 1984, for example, have admitted to earning some 1,000 forints an hour in clear profit just by including illicit video tapes in their programs.[20] Since the authorities consider video as a threat to socialist morality, the government regulators are busy in their search to find solutions how to curb such practices, how to keep pace with and eventually overtake the blackmarket. To counter the negative effects of video products, the authorities developed their own video program in four major areas: party propaganda, public and higher education, entertainment, and propaganda directed abroad.[21] In other words, the party and state authorities have reluctantly accepted the fact that the video boom and the general communications revolution that it represents can no longer be brought under full control in the traditional totalitarian sense; hence the party and state are trying to compete with the black-marketeers for the potential clients by giving the regime a controlling edge through tighter laws and law enforcement.

THE PLEASURES OF LIFE REGULATED BY SOCIALIST MORALITY

It would be no exaggeration to claim that most Hungarians like good food and "a good time." For men "a good time" means good wine and good-looking women; for Hungarian women "a good time" usually means to wine and dine in good restaurants and be entertained by exciting Gypsy music. The latter, they claim, turns on the passion of the Hungarian lover that is equal only to the myth of a Casanova.

Most Hungarians are as temperamental as the Gypsy music: they are either exceedingly gay and exuberant or very low and morose. Most Hungarians prefer to deal with their emotions in public places over food and drinks rather than on a psychiatrist's couch. Entertainment in Hungary is very seldom confined to the home. Even those who do have the space and means to entertain in their own house or apartment prefer to dine out. This is true not only for the cities but also for smaller towns as well.

Budapest has a great many restaurants; almost every corner is occupied by one. They can be state-operated, privately-operated, or somewhere between the two. The state-operated establishments run on the principle of "tight business." Employees work for fixed incomes, their salaries do not depend on the amount of business they do. Thus, their interest is to receive their money by working the least. In other words, they want to see as few customers as possible. The average luncheon runs like this. The customer comes in and sits down. Unlike in the United States, there are no seating hostesses in Hungary, so he sits anywhere he wants to. One can reserve a table, in which case they place a sign on the table saying "Reserved." There are places where more signs are placed on tables than there are actual reservations; this is another method by which potential customers can be kept away. In about half an hour, the waiter comes out, and one can order drinks. In about 15 minutes, he will bring the drinks, and now one can order the food. Another 15 minutes, and the food arrives; another 15 minutes is spent on eating, and then 10 minutes on waiting for the bill. Total time spent is about one and a half hours.

In state-operated restaurants prices vary according to the classification of the establishment. In "*maszek*" places not only is the quality of the food better, but so is the service; the prices, however, are higher. The semi-private restaurants are owned by the state, but leased by their managers. The employees receive a good portion of the profits in accordance with the contract signed. The state declares the least successful restaurants to be up for lease, setting a relatively high price commensurate with the profits of the place. There is an open auction, and the winner gets the lease. Each year he has to pay a fixed amount to the state. Otherwise the state does not interfere in the operation of the business; everything is left up to the leaseholder, from the purchasing of utensils to the advertising. If, after a year, the manager fails to show a profit, the state reclaims the restaurant and holds another auction. Thus, the only choice the manager has is to do everything possible to make a profit from a business that in the past has been a loser. There are two legitimate ways of making a profit: to charge higher prices to fewer guests, or lower prices to many guests. There is, of course, a third alternative: to charge higher prices to many guests, but this does not work, because if someone is ripped off once, he is not likely to return to the same place. By "rip-off," Hungarians do not mean only that the waiter adds up the bill wrong, but also that the prices are too high compared with the service. The managers of so-called "rubber" establishments figure they can always take the naive or foreign customer by charging high prices. Their business is not brisk, but the service is good; they do anything to please the customer, that is, to get his money. The menu features a wide selection of foods; most of the dishes have fantastic names. This way the "honored customer" does not feel that he is paying a high price for a simple roast beef, but for something that has a French name. Of course, the two are identical; at most the latter has additional spices. Sometimes, however, there is also outright cheating. An order of wild boar stuffed with blueberries can turn out to be in fact plain pork stuffed with canned cherries. In Budapest, there have always been fashionable restaurants, but they remain so only for a brief period. Much more pleasant are the (usually privately-owned) places where the food is good and the prices are moderately acceptable. For example, the Kis-Pipa (Small Pipe) in Pest is like that, and is one of the most popular restaurants. One has to make reservations 2–3 weeks in advance. The choice is wide: more than 50 main dishes, 20 roasts, 8–10 soups, and the same number of salads appear on the menu. One can eat there for 150 forints (about U.S. $3.00) and have something to drink, too. This is about one-thirtieth of the average Hungarian daily pay, so it is still expensive, but every once in a while one can afford it.

An average Hungarian family with 3 children and a total monthly income of 11,000 forints seldom goes to restaurants, unless it is a special occasion. A family of five cannot eat out for less than 500–600 forints, and few people can afford that regularly. Each month about 2,500 forints go for repayment of loans, another 1,000 is spent on gas and electricity, 6,000 on groceries, 1,200 for gasoline—this totals already 10,700 forints without allowing for clothing and other essentials. Of course, for wealthy people the situation is different. For example, an auto-parts merchant eats in restaurants often, because his wife hates to cook. Or else the husband brings food home from the Kis-Pipa. This is about 8–9 thousand forints a month, just in dinners, but it is a comfortable solution.

Even if one wants to seduce someone in Hungary, one must make use of restaurants, bars, or espressos. The latter are small places where, in addition to drinks and coffee, one may get snacks. The first few meetings always take place in espressos, and often the getting acquainted also occurs over coffee or drinks. The sight of young people kissing and embracing in espressos is routine. After a few meetings, the time comes when the lady can be taken to one's apartment for a few hours of increased intimacy. After that, it is less and less frequent that the couple meets outside the apartment. Of course a few drinks are consumed there, too, but that is only a side attraction. As the saying goes: "What are the

3 best things in the world?" Answer: "A glass of vodka before, a cigarette afterwards, and in between. . . . "

In addition to the more sophisticated eating/drinking places with entertainment, there are also the less elegant wine and beer cellars and stand-up joints. The Hungarian authorities are taking all sorts of measures to curb the rise of alcoholism in the country, but at the same time they are also selling as much alcohol as possible. The monopoly on alcohol sales brings in a sizeable income (52 million forints in 1985). In view of this contradiction, anti-alcoholism speeches seem like empty rhetoric. The wine cellar *(kocsma)* is a place where the lowest strata of society get regularly drunk, day after day. Sitting or standing (as long as he can stand), the Hungarian can spend his money on booze. Places like this can be recognized from afar by the smell of alcohol. Police raids are regularly held, because wanted criminals can usually be found in these places. Fights are also frequent. More sophisticated people usually avoid these places, not only because of the fights and the level of prevailing conversation, but also because if one is seen around one of these places, his prestige takes a dive.

For the few privileged Hungarians, and for foreigners, there are night-clubs and cabarets (even casinos) operating in Budapest; for instance, the "Maxim." They are expensive and employ quality entertainment, often from abroad. For most Westerners, however, the night clubs are primitive, and for most Hungarians they are beyond reach.

There are also a number of clubs in the country (not to be confused with "night clubs"). Many of them are attached to various enterprises, while others are open to anyone. They are subsidized by the state and serve the cause of "public culture" *(közmüvelödés)*. The scale of their programs is wide. One of the most successful of these clubs in Budapest is attached to the University of Gardening *(Kertészeti Egyetem Klub)*. Commonly known as the KEK, this club is open almost every evening, featuring such programs as Commodore 64 Club, one-man programs by a famous actor, travel reports by a political newsman, "Country Club," jazz club, club for lovers of classical music; video-club; club for poetry lovers; and, of course, the Saturday night parties, at which one of the popular rock groups performs, and some 1,000–1,500 youth dance and go crazy. This club had its problems. For one thing, it was forbidden by law to pay more than 1,000 forints to any performer per night. Of course, a well-known actor or writer will not come for such a low fee. What to do? For years the KEK adopted the following practice: they maintained two sets of books. One showed the official costs, expenses, and incomes, and the other the actual costs and incomes, which were much higher. Of course, they had to make money somehow. The Saturday-night parties were the best occasions for this. Tickets were generally 60 forints per person. Two-thirds of the tickets were official, while one-third were home-made pieces of paper, made to look official by attaching rubber stamps to them, and unaccountable for higher authorities. The extra income thus derived was often as high as 60,000 forints, and this money could be used for purposes that the official income could not cover. As long as the leadership of the club was unified, everything went smoothly. However, when two of the leaders quarrelled over a woman, one of them squealed to the president of the university. Of course, nobody called the police. The president called in the manager of the club and told him to look for other employment quickly. Within two weeks the man left the university, and a new manager—the niece of the party secretary—was appointed. In other words, they got rid of a resourceful and bold individual, and they solved the employment problem of a "kinfolk."

Around Lent (or *farsang* in Hungarian), every February–March, there are many balls organized. For example, almost every high school has a "ribbon-dedicating" ball. The name comes from the fact that every senior receives a piece of blue ribbon, with the year of his or her graduation on it. They are very proud of this ribbon, especially the girls, because they feel that it makes them adults.

For the highly sophisticated Hungarians, the favorite means of entertainment are concerts and theatres. The theatres hire actors for a season, and not for one play. As a consequence, the plays are often adjusted to the available actors, and not vice versa. The situation is similar with the two opera houses of Budapest, the two operetta theatres, and many of the concert halls. In addition to its two professional concert orchestras, the city also has 5–6 semi-professional orchestras. One may buy tickets for the specific performance or for the entire season. However, to acquire season tickets for the world-famous Budapest Opera (which re-opened in 1984 after several years of renovation) is nearly impossible, unless one is a previous season-ticket holder. Even the exact program is not known in advance; 15 pieces are indicated, of which 10 will appear on the coming year's program. Season tickets are not easy to buy for the other theatres, either. Single tickets are also difficult to come by. What is most interesting is that in spite of the fact that the ticket windows have the "sold out" signs posted, the houses are often, though not always, only partly filled. The reason? The audience—for example, the ironworkers—are compelled by their trade union to purchase theatre tickets, so they can say that the Hungarian workers are hungry for culture. They place the tickets in the official records of their brigades, and then go to the neighborhood bar instead.[22] Thus it is difficult to sell culture, even if one can sell tickets. At the same time, those who really want to see the play cannot get tickets. This is one of the problems of cultural centralization. The special cases are when a great soloist or a great foreign orchestra shows up. At times like that, the house is full and tickets are at a premium. The average price of a concert ticket is 70–80 forints, but for something like a Leonard Bernstein or the Amsterdam Concert, the cheapest ticket is 500 forints. This is too expensive for the "culture-hungry" brigades, so only the seriously interested people will purchase tickets. In the past there used to be many more events like this; but in the 1983/84 season, the only similar guest performance was by the Amsterdam orchestra mentioned above. More and more frequently, Hungarian artists living abroad visit home for a performance (e.g., Antal Dóráti, György Solti, Árpád Joó, etc.). Budapest, which used to be called the Paris of Eastern Europe, offers a broad scale of cultural events, and the foreigner with hard currency can always get tickets for a first-rate performance. For example, it was almost impossible to get tickets to the performance of "Cats," but in every hotel there were plenty of tickets, for 50 Deutschmarks. There was a Vienna firm that organized 2–day trips to Budapest, which included sightseeing and tickets to "Cats." Any way one looks at it, Hungary is inexpensive for the Western visitor, and the authorities, interested in hard currency, make it known through their appeal to potential tourists. The dollar/forint ratio of roughly 1:50 is a great bargain for the Westerners, but very bad for the Hungarians. The prices of all imported articles depend on this ratio, and the Hungarian who wants to travel abroad has to purchase dollars at this rate. While the West buys Hungarian products at a low price, it sells its own products high. This is considered poor business, but it maintains the frequently mentioned "liquidity" of Hungary and guarantees that the loans will be repaid. Thus, even culture and entertainment are closely tied to the principles of economics. What better proof of this incongruity than the beauty contest and the selection of the Belle of Hungary in 1985.

After a break of 49 years, before an audience of 1,700 people who paid 500 forints each (including dinner), "The Belle of Hungary" was chosen. The winner was a 16–year old schoolgirl, Csilla Andrea Molnár, from Fonyod on Lake Balaton. The 20 judges included one woman as well as a Communist Youth League CC member. "The revival of the custom of electing a beauty queen seems to have fulfilled a mass requirement."[23] The initiative came from Magyar Media, an affiliate of the state-owned Lapkiadó Vállalat [Newspapers Publishing Co.], which is under the control of the Ministry of Culture. Several sponsors (many from abroad) financed the beauty contest and, according to observers, Magyar Media made a handsome profit on the contest. The Director of Magyar Media, István Fodoros, objected to the term "money-making venture" and referred to the contest as "an enterprise counting on profits" with certain "moral and political obligations."[24]

Those obligations, claimed the winner, meant Magyar Media had a monopoly on her while the expense of her photographs she had to pay out of her own pocket: "Just imagine, I make a small error, my photo appears somewhere without the permission of Magyar Media and I have to pay a fine of several hundred forints. It's like being a prisoner... I don't even know what I signed in that contract. I was forced to do so, otherwise I would have been excluded from the contest...."[25] Another contestant revealed to the *Ifjúsági Magazín* [Youth Magazine] that her only objective in competing was to earn enough for a furnished room or apartment of her own, away from her boyfriend whom she had been trying to leave for the past three years. She, like all the other competitors, had to sign a statement agreeing that if they wished to take jobs as models or hostesses, they would only do so through Magyar Media and that to do otherwise would obligate them to pay heavy penalties. "A contract of a sort might help me. I'm no better nor worse than most of the girls here. But look at us: we all have some defect or other, visible or invisible. A healthy, sane, and well-balanced person would never, on her own account, come here and show her body. Those who are in good order physically and mentally have already won their prize, somewhere and with someone...."[26] The real winner it would seem was the contestant who won Fotex's independent prize of a year's photo modeling course in California and 100,000 forints in cash. What the Belle of Hungary received, in addition to flowers, clothes, and other gifts, is not quite clear, but the prize does include a week's visit to Egypt and some sort of contract.

Despite all the controversy generated by the beauty contest, the custom of selecting beauty queens is here to stay. In August 1986, for example, when the Grand Prix Formula One car race was held near Budapest, there was also a contest for "Miss Grand Prix."

SPORTS—ARE THEY FOR FUN?

Among the many traits and virtues, one that is dominant with all Hungarians is their love for sports. Hungarians are very competitive and that shows on their athletic score cards as well. In the sports world, Hungary is considered a major competitor. Among the nations of similar size, Hungary always finished best at the Olympic Games, provided, of course, it was a participant. There are times when Hungary will abstain from participation, as was the case in 1984 in Los Angeles. The decision not to participate in the XXIII Olympiad was handed down in Moscow, not in Budapest. Of course, to make it look like a genuine Hungarian decision, the Hungarian Olympic Committee was convened—two days after the Soviet Union announced its nonparticipation—and reached, in solidarity with the Soviet bloc leader, a pseudo-decision to boycott the Los Angeles games. There have been rumors to the effect that several Hungarian delegations tried to influence the "Great Eastern Neighbors" into participating, but without success. In order to pacify the disappointed public, the authorities then permitted a daily one-hour TV coverage of the Olympic events from Los Angeles. Therefore, it is appropriate to ask, what role do sports play in Hungarian society?

The much-heralded socialist principle of "sports for the masses" or "mass involvement in sports" is only for outward appearances, because in reality it amounts to no more than a cliché. For example, if one wants to participate in a sport purely out of love of sport, he or she is out of luck. There is not room for bourgeois individualism and self-aggrandizement in a political system that claims to produce better athletes and superior achievements than its capitalist competitors. Sports in Hungary, like in other socialist countries of the Soviet bloc, are pure and simple politics. The system tries to prove its superiority vis-à-vis the outside world by breaking new athletic records, and by providing people at home a form of inexpensive entertainment, lavishly adorned with political objectives to mobilize the public, especially the young people, toward the achievement of socialist goals. Sports unions not only manage the country's sports life, but also engage in party-oriented activity of a mobilizational character. There is hardly any club that can support itself without state subsidy. Even the popular soccer (in Hungary called football) clubs receive significant support from the state. In Hungary there are no professionals; thus, on paper, every soccer player is an amateur. What this means is that each player holds down a job, which is a hidden, so-called "sport position," created by the company or industry supporting the team and the club. In this position the player receives a permanent monthly salary. Naturally not only does he not have to work for this money, but he does not even have to go in to pick it up. The money (i.e., salary) is simply mailed to the address of the club, where it is handed over to the player. In addition to this, the players receive "calorie money," and "victory bonuses." In other words, they are professionals, while maintaining the facade of amateur status. The problem is that these so-called "amateur" players are allowed to participate in any amateur event and usually they beat the real amateurs in unfair competition. An individual playing for a Class One team usually earns 10–15 thousand forints monthly. Any outstanding player will receive additional benefits. If the team is good, it may be invited to play abroad, which is very good business for both the players and the club. Outside the borders, the players receive their daily expense monies as well as a certain amount for each match, in hard currency. This applies even to the noncompetitive (so-called "friendly" or exhibition) matches. In the case of World Cup soccer matches, the benefits can be of two kinds. If the playoffs consist of several rounds, the bonus is increased, usually doubled after each round. If the team defeats a famous foreign team, there is even additional money. The trouble is that the previously promised money is not always delivered. This is what happened during the 1974 World

Championship in Argentina. During the preliminaries, the players were promised U.S.\$2,000, to be received during the finals; and customs-free status for anything they purchased with that money. The team made the finals, but in Argentina they found out that the money was no longer available. Their disappointment was noticeable both on and off the field.

Members of the national team often receive favorable treatment at the border by the customs officials. This may be legal or illegal, the fact is that they bring in stuff bought abroad without paying duties on it. Evidently this is how they were going to bring in the stuff they were stealing in a London department store, except that the wives of two team members were caught. During a subsequent match involving the Ferencváros team, a choir from the stands began to chant: "Mrs. Fazekas went to steal . . ." for it was the wife of the Dózsa club player, Fazekas, who was caught shoplifting in London. The members of the national team also enjoy preferential treatment by the courts. Almost everyone in Hungary knows, for example, that the center forward, Torocsik, ran someone down while driving drunk, yet he was not jailed. An average citizen would have been locked up and would have lost his license, too. But in the case of a national team member, who also plays for the team of the police, the story is quite different. Incidentally, every club is supported by one of the national organizations: Honvéd by the army; Dózsa by the police; Vasas by the party; MTK by the Hungarian Jewry; FTC [Ferencvárosi Torna Klub or "Fradi"] by the food industry; and so on. Other clubs are known by the name of their sponsors, for example, the VIDEOTÓN TV factory in Székesfehérvár or the name of a city or town. There is a certain amount of political irony in this; for example, the dissident citizen usually roots for the FTC team, which wears the green and white colors. A match involving the "Fradi" is always a mass social event, and fights are frequent. Many people find this the only way to exhibit their anti-regime feelings. The police always take the troublemakers in for 2–3 days of interrogation as the "guests of the Yard," after which they are free to go, but they are forbidden to attend sports events for a certain period of time. Of course these scandals are mild when compared with similar events taking place in Italy or Latin America. The political tendencies connected with the teams have other consequences, as well. By manipulating the contingents of the teams, the authorities can make champions out of any team they desire. For example, in 1969 the "Fradi" was at the top with practically no competition. The authorities drafted every one of their players and turned them into the famous Honvéd team; the authorities also formed the nucleus of the national "Golden Team." Nowadays this is not done quite so openly; nevertheless, the hand of the authorities pulling the strings is still obvious.

When a player reaches the age of 30, he is allowed to sign a contract with a foreign team. He is obliged to turn over 20 percent of his earnings to the state and he can keep the rest. Whatever he purchases abroad, he can bring back to Hungary without paying duties. For example, two of the "Fradi's" players, Szokolai and Nyilasi, were allowed to sign contracts in Austria, which almost removed "Fradi" from the Class One [Nemzeti Bajnokság I] championship.

Corruption and the "pulling of strings" do not always originate at the top; sometimes they happen on a lower level, too. They include such practices as the manipulation of tickets and rewards, the bribing of officials, game and lottery fixing—to mention a few. One of the more interesting cases of corruption was discovered when the Nyíregyháza (a town in eastern Hungary) team was investigated. It became apparent that the income of the stadium suddenly decreased, even though the seats were always full. A thorough investigation proved to be quite revealing. A certain portion of the tickets were not real tickets, but simply printed forms that could be purchased in any stationery store. Thus there were no records for the sale of these tickets. The club did not report this amount to the (national) Football Association, but instead utilized it to reward the players or to payoff opponents to "throw" certain games. This was corroborated by several players who then told the rest of the story. Around the end of the 1983/84 season, the Nyíregyháza team beat the Csepel team at the latter's home, with the score of 3 to 0. This was a fantastic and surprising upset. After observing the playing of the teams, the head referee reported his suspicions to the Football Association. Following a preliminary investigation, the coach of Csepel team admitted that he and several key players on his team received a significant amount of money for "throwing" the game. As a result, the participants have been suspended from any sport activities for many years. The upshot of the whole affair was the suspension of Nyíregyháza from the Class One championship. Rumors have it that the Football Association's intent to castigate Nyíregyháza was to set an example for the future. However, cases like this are frequent in Hungary today; everyone talks about them, but nobody does anything about them. According to "Fradi" players, for example, the matches between their team and the Dózsa team have for years been ending in a fix. Only if there are no special pre-game agreements, the two teams will play to a tie. If, however, one of the teams needs the two points (i.e., to win), then the game will not end in a tie. There is no payment involved here; the two points are simply "borrowed." They can be "returned" when the losing team needs to win. It is not unusual, therefore, to see the same year "Fradi" as the national champion and Dózsa the winner of the national cup. This way, both teams end up with prestige and awards. If for some reason there is no agreement (on fixing the outcome of games), then the viewers are in for the rare treat of a "lively" match. According to one of the interviewed subjects, during the late 1960s, as a fervent "Fradi" fan, he used to attend not only every match but every training session of the team. One of the players, who became the subject's close friend, was apparently boasting that he used to be able to name not only the winning team, but the score and the "script" of the game, that is, the order in which the goals were to be kicked, and who would kick them. This was important to him, because the high scorers receive awards, which means prestige and money.

If a soccer player wants to transfer from one club to another, this can be accomplished through official or unofficial channels. The former method consists of an agreement between two clubs that spells out the terms affecting the player, moneys, rights, and obligations. In addition to this, there are certain benefits provided for the player "under the table," which are not part of the written agreement—they are simply transacted verbally between the player and the new club. In most cases the player receives an apartment free of rent and a lump sum of money, which can be as high as 500,000 forints. If one considers the kind of sacrifices an average Hungarian must make in order to obtain an apartment, and the average monthly income of less than 5,000 forints, then the "under-the-table" benefits of a soccer player are far too excessive. Yet there are also other privileges and benefits that go with the position of a well-known player. For example, there was a player on the team of Györ (a city in western Hungary), named Korsos. He was not only an excellent soccer player, but also somewhat of a "swinger," who literally liked wine, women, and songs. Once he became involved in some brawling incident that became a police matter and could not be "taken care of" in the usual manner of speaking. In September 1984 the club suspended the player for 6 months, for conduct unbecoming a sportsman. The Football Association immediately had him transferred to the party's team, the Vasas, and one week later, due to a happenstance, he played against his former team. Similar cases took place in other sports as well, with the result that a successful, well-known sportsman cannot be disciplined. However, conventional wisdom in Hungary is very much concerned that if you cannot enforce discipline on one player, how can you expect the other players to follow? Thus, the behavior of outstanding Hungarian sportsmen abroad causes serious problems. The above-mentioned case of shoplifting in a London department store is just one such case. But there were also brawls, drunken scenes, and, most recently, another shoplifting case involving the Hungarian boxing team. Of course, most Hungarians consider their sportsmen as decent and honorable members of society, but then there are those Hungarians who are more envious and less forgiving.

The most significant case in recent years was the scandal involving the TOTO—a state-guaranteed, state-organized mass gambling involving sports events. During the summer months there are matches that have no bearing on the season's standings. There are 14 matches on a betting ticket and one has to guess the results. One means that the bettor picks team No. 1 as the winner, 2 means team No. 2, and X means he calls it a tie. 14 correct guesses (called "13 + 1") means that the player wins several hundred thousand forints. A handful of people became rich by making sure that 9–11 matches out of the 14 were sure bets. They used several methods. The simplest was to find out the line-up from insiders. Due to the lack of interest, the clubs often started their second lines or even their youth teams. In cases like this, there was little doubt about the outcome of the match. The other method was the simple purchase of the match. This could be done by approaching the players, coaches, or the referees. An agreement with a few key players was usually sufficient; they simply made some mistakes in a few crucial situations, and the resulting one or two goals usually sealed the outcome of the game. They used this method when two evenly matched teams faced each other; in the case of significant differences, they could guess the outcome themselves. However, in the case of well-matched teams, 1 or 2 goals make all the difference. Payments to referees served the same purpose: a little tendentious refereeing, a few overlooked off-sides, one or two wrongly-awarded free kicks could decide the outcome without arousing suspicion. All of the information centered in the hands of 3–4 persons; the "flunkies" only knew about one or two matches. Thus, within a few weeks a few men pocketed huge amounts of money by having to play only a few variations. For example, in the case of four undecided, unfixed matches, the possibilities are only $3 \times 3 \times 3 \times 3 = 81$. Filling out this many tickets (at 5 forints apiece) guarantees a 13 + 1 result. This went on until someone became suspicious. The "fixers" were careful enough not to have the same persons pick up the money week after week. Therefore, winning tickets were sold to private businessmen or entrepreneurs, who used these "winnings" to document their (unreported) earnings. Then came the slip-up, caused by the numbering of the tickets. Week after week, tickets having the same or nearly the same serial numbers won. This was detected by someone from the group that checks the tickets. After this, they started to watch the winnings, and finally some insider broke down and spilled the beans. There were a series of arrests, and Budapest witnessed the "TOTO trial of the century." The participants received several years in prison and the state even ordered large confiscation of their wealth. Thus, even though the other bettors were the victims, it was the state that made significant profits out of the case.

There was another similar case a few years earlier, but this one was much larger in scope and operation. The affair had an interesting follow-up. In the summer of 1985 one of the few existing private theatrical companies announced a humorous program: "Why is Soccer Ruined, or 'Did You Also Play TOTO, Buddy?' " The play was written by Antal Végh, who also authored an earlier book, *Why Is Hungarian Soccer Sick?* The play attempted to make fun of the shady sides of Hungarian soccer on the stage. However, weeks before the premiere, there were threatening letters to the organizers, and warnings that some people would try to disrupt the event. At the premiere, a group, well-equipped with vegetables, eggs, and tomatoes, did indeed break up the performance. Afterward the newspapers wrote the whole thing off as a theatrical failure, though obviously the group of demonstrators was operating with state support. There was never any mention of the scene being prearranged; the information about the threatening letters came from a former player of the national team, who was personally involved in the program.

It should be obvious by now, whether for good or bad, party or government authorities are involved in every sports event. This is also true for the first Grand Prix Formula One car race, which took place on August 10, 1986. The race was held on a newly-built track known as the "Hungaroring," which is 18 kilometers outside Budapest. The four kilometer track was built in a record time of 8 months at an estimated cost of 500 million forints. The race was attended by an estimated 200,000 people and was covered by 27 television stations, mostly from Western Europe but also from the Soviet Union, Czechoslovakia, Bulgaria, Poland, and Yugoslavia.[27] The sponsors for international motor racing, the Formula One Constructors' Association (FOCA), as well as all Hungarian media, declared the race a success.[28] It is interesting to note that the president of FOCA, Bernie Ecclestone, opted for Hungary after unsuccessful attempts to persuade Moscow and Prague to build a track and after his associate, a former emigré, suggested that he try Budapest. The contract was signed and sealed in 1985. Under the contract with FOCA, Hungary did not share in the television rights and advertisements; its only source of hard currency income came from the sale of tickets in Western Europe. Instead of the expected 30–40 thousand Westerners, however, only about 10,000 came, leaving Hungary with less than one-quarter of the expected U.S.$2.5 million in hard currency revenue.[29]

It is possible that fears of radiation from the Chernobyl reactor accident had something to do with the low number of Western visitors. According to *Heti Világgazdaság*, by the spring of 1986, 15,000 hotel reservations had been booked in Budapest for the day of the race; but reservations were cancelled in May and June.[30] Perhaps to pull Hungary out of the financial hole, about 30,000 tickets each were sold in the G.D.R. and Czechoslovakia. However, none of this helped to pay the $900,000 committed to FOCA for the rights to organize the race under its auspices. Therefore, the Hungarian National Bank had to step in. As for the future, it was assured by sports officials and government authorities as well that the investment in the race track complex would be recovered in the next five years or so.[31] While the Soviet Sports daily *Sovetskii Sport* praised the race,[32] an article in the Budapest daily *Magyar Hírlap* criticized some Western newspapers for depicting the race as in indication of Hungarian "independence" or movement toward a capitalist way of life. Hungary was merely trying to "catch up with the West" the article said, defensively.[33]

CONCLUSIONS

In order to assess the quality of life in Hungary, one would have to ask every Hungarian how he or she feels about their present life, or perhaps about the whole course of their life. Obviously this would be an impossible task. The enumeration of personal reasons for being content or discontent with life, even if people do express in some way the relative weight or priority they attribute to one or another factor that plays a role in their life, will never be complete. Neither are people conscious of all factors that influence their feelings or judgment about life, nor are they willing to speak about everything they may have on their mind—success or failure in marriage, trouble with children and relatives, the general political situation, and so on. For these and other reasons, no social scientists have tried to measure the quality of life of an individual person. Instead they gather data that relate to quality of life as a collective attribute that adheres to groups or categories of people, not to individuals. Consequently, any measure or indicator of the quality of life is regarded as a social indicator inasmuch as it characterizes (in quantified terms) the well-being of certain groups or categories of people. In our case, the selected indicators of life quality in Hungary are based both on objectively observable facts and conditions of life in Hungarian society, and on Hungarians' own subjective perceptions and assessments of the life they live under the given circumstances.

On the previous pages an attempt was made to give a sample of the subjective perception of Hungarians as far as entertainment in restaurants, wine cellars, espressos, clubs, concerts, theaters, beauty contests, and various sports is concerned. It should have been obvious in all cases that public entertainment of all types is subject to party and government controls with the aim to provide a variety of outlets for the release of tension and stress of all individuals and social groups and for the mobilization of society to support the national programs. In all instances, because of the socialist morality imposed on entertainment, the existing loopholes have given rise to exploitation that led to corruption and all manner of abuse. Thus, again as in similar situations (mentioned in preceding chapters), many Hungarians took advantage of the opportunities to enhance their own position in society. As far as the authorities are concerned, they face the same dilemma in the entertainment field as they do in the economic one: Either to tighten the controls and thereby risk the suppression or elimination of incentives responsible for the improved economic conditions in the country, or to ignore the spread of questionable practices in entertainment and hence allow for a superficially content society. Just how important these incentives are can be seen from a few examples. Household plot [*háztalyi föld*] farmers account for about 20 percent of Hungary's poultry production, 40 percent of its pork production and over 50 percent of the country's egg supply. Over 15 percent of the total working hours are accounted for by the second economy, which generates 30 percent of the population's income. Reported personal savings have climbed from $1.4 billion in 1970 to almost $5 billion in 1985—more than four annual salaries per individual. In 1960 there were about 18,000 automobiles in Hungary. Today there are more than 1.2 million privately-owned cars, and more than 200,000 people are on a waiting list to acquire one. There are more than 3 million television sets in Hungary—about 15 percent color sets. Of the 70,432 dwellings built in 1985, about 60,000 were built by the private sector with state loans. While in 1958 only 18,000 Hungarians traveled abroad to both socialist and nonsocialist countries, in 1986, for example, Hungarians made 6.3 million trips abroad. There were similar increases in the number of tourists visiting Hungary: from 39,000 in 1958 to 16.6 million in 1986. Therefore, it is not surprising that the demand for travel far exceeds the supply of Hungarian tourists booked on tours to such exotic places as Peru, Australia, and India—tours that cost between 50,000 and 100,000 forints. This, in a country where the average official wage is only some 70,000 forints a year. It is equally unsurprising to learn that about 45 percent of Hungary's trade is with the West.[34]

Hungary's quiet economic reform, which started in 1968 and triggered the creation of the second and third economies in the country, looked very successful on the surface. From the mid-1960s to the mid-1970s the Hungarian GNP grew at 6 percent or better per annum. Real income grew by 5.6 percent. Almost everyone was getting cars, refrigerators, and TV sets; and Hungary witnessed an unprecedented 4–4.5 percent agricultural growth. It was an unparalleled period in Hungarian economic history. It lifted the expectations of all Hungarians to a level of even greater ambitions and incentives because the opportunities for a better life were just around the corner.

However beneath the surface the party and government authorities, still suffering from ideological restraints, were only half-heartedly supporting the reforms. Only the more efficient firms were subjected to some market discipline. The inefficient firms, which should have been closed down, were kept afloat on a burgeoning river of subsidies. In one year, subsidies to inefficient operations nearly doubled, to about $2 billion. The dogmatists, advocating strict central planning, regained some power in 1972, allowing them to set the reforms back, but not for long—OPEC saved them from that fate. Hungary's ratio of its export price increases to its import price increases plummeted by some 25 percent. To finance that, Hungary began piling up debt; from 1973 to 1978 the country's hard currency debt quintupled to $7.5 billion—almost triple the value of its exports.

Although the dogmatists were able to arouse the national anger at the new class of rich managers and peasants, the Kádár leadership had no choice but to forge ahead with the reform movement by giving priority to hard-currency-earning export projects. The result: Hungary's hard-currency account registered a small surplus (about U.S.$150 million) in 1980, but Hungary was not out of the woods yet. According to an unpublished semi-official report compiled in November 1986, under the auspices of Hungary's PPF, by a large group of Hungarian economists, sociologists, and other experts (and excerpted in the supplement to the *Financial Times*, February 20, 1987), the economic results of the 1980s, especially those for 1985 and 1986, have shown a sign of enfeeblement and disarray among the party and government authorities charting the course of the Hungarian reforms. The experts pointed out that: labor, energy, raw material, and capital are being squandered; Hungary has been unable to adjust to new trends in the world economy; CMEA deliveries are no longer secure; tension within the economy is not caused by external factors but by basic domestic problems and the postponement of further reforms; and waste has led the system of allocating funds into a serious crisis. The economic hardship still continues and the Kádár regime has told the Hungarian people to tighten their belts. There were numerous steep price increases since 1979, the most drastic one in July 1987, while wage increases were held down to a minimum. The economic hardship still continues and the Kádár regime has told the Hungarian people to tighten their belts. There were numerous steep price increases since 1979, while wage increases were held down to a minimum. Real income rose by less than the projected 7 percent during the 1981–1985 Five-Year Plan. It is therefore understandable that many Hungarians today are disgruntled; their expectations for greater opportunities and a noticeably improved lifestyle are presently not being realized.

Remembering that the great disparities between word and deed, between the egalitarian self-image of the party and the new class of the political elite, were the main cause of the 1956 Revolution, the authorities under János Kádár's leadership are extremely sensitive to the socioeconomic problems that can trigger a new upheaval in the country. Therefore the policy of reconciliation after 1956 continued to aim for the eradication of the glaring inequalities of the past. The problem, however, remains that while the standard of living and the lifestyle of the working class has improved considerably during the period of economic reform, the same economic miracle has created an upper class that is also responsible for an "anti-rich" mood in Hungary.[35] In Budapest and other Hungarian cities, the latest shibboleth is "the socialist millionaire." The lack of statistical data makes it difficult to estimate the number of millionaires presently in the country, but according to official sources there are quite a few and their number is growing. The authorities' response to the critics who regard these developments in Hungary as contradictions in the values of socialism is short and simple: We act according to the principles of Marxism-Leninism, not by a course of "penurious equalization but by not allowing our economy to lag behind, and by creating the conditions for a new prosperity."[36] At what cost or price? That still remains an open issue.

What is clear so far is Hungary's determination to adapt to changed conditions that have created a new political culture of "socialist pragmatism" with its own subculture consisting of unsanctioned practices of an underground economy.[37] It is also clear that so far the socialist system and its subsystem seem to be working smoothly side-by-side, and while the party and government authorities are convinced that they are creating the conditions for a new prosperity by redefining socialism, the Hungarian people at large feel that *they* are responsible for forcing the hand of the authoritative decision makers to adopt more liberal policies. This is especially true when one examines the consumption levels in Hungary.

Take foodstuff consumption, for example: in 1984, every Hungarian consumed 78 kg of meat and fish; 185 kg of milk and dairy products; 33 kg of fats; 58 kg of potatoes; 327 eggs; 3 kg of coffee; 30 litres of wine; 87 litres of beer; 9.9 litres of hard liquor; and 2 kg of tobacco.[38] Compared with the pre-reform period and with other socialist countries in the Soviet bloc, these figures are certainly impressive. In 1984, Hungary's citizens realized the monetary income of 634 billion forints. Approximately 28 percent of this sum was spent on foodstuffs; 15 percent on pleasure items; 30.9 percent on durable consumer goods; and 25.9 percent on service-related items.[39] It is also interesting to note that workers and pensioners spent far more on foodstuffs than the white-collar group.[40] In January 1985 there were 4,940,000 working people in Hungary; of that total 2,247,000 worked in light industry. Physical work was done by 3,322,000 people of which 1,416,000 were skilled workers.[41] While the lowest income groups spend 86 percent of their income on necessities, the upper income groups spend only 50 percent. Thus luxury items, including cars, are the prerogative of the high income groups.[42]

Next to income, housing is the second most important indicator of the quality of life in Hungary. In 1982, 59 percent of the workers, 88 percent of the collective peasantry, 37 percent of the white-collar group, and 70 percent of the pensioners lived in a one-family house.[43] Living space is still scarce, especially in cities like Budapest. Apartments with central heating or heating from a remote source are owned by 17 percent of the workers and 8 percent of the pensioners, as opposed to 27 percent of the white-collar families.[44] While in 1985 every 1,000 dwellings built had electricity and water, only 319 had gas heating.[45] In terms of household equipment and facilities the quality of housing is much higher in urban areas than it is in the rural regions. However in terms of the availability of living space, it is just the opposite. Perhaps the greatest difference between the social groups is in the possession of telephone service. Only 6 percent of the unskilled workers have a telephone, as opposed to 40 percent of the professionals.

Despite all the social differences that exist in Hungarian society today it is safe to argue that the progress achieved since 1968 has created an awareness of general satisfaction. The lifestyle of the average Hungarian has improved considerably in the last two decades. By making this point, however, it would be shear folly to underestimate the growing dissatisfaction among the majority of the people concerning equality in Hungarian society. All of the surveys conducted on this subject for the last 5–10 years show that an overwhelming percentage of people interviewed (85–90 percent) are of the opinion that "there are some who are too well off." However opinions differ as to whether or not there are also some who are "not well enough off." Neither is there complete agreement about what sections make up society today. The growing public awareness and widespread discontent with continued economic and social inequalities in Hungarian society, was finally tackled on July 2, 1987, by an "action programme" of the HSWP CC which endorsed a wage reform, stating that "salaries and wages should be made proportional to the social usefulness of the work performed," to be reflected in an income tax and value-added tax. After some opposition from the Academy of Sciences, the PPF, the trade union council, and the state office of wages and labor, the Hungarian Parliament approved, on September 18, 1987, the Central Committee's recommendation, and thus, Hungary will be the first socialist country to introduce value-added tax and personal income tax beginning January 1, 1988. The objectives of the tax reforms are: to shift the burden of taxation from producers to consumers, to reduce subsidy of loss-operating enterprises, to enable successful enterprises to reinvest in modernization, and to make Hungarian industry more responsive to world market conditions. It will also tap the estimated 30 percent income from the second and third economies.

Because of the slowdown of economic growth and, therefore, the near stagnation of resources, the core of the controversy concerning the quality of life in Hungary today is the clash between economic interests and social policy. There are some who argue that full employment is the cause of many economic shortcomings. There are criticisms directed against the subsidized social services, saying that people do not value what they get free, that they overuse or abuse services that are very costly to provide, and that they constitute a disincentive to work more and earn more. Therefore they advocate more market-oriented solutions, assuming that this will improve the services and create new incentives to produce more.[46]

NOTES

1. Elemér Hankiss, "Második társadalom? Kísérlet egy fogalom meghatározása és egy valóságtartomány leírása" [The other society? Attempt to define a concept and to describe a Province of reality], *Valóság* 5 (1984): 25.

2. Endre Hánn and Lázár Guy, "The balance of five years," *Jel-Kép* 3 (1985).

3. Drago Buvać, "How to warm up cooled down 'goulash socialism'," *Vjesnik* (July 12, 1986).

See *Nemzetközi Szemle* [International Review] (January 1985): 9–23.

5. *Napló* (Veszprém) (May 12, 1970).

6. *Népszabadság* (May 23, 1986).

7. See *Népszabadság* (May 29, 1986) and *Magyarország* (June 22, 1986).

8. *Népszabadság* (March 21, 1986).

9. Ibid.

10. *Magyar Hírlap* (March 12, 1986). For the deficiency of the law and recommendations for media reforms, see *Népszabadság*, June 27, 1987.

11. June 11, 1985, 9:30 p.m.

12. *Süddeutsche Zeitung* (May 10, 1985).

13. *Népszabadság* (May 10, 1985).

14. *Die Presse* (May 8, 1985).

15. *Der Spiegel* (May 20, 1985).

16. *Népszabadság* (May 11, 1985).

17. *Magyarorzág* (March 3, 1985).

18. *Dunántúli Napló* (April 22, 1985).

19. See *Munka* (March 1985) and *Népszava* (June 7, 1985).

20. *Magyar Hírlap* (May 4, 1984).

21. *Dunántúli Napló* (March 3, 1985).

22. See Péter Bogáti's article "The collective community marches in four columns," *Valóság* 5 (1984); 63–75.

23. *Népszabadság* (April 20, 1985).

24. *Magyar Hírlap* (Illustrated Supplement) (September 21, 1985).

25. "Hundred sixty eight hours," *Radio Budapest* (October 12, 1984, 4:00 p.m.).

26. *Ifjúsági Magazín* (September 19, 1985).

27. *The Times* (August 12, 1986).

28. *Népszava, Magyar Nemzet,* and *Magyar Hírlap* (August 11, 1986).

29. *Héti Világgazdaság* (August 16, 1986).

30. *Heti Világgazdaság* (August 2, 1986).

31. *Magyar Hírlap* (Supplement) (August 2, 1986).

32. August 13, 1986, p. 4.

33. *Magyar Hírlap* (August 16, 1986).

34. The above data are derived from various annual issues of *Magyar Statisztikai Évkönyv* [Hungarian Statistical Yearbook] and *Statisztikai Zsebkönyv* [Statistical Pocket Book], both published in Budapest by the Central Statistical Office.

35. *Magyar Hírlap* (September 15, 1984).

36. Iván T. Bérend, "Catching up or falling behind? The lessons of a decade," *Magyar Nemzet* (December 24, 1983).

37. See interview with István Huszár, director of the Hungarian Party History Institute and a member of the HSWP Central Committee, in the Zagreb (Yugoslavia) weekly, *Danas* (December 3, 1985).

38. See *Statisztikai Zsebkönyv, 1984* [1984 Statistical Pocket Book] (Budapest: Central Statistical Office, 1985).

39. See *Magyar Hírek* 38 (July 6, 1986); 5.

40. Nyitrai, Ferencné, "Gazdasági élet" [Economic life] in *Mit kell tudni Magyarországról* [Essential Facts About Hungary] (Budapest: Kossuth Könyvkiadó, 1984), 243.

41. *Magyar Hírek* 38 (July 6, 1985); 5.

42. József Bálint, *Társadalmi retegezödés és jövedelmek* [Social Stratification and Incomes] (Budapest: Kossuth Könyvkiadó, 1983), 246.

43. Bálint, op. cit., 264.

44. Nyitrai, Ferencné, op. cit., 245.

45. *Magyar Hírek* 38 (July 6, 1985); 5.

46. See Zsuzsa Ferge, "Main trends in Hungarian social policy," *The New Hungarian Quarterly* 23 (Summer 1982); 137–149.

PART IV
NEW SOCIETY WITH OLD TRADITIONS

7
The Hungarian Social Character

In the Introduction to this study the point was made that Hungarians today enjoy greater economic and political freedom than their counterparts in the Soviet bloc. The reason given for this phenomenon was the peculiarity of the Hungarian social character. In this chapter an attempt will be made to explain this concept within the framework of contemporary Hungarian society.

Since this study assumes that character structure is a more or less permanent, socially and historically conditioned organization of an individual's drives and satisfactions, it also takes for granted that character is socially conditioned and man is made by his society. Hence we speak of character as "social character,"[1] that is, the patterned uniformities of learned response that distinguish people of different backgrounds, experiences and convictions. Character structure, like social structure, serves not only to limit choice but also to channel action by foreclosing some of the otherwise limitless behavior choices of human beings; in like manner the social character permits human beings to live in some sort of working harness. As a result, the function of social character is to ensure or permit conformity in society. There are various modes of conformity that are developed in social character. In the previous chapters an attempt was made to identify some of these modes as they apply, for instance, to the institutions of family and religion; in this chapter we will endeavor to construct an index to characterize Hungarian society through an analysis of class structure and attitudinal responses to sensitive social and cultural issues.

It is further assumed in this study that people of radically different types (background and experience) can adapt themselves to perform a number of complex tasks. That is to say, social institutions can harness a variety of different motivations, arising from different character types, to perform very much the same kinds of socially demanded jobs. Therefore we must take into account the possibility that people may be compelled to behave in one way although their character structure spurs them to behave in an opposite way. This behavior is particularly noticeable in authoritarian societies where the vertically imposed new norms and practices are in direct conflict with old traditional values and practices that are deeply rooted in character structure. Such a resolution to radically revamp a society, without a successful process of socialization, usually ends in an open conflict at an opportune time. This was the case in Hungary in October 1956 when the traditional forces of Hungarian society—betrayed, and with their values threatened—chose to risk their lives in a revolt against the small but powerful group of Stalinists who were determined to mold a new society with a social character conforming to the rigid ideological tenets of Marxism-Leninism. Today, the character structure in Hungary is more consensual than conflictual; it reflects the changes in party policy and methods of operation initiated by the Kádár regime. The party has become socialized and has embraced many "old" values; even so, there are still two societies, each of them characterized by different structural properties.[2]

The social sciences are rich in methods for classifying societies. For example, David Riesman in his well known study of the changing American character, *The Lonely Crowd,* emphasized the relationship between population growth of the American society and the historical sequence of character types. He and his associates explored the correlations between the conformity demands put on people in American society and the broadest of the social indexes that connect people with their environment—the demographic indexes. Riesman makes the point that a useful key to those indexes is the population theory, according to which all societies are located in and moving along a curve of population growth and distribution. Because the United States has a long history of industrialization, Riesman used a particular kind of S-shaped curve for population analysis as an approach to the study of American society and character.[3] Consequently he developed a typology of American character that he calls tradition-directed, inner-directed, and other-directed. It is the latter that has some significance for this study because "other-directed" people, according to Riesman, live in a society of *incipient population decline* with "a social character whose conformity is insured by their tendency to be sensitized to the expectations and preferences of others."[4] As pointed out in Chapter 5 under "Changes in the Family Structure," projections of population decline in Hungary are so alarming that party and state authorities have decided to give priority to population policy over socialist policy. The authorities are not only encouraging large families but rewarding them with money and other benefits, even if this means in many instances a return to the asymmetrical model of family structure based on traditional values. However, when one considers the unprecedentedly high rate of alcoholism, suicide, and divorce—coupled with other contributing factors to the decline of population, such as the catastrophic housing situation, the aging population, fewer marriages, more frequent abortions, stillbirths, and the rising cost of living—then the rational choice of seeking to stabilize population growth in Hungary is understandable. Another way of making this point is to suggest that by October 1956 the party authorities had learned from past experience that the attempted destruction of the traditional hierarchical structures and the replacement of the latter by strict ideological uniformity ended in complete failure and, therefore, that they had no choice but to initiate a policy of cooperation with the populace rather than coercion. By 1962 the conditions were ripe for Kádár to formulate his famous slogan: "Whereas the Rákosiites used to say that those who are not with us are against us, we say those who are not against us are with us."[5] The same year Kádár's "alliance policy," promising liberalization for the future, received the highest accolade from the HSWP's 8th Congress.[6] By then, the population growth in the country had reached a new low and all the indicators were signaling a steady decline. In anticipation that this trend could be reversed, the authorities introduced a series of measures making their population policy one of several ploys to appease a large segment of Hungarian society. Of course it would be sheer folly to argue, as the population theorists do, that all societies (including Hungary) are moving along a curve of population growth and distribution and, therefore, changes in population are correlates of changes in the social character.[7] In addition to changes in population, there are many other factors and variables contributing to changes in the Hungarian social character; for example, the size and location of the country, the distribution of the changes among social classes, sex, education, and income distributions, the persistence of customs and traditions, nationalism and anti-minority attitudes, alcoholism, suicide and divorce, and above all, the limitations of basic freedoms imposed on society by the ruling elite. The latter is particularly important, since Hungary, as a Marxist-Leninist political system, is deeply committed to the socialist camp under Soviet leadership.

SOCIAL CLASSES

Officially, Hungarian authorities recognize three "friendly" classes: the workers, the peasants, and the intelligentsia—all cooperating in the process of socialist production. The party as the leading and guiding force of Hungarian society sees itself as the builder of a classless society that is to be achieved through the expansion of the working class, which is the backbone of society. According to Hungarian semantics, the term *munkás* (worker) includes both agricultural and industrial laborers—a political advantage for the party because it inflates the ranks of the working class in a society that has a strong agricultural/rural background. Thus the category "working class" includes: (1) blue-collar workers in state enterprises and cooperatives (including agriculture and forestry); (2) skilled workers, technicians, and foremen; and (3) pensioners from the above occupations and persons who have transferred from this category to other jobs (e.g., state and party bureaucracy). In 1984 the proportion of the working class in the economically active population stood at 55.7 percent—only 2.1 percent above the 1941 level. In 1949, however, blue-collar workers made up only 38.8 percent of total wage earners. The reason for the large decline in the number of the blue-collar workers between 1941 and 1949 (14.8 percent) is the large population shift from urban to rural areas after WWII to take advantage of the large-scale land reform in Hungary.

A similar trend, but in reverse, can be seen among blue-collar workers in agriculture and forestry. Here the trend has been a steady decline, from 23.5 percent in 1949 to 7.6 percent in 1980.[8] As a result of restructuring the traditional character of agricultural work, the technical, legal, and economic skills needed for efficient operation of farms have steadily increased. Another characteristic of the development of collective peasantry is the rise of the "employed" category to the detriment of the collective farm members themselves. Between 1973 and 1980, the proportion of manual workers who had contracted for work on a collective farm rose from 12 to 23.9 percent.[9] As employees, the workers enjoy greater prestige and the simple labor contract gives them greater freedom and mobility, especially to the young people.

Another segment of Hungarian society cooperating in the process of socialist production is the white-collar stratum, or intelligentsia. It encompasses a variety of professions and occupations in the large spectrum of productive and nonproductive branches of the economy. In 1981 Hungarian intellectual resources reached a figure of 1,399,200, or about 28 percent of the active wage earners, which represents an increase of 287,000 people or 25.8 percent since 1970.[10] Some 330,000 people worked in technical fields, 377,000 in business and administrative jobs, 332,000 in cultural and health services, and about 361,000 in accounting and clerical jobs; 29 percent of all white-collar workers were university graduates.[11] There are several implications that follow from these statistics. First, the "old" intelligentsia has either been deprived of its position or has retired because of age; thus a "new" intelligentsia is in existence that has been exposed to sociopolitical influences after the war. Nevertheless, nowadays, just as before the communist takeover of power, a large number of professional people try to play the role of an elite in the cooperative model of the social classes, while an equally large number of blue-collar workers are of the opinion that professional people are subordinate to the working class. Secondly, there is a disproportion of white-collar workers who favor authority positions; the ratio of "leaders" (department or division heads) to untitled personnel is 1:3.6. In 1981 there were 323,100 "bosses" in Hungary—more chiefs than Indians. According to sociologist József Bálint, the inflated number of "leading and directing positions is a consequence of...sources of income and prestige" rather than necessity.[12] Thirdly, the unusual increase in intellectual resources (25.8 percent between 1970 and 1981) can be equated with the early rise in bureaucracy during the period of central planning (1949–1968). However, due to the introduction of the NEM in 1968, there have been drastic shifts in the make-up of white-collar jobs. Whereas the number of accounting and clerical jobs as well as cultural and health services declined by roughly 22 percent between 1970 and 1980, the jobs in technical fields and state and business administration increased by a whopping 164 percent.[13]

Although Hungarian authorities do not officially consider the small commodity producers, shopkeepers, and small farmers (whose holdings do not exceed three hectares) as members of either the working class or the intelligentsia, unofficially they accept them as contributing economic forces to the process of socialist production. As pointed out in the preceding chapters, especially Chapters 3 and 6, ever since the economic reform of 1968 the party and state authorities have encouraged enterprise autonomy and small entrepreneurship, to the extent that today Hungary has not one but three economies. As a result, private enterprise has mushroomed and a majority of the *maszek* enterprises pursue all sorts of valuable service activities. Over 15 percent of the total working hours are accounted for by the second economy, which generates 30 percent of the population's income. It is not surprising, therefore, that the July 2, 1987, decision of the HSWP CC had not only encouraged the creation of "new, flexible, and profitably operating small and medium-sized enterprises", but also considered them an organic part of the socialist economy. For this reason, it also recommended raising the number of workers in private enterprise from 12 to 24.

Over 50 percent of housing was constructed by the private sector in the last 10 years and *maszek* is also responsible for more than half of all car, watch, radio, and TV repairs in the country. In agriculture the private sector contributed 75,794 million forints or 31.4 percent of the total 1982 value of gross agricultural production, which is twice the value produced by the state sector (15.8 percent).[14] In addition to producing approximately one-third of the gross agricultural output, the share of the small farms in net agricultural production amounts to 49 percent[15]

Table 7.1

Occupational Groups, by Place and Residence (in percentages)

	Budapest	Towns	Villages
Blue-collar	17.7	36.3	46.0
Collective peasantry	4.2	12.3	83.5
White-collar	33.1	41.1	25.8
Small commodity producers	12.8	26.9	60.3

Source: Népszabadság, November 23, 1983, and Hans-Georg Heinrich, Hungary (London: Frances Pinter, 1986), 106.

and they contribute 25 percent of all agricultural exports to the dollar sector.[16] Because of these achievements, the party and state authorities have rehabilitated the small farms in the last decade. Recognizing and accepting their importance, official statements today describe small farms as permanent rather than temporary. While the small commodity producers and shopkeepers are middle-aged men and women on the rise, the small farmers are mostly older people on the decline—representing the skeleton of what was the largest population group in Hungary in 1949. Nevertheless they also represent the backbone of the traditional Hungarian culture, which was systematically decimated by Rákosiite policies in the early 1950s and then again by Kádár after the October 1956 Revolution.

The many peasant workers joining the agricultural cooperatives did not take their traditional values with them, and those migrating to the cities soon lost their cultural identity and pride as they were absorbed into the dark masses under the neon lights. It is not surprising, therefore, that while in 1949 only 31 percent of the skilled and 42 percent of the unskilled workers in industry were of peasant origin, in the mid-1960s these percentages had risen to 36 and 68, respectively.[17] Almost all workers have strong ties to the villages, mostly by virtue of their origin. Thus in spite of the rapid industrialization (which was inevitable even without communist acquisition of power) and collectivization of the farms that resulted in far-reaching social transformations, the village is still present in the Hungarian psyche. Only seven cities in Hungary have a population of over 100,000. With the exception of Budapest, even the bigger towns have a distinctly rural character; the occasional modern multi-level apartment houses on the outskirts of these towns are reminders of the changes that had been ushered in by the industrialization drive. Yet the village lifestyle in socialist Hungary is deep and pervasive. In 1985, only 19.5 percent of Hungary's population lived in Budapest; 43.6 percent lived in villages and the rest lived in smaller towns. About one half of the workers lived in villages. The distribution of the occupational groups to places of residence (Table 7.1) shows that all groups are affected by the village or smalltown lifestyle.

It would, however, be misleading to argue that this influence bears a close resemblance to the "old" traditional values and social characteristics of rural Hungary before the war. Not at all. In the last ten years some fundamental changes have occurred in the development of villages and in the village population itself. In addition to the world economic conditions—which made Hungarian agriculture more important in the national economy—and the recent rise in farm employment, the most noticeable impact on the changes in village development and lifestyle has been the effect of the economic reform introduced in 1968. The aim of the Rákosi policies to transform the staunch and stubborn population of the Hungarian working class had failed through the method of coercion, but succeeded through the economic reform. Today the social structure of the villages can no longer be differentiated in terms of two main social categories: workers and peasants. Within the two major social classes numerous smaller strata, especially if one looks at the composition of active wage earners in the villages, have become distinguishable. Nearly half of the active wage earners in villages cannot remember either what village conditions were or what happened in the villages in the years between 1945 and 1956. Thus the background and experiences of the younger generations in villages are different, and consequently they have ambitions and aspirations other than those of older generations.

There were several recent studies dealing with the changes in and prevailing conditions of rural society in Hungary;[18] they all seem to be in agreement that villages are just as much workers' settlements as they are peasant settlements. As Table 7.2 shows, the social composition of active wage earners living in villages in 1980 was made up of white-collar workers, manual workers, cooperative peasantry, and small-scale commodity producers; they all include smaller strata, which in organizational terms tends to result in lack of cohesion in interest articulation.

In Hungarian villages in 1980, 51.1 percent of the population were skilled, semi-skilled, or unskilled manual (blue-collar) workers, only 19.3 percent were skilled, semi-skilled, or unskilled cooperative peasantry, and as many as 16.1 percent were white-collar workers. The remaining 17 wage-earning categories in villages totaled 13.5 percent. It would be difficult to consider 91,000 manual workers on state farms, 31,000 forestry workers, and 443,000 cooperative farm members as peasants, either in the traditional sense of the word or in that used in the West. Among men, nonagricultural manual workers are in the majority. They include, for example, 32,000 fitters, 31,000 truck drivers, 20,000 transport work-

Table 7.2
Social Composition of Active Earners Living in Villages (1980)

Social class, stratum	Men		Women		Total	
	'000s	%	'000s	%	'000s	%
WHITE-COLLAR WORKERS						
Professional, manager	49.4	3.7	33.6	3.6	83.0	3.6
Other non-manual	92.1	6.8	194.9	20.8	287.0	12.5
MANUAL WORKERS						
Foremen	26.7	2.0	4.4	0.5	31.1	1.4
Skilled	390.9	28.9	73.8	7.8	464.7	20.3
Semi-skilled	240.5	17.8	279.2	29.7	519.7	22.7
Unskilled	96.4	7.1	89.2	9.5	185.6	8.1
Skilled, state farms	33.2	2.5	1.3	0.1	34.5	1.5
Semi-skilled, state farms	25.2	1.9	15.2	1.6	40.4	1.7
Unskilled, state farms	10.8	0.7	5.7	0.6	16.5	0.7
Skilled, agricultural services	1.4	0.1	0.0	0.0	1.4	0.1
Unskilled	2.4	0.2	1.2	0.1	3.6	0.2
Skilled, forestry	8.9	0.7	0.1	0.0	9.0	0.4
Semi-skilled, forestry	10.5	0.8	5.5	0.6	16.0	0.7
Unskilled, forestry	3.7	0.2	1.9	0.2	5.6	0.2
Occasional farm worker	0.7	0.1	0.4	0.0	1.1	0.1
Assisting member of worker's family	0.4	0.0	26.8	2.9	27.2	1.2
COOPERATIVE PEASANTRY						
Manager, foreman	8.9	0.7	0.7	0.1	9.6	0.4
Skilled	133.4	9.8	6.5	0.7	139.9	6.1
Semi-skilled	129.9	9.6	102.3	10.9	232.2	10.1
Unskilled	45.9	3.4	25.1	2.7	71.0	3.1
Assisting family member	1.2	0.0	54.1	5.8	55.3	2.4

Table 7.2 (Continued)

SMALL-SCALE COMMODITY PRODUCER					
Self-employed peasant	13.6	1.0	3.6	0.4	17.2	0.7
Assisting member of peasant family	0.4	0.0	3.4	0.4	3.8	0.2
Self-employed artisan, shop-keeper, etc. and assisting member of family	25.0	1.9	9.3	1.0	35.1	1.5
Total	1,353.1	100.0	938.4	100.0	2,291.5	100.0

Source: Rudolf Andorka and Istvan Harcsa, "Changes in village society during the last ten years," *The New Hungarian Quarterly*, 24, No. 92 (Winter 1983): 32.

ers, 16,000 carpenters and other wood workers, 14,000 bricklayers, 9,000 car mechanics, and so on. Some of them work on the auxiliary units of the large farms and others in jobs servicing agriculture (e.g., repairs, construction, transportation). These fitters, bricklayers, drivers, and so on performed their jobs more like skilled workers in industry, construction, and transport and are therefore more identified with the workers than with the peasants in the traditional sense of the meaning. As a consequence, the composition of those who perform manual work in large agricultural units as well as the characteristics of their work are becoming both more and more like those working in other sectors of the economy and less and less like the peasantry who used to farm independently. The number of small farmers and their helping family members (a total of about 63,000) are a dying species; even by 1970 the majority of them were elderly people farming on poor land where organization into large farms (cooperatives) would have been unprofitable. While on the whole the share of those belonging to agricultural categories diminished, the nonagricultural worker strata increased in the villages; the largest increase was recorded by the semi-skilled workers.

The breakdown of the 411,000 white-collar workers (including foremen) living in the villages also demonstrates a modernization of the social structure of the villages. In 1980, among the various categories, there were 61,000 teachers (and others engaged in cultural occupations), 3,000 priests and ministers, 33,000 district doctors and others providing health services, 99,000 technicians, 98,000 in administrative and business jobs, and 117,000 in accounting and clerical jobs. This breakdown indicates that the social composition of villages in 1980 bears very little resemblance to the villages of the past.

Another unusual development in the transformation of the social structure in the villages is the upward social mobility.[19] A large number of persons and families who leave agriculture, and are thus mobile in the social sense, have remained village inhabitants. Consequently, they have added to the number of manual and white-collar workers in the villages. Many of them had been commuting to their new workplaces from their village residence. According to Hungarian sources, there were over one million commuters at the end of the 1970s.[20] The other consequence is that these commuting workers who reside in villages have kept, and in many instances even cultivated, their own household plots or auxiliary farms. This has led to nonagricultural workers becoming an even more marked majority among those engaged in small scale production, when compared with cooperative peasants and the workers of the state farms. About 90 percent of the village dwellers are involved in some way in agricultural production.[21] More than half of Hungary's population pursues agricultural activities in addition to their main occupation. Therefore, there is a strong overlap between agricultural and industrial work in Hungary, which is unusual for a highly specialized modern society. In spite of industrialization and modernization of the rural communities, it would appear that the ties to the soil in Hungary are still very strong.

This phenomenon is also substantiated by the social composition of households. In 1981, 14 percent of the five million or so village inhabitants lived in households where there was no active wage earner (only pensioners and dependents); in 29 percent of households there was only one active wage earner. In the remaining 57 percent of households there were two or more active wage earners. A little over half of these households were of a mixed composition; as a result, 29 percent of the village population lived in mixed households, which makes class and stratum distinctions somewhat blurred. If, for example, a manual worker lived in a household with a member of a cooperative, he obtained a household plot through the latter, in the working of which he or she of course participated and also shared in the income. It is interesting to note that only 28 percent of those belonging to households engaged in small-scale farming were "peasants" in 1978, while 31 percent were workers and 17 percent were members of households with two types of income.[22] Therefore, it is reasonable to argue that certain contradictions between the modernization of production and the social structure in the villages still exist. Many attitudes and habits characteristic of the past have survived in the way of living of the village population: long working hours, widespread small-scale production, and the straightforward spending of leisure time. To put it differently, most Hungarians are highly motivated to improve their lot and therefore they will take advantage of every opportunity to maximize their ambitions. The NEM created such opportunities for most village inhabitants. As a matter of fact, in 1977 income per household was higher in the villages than in the towns. (However, since village households were larger, income was divided between more individuals.) Today per capita income of the workers on cooperative farms is practically the same as the income of factory workers.[23] However without the complementary income from self-employment (small-scale production), the level of income in villages would lag considerably behind the average for towns and the capital city. In 1979, for example, cities used up 88 percent of the country's total communal development funds (42 percent by Budapest alone) even though 47 percent of Hungary's population lived in villages. Consequently, the majority of the villages designated as lower priority centers made very little progress.[24] Of course, the authorities are delighted about the self-motivation of the villagers and are encouraging them to work hard, long hours, and with great efficiency. After all, the hard-earned income does not go into low-interest savings accounts but is being spent by village families on the construction and modernization of their homes, the improvement of their utility equipment, and on durable consumer goods. In 1980, 38 percent of village dwellings were less than 20 years old and almost two-fifths of the housing stock in villages has changed since the collectivization of farming. But in spite of these modernizations, housing conditions in the villages are still behind those in towns.[25] In other words, the village population has by great additional efforts (income obtained from household and auxiliary farming and the building of their own homes) reduced the gap between themselves and town dwellers with regard to living conditions; however, they are still behind and their way of life can hardly be called modern.

The worst conditions, however, can be found in the "dwarf villages" (or hamlets, i.e., settlements of less than 500 inhabitants). According to the latest census, there are 832 dwarf villages in Hungary inhabited by less than one-quarter million people, or only 1.5 percent of the total population of working age.[26] These settlements were totally neglected before and after the October 1956 Revolt. Only after 1981, when they were renamed "basic settlement units," was more and more attention given to these hamlets. The growing concern about the fate of the hamlets has its roots in the problem of finding a solution to the growing influx of rural population into towns where the infrastructure is unable to cope with this exodus. A growing imbalance is taking place in the distribution of population, not only in terms of settlement size but also in the social character of villages. The migration from the villages to towns shortly after the mechanization and industrialization of the rural areas was the strongest in those parts of the country where the agricultural jobs were least available and where commuting proved to be especially inconvenient. The most capable young people and skilled workers left the villages, which robbed the countryside of its demographic potential, causing a drop in its birthrate. The change in the population structure had several negative repercussions, one in the employment structure and another in the creation of common councils. In the 1970s, when the administrative measures merged both the agricultural cooperatives and the communities into one large entity, 55 percent of communities consisting of small settlements were deprived of their own independent councils.[27] As a result, small settlements are not in a position to determine their own fate but are left at the mercy of central decision making. This seems to be one of the greatest obstacles to development by some reformists, who call for the strengthening of popular participation in the decision-making process and suggest that the opinion of the representatives of small communities be taken into account. Thus the economic, social, and political inequalities that existed between the capital city of Budapest and the small villages, especially the hamlets, during the pre-communist rule still exist today, albeit in a different form and shape.

COMMUNITY VALUES AND TRADITIONS

In the life of every community there are periods when more or less uniform behavior by members of the community—patterns not arising simply from the division of labor—are legitimized or required. Such behavior on special occasions is generally value-rational, in the Weberian sense of the term, and it often contains symbolic elements as well. In other words, such behavior usually reveals concrete manifestations of the abstract sense of belonging that is being felt by individuals toward their community, or the community's own identification with certain values and ideals.[28]

Sophisticated scholars in Hungary have used several approaches to identify and clarify underlying values and their role in society. Hankiss, for example, argues that it is impossible to draw a sharp dividing line between the study of values in society and the study of values as they are reflected in the field of literature, which is always organically and inseparably built into social practice. The gist of the argument is that certain key experiences can be captured only through observation of deeply-rooted customs and habits or through works of literature, in which the written language serves as a special instrument for the registering of information pertaining to cultural patterns. In this regard even the "joking behavior" studied by social anthropologists is a valid way of gauging social values because, they claim, in Marx's opinion comedy and ridicule are a means of eliminating incongrous survivals from the past, in the general cause of historical development. According to Hankiss, the social and psychological functions of the joke are to attack distortions in the relation between language and reality and thus make these distortions look ridiculous. As illustrated in previous chapters, Hungarians are exceptionally gifted with this art of expression.

Another way of measuring community values is through the observance of holidays. The assumption is that in order for the holiday to become a major event in the life of the community, relatively uniform behavior is required. Holidays are also necessary for a community to demonstrate that it can mold and guide the actions of its members into certain ways of paying respect to meaningful symbols. There have been numerous studies by Hungarian scholars dealing with holiday customs and folklore traditions and their impact on social behavior. For example, in 1978 Miklós Hernádi surveyed 1,285 employees of the V.B.K.M. Battery Factory in Budapest's 13th District, where two-thirds of the respondents were blue-collar workers and the remaining one-third was composed of engineers, technicians, and clerks. One-third of the sample was commuters from nearby villages. Although this working population of a factory does not represent a cross-section of Hungarian society, it is representative of the working class.[29]

All holidays, without any exception, were valued by the respondents because of the abstention from work. Most respondents still remembered with resentment the practice of "celebration by work" and "voluntary" (meaning obligatory) work on holidays in the early 1950s under the Rákosi regime. About half of the respondents rejected the idea of a job that would require working on holidays. In justifying their negative answers, men stressed the value of their free time and women stressed the need to be together with their family. Very few respondents used the justification of the traditional, Christian prohibition of working on holidays. There was no significant difference in the condemnation of holiday-work between those who lived in the city and those from the country. There are seven holidays with nine rest days, excluding Sundays, in Hungary. More than a quarter of the respondents, all blue-collar workers, felt that the number of holidays was too low; however, most of them followed up with a comment: "You see, it's not up to us to decide."

One tradition that still continues and was identified as a natural linkage to holidays is eating and drinking. Members of larger families were more inclined to view the holiday in this light than those with a less sizeable family, and inhabitants of villages with lesser schooling tended to spend their holidays at home whereas younger, more educated, smaller families spent their holidays elsewhere. There was a strong correlation between car ownership and mobility at holiday periods. It is interesting to note that traditional house visiting within the local community no longer characterizes the majority of contemporary holidays (including Sundays).

Another departure from tradition is the timing of major cleaning activity in the apartment or house to coincide with the Easter holiday. In the past, in most places, the most thorough housecleaning occurred in the spring; the reason for this goes back to ancient times. Only 13 percent of the factory people viewed the Easter holiday in this context; 32 percent stressed only the season and 6 percent mentioned both the holiday and the season. Over a third of the respondents answered that such activity was unrelated either to the season or to the holiday, which suggests a considerable weakening of the old tradition.

A tradition that is still meaningful to the population—the wearing of clean, best clothes—was also reflected in this sample. At a wedding or funeral or on major holidays, it is highly unusual to see anyone inappropriately dressed. Of the respondents, 40 percent would judge such a person intolerantly, 31 percent were indifferent, and 29 percent would want to know more about the circumstances before stating their opinion. Factory people with religion (one-seventh of the respondents) were more tolerant about sloppiness in attire on holidays than were the rest of the workers.

The respondents were less critical of a costly wedding than a costly funeral—both symbols of very traditional values. Here again villagers were much more tolerant than residents of the capital city. About 8 percent approved both lavish weddings and costly funerals, while 30 percent felt it is their own concern and 62 percent referred to it as extravagant.

The most interesting findings in the survey were the attitudes toward celebrating holidays in the enterprise and the ranking of the holidays within the community. Only a small minority of the sample approved of the celebration of four holidays (Liberation Day, April 4; May Day; Constitution Day, August 20; and the anniversary of the October Revolution, November 7) within the enterprise. Unskilled workers, the majority of whom commute, seldom attended such celebrations or stayed to their end. The greatest critics, however, were the subgroups with the highest level of education: the technical employees. The greatest support for such celebrations came from the semi-skilled workers, who are mostly women; their choice, however, was the celebration of Women's Day. The celebration of a name day, also traditional, is common only among the Catholics, though declining somewhat. There always has been and still is great support for "solitary celebration" in Hungary. Only those respondents with large families were less likely to accept the possibility of solitary celebration. Some of the negative comments included statements that "only the ox drinks by itself" (a well-known Hungarian proverb), which implies that the individual celebrating (drinking) by himself enjoys solitude and certain emotions he is not willing to share with others.

Perhaps the greatest emotive aspect of celebration that affects community life can be observed among Hungarians reacting to the Hungarian National Anthem. In this sample, 92.4 percent of the respondents reported a deep emotion when the anthem was played. They explained their emotions in the most positive and logical terms; for example, that through the anthem great sporting events were transformed into festive occasions in popular consciousness. In other words, the anthem arouses a feeling of nationalism that in turn evokes an awareness of belonging and community identification. Yet most of the respondents had no clear understanding of the origin, history, or significance of most holidays. The importance of holidays experienced in an actual or symbolic religious community is receding. Most respondents believed holidays had some repercussions in the realm of their private lives (e.g., additional leisure, rest and recreation, cooking and baking, visiting, giving gifts, eating and drinking, etc.). Attributes that could be considered partly or wholly "public" (e.g., socialism, joint commemoration, or universal festive symbols), were not cited by the respondents. Additional free time figured more frequently than other attributes. As to the most festive occasion in the lives of the respondents, one-quarter referred to an experience connected with love or marriage, more than one-third to childbirth, and one-tenth to some form of initiation (e.g., oath, admission to a community). All these occasions reflect the "rights of passage" studied by anthropologists.

Although Christmas was considered the most popular of the seven major public holidays, traditional religious or secular values have diminished and the importance of the neighborhood and one's place of work in celebrations was conspicuously low. The intermediate sphere of the community, which in the past linked the family feast with the holiday culture of the whole of society, was almost entirely lacking in the holiday culture of the respondents. This has been offset, however, by an increase in the desire for free time combined with a variety of pleasurable occurrences in the lives of individuals.

Another survey seeking to identify community values in a changing environment in the 9th District of Budapest is equally revealing in the study of the Hungarian social character. The focus of the study is on the way of life of families living in three huge tenement houses with outside corridors containing 424 apartments, built in 1937, on a small street called Illatos út ("Fragrant Street,") in Hungarian. The reason it was called Fragrant Street was its location near chemical works and tanneries whose outpouring polluted the air all around. The waste waters from these plants and from the nearby pig slaughterhouse were drained into an open ditch and the street that ran parallel to that ditch was accordingly named Fragrant Street. The surrounding area consisted of smoking factories, nowhere a spot of green, hardly any shops at all—only the *kocsma* (saloon)—which offered some comfort and freedom to men and women who wanted to escape their reality by heavy drinking. The apartments were nicknamed "Dzsumbuj," which in Hungarian means chaos and danger of a jungle. In 1967, when the first survey on Dzsumbuj was taken, 62 percent of the inhabitants were unskilled workers. There were many who were living on small pensions or were dependents, old, or invalid; there were also many families with many children who lived in poverty. Most of them were uneducated and lacked cultural interests. Their housing conditions were far below standard; the average density per room was 3.6 persons but half of the tenants lived 5–10 to an apartment. Between 1937 and 1967 the apartments had been remodeled into one room-plus-kitchen and now had natural gas. When the second survey was taken in 1972, it seemed that nothing had changed; only the density had increased because with additions to the families several generations were squeezed into the same small apartments under intolerable conditions. The majority of these families had been living in those cramped quarters for over 30 years without a glimmer of hope.[30] By 1972 they had become conditioned to the scorn of the outside world and their own under-privileged status and rigid habits; they were hostile to a world that had shut them out.[31]

Between 1972 and 1975, some 150 families were relocated from Dzsumbuj to the new housing development of Köbánya-Újhegy. Of course, these families of unskilled workers brought their old habits with them. The bonds with the Dzsumbuj environment proved to be practically unbreakable. Former inhabitants still visit relatives and friends there and this, too, helps to revive old habits. Most of the apartment dwellers are lost in the new environment. They miss complaining to each other, asking somebody to take care of the children or asking for a small loan to keep them going until the next payday. Those were normal habits in "Fragrant Street," but nobody in the new environment can be asked for a loan, and the relationships with others are not on a level that enables people to learn how to make ends meet. They must fend for themselves. Poverty and impotence arouse suspicion in the new environment; their financial ups and downs and happy-go-lucky way of life find no sympathy at Köbánya Újhegy. Many of them still go back to Dzsumbuj to ask for small loans or just to feel at home among their own.

The impact of displacement was even more severe on the teenagers. On "Fragrant Street" they used to form groups and roam the streets or play soccer in the open space around the buildings. If they became bored, they would always come up with an idea, a good little hoax, gang fights, or some petty burglary; and when the weather was bad, they would meet in any of the apartments. But at Köbánya-Újhegy the housing rules prohibit such gatherings; what remained for them was the street and glue sniffing, with gangs of youth loitering on the streets and in doorways. At Dzsumbuj nobody objected to the noise, created by these gangs; here there were objections to the slightest noise and young people gathering in groups. Those teenagers who would rather face confrontation than adjustment made frequent visits to their old environment at Dzsumbuj where they felt at home.

The school records of these children are poor or mediocre, which, of course, limits their future opportunities for a successful beginning. Many do not even learn a trade; they drop out because studying is a burden or there is a lure of immediate money. Their role models are pals who are unskilled workers and make good money, usually by becoming truck drivers' mates. This means they can become independent of their parents and enjoy more freedom than in a factory. The aspiration for social mobility among these youths is very small. They choose and quit jobs at random and for weeks or months between jobs they engage in idleness and petty crime. They become used to an irregular lifestyle and adjust with difficulty to steady employment. Their chances of promotion and improvement in social status are very low.

It would appear from the above two surveys that the attempt to solve a serious social problem by allocating apartments to tens of thousands of underprivileged families has itself raised new problems. It proved that a decent apartment was a necessary but not sufficient condition for changing the attitudes and behavior of these people—especially the youth.

As in other societies undergoing rapid changes due to economic modernization, so in Hungary, too, there seems to be a generation gap between the young and old. While the young seek to change the world according to their needs, the old try to avoid unnecessary changes that could jeopardize their needs. Since Hungary is a young society—in 1984, 41.8 percent of the population was under 30 years of age—the preponderance of the young causes concern and a focus of attention at the highest levels of authority. According to numerous surveys taken in recent years, Hungarian authorities have cause for concern about the future of the young people in their country. For example, a 1984 survey conducted at the Budapest Technical University revealed some very discouraging attitudinal information about the youth. Three-quarters of the respondents felt that Hungary's public life had not become more democratic, and for 40 percent the current political system was not adequate to allow the will of the public to assert itself. According to the majority, however, some progress had been made in many areas, including the freedom to express one's opinions. The majority of the respondents were dissatisfied with ideological courses. According to 70 percent of the sample, KISz's work consisted only of performing "tasks assigned from above." As to the question whether or not an engineer needed firm Marxist convictions, only 15 percent answered in the affirmative (compared with 77 percent in 1976). Many (66 percent) disagreed that "there are no social differences in Hungary," and the majority (67 percent) considered great personal wealth something that should not be permitted. Nevertheless, 65 percent of the respondents felt that private enterprise was not harmful for the country's "socialist" character; and 81 percent agreed with the creation of private enterprises, although some raised the question of "whether this represented a revival of capitalism." While 42 percent responded that materialism "hinders the development of socialist consciousness," 67 percent felt that more efficient work could help maintain the current standard of living. The majority of the sample condemned corruption, unearned income, materialism, and an inflated bureaucracy as well as selfishness. For 81 percent of the respondents, religiousness was compatible with a career in engineering.[32]

Disenchantment with Marxist-Leninist ideology and a gravitation toward religion by young people is well known to the party authorities.[33] According to the findings of the HSWP/CC, the great majority of young people have no political convictions. Young Hungarians have what some sociologists have referred to as a "secondary ideology" or an "everyday ideology," characterized by abstention from politics. In most surveys it was pointed out that young people favor individualism and independence and reject collectivism imposed from above. The idea of forming communities or thinking in terms of community rather than in terms of the individual is foreign to most young people. The growing religious influence among young intellectuals can be partially explained, according to *Társadalmi Szemle*, by their unfulfilled needs for a genuine independent community life, since KISz cannot offer interesting programs and therefore is not successful in attracting young intellectuals.[34]

The drop in party membership among the younger generation is due, according to these surveys, to their dissatisfaction with specific party programs and to the deterioration in the standard of living.[35] Young people are especially dissatisfied when they see their income is not commensurate with the work performed and are frustrated because their income is not high enough to finance a home or to give their children a comfortable life. If parents are unable to give them financial support, many young people (25 percent) are unable to own an apartment even after eight years of marriage. The cost of raising children has doubled in the past six years, since the state no longer subsidizes certain articles for children. Some young couples with more than one child are therefore unable to sustain themselves without outside help. Thus, a majority of respondents to a survey taken in 1982 designated the periods of starting a career, founding a family, finding an apartment, and raising children as the most difficult stages of their life cycle.[36]

Concern about the the negativism of the students prompted the party and state authorities to take measures to strengthen state intervention in academic life by enabling the authorities to bring in a nominee for a university post even if the university council objected to it.[37] Other measures concerning non-student youth were discussed at an international conference on ideology held in Budapest in October 1984 under the auspices of Hungarian Academy of Sciences, the Institute of Party History of the HSWP's CC, the Political Academy, and the CC of the Communist Youth League.[38] At that conference, István Huszár, head of the HSWP/CC's Party History Institute urged that a "new educational strategy" be devised to counter "views, changes of lifestyle, and behavior" among young people that were "downright dangerous to socialist development." Other party officials were more conciliatory and felt that young people needed "concrete and immediate answers to real questions." The conferences appealed for a new ideological approach involving not only the "criticism, exposure, and rejection of hostile views" but also more effective means of analyzing "socialist reality, with its contradictions and the offensive propagation of Marxism-Leninism."[39]

Although Hungary's planned labor market is supposed to eliminate unemployment by providing a job for everyone, the choice of an appropriate education, career path, and general future identity in adult life poses a serious problem for Hungarian youths. The graduates of technical schools, for example, have no problem finding jobs that are in line with their qualifications. Skilled workers are in high demand for an annual offering of 50,000 jobs. Young graduates are absorbed into the job market without difficulties. The same applies to the graduates of technical high schools, numbering about 25,000 per year, although about one-quarter of them do not match their qualifications. The greatest problems exist for graduates with liberal arts degrees, who have difficulties not only finding suitable jobs but any jobs at all in the white-collar category.[40] While officially there is no unemployment in Hungary, it is well known that many young people in white-collar positions just loaf on the job because there is no work for them to do. It is also well known that there is unreported unemployment in Hungary. Consequently, in the fall of 1985 two Hungarian counties—Szolnok and Baranya—introduced an experimental employment project allegedly to provide work for people who, because of their own fault, were finding it difficult to get a job. Although it was claimed to be an assistance project, there are indications that the scheme was intended as a new way of cracking down on shirkers and of creating a pool of manpower.[41] Yet according to the economic weekly, *Figyelö [Observer]*, in July 1985 there were 10.8 percent fewer job vacancies and 12.1 percent more jobless than in the previous month.[42] Several cities, including Debrecen and Ózd, registered unusually large increases in the number of job seekers, but the problem was most acute in the small towns of Nyirbátor and Kisvárda, where in July 1985, 2.5–3 percent of the working age population was without work.[43] According to the Hungarian news agency, in 1985 of the 122,000 young people entering the job market, 3,000 had not been able to find work. However a few months earlier the trade union daily, *Népszava*, unequivocally stated that "full employment is an inseparable part of socialism" and that "the threat of unemployment is not a real one in our country."[44] Of course, if there is no unemployment, there is no need for unemployment compensation![45]

Full employment has been attained by the creation of jobs and by certain aspects of wage policy. Full employment, however, has always been a costly undertaking; in many cases more people were engaged in certain jobs than are actually needed. Some economists maintain that overemployment is one of the major causes of economic inefficiency. However, there were other social policy measures that also contribute to full employment.[46] Among these policy measures are the childcare allowance, early retirement for medical reasons, and the various income policies and social benefits (all covered in Chapters 5 and 6). Nevertheless, there are certain shortcomings in the existing social policies that result in failure to satisfy certain needs in Hungarian society and thus help to shed light on the Hungarian social character. For example, the continuing housing shortage or the overcrowding of certain institutions; the lack of provisions for public assistance to care for children of ill mothers or assistance to families who have a permanent invalid to care for and who cannot or do not want to place him or her in an institution; the social inequalities in the standards and access to services; and so on. It is well known that groups in better position to assert their interests (because of more knowledge, more influence, etc.) are likely to get more and better services than those with limited knowledge and influence in their communities. The issue of inequality—social as well as economic—is the subject of a long-lasting debate and controversy among the economic and social policy interests of the Hungarian policymakers. The main issues are the following:

1. Some critics maintain that full employment is at the root of many economic shortcomings in Hungary today. They point at inefficiency in production, lack of work ethics and work discipline, and so on. On the other hand, those favoring the present policy maintain that the threat of unemployment does not seem to improve the work ethic or low discipline in other countries and that the high cost of unemployment is equally bad.

2. The critics are also opposed to fully or heavily subsidized social services, reasoning that the recipients do not value what they get free; that they overuse and abuse services that are free to them but very costly to the state. Hence they support market-oriented solutions that would be a greater incentive to work and earn more. The advocates of the existing system, however, argue that those services are viewed by the people as their constitutional rights and that the market has in fact never helped to cover their needs in a general way; besides, a two-tier system (parallel paying and free systems) would be socially divisive and lead to an increase in social inequalities.

For the time being the economic argument has a fairly good chance to gain some ground in various minor matters. For example, cutting pensions to the highly paid; introduction of family allowances for reasons of fairness and to improve the breeding and rearing of offspring; and many modifications that would improve economic efficiency. Nevertheless, some basic values, such as full job security and the necessity of universal social services seem to be firmly established and the party authorities are determined not to tinker with them.[47]

SOCIAL DIFFERENTIATION AND UPWARD MOBILITY

While it can be argued that socialist transformation after 1947 brought an end to the former ruling classes and a substantial reduction of inherited class inequalities, social inequalities have continued to exist and in recent years they have become a major problem for the decision makers. As pointed out by sociologist Tamás Kolosi and Edmund Wnuk-Lipiński, "If private ownership of the means of production is replaced by collective ownership, some types of inequality are eliminated, some others remain, and some new sorts of inequalities emerge in social life."[48] According to a multinational comparative research project undertaken by the academies of science of seven European socialist countries in 1979–1980, the inconsistencies and inequalities between the Hungarian social strata are many and varied. They can be found in the area of work and working conditions; the material living conditions; cultural activities; social mobility; and the sociodemographic situation. The "divergent" differentiation of material living conditions in Hungary causes considerable status inconsistencies. For example, the cluster of workers in heavy manual jobs with several shifts (i.e., unfavorable work schedules) and the high proportion of workers living in villages form a separate and distinct group within the occupational structure. The unfavorable housing conditions of this group largely account for the differentiation in housing situations among the total population.

As far as convergence between manual and nonmanual workers is concerned, it exists, but only among one-fifth of the working population. With regard to material living conditions, the financial situation of the unskilled group, administrative workers, subordinate professionals, and skilled workers is extremely differentiated. The material living conditions of almost one-third of each group are similar to groups above or below them in the division of labor.

Status inconsistency is particularly high in areas where living conditions are inconsistent with other elements of social stratification. There is also extensive inconsistency between individual elements of material living conditions. Social differentiation within the manual and nonmanual categories surpasses the average differences between the two categories. There is a definite layer in the manual worker categories, particularly among skilled workers, that is above-average on every dimension examined. The social situation of this group is very similar to the average social situation of the professionals. There are no significant differences in cultural activities between the manual and nonmanual workers. There are, however, noticeable differences between unskilled and skilled workers. For example, there were 28.5 percent nonreaders among the unskilled workers but only 14.2 percent among the skilled workers. The reading of literature gains in intensity with growing participation in other cultural activities. The data show, however, that the majority of cultural activities are connected with only a small group of people. Music (opera, operetta, classical) has the smallest audience; 91 percent of the respondents were nonparticipants in opera, 87 percent in classical music, and 83 percent in operettas. On the other hand, only 32 percent were nonparticipants in movies, and 36 percent in museums. Consequently, only 10.9 percent of the unskilled workers and 16 percent of the skilled workers were active recipients of culture. In other words, there is a considerable differentiation among manual workers as a whole, since there is a big gap between the elite and the unskilled, deprived strata of workers.[49]

The emergence of a "new sort of inequality" in Hungarian social life is monitored carefully by the party leaders because the events of October 1956 are still vivid in the memory of most of these leaders. They remember well the empty promises made by the Rákosi regime that remained only promises and hence triggered the mass uprising against the Rakosi-Gero clique; and they have not forgotten that the first resolution of the new provisional Central Committee of the HSWP in December 1956 was commitment to dismantle the doctrinaire Stalinist extremism and to introduce a new economic policy tailored to Hungarian conditions with the aim to improve the standard of living through private initiatives and expertise as well as to strengthen the alliance between workers and peasants.[50] Thus the Kádár regime in the 1980s is caught between a rock and hard place: on the one hand, it seeks to satisfy the demands for improved economic conditions leading to a higher standard of living, and on the other, to narrow the existing gap in social inconsistencies and inequalities between the social classes or, as Hans-Georg Heinrich observed, "The main problem is probably not so much the continuing existence of inequalities and disparities, but rather their high viability. Wealth is openly displayed in contemporary Hungary and it exists side-by-side with distressing poverty."[51]

As pointed out in Chapter 4, the growing differentiation of incomes and the accumulation of wealth in certain segments of society is one of the main concerns of the Hungarian authorities. In 1982, the overwhelming majority of the Hungarian people (90 percent) distinguished between rich and poor in terms of financial inequity.[52] In 1984, individuals earning ten times the official average wage (4,800 forints per month) amounted to about 5 percent of the economically active population.[53] In 1983, however, 28.2 percent of the same population had an income below the accepted minimum poverty level (2,500 forints per month).[54] Among the rich are lawyers, engineers, writers, party apparatchiks, top-level bureaucrats, house painters, collective farmers, electricians, business contractors, doctors, boutique owners, small manufacturers, building contractors, prostitutes, and all sorts of individuals specializing in goods or skills that there are in short supply; among the poor are retirees, single parents, petty bureaucrats, unskilled white-collar workers (mostly women), young teachers with families, and many people without apart-

Table 7.3
Income Groups, 1978–1982

Forint per month	1978	1980	1982
2,000 and lower	3.0	1.3	1.7
2,001–4,000	20.0	23.9	23.0
4,001–5,000	22.1	25.3	23.5
5,001–6,000	19.3	16.1	17.3
6,001–7,000	9.8	9.3	10.2
7,001–8,000	7.8	5.2	5.4
8,001–10,000	4.7	3.6	4.3
10,001–12,000	2.6	2.2	2.2

Source: *Népszabadság* (May 30, 1984); and Heinrich; op. cit., 113.

ments living in sublet rooms and those unable to cope with their lives, such as alcoholics, compulsive gamblers, bag women, and young people living on the streets.[55]

The problem is vividly and dramatically manifested against a background of a failed communist utopia. The contrast between the rich and poor is so visible that the lower economic strata refuse to accept the nouveau riche class as equals. It is the conspicuousness of wealth that has resulted in the "anti-rich" mood in contemporary Hungary.[56] It is not surprising, therefore, that income differentials have been gradually leveling out in the early 1980s. As Table 7.3 shows, between 1978 and 1982 income has been redistributed toward the middle in order to reduce the extremes.

Of course it should be pointed out, official statistics inflate income figures by adding fringe benefits and other transfer payments in order to reduce the proportion of the poor, especially families with more than 3 children and old age pensioners.[57] The problem is further compounded by continuous gaps in income differentiation between generations and sexes.

As Table 7.4 shows the generational gap in income is quite evident, using the mid-life point of 40 years as the dividing line between younger and older generations. The income for young families is very low, when one considers the unannounced inflationary increases in consumer prices prior to 1984, when the monthly per capita income was published. In spite of the attempts by party authorities to eradicate the deep-rooted feelings of a male dominated culture, socialism has not been able to remove the wage differentials between male and female earners. Discrimination against the female sex is noticeable in unequal wages for

Table 7.4
Monthly Income per Capita by Age of Family Head, 1983

Household heads by age brackets	Average	White collar	Foremen	Prof. workers	Non-agr. workers	Agr. blue collar
20-29	2,881	3,293	3,277	3,522	2,815	2,663
30-39	2,956	3,366	3,303	3,530	2,838	2,463
40-49	3,592	4,095	3,987	4,319	3,452	3,328
50-59	4,199	5,089	4,737	5,154	4,033	3,991
Average	3,385	3,952	3,817	4,066	3,218	3,214

Source: *Társadalmi Szemele* 39, Nos. 7–8 (1984): 75; and Heinrich, op. cit., 117.

equal work, unequal opportunities for higher positions (particularly in party organizations), and unequal advancement in the technical fields. The only places where there is practically no discrimination are in the health fields.

There still exist inequalities in career opportunities and other areas of social activity, which is largely due to attitudinal prejudices characteristic of a closed society. Although the forced equalization policies of the Rákosi era and the more conciliatory policies of the Kádár regime have resulted in radical social transformation of society, the semi-skilled and unskilled workers appear to be the only stable socio-occupational category in Hungary today. As Table 7.5 shows, there was considerable upward mobility into the white-collar stratum from this category in 1979.

Two-thirds of the professionals, 40 percent of the skilled workers, and about one-third of the white-collar workers are higher in the hierarchy than were their fathers.[58] The highest ratio of "immobiles" was found among the unskilled and semi-skilled workers: 55 percent.[59] The same findings show that inter-generational mobility is much higher in Hungary than intra-generational mobility. Interestingly enough, intra-generational upward mobility is more frequent among males whereas inter-generational upward mobility is more frequent among females. Yet there is a larger percentage of unsuccessful attempts to rise among women than among men. Looking at family occupational homogeneity as an indicator of upward mobility, the proportion of homogenous families, where parents and children are in the same socio-occupational category, "is about 10–12 percent among manual workers, 9 percent among professionals and about 2 percent among white-collar workers."[60] Upward mobility among skilled workers is the highest, followed by the white-collar group and professionals—unskilled and semi-skilled work-

Table 7.5
Intergenerational Mobility, 1979

| | Present Occupation | | | |
Father's Occupation	Unskilled or Semi-skilled workers (%)	Skilled workers (%)	White collar workers (%)	Profes-sionals (%)
Individual farmers	13	9	5	2
Unskilled or semi-skilled workers	52	42	33	17
Skilled workers	24	37	39	32
White-collar	2	3	8	13
Professionals	3	4	10	32
Merchants, craftsmen	6	5	5	4

Source: Akszentievics, "Mobility and social relations," 58; and Heinrich, op. cit., 132.

ers are at the bottom. For whatever reason, unskilled and semi-skilled male workers have fewer friends than their wives in the same category; they tend to be inward oriented, toward their "own," in a closeknit relationship—either feeling inferior to the professionals and white-collar workers or distrusting them. Skilled male workers keep their friendship relations within their own socio-occupational category. Friendships with unskilled and semi-skilled workers, or with white-collar workers and professionals, are more common than marital relations with them: 45 percent of skilled workers have a skilled worker wife but 79 percent have a skilled worker friend. In the choice of friends, there is a distinction between manual and nonmanual workers. The former have practically no friends among professionals; the same is almost true for women because of the dominant role of men in the choice of friends: a large number of male manual workers have no friends among white-collar workers, yet some of them have white-collar worker wives.[61] It is important to point out that the concept of "friend" has a different connotation in the Hungarian culture than in the American context. In Hungary, "friend" implies intimate relationship based on trust and dependability, confidence, and sharing in such things as information, knowledge, advice, emotional support, and financial assistance in social relations. For example, it is one thing to have "connections," and quite another to have "friends."

MAGYAR NATIONALISM AND CULTURAL DIVERSITY

During the Austro-Hungarian monarchy, Magyar nationalism was an ideological movement spearheaded by the aristocratic elites who sought to embark on the path of modernization while remaining free from Austrian interference. Between the two world wars, Magyar nationalism was an expansive type of nationalism, seeking to regain the territories lost as a result of the defeat suffered in World War I. Today, Magyar nationalism represents a reaction against two compelling phenomena: the loss of some of the regained territory and population at the end of World War II, and the predominance of Soviet power in Hungary. More precisely, it represents a feeling of frustration at not being able freely to exercise the sources of national identity and national aspirations. It is a means of mobilizing all segments of society in a unified effort to repel—through expediency and other peaceful means—any alien or parochial interests and forces opposing Hungarian cultural traits and economic well-being. In this respect Magyar nationalism is more of a patriotic movement equipped with pragmatic formulae rather than a rightwing ideology seeking the glorification of nation and state. It is quite different from the national sentiments prevailing during the October 1956 Revolution when the "counterrevolutionaries" (or "Freedom Fighters" as they were know in the West) were struggling for freedom from communist (i.e., Soviet) control. The threat to party control and alliances within the Soviet bloc transformed national communism into anticommunist nationalism (i.e., "counterrevolution").[62] This observation is based on the assumption that there is no inherent contradiction between nationalist and communist sentiments in Hungary. It is further assumed that whatever vitality persists in contemporary communism in Hungary actually derives from its national orientation. The marriage of communism and nationalism in Hungary is based on the 1957 principle that each communist party can determine its own future in the context of unique national conditions prevailing in the country. By the same token it can be argued that there is no other communism in the world today than national communism. The case of Hungary is, therefore, nothing more or less than a variation of national communism.

As explained in previous chapters, after the armed suppression of the October 1956 uprising, the Kádár regime skillfully exploited Magyar nationalism by addressing the collective social and economic grievances and by committing the party to seek an alliance policy with all social strata for achieving the greatest good for the greatest number of people in the post-1956 period. Of course, what was "good" and who should benefit from it was determined—and still is determined—by party authorities. There were many elements of national communism in Hungary during the Kádár era that brought about cooperation and harmony among the various groups of Hungarian society; they all come under the heading of "reform" discussed earlier in this book. These reforms brought reconciliation, work initiative, profit incentives, increased productivity, entrepreneurship, improved standard of living, more relaxed political environment, and increased hope for well-being. But they also created an environment in which the visibility of income differentiation and the widening gap in living standards and social services caused rumblings at the grassroots level and serious concern among the decision makers.

From the point of view of its ethnic make-up, Hungary is a relatively homogeneous country. National minorities constitute less than 5 percent of its total population. Of the country's 10,700,000 inhabitants, about 230,000 are of German, a little over 100,000 of Slovak, about 95,000 of Southern Slav (Serbs and Croats,) and approximately 30,000 of Rumanian origin.[63] In addition, the country has a Gypsy population of about 500,000, or 5 percent, and an estimated 150,000 Jews—neither of which is recognized as an official minority.

According to the 20th Semiannual Report on the implementation of the Helsinki Final Act, in 1986, "Hungarian minority policy is liberal in theory and practice."[64] The Kádár regime has followed a carefully balanced nationality policy aimed at projecting an image of fairness. The national minorities have their own nationality federations under the auspices of the Patriotic People's Front (PPF), proportional representation in the powerless National Assembly, radio and TV studios, and press organs.[65] The support for or at least tolerance of minority cultures has been cited by party and state authorities on numerous occasions as examples to be followed by the country's neighbors with large Hungarian minorities. There are almost 4,000,000 Hungarians living in the neighboring countries—about 2,250,000 in Rumania, approximately 650,000 in Czechoslovakia, and a little over 1,000,000 in Yugoslavia, the USSR (Ruthenia), and Austria.

One problem, however, that continues to haunt Hungarian authorities is the plight of the Gypsies. With a birthrate more than twice that of the rest of the population, Gypsies account for a rapidly increasing portion of the Hungarian population—according to the 1971 census, about 500,000 (or 5 percent) today. Although they are not recognized as an official minority on the grounds that 75 percent of them speak only Hungarian, they do have equality before the law. The state provides many programs designed to absorb the Gypsies into the mainstream of Hungarian life.[66] In practice, however, the gradual acculturation is laced with conflict, alienation, and discrimination. About 30,000 Gypsies still live in slums.[67] Economically, Gypsies, mostly unskilled workers, hold the lowest-paid jobs. The last survey, taken in 1971, indicated that 39 percent of adult Gypsies were illiterate. Unskilled workers made up 12 percent of the overall population, but in the case of Gypsies the share was 50 percent. Only 8 percent of Gypsies worked as skilled workers, in contrast with 30 percent of non-Gypsies; and only 37 percent of Gypsy children finished 8th grade, while 94 out of every 100 non-Gypsy children continued their studies after elementary school.[68] As a result, the crime rate among Gypsies is very high: 7,000–8,000 of them commit an offense each year.[69] An in-depth study conducted in Borsod-Abaúj-Zemplén county produced the following statistics about crimes committed by Gypsies: 40 percent of all burglaries, 60–65 percent of all thefts, half of all instances of rowdiness and rape, and 30–40 percent of homicides and attempted homicides.[70]

It is not surprising therefore that Mrs. István Kozák, head of the Council Office of the Council of Ministers and secretary of the interdepartmental committee dealing with Gypsies, admitted that the Hungarian population was less tolerant of the Gypsies under communist rule than before World War II.[71] Her opinion was confirmed in a study entitled "Gypsies in Public Opinion" by Endre Hánn.[72] According to Hánn's study, 28 percent of the respondents gave criminal behavior as the reason for their negative feelings toward Gypsies; 21 percent mentioned the exploitation of society, parasitism, begging, prodigality, and taking advantage of their situation; and 11 percent perceived the high incidence of alcoholism among Gypsies as the major cause of their own animosity towards them.

Most studies are in agreement that prejudice is the major obstacle to the improvement of the Gypsies' social conditions. It leads to widespread discrimination, which is reinforced by claims that even though the regime is making enormous efforts to help them, the Gypsies are unwilling to change and are content to be living off others. Popular resentment of Gypsies continues to grow and the behavior of the Gypsies continues along the lines of the old traditions of a nomadic culture. It is not unusual to find government-sponsored programs, such as the one in Budapest's 13th District, designed for providing assistance for Gypsies in cultural and social areas, but such programs are poorly attended by non-Gypsies and, interestingly enough, by no Gypsies.[73]

On the other hand, the issue of unfair treatment of Hungarian ethnic minorities abroad, especially in Rumania, is an acute problem with most people from the bottom to the very top of Hungarian society. At the 13th Congress of the HSWP, János Kádár was the seventh speaker to mention the fate of the Hungarian ethnic minorities: "These minorities often had to remain silent when the topic of Hungary was raised, so the Congress should remember the existence of those of Magyar origin and nationality and hope that they would not be ashamed when their mother tongue was spoken but would listen to it without fear and with their heads raised high."[74] While the official Rumanian position is that a minority problem no longer exists in that country and that reference to it represents nationalist and chauvinist views, the Hungarian public at large as well as the party leadership keep pressing for a fairer treatment of its minorities abroad. Márton Klein, a department head in the Ministry of Foreign Affairs, was among many high ranking Hungarian officials condemning "nationalism, prejudice, and every form of forced assimilation." He warned that "it is the primary duty of those countries having minorities living on their territory to provide the necessary conditions for them to have access to their cultural rights."[75] It would appear that amidst their economic difficulties the party and state authorities are forced to respond to the growing pressure of nationalism and thus to show genuine concern for the treatment of ethnic Hungarians abroad.

With somewhat lesser intensity the issue of fair treatment of ethnic Magyars also prevails with regard to Czechoslovakia (or more precisely, Slovakia). There the issue has become exacerbated with the re-arrest on May 10, 1984, of the 40-year-old geologist and writer Miklós Duray. He was first arrested in November 1982 for representing the case of the Hungarian minority within constitutional limits. Duray's trial in 1983 was suspended after provoking the intervention of prominent Hungarian intellectuals and reportedly (behind-the-scene) of the Budapest government itself. He was re-arrested for leading a campaign against plans to reduce native language instruction for the Hungarian minority in Slovakia. Hungarian human rights activists formed the Duray Committee and started a letter writing campaign seeking Duray's reprieve. The Hungarian public displayed great sympathy for Duray, who became the symbol for advocacy of Hungarian minority rights in Czechoslovakia.

Another burning issue arousing the sentiments of nationalism among Hungarians is the controversial construction of the Bös (Gabčikovo) Nagymaros hydroelectric power and navigation system on the Danube River, which forms the border between Hungary and Czechoslovakia. In May 1984 a full-scale nongovernmental ecological movement was formed to protest the contemplated construction of the hydroelectric power dam and stations. Fifty prominent cultural and scientific figures started a signature-gathering campaign.[76] According to the protest letter, the construction of the dam system will cause serious damage to the potable water supply, agriculture, forests, and settlement networks of both countries and irreparable damage to the landscape and natural environment of several regions in northwestern Hungary. The petition called for a halt to the construction and for the working out of plans for the regulation of the joint section of the Danube that take into account the ecological, social, and economic role of the river. The project is moving at a slow pace—the original completion date of mid-1980s has been pushed back to 1994—and the opposition to the construction is gaining momentum among the environmentalists not only in Hungary but in Czechoslovakia and Austria.[77]

It would be inconceivable to write about the Hungarian social character and Magyar nationalism without identifying and analyzing the role of Jews in Hungarian society. For centuries the Jews have played a very significant and unique role. Before the Nazi occupation of Hungary in March 1944, Jews constituted the only middle class between a large land owning aristocracy and an impoverished gentry on the one hand, and millions of landless peasants on the other. Hungarian Jewry was not only fully assimilated but reached a position of prominence in economic, social, and political life.[78] From 1880 to 1944 more than one-fifth of the population of Budapest—the power and cultural center of Hungary— was Jewish. Hungarian Jews were much more than commercial middlemen; they were also in the forefront of Hungarian intellectual, professional, and political leadership. They were founders of the first labor party in 1878, which was renamed the Social Democratic Party in 1890. Béla Kun and his mainly Jewish associates (out of 49 Commissars 31 were of Jewish origin) were responsible for the creation of the first "dictatorship of the proletariat" in 1919.[79] Because of full assimilation, Jews in Hungary were stratified into various economic and social classes as well as varied political orientations. Thus Jews, like non-Jews, were at both ends of the political spectrum and were divided on social and economic issues until March 1944, when Nazi Germany invaded the country while the Regent of Hungary, Miklós Horthy, was under house arrest at Schloss Klessheim. Until then, Hungarian Jewry enjoyed considerable freedom in spite of some anti-Jewish laws (e.g., admissions quotas to the universities) that were imposed on them during the so-called "White Terror" to eradicate Bolshevism in Hungary. According to Holocaust documentation, Hungary became a haven for thousands of Jews from neighboring countries during the war years, until Nazi occupation of Hungary in March 1944. By July 7, 1944, when the Regent ordered a halt to the deportation of Hungarian Jews, the solution to the "Jewish problem" was near completion. The overall losses of Hungarian Jewry as a result of deportations, massacres, hunger, disease, and other causes came to about 300,000 from present-day Hungary (about 100,000 from Budapest alone), and about 260,000 from the ceded territories.[80]

After World War II, the decimated Jewish population of Hungary welcomed with open arms their Soviet "liberators" who, because of their ideological commitment to internationalism, were regarded by most Hungarian Jews as the guarantors of equality and protection from anti-Semitism. The Soviet occupation forces skillfully exploited these perceptions by recruiting large numbers of Jews into the ranks of the ruling bureaucracy, especially the much hated secret police. "In fact, Jews were elected on the slates of almost every party in November 1945, the only free election ever held in Hungary's history."[81] Within four months after the Red Army's entry into Budapest the Communist Party of Hungary increased in membership from 2,000 to 150,000; and by September 1946, to 653,000.[82] A Moscow-trained "general staff," consisting almost entirely of Jews, headed the party whose ranks were swollen by tens of thousands of former Nyilas [Arrow Cross], fascist "activists."[83] By building a mass party, the top communist leadership, which was "Jewish," was now divided between the "Muscovites" and the "home communists." It was the Muscovites, or the so-called communist "court Jews" (i.e., Matyás Rákosi, Ernö Gerö, Mihály Farkas, and Gábor Péter),[84] who secretly initiated and sponsored the summer 1946 pogroms at Kunmadarás and Miskolc. "On both occasions party members were involved in the anti-Semitic outrages that caused the death of five Jews."[85] Ironically it was the communist Minister of Interior, László Rajk (also a Jew), who sabotaged court proceedings and criminal investigations against the perpetrators of the pogroms. According to Paul Lendvai, however, "Rajk was simply carrying out the Party's instructions. Moreover, the political police proper was headed by the Jewish Gábor Péter, a former tailor, and was staffed at its command level mainly by Jews."[86] Three years later, in May 1949, Rajk, now Minister of Foreign Affairs and a member of the Politburo, was arrested along with more than 200 prewar communists (among them many Jews) on charges of "Titoism." The following Rajk trial carried the indictment not only of "Titoism" but of a "world-wide Zionist conspiracy," which was tailored to compliment the Stalinist line after Moscow's breach of diplomatic relations with Israel. "Rákosi and other 'court Jews' were running the country as Moscow's agents and were seen by the population as Jewish stooges of a hated foreign oppressor."[87] However it is interesting to note that the proportion of Jews was as high among the purgers as it was among the purged; therefore, the trials and purges coincided with a struggle for power within the party, divided between the "Muscovites" and "home communists." In 1951, for example, after the bulk of the "home communists" were arrested—including János Kádár, Gyula Kállai, Géza Losonczy, and Ferenc Dónáth—the party was purged of the last of the prominent home communists. Following the example of his Soviet master, in late 1952 and early 1953 Rákosi began his own anti-Semitic frenzy by arresting Gábor Péter, Lajos Stöckler (the communist-sponsored leader of the Jewish community), István Szirmai (head of the Hungarian Radio), and scores of Jewish doctors, journalists, and executives. Moscow, of course, was delighted because the Soviet party leaders, after Stalin's death, considered it a mistake to have so many Jews at the helm of the party in a country where anti-Semitism had strong roots.[88] Yet there were no systematic anti-Semitic excesses in Hungary during or after the October

1956 revolution. However, the official propaganda referred in a White Book to "anti-Semitism and anti-Jewish violence during the Hungarian counterrevolution."[89]

While there were several Jewish Muscovites who paid the price for their crimes during the 13 days of the uprising, there were no pogroms or other visible signs attempting to turn the revolution into an anti-Semitic movement. About 18,000 Jews, or about 7 percent of the refugee total, left the country.

The trauma of the 1956 revolt and the Rákosi era of terror led almost automatically to a numerical reduction of the Jewish element in the leadership role of the Kádár regime; it split the ruling elite into three main groups: Stalinists (the minority), reformists (the majority), and centrists. As pointed out earlier in this chapter, the first resolution of the new provisional Central Committee of the HSWP in December 1956 was a commitment to dismantle the remnants of Stalinist extremism and to introduce a new economic policy tailored to Hungarian conditions. There were several Jews in the new party and government leadership under Kádár, most of whom joined the reformist movement. The Jewish community as a whole had profited as much, or more, as non-Jews from the liberal, reformist policies that were inscribed into the New Economic Mechanism. Similar benefits were achieved in social and cultural areas. Today the assimilated Hungarian Jews enjoy greater freedom and well-being than Jews in any other state within the Soviet bloc. They have a rabbinical seminary, a high school, a library and museum, numerous kosher butcher shops, a factory producing unlimited quantities of mat-zoh, an orphanage, a home for the elderly, about 30 synagogues, several publications, including newspapers, and so on. During the summer of 1987, Hungary established an "interest section" in Tel Aviv, which is the lowest level of diplomatic representation between the two countries. All this does not mean, however, that there is no anti-Semitism in Hungary.

Anti-Semitism in Hungary existed before as well as after the 1956 revolt—and it still exists today. The reasons for anti-Semitic feelings in Hungary are many and varied. Some are more convincing than others, but in the final analysis they are all irrational and bigoted. There were two areas of power—political and economic—that were exploited by some Hungarians to foster anti-Semitic feelings. The so-called "Jewish rule"—a reference to the highly disproportionate position of Jews in party politics (especially the communist party), the secret police, and other top and middle levels of the governmental bureaucracy—served as an example to equate the Rákosi dictatorship with "the revenge of the Jews." There were some isolated cases of revenge by some Jews who were then in a position of authority and who only a few years earlier were themselves victims of ghettoism, humiliation, and deprivation; thus there were also some innocent Hungarians who became victims of this revenge. However, the ascendence of several people to high positions did not mean the development of a Jewish power structure; these positions were gained due to personal connections and the political circumstances of that time. Their "Jewishness" was not the sole determining factor. Jews who were in positions of power during the Rákosi era owed their loyalties to Marxism-Leninism and its fountainhead, the Kremlin.

The economic source of power as a cause for anti-Semitic feelings was exploited by some Hungarians who pointed their finger at the wealth of many Jews who survived the war and had managed to save it. According to statistical reports, not many poor Jews survived the ordeal of the concentration camps, and those who were permitted to remain in the ghettos were Jews of means or influence with the Central Jewish Council. Mutual aid and care for each other among the decimated Jewish population in the confused economic situation after the war was perceived by some Hungarians as exploitation and discrimination against non-Jews who were also destitute.

During the Kádár era anti-Semitic feelings abated considerably but did not disappear. In Hungary, every Jew is officially a Hungarian. Unlike in the USSR, where Jews are considered an ethnic minority, in Hungary they constitute a religious denomination and the official position is that there is no Jewish culture independent of Jewish religion. Anti-Semitic speeches are unlawful and classified as "anti-denominational incitement"; a few months' imprisonment can be meted out for this unlawful act. Laws of this type are used by the anti-Semites as one of their chief complaints: while they are forbidden to organize openly, Jewish organizations are tolerated. There are no officially permitted Jewish organizations, but members of the local Jewish communities meet frequently, and their attitudes toward non-Jews is often discussed at these meetings. In university circles of Budapest, for example, the acronym of "OH" (*Optimális Halmaz* or Optimal Mass) stands for a well-known organization of mathematicians under Jewish leadership. Its members indicate their OH affiliation in their publications, they use their connections at home and abroad, and they are allowed to operate openly.

While anti-Semitic activities are prohibited by law, anti-Zionism is encouraged and represents the official policy of the Hungarian government. With the fervent support of the Soviet Union, Isreal has become a veritable pariah and is denounced as the root of all evil regarding the Palestinian and other Middle Eastern issues. In this regard most Hungarians follow the dictum: "The enemy of my enemy is my friend," and consequently are supportive of pro-Israeli Jews. For example, when Pál Ipper (a former secret policeman before 1956, and today one of the best known TV commentators) talked about the Israeli raid on Iraq's nuclear power plant, he spent five minutes stating the official line, and then ten minutes describing how the Israeli air force through precision bombing damaged the Iraqi and Syrian defenses. Another sign of subdued anti-Semitism in contemporary Hungary is the support for Jewish dissidents, among them László Rajk, son of a victim of the Rákosi purges and now one of the leaders of a group called "Shalom." Shalom attacks the National Representation of Hungarian Israelites for complying with the totalitarian system and its Soviet mentors. Shalom believes that Hungarian Jews deserve recognition as a minority group with equal rights and representation, rather than as a religious group with no political privileges; and that they should be integrated into Hungarian society. He rejects classifying individuals as Jews merely on the basis of race or religion. Jews, according to Shalom, should be regarded as a community shaped by historical, cultural, ethnic and social factors, within which unity varies in intensity and character.

According to Shalom, the Jews in Hungary fell into the trap of history twice. The first time was in 1945, when they backed the extreme Left and in order to prevent anti-Semitism filled the high posts of power in the state machinery.[90] The second trap was in 1956, when fearing pogroms, they supported the Kádár rather than the Imre Nagy regime. Shalom contends that the Hungarian Jews should show loyalty toward the sovereign Hungarian state and the nation and not the government in power. Shalom condemns the Hungarian Jews who follow in the footsteps of such political leaders of Jewish origin as György Aczél, Ernö Lakatos, and Péter Rényi.[91] Yet even the staunchest party loyalists of Jewish origin sometimes engage in Jewish favoritism, which can backfire on them. The case in point is György Aczél. As the chief ideologue and the man in charge of cultural life, Aczél used his personal intervention during the past few years in cases where the issue was the promotion of Jews or pro-Jewish men. He interfered in the appointment of theatre directors, the naming of local cultural and culture/political functionaries, and even trod on the privileged internal affairs of universities. The so-called mathematics case at the Eötvös Lóránd University created quite a stir.

For decades there existed, in relative peace, two groups of mathematicians, each containing several chairs. One of them was made up of the so-called "Jewish urbanists," while the other, the "populists," at times openly exhibited evidence of anti-Semitism. With the knowledge of both groups, the university authorities petitioned the Ministry of Education to request the creation of two institutes, one dealing with pure mathematics and one with applied math. In fact, the creation of these would have meant the institutionalization of the division. At the personal intervention of comrade Aczél, the minister, Béla Köpeczi, decreed the creation of a single institute in September 1983. In the new institution full control was given to the "Jewish, urbanist" group; the "populist" group's chairs were dismantled, their leaders were removed, and so on.

After the declaration of the decree, the party organization of the university addressed a petition to the president of the Supreme Court, complaining that the Minister of Education acted in an unlawful manner in interfering with the university's internal affairs. This petition was, of course, rejected with the reasoning that in accordance with the Constitution, the minister has the right to interfere in exceptional cases. Still, László Maróthy, then first secretary of the Budapest party committee, went to the university to look over the situation and, based on his experiences there, attacked Aczél during the next meeting of the Politburo. He claimed that such crude interference into the scientific-cultural life should not be allowed. The meeting turned into an open confrontation; in the end even Kádár himself is reported to have said, "Georgie, this time you went too far." At the 13th Party Congress Aczél was removed from the post of CC Secretary and on July 1, 1985, the previously eliminated positions in mathematics were reinstated.

CONCLUSIONS

In this chapter an attempt was made to identify and explain contemporary Hungarian society in terms of the changing social structure since 1947. As we have seen, these changes impinge directly on the character of Hungarian society, and therefore they have enabled us to construct an index to characterize the dominant features of the attitudinal responses of certain groups to sensitive social and cultural issues. In spite of the changes in strategy and tactics of the party under the Kádár regime to transform the structure of the Hungarian social character from a conflictual to a more consensual one, today there are still not one, but two, societies in Hungary—each characterized by different structural properties. Officially there are only three friendly classes (the workers, the peasants, and the intelligentsia) cooperating in the process of socialist production. Unofficially, however, there are not only competing but conflicting interests and differentiations among several stratified groups in today's Hungarian society. The latter is referred to by contemporary sociologists as the emergence of "new sorts of inequalities."

As we have seen, Hungary underwent a drastic restructuring of the traditional organization of its society. This is particularly true with regard to the modernization of the social structure of the villages. There were considerable increases in the proportions of manual, skilled, and unskilled workers in rural Hungary. Villages in Hungary are no longer peasant communities; they are just as much workers' settlements as they are peasant settlements. Many of the nonagricultural workers perform their jobs like skilled workers and therefore they identify less with the peasants in the traditional sense of the meaning. The improved upward social mobility has enabled many individuals who left agriculture, and thus became more mobile in a social sense, to remain village inhabitants. There are over 1 million commuters in Hungary who work in the cities but reside in villages. Today's rural communities include not only workers and peasants but a large number of white collar workers: doctors, teachers, the clergy, technicians, businessmen, administrators, accountants, and clerks. The small farmers (about 63,000 of them) are a dying species. The majority of them are elderly people farming on poor land. The village of today bears little resemblance to the villages of the past, yet 90 percent of the village dwellers are involved in some way in agricultural production. More than half of Hungary's population pursues agricultural activities in addition to their own main occupation. The authorities are, of course, gratified because self-motivation (under the auspices of the economic reform), hard work, and increased productivity mean less burden and less subsidy for the state. Many attitudes and traditions characteristic of the past have survived in the way of living of the village population: long working hours, widespread small-scale production, and the straightforward spending of leisure time. The village is still present in the Hungarian psyche; all groups are affected by the village or smalltown lifestyle. The traditions that pervade and in some ways control the life of Hungarians, especially in the villages, form a complex expression of emotions, ideas, morals, and beliefs that are in many ways antithetical to the rigidities of Marxism-Leninism. This is also evident among the younger generations, who grew up under the socialist system.

There is a general disenchantment with Marxism-Leninism and a movement toward religion by young people. Many young Hungarians have no political convictions; they have a "secondary (everyday) ideology" characterized by abstention from politics. The young people of Hungary favor individualism and independence and reject collectivism imposed from above. The idea of forming communities or thinking in terms of community rather than in terms of the individual is foreign to most young Hungarians. The overwhelming majority of university students are dissatisfied with the teachings of Marxism-Leninism; they condemn materialism, selfishness, corruption, and the inflated bureaucracy. While they consider private enterprise as not harmful to the country's socialist character, they do condemn unearned income and the accumulation of great personal wealth. Most of them disagree with the official allegation that public life in Hungary has become more democratic. In search of a genuine independent community life, Hungarian youth are more and more turning to religion as an answer to the unfulfilled spiritual needs denied to them by the teachings of Marxism-Leninism.

Other disenchantments and criticisms are noticeable in contemporary Hungarian society by groups and individuals who were victims of the "new sorts of inequalities." They can be found in the housing shortage, criticized by young couples with low incomes, pensioners, and old people. They also can be found in the standards of and access to services (i.e., those with means and influence have the best in health care and leisure time). These criticisms can also be found in work and work conditions (e.g., manual workers with several shifts and unfavorable work schedules or workers commuting several hours a day to work from villages). There are also noticeable differences in cultural activities between skilled and unskilled workers. Only a small percentage of manual workers are active recipients of culture. There is a considerable differentiation among manual workers because of the big gap between the elite and the unskilled, deprived, layer of workers.

The "new inequalities" can be found in the material living conditions among the unskilled group, administrative workers, subordinate professionals, and skilled workers, whose financial situation is extremely differentiated. The differences in material living conditions are particularly noticeable between the smaller group of high income entrepreneurs in the second economy (accompanied by the bureaucratic elite, speculators, and black marketeers in the third economy) and the large segment of the low income population. The visible differences between the rich and the poor in terms of financial inequality and living standards is one of the main concerns of the Hungarian authorities today. They are keenly aware that the widening gap between the two groups, coupled with other inequities, could rekindle mass protests leading to a new uprising. Thus the policymaking authorities are making great strides to alleviate sharp differences serving as irritants in the social structure. The party's "alliance policy" acts as a safety valve to permit the disgruntled elements of Hungarian society to lodge their dissatisfaction through a channel of command to be heard at the very top of the political structure. The price, however, for this socialist pluralism is the creation of a new party that has become socialized and has embraced many "old" values. Void of the "Muscovites," as "home communists" the party leadership—divided into pro-reformists and anti-reformists—is fully committed to anti-Stalinism and to the New Economic Mechanism, tailored to Hungarian conditions with the goal of improving the standard of living through private initiative and new technology. In other words, the vitality of contemporary communism in Hungary is actually derived from its national orientation. The reforms, which started with the NEM in 1968, are the cornerstone for stability, success, and hope for the future. The party knows, as do the people at large, that there can be no turning back on the road to radicalism without risking a new upheaval. Hence the road ahead is a rocky one but clear as to the destination and the mode of travel.

The personal experiences of such top "home communists" leaders as János Kádár and György Aczél are guarantees that Hungarian needs will never again be sacrificed for alien interests. On the other hand, the Hungarian people at large have learned from the experience of October 1956 that they cannot depend on outside support to guarantee their independence, and therefore are very cautious about how far they can push their demands short of losing their bargaining position. It is within this context that the Kremlin leaders are fully endorsing the Hungarian reforms, because they perceive economic well-being as a guarantee to political stability and commitment to the socialist community. Thus Hungary is in a peculiar position, which allows her to enjoy greater economic and political freedom than any other socialist country in the Soviet bloc. These peculiarities include not only the traumatic experience of the October 1956 Revolution, but the strong national feelings of the party leaders, the declining population, the skillful role of the intelligentsia and managerial leadership in the modernization process of the Hungarian society, the unusual élan and initiative of the Hungarian entrepreneurs, and the cultural heritage of Hungarian resourcefulness; they, and others, are all attributes of a potpourri of interests that have made Hungarian national communism a success, regardless whether it is the party rulers or the multitude of the ruled that claim credit for it. So far no other country in the Soviet bloc has been able to play this political game by emulating Hungarian rules successfully.

Part of the credit for the Hungarian success belongs to the small but influential group of Hungarian Jews. Just as the small but powerful circle of Hungarian Jews at the end of WWII introduced Stalinism to Hungary, after October 1956 many of the liberal, pro-reformist Jews were in the forefront advocating economic and social changes that led to the establishment of the NEM in 1968.

Since introducing the NEM, the Kádár regime has attempted to combine central planning of the economy with a major decentralization of economic decision making at the enterprise level. With this goal in mind, the pro-reformist managerial group has increased its reliance on indirect controls (economic regulators) and market forces, as opposed to central directives, to guide the enterprises. At the same time, however, the authorities have preserved a number of the bureaucratic structures that are characteristic of the more traditional socialist economies and have retained a commitment to such socialist principles as full employment, equity in income distribution, and a subsidy system. In other words, the reform process has not been linear. Changes in the international economic environment in the 1970s and 1980s have led the policymakers periodically to modify the system of economic management. They now confront the complex task of developing a technologically advanced socialist economy that is capable of adapting rapidly to changing world conditions. There are several dilemmas facing Hungary's policymakers today. Will the authorities opt for continued equity in income distribution even if it means reducing workers' incentives and productivity? Will they opt for continued guarantees of full employment, which may reduce competition, and call for increased subsidies for enterprises that are deficient and unprofitable? Will they opt for a further decentralization of the economic system, stability of the policy environment, greater control over resources by enterprises, and their greater accountability for the use of resources? In other words, will the reforms continue to bring about technological change that will make Hungary more competitive in the international markets of the future, and if so, at what costs and with what speed?[92]

A resolution to these dilemmas will also explain to what extent the national orientation of communism in Hungary will continue to be successful in achieving industrial and technological modernization without any major crises or internal upheavals. The concept of modernization presupposes structural as well as attitudinal changes in society. Hungary has already witnessed the failure of an attempt to remold its society into a classless, faithless, egalitarian, and symmetrical shape through imposed dictates of the Rákosi era. The Hungarian October of 1956 was a clear admission that the creation of a "new socialist man" with all its attributes prescribed by Marxist-Leninist ideology ended in failure. Hence the Kádár regime was perceptive and pragmatic enough to induce changes in the Hungarian social character that call for modernization without uprooting the character structure of the Hungarian society. Thus, it is conceivable to argue that in Hungary today there is a new society (or social structure), but one adhering to many of the old traditions.

NOTES

1. See Eric Fromm, "Individual and social origins of neurosis," *American Sociological Review* 10 (1944); 380; reprinted in *Personality in Nature, Society and Culture,* ed. by Clyde Kluckhohn and Henry Murray (New York: Alfred A. Knopf, 1948), 407, 409–410.

2. See Hans-Georg Heinrich, *Hungary* (London: Frances Pinter, 1986), p. 93 and Chapter 2, "The Rulers and the Ruled," which identifies the two societies in terms of the structure and function of power in the state.

3. See David Riesman, *The Lonely Crowd* (New Haven: Yale University Press, 1950).

4. Ibid., 9.

5. See *Népszabadság* (January 21, 1962).

6. See *A MSzMP VIII kongresszusának jegyzökönyve* [Protocols of the HSWP 8th Congress] (Budapest, November 20–24, 1962).

7. Riesman, op. cit., v.

8. See József Bálint, *Társadalmi rétegezödés és jövedelmek* [Social Stratification and Incomes] (Budapest: Kossuth Könyvkiadó, 1983), 29–39; and *Statisztikai*

Zsebkönyv [Statistical Pocket Book] (Budapest: Központi Statisz kai Hivatal, 1985).

9. See Heinrich, op. cit., 103.

10. See Bálint, op. cit., 75.

11. See Rezsö Nyers, "The efficiency of the intellectual resource," *The New Hungarian Quarterly* 23 (Autumn 1982); 38.

12. Bálint, op. cit., 71.

13. Bálint, op. cit., 76; and Nyers, "The efficiency of the intellectual resource," op. cit., 38.

14. *Mezögazdasági Statisztikai Évkönyv 1982* [Agricultural Statistical Yearbook 1982] (Budapest: Magyar Központi Statisztikai Hivatal, 1983).

15. *Valóság* (May 1984).

16. *Heti Világgazdaság* (May 19, 1984).

17. See Kálmán Kulcsár, "A társadalmi struktúra" [The social structure] in *Mit kell tudni Magyarországról* [Essential Facts About Hungary] (Budapest: Kossuth Könyvkiadó, 1984), 104.

18. See, for example, Rudolf Andorka, *A magyar község társadalmának átalakulása* [Social Change in Hungarian Villages] (Budapest: Magvetö Könyvkiadó, 1979); Rudolf Andorka, "A községi népesség társadalmi jelemzöi" [Social characteristics of the village population], *Társdalmi Szemle* 8–9 (1974); Rudolf Andorka and István Harcsa, "A községben zajló társadalmi változások az elmúlt másfél évtizedben" [The social change in the villages in the past decade and a half], *Társadalmi Szemle* 5 (1979); György Enyedi, "Development regions on the Hungarian Great Plain" in A.F. Burghardt, ed., *Development Regions in the Soviet Union, Eastern Europe and Canada* (New York: Praeger, 1975), 65–74; C.M. Hann, *Tázlár: A Village in Hungary* (Cambridge: Cambridge University Press, 1980); and Tibor Simó, *Társadalmi tagozólás a mezögazdasági termelöszövetkezetekben* [Social Stratification in Agricultural Producers' Cooperatives] (Budapest: A Magyar Szocialista Munkáspárt Központi Bizottságának Társadalomtudományi Intézete, 1980).

19. For a thorough and detailed analysis, see Rudolf Andorka, *A társadalmi mobilitás változásai Magyarországon* [Changes in Hungarian Social Mobility] (Budapest: Gondolat Könyvkiadó, 1982); and György Akszentievics, "Mobility and social relations" in Tamás Kolosi and Edmund Wnuk-Lipiński, eds., *Equality and Inequality Under Socialism* (London: Sage Studies in International Sociology, 1983), 50–77.

20. Bálint, op. cit., 91. See also *Népszabadság* (April 4, 1981).

21. *Népszabadság* (November 23, 1983).

22. See E. Csizmadia, "A háztáji termelés új vonásai" [New features of household farming], *Valóság* 2 (1978).

23. Tibor Simó, "Social stratification in cooperative farms," *The New Hungarian Quarterly* 22 (Winter 1981); 145.

24. See György Enyedi, "A magyar településhálózat átalakulasi tendenciái" [Transformation tendencies in the Hungarian settlement network], *Magyar Tudomány* [Hungarian Science] 10 (1981); 727–734.

25. In 1978 there was a bathroom and watercloset in 23 percent of village households, compared with 64 percent in town households and 71 percent in Budapest households.

26. *Népszabadság* (February 9, 1984) and *Élet és Irodalom* (February 10, 1984).

27. *Ötlet* (October 20, 1983).

28. For an analysis of works of creative art and culture representing social values in Hungary, see Elemér Hankiss, *Érték és társadalom: Tanulmányok érték-szociológia köréböl* [Value and Society: Studies in the Sociology of Values] (Budapest: Magvetö Könyvkiadó, 1977). For a description of many interesting customs still in existence in Hungary, see Telka Dömötör, *Magyar népszokások* [Hungarian Folk Customs] (Budapest: Corvina, 1972; tr. into English by Judith Elliott, Kossuth Printing House, 1977).

29. See Miklós Hernádi, "Festive behavior in Hungary," *The New Hungarian Quarterly* 21 (Autumn 1980); 130–37.

30. This mood of misery, destitude and jungle-like behavior was brilliantly captured in a short story written by Erzsébet Galgóczi, *Félemelet* [The Mezzanine] which is presently being translated into English for publication in the United States.

31. Júlia Juhász, "Old habits in new surroundings," *The New Hungarian Quarterly* 24 (Spring 1984): 142–48.

32. See Dr. Géza Denke, "Teaching Marxism-Leninism: Findings about the ideological and political education of university students," *Felsöoktatási Szemle* [Review of Higher Education] (November 1984); 662–667.

33. See, for example, Ágnes Dus, ed., *A magyar ifjúság a 80 években* [Hungarian Youth in the 1980s] (Budapest: Kossuth Könyvkiadó, 1984); and several articles in the *Társadalmi Szemle* [Social Review] (July/August 1984).

34. See András Knopp and Katalin Radics, "Concerning the situation of young intellectuals," *Társadalmi Szemle* (July/August 1984): 52–68.

35. See *Napjaink* [Our Days] (October 1984); 22–23.

36. *Népszabadság* (December 3, 1983).

37. *Magyar Közlöny* 3 (February 29, 1984), articles 1–4.

38. See Pál Berényi and Peter Schiffer, "Ifjúság, Társadalom, Ideológia" [Youth, society, ideology], *Társadalomtudományi Közlemények* [Sociological Reports] 1 (1985).

39. See also *Magyar Ifjúsag* [Hungarian Youth] (September 20, 1985): 26–27.

40. *Népszabadság* (December 22, 1983).

41. See *Vasárnapi Hírek* [Sunday News] (August 25, 1985).

42. *Figyelö* (September 12, 1985).

43. See *Heti Világgazdaság* [World Economic Weekly] (September 21, 1985).

44. *Népszava* (April 6, 1985).

45. *Figyelö* (July 11, 1985).

46. "Social policy" covers instances where resources are allocated or re-allocated by the state in order to assure the satisfaction of certain needs, independently of the market mechanism. Social policy is essentially an ex post facto intervention in distribution, designed to correct the socially problematic or harmful aspects of the market.

47. See Zsusza Ferge, *A Society in the Making. Hungarian Social and Societal Policy, 1945–1975* (White Plains, NY: M.E. Sharpe, 1980); and Zsusza Ferge, "Main trends in Hungarian social policy," *The New Hungarian Quarterly* 23 (Summer 1982); 137–149.

48. Kolosi and Wnuk-Lipiński, op. cit., 3.

49. See Tamás Kolosi, "Concluding remarks: Inconsistencies and inequalities" in Kolosi and Wnuk-Lipiński, op. cit., 181–193.

50. See Iván T. Berend and György Ránki, *The Hungarian Economy in the 20th Century* (Sydney: Croom Helm, 1985), 227–228.

51. Heinrich, op. cit., 113.

52. *Jel-Kép* [Symbol] (January 1984).

53. *Magyar Hírlap* [Hungarian News] (September 15, 1984).

54. *Magyar Statisztikai Zesbkönyv* [Hungarian Statistical Pocketbook] (Budapest: Központi Statisztikai Hivatal, 1985); and *Heti Világgazadaság* [World Economic Weekly] (November 19, 1983).

55. Szikra Katalin Falusné, "A vagyonosodásról" [On the accumulation of wealth], *Közgazdaśagi Szemle* [Economic Review] 11 (1982): 1314–1330.

56. *Magyar Hírlap* (September 15, 1984).

57. József Bálint, op. cit., 235.

58. Akszentievics, "Mobility and social relations," op. cit., 60–61.

59. Ibid., 61.

60. Ibid., 65.

61. Ibid., 73.

62. For documentary evidence of the events of the 1956 Revolution in Hungary, see Paul Zinner, ed., *National Communism and Popular Revolt in Eastern Europe: A Selection of Documents on Events in Poland and Hungary, February–November 1956* (New York: Columbia University Press, 1956).

63. See Gerhard Seewann, "Minority question seen from Budapest's viewpoint," *Suedosteuropa* 23 (1984): 1–14.

64. See *Special Report No. 146* (Washington: U.S. Department of State, Bureau of Public Affairs, 1986), 40.

65. *Népszabadság* (November 1, 1984).

66. Ibid., 40.

67. *Heti Világgazdaság*, (July 20, 1985).

68. *Mozgó Világ* 6 (1985): 74–77.

69. *Heti Világgazdaság* (July 20, 1985).

70. Albert Porkolov, "The situation of the Gypsy population in Borsod-Abaúj-Zemplén County," *Borsod Szemle* [Borsod Review] 1 (1985): 72–78.

71. *Mozgó Világ* 6 (1985): 74–77.

72. *Magyar Hírlap* (July 6, 1985).

73. *Népszabadság* (April 10, 1985).

74. *Népszabadság* (March 30, 1985).

75. *Népszava* (November 16, 1985).

76. *Die Welt* (November 23, 1984).

77. *Magyar Hírek* 33 (July 6, 1985); 29.

78. Oszkár Jászi, *Magyar Kalvária, Magyar Feltámadás [Hungarian Calvary, Hungarian Resurrection]* (Vienna: Bécsi magyar kiadó, 1920), 121; Francois Fejtö, *Les Juifs et l'antisémitisme dans les pays communistes* [The Jews and Antisemitism under the Communists] (Paris: Plon, 1960), 91; and Eugene Duschinsky, "Hungary," in *The Jews in the Soviet Satellites* (Syracuse, NY: Syracuse University Press, 1953), 374–76.

79. See Árpád Szélpál, *Les 133 jours de Béla Kun* [133 Days of Béla Kun] (Paris: A. Fayard, 1959), 235; and Kun Béláné, *Kun Béla* (Budapest: Magvetö, 1966).

80. See Randolph L. Braham, *The Hungarian Jewish Catastrophe* (2nd ed., New York: Columbia University Press, 1984), 2.

81. Paul Lendvai, *Anti-Semitism Without Jews* (Garden City, NJ: Doubleday, 1971), 304.

82. Peter A. Toma, "Revival of the Communist Party in Hungary," *Western Political Quarterly*, 14 (March 1961); 87–103.

83. Lendvai, op. cit., 305–306.

84. Ibid., 66 and 321. For a very perceptive description of the "Muscovites," see Tamás Aczél and Tibor Meray, *The Revolt of the Mind* (New York: Frederick A. Praeger, 1959), 7–15.

85. Ibid., 307; see also Hugh Seton-Watson, *The East European Revolution* (3rd ed., New York: Praeger, 1956), 196.

86. Lendvai, op. cit., 307.

87. Ibid., 309.

88. Ibid., 313.

89. *Ellenforradalom Magyarországon, 1956* [Counterrevolution in Hungary, 1956] (Budapest: Kossuth Kiadó, 1958), vol. 2.

90. This observation was made as early as 1948 by a well respected scholar, the late István Bibó, who wrote a remarkable sociological essay reviewing the catastrophe of Hungarian Jewry and the causes of anti-Semitism in Hungary after WWII. See István Bibó, "Zsidókérdés Magyarországon 1944 után" [Jewish question in Hungary after 1944] in *Bibó István öszegyüjtött munkái* [The Collected Works of István Bibó] ed. by István Keményi and Mátyás Sárközi (Bern: Az Európai Protestáns Magyar Szabadegyetem Kiadása, 1982), 391–504.

91. See *A Hírmondó* (May–June 1984).

92. See Berend and Ránki, op. cit., 227–291; and Peter T. Knight, *Economic Decisionmaking Structures and Processes in Hungary* (Washington, D.C.: The World Bank, 1984), 68–79.

Bibliography

PRIMARY SOURCES: BOOKS AND JOURNALS

Aczél, György. "The challenge of our age and the response of socialism." *The New Hungarian Quarterly* 24, No. 90 (Summer 1983).

———. "A new system of values." *The New Hungarian Quarterly* 21, No. 77 (Spring 1980).

———. "The stages and crises of socialism." *The New Hungarian Quarterly* 23, No. 87 (Autumn 1982): 10.

Ádám, M., G. Juhász, and L. Kerekes. *Magyarország és a második villágháború* [Hungary and the second World War] (Budapest: Kossuth Könyvkiadó, 1961).

Akszentievics, György. "Mobility and social relations," in Tamás Kolosi and Edmund Wnuk-Lipínski, eds., *Equality and Inequality Under Socialism: Poland and Hungary Compared* (London: Sage Studies in International Sociology, 1983).

Andorka, Rudolf, "A Községi népeség társadalmi Jelemzöi" [Social characteristics of the village population]. *Társdalmi Szemle* 8–9 (1974).

———. "Alkoholizmus a mai Magyar társadalomba" [Alcoholism in today's Hungarian society]. *Pártélet* [Party Life] (May 1986).

———. *A magyar község társadalmának átalakulása* [Social Change in Hungarian Villages] (Budapest: Magvetö Könyvkiadó, 1979).

———. *A társadalmi mobilitás változásai Magyarországon* [Changes in Hungarian Social Mobility] (Budapest: Gondolat Könyvkiadó, 1982).

Andorka, Rudolf, and István Harcsa. "A Községben Zajló társadalmi Változások az elmúlt másfél évtizedben" [The social change in the villages in the past decade and a half]. *Társdalmi Szemle* 5 (1979).

Bállai, László. "The development of enterprise management." *Pártélet* (October 1984).

Bálint, András. "Népmozgalmi Statisztika" [Demographic statistics]. *Heti Világgazdaság* (March 31, 1984).

Bálint, József. *Társadalmi retegezödés és Jövedelmek.* [Social Stratification and Incomes] (Budapest: Kossuth Könyvkiadó, 1983).

Bauer, Tamás. "A második gazdasági reform és a tulajdonviszonyok: Szempontok az új gazdasági mechanizmus továbbtejlesztéséhez" [The Second Economic Reform and ownership relations: Some considerations for the further development of the NEM]. *Mozgó Vilag* [Moving World] 8, No. 11 (November 1982).

Benke, Valéria. "Social policy, reality, socialism." *Társadalmi Szemle* [Social Review] 2 (1982).

Berend, Iván T., and György Ranki. *The Hungarian Economy in the 20th Century* (Sydney: Croom Helm, 1985).

———. *Underdevelopment and Economic Growth: Studies in Hungarian Economic and Social History* (Budapest: Akadémiai Kiadó, 1979).

Berényi, Pál, and Peter Schiffer. "Ifjúság, Társadalom, Ideológia" [Youth, society, ideology] *Társadalomtudományi Közlemények* [Sociological Reports] 1 (1985).

Bibó, István. "Zsidókærdés Magyarországon 1944 Után" [Jewish question in Hungary after 1944], in István Keményi and Mátyás Sárközi, eds., *Bibó István Öszegyüjtött munkái* [The Collected Works of István Bibó] (Bern: Az Euŕopai Protestáns Magyar Szabadegyetem Kiadása, 1982).

Bihari, Mihály. "Political mechanism and socialist democracy." *The New Hungarian Quarterly* 29, No. 88 (Winter 1982).

Bogáti, Péter. "The collective community marches in four columns." *Valóság* 5 (1984).

Cseh-Szombathy, László. "The family, its members and society." *The New Hungarian Quarterly* 22, No. 82 (Summer 1981).

Czernák, Magda. "Születési Kohorzok elsö házasság Köteseinek alakulása Magyarországon a második világháború után" [First marriages in Hungary after the Second World War in terms of both cohorts]. *Demográfia* 4 (1982).

Csizmadia, E. "A háztáji termeles új vonásai" [New features of household farming]. *Valóság* 2 (1978).

Denke, Géza. "Teaching Marxism-Leninism: Findings about the ideological and political education of university students," *Felsöoktatási Szemele* [Review of Hungarian Education] (November 1984).

Dömötör, Tekla. *Magyar népszokások* [Hungarian Folk Customs] (Budapest: Corvina, 1972). Translated into English by Judith Elliott (Budapest: Kossuth Printing House, 1977).

Dus, Ágnes (ed.). *A Magyar Ifjúság a 80 években* [Hungarian Youth in the 1980s] (Budapest: Kossuth Könyvkiadó, 1984).

———. *Tárrsadalma beilleszkedési zavarok Magyarországon* [Problems of Social Adjustment in Hungary] (Budapest: Kossuth Könyvkiadó, 1986).

Ellenforradalom Magyarországon, 1956 [Counterrevolution in Hungary, 1956] (Budapest: Kossuth Kiadó, 1958).

Enyedi, György. "A magyar településhálózat átalakulasi tendenciái" [Transformation tendencies in the Hungarian settlement network]. *Magyar Tudomány* [Hungarian Science] 10 (1981).

Erdei, Ferenc, et al., eds. *Information Hungary* (New York: Pergamon Press, 1968).

Falusné, Szikra Katalin. "A Vagyonosodásról" [On the accumulation of wealth]. *Közgazdásagi Szemle* [Economic Review] 11 (1982).

Fehér, F., A. Heller, and G. Márkus. *Dictatorship Over Needs* (London: Basil Blackwell, 1983).

Fejtö, Francois. "Les Juifs et l'antisémitisme dans les pays communistes [The Jews and anti-Semitism under the communists] (Paris: Plon, 1960).

Ferge, Zsuzsa. "Main trends in Hungarian social policy," *The New Hungarian Quarterly* 23 (Summer 1982).

———. *A Society in the Making: Hungarian Social and Societal Policy, 1945–1975* (White Plains, NY: M.E. Sharpe, 1980).

Fónay, Jenö. *Megtorlás* [Revenge] (Zurich: Svájci Magyar Irodalmi és Képzö- müvészeti Kör, 1983).

Foreign Broadcast Information Service. *Daily Report, Eastern Europe* (April 26, 1984).

Galgóczi, Erzsébet. "Félemelet" [The mezzanine], in *Közel a Kés* [Near the Knife] (Budapest: Szépirodalmi Könyvkiadó, 1978).

Gergély, Mihály. *Röpírat az Öngynilkosságról* [Leaflet on Suicide] (Budapest: Med- icina Publishers, 1981).

Guy, Lázár and Endre Hanna. "Az Ötéves mérleg" [The balance of five years] *Jel-Kép* [Symbol] 3 (1985).

Hankiss, Elemér. *Érték és társadalom: Tanulmányok értékszociológia köréböl* [Value and Society: Studies in the Sociology of Values] (Budapest: Magvetö Kö- nyvkiadó, 1977).

———. "Felületes Társadalom?" [Sloppy society?]. *Valóság* (February 1986).

———. "Második társadalom? Kísérletegy fogalom meghatározása és egy Va- lóságtartomany léirasa" [The other society? Attempt to define a concept and to describe a province of reality]. *Valóság* 5 (1984).

———. "Variations on corruption—One of the most dangerous forms of envi- ronmental pollution." *Valóság* 4 (June 1983).

Harcsa, István. "Concerning the living standard of young workers." *Társadalmi Szemle* (July/August 1984).

Hernádi, Miklós. "Festive behavior in Hungary." *The New Hungarian Quarterly* 21, No. 79 (Autumn 1980).

———. *Olyan, Amilyen?* [Should we accept it as it is?] (Budapest: Kozmosz, 1984).

Héthy, Lajos. "A 'második gazdaság,' a Kisvállalkozás és a gazdaságiranyítós" [The 'second economy,' the small enterprise, and economic control]. *Tár- sadalomkutatás* [Social Research] 1 (1983).

Huszár, István. "The transformation of social structure." *Valóság* (February 1985).

Jászi, Oszkár. *Magyar Kalvária, Magyar Feltámadás* [Hungarian Calvary, Hun- garian Resurrection] (Vienna: Bécsi Magyar Kiadó, 1920).

Juhász, Júlia. "Old habits in new surroundings." *The New Hungarian Quarterly* 24, No. 93 (Spring 1984).

Kádár, Janos. "The basis of consensus." *The New Hungarian Quarterly* 23, No. 86 (Summer 1982).

Kázmér, Nagy. *Elveszett alkotmány: A hidegháború és a magyar Politikai emigráció*

1945–1975 [The Lost Constitution: The Cold War and the Hungarian Political Emigration, 1945–1975] (London: Gondolat Kiadó, 1982).

Klinger, András. "Population policy in Hungary: Scope and limits." *The New Hungarian Quarterly* 23, No. 86 (Summer 1982).

Knopp, András, and Katalin Radics. "Concerning the situation in young intellectuals." *Társadalmi Szemle* (July/August 1984).

Kolosi, Tamás. "A strukturális viszonyok Korvonalai" [Outlines of structural conditions]. *Valóság* 11 (1982).

Kovács, Lajos. "Causes of administrative and public violations as reflected in an empirical study." *Magyar Jog* [Hungarian Law] (February 1984).

Kulcsár, Kálmán. *A mai magyar társadalom* [Contemporary Hungarian Society] (Budapest: Kossuth Könyvkiadö, 1980).

———. "A társadalmi Struktúra" [The Social Structure], in *Mit Kell tudni Magyarországról* [Essential Facts About Hungary] (Budapest: Kossuth Könyvkiadó, 1984).

Kun, Béláné. *Kun Béla* (Budapest: Magvetö, 1966).

Lackó, Miklós. *Ipari munkásságunk összetételének alakulása 1867–1949* [The Formation of Our Industrial Workers' Movement, 1867–1949] (Budapest: Akadémiai Kiadó, 1961).

Lenin, V.I. *Collected Works* (Moscow: Foreign Languages Publishing House, 1960).

Lisagor, Nancy. "The new Hungarian Criminal Code," *The New Hungarian Quarterly* 23, No. 87 (Autumn 1982).

Lukács, György. *Lenin: A Study on the Unity of His Thought* (Tr. from German by Nicholas Jacobs) (London: N.L.B., 1970).

Magyar Statisztikai Évkönyv [Hungarian Statistical Yearbook] (Budapest: Központi Statisztikai Hivatal, various years).

A MSzMP VII Kongresszusának jegyzökönyve [Protocols of the HSWP 8th Congress] (Budapest, November 20–24, 1962).

A Magyar Szocialista Munkáspárt Központi Bizotságának elözetes Jelentése a XIII Kongreszus Küldötteinek [Preliminary Report of the HSWP/CC to the Delegates of the 13th Congress] (Budapest, 1985).

Mészáros, Árpád, and István Monigl. "A házasságon kívüli születések és ezek demográfiai összefüggesei" [Birth to unmarried mothers and their relationship to other demographic factors] *Demográfia* 2–3 (1982).

Mezögazdasági Statisztikai Évkönyv [Agricultural Statistical Yearbook] (Budapest: Magyar Központi Statisztikai Hivatal, various years.

Molnár, Edit S. "Birth control, abortion and public opinion." *The New Hungarian Quarterly* 23, No. 86 (Summer 1982).

Nyers, Rezsö. "The efficiency of the intellectual resource," *The New Hungarian Quarterly* 23, No. 87 (Autumn 1982).

Nyitrai, Ferencné. "Gazdasági élet" [Economic life], in *Mit kell tudni Magyarországról* [Essential facts about Hungary] (Budapest: Kossuth Könyvkiadó, 1984).

Oszlányi, Zsolt. "Mai lakáshelyzet Magyarországon" [The housing situation in Hungary today]. *Társadalmi Szemele* (June 1985).

Porkolov, Albert. "The situation of the Gypsy population in Borsod-Abauj-Zemplén County." *Borsod Szemle* [Borsod Review] 1 (1985).

Papp, Gábor. "The aged in Hungary." *The New Hungarian Quarterly*, 24, No. 89 (Spring 1983).

Petsching, Mária. "On medical gratitudes—Not on an ethical basis." *Valóság* (November 1983).

Rácz, Attila. *Courts and Tribunals* (Budapest: Akadémiai Kiadó, 1980).

Ránki, György. *Magyarország gazdasága az elsö 3 éves terv idöszakábam* [Hungary's Economy During the First Three-Year Plan] (Budapest: Közgazdasági es Jogi Könyvkiadó, 1963).

R.R. "Az idös lakósság problémai" [Problems of the older population]. *Magyar Tudomány* (March 1984).

Samu, Mihály. *Hatalom és állam* [Power and State] (Budapest: Közgazdaságvés Jogi Könyvkiadó, 1982).

Schmidt, Péter. "The direction in which the political system develops." *Pártélet* (February 1984).

Simai, M., and L. Szúcs. *Horthy Miklós titkos iratai* [Nicholas Horthy's Secret Documents] (Budapest: Kossuth Könyvkiadó, 1962).

Simó, Tibor. "Social stratification in cooperative farms." *The New Hungarian Quarterly* 22, No. 84 (Winter 1981).

———. *Társadalmi tagozólás a mezögazdasági termelöszövetkezetekben* [Social Stratification in Agricultural Producers' Cooperatives] (Budapest: A Magyar Szocialista Munkás párt Központi Bizottságánok Társadalomtudományi Intézete, 1980).

Soltész, Anikó. "Whose sin is it?" *Ifjúsági Szemle* [Youth Review] (July–September 1984).

Statisztikai Havi Közlemények [Annual Statistical Reports] (Budapest: Központi Statisztikai Hivatal, various years).

Statisztikai Zsebkönyv [Statistical Pocket Book] (Budapest: Központi Statisztikai Hivatal, various years).

Székely, Zsuzsanna. "Building a house," in Gusztáv Hegyesi, ed., *Író Szemmel* [With the eyes of the writer] (Budapest: Kossuth Kiadó, 1982).

Szélpál, Árpád. *Les 133 Jours de Béla Kun* [133 days of Béla Kun] (Paris: A. Fayard, 1959).

Tomka, Miklós. "Vallásszerep a társulatunkban" [The role of religion in our society]. *Kritika* (January 1985).

Varga, Csaba. *A jog helye Lukács György világképében* [The place of law in György Lukacs's thought] (Budapest: Magvetö, 1981).

NEWSPAPERS AND MAGAZINES

Élet és Irodalom [Life and Literature].
Esti Hírlap [Evening News].
Magyar Hírek [Hungarian News].
Magyar Hírlap [Hungarian News].
Magyar Nemzet [Hungarian Nation].
Népszabadság [People's Freedom].
Népszava [People's Voice].
Új Tükör [New Mirror].

SECONDARY SOURCES: BOOKS AND JOURNALS

Aczél, Tamás, and Tibor Meray. *The Revolt of the Mind* (New York: Frederick A. Praeger, 1959).

Avineri, Shlomo. *The Social and Political Thought of Karl Marx* (London: Cambridge University Press, 1968).

Berlin, Isaiah. *Karl Marx, His Life and Environment* (New York: Oxford University Press, 1959).

Betts, R.R., ed. *Central and South East Europe* (London: Royal Institute of International Affairs, 1950).

Borkenau, Franz. *World Communism: A History of the Communist International* (New York: Norton, 1939).

Braham, Randolph L. *The Hungarian Jewish Catastrophe* (2nd ed.; New York: Columbia University Press, 1984).

Conquest, Robert. *V.I. Lenin* (New York: Viking Press, 1972).

Duschinsky, Eugene. "Hungary" in *The Jews in the Soviet Satellites* (Syracuse, NY: Syracuse University Press, 1953).

Enyedi, György. "Development regions on the Hungarian Great Plain," in A.F. Burghardt, ed., *Development Regions in the Soviet Union, Eastern Europe and Canada* (New York: Praeger, 1975).

Esposito, Vincent J. *A Concise History of World War II* (New York: Praeger, 1964).

Faris, Robert E.L., ed. *Handbook of Modern Sociology* (Chicago: Rand McNally, 1964).

Fischer, Louis. *The Life of Lenin* (New York: Harper and Row, 1964).

Fromm, Eric. "Individual and social origins of neurosis." *American Sociological Review* 10 (1944); reprinted in Clyde Kluckhohn and Henry Murray, eds., *Personality in Nature, Society, and Culture* (NY: Alfred A. Knopf, 1948).

Gitleman, Zivi. "The politics of social restoration in Hungary and Czechoslovakia." *Comparative Politics* 13, No. 2 (1981).

Gregor, A. James. *A Survey of Marxism* (New York: Random House, 1965).

Hann, C.M. *Tázlár: A Village in Hungary* (Cambridge: Cambridge University Press, 1980).

Heinrich, Hans-Georg. *Hungary* (London: Frances Pinter, 1986).

Helmreich, Ernst C., ed. *Hungary* (New York: Praeger, 1957).

Hook, Sidney. *Marx and the Marxists: The Ambiguous Legacy* (New York: D. Van Nostrand, 1955).

Ignotus, Paul. *Hungary* (New York: Praeger, 1971).

Kenedi, János. *Do It Yourself: Hungary's Hidden Economy* (London: Pluto Press, 1981).

Kertész, Stephen D. "The methods of Communist conquest: Hungary 1944–47." *World Politics* 3 (October 1950).

Knight, Peter T. *Economic Decisionmaking Structures and Processes in Hungary* (Washington, D.C.: The World Bank, 1984).

Lendvai, Paul. *Anti-Semitism Without Jews* (Garden City, NJ: Doubleday 1971).

Lévai, Jenö. "The war crime trials relating to Hungary," in Randolph L. Braham, ed., *Hungarian Jewish Studies* (New York: World Federation of Hungarian Jews, 1969), Vol. 2.

Lindblom, Charles. *Politics and Markets: The World's Political–Economic Systems* (New York: Basic Books, 1977).

Lobkowicz, Nicholas, ed. *Marx and the Western World* (Notre Dame: University of Notre Dame Press, 1967).

McCartney, Carlil Aylmer. *October Fifteenth: A History of Modern Hungary 1929–1945* (Edinburgh: Edinburgh University Press, 1957 and 1961), 2 Vols.

McLelland, David. *Karl Marx: His Life and Thought* (New York: Harper and Row, 1974).

Mars, Gerald. *Cheats At Work* (London: George Allen and Unwin, 1982).

Mayer, Alfred G. *Leninism*. (New York: Praeger, 1962).

Mosca, Gaetano. "Elementi" in James H. Meisel, *The Myth of Ruling Class: Gaetano Mosca and the "Elite"* (Ann Arbor: University of Michigan Press, 1985).

Nagy, Károly. "The impact of communism in Hungary." *East Europe* 18 (March 1969).

Radio Free Europe Background Reports.

Radio Free Europe Situation Reports.

Rejai, Mostafa. *Comparative Political Ideologies* (New York: St. Martin's Press, 1984).

Révai, József. "The character of a people's democracy." *Foreign Affairs* 28 (October 1949).

Riesman, David. *The Lonely Crowd, A Study of the Changing American Character* (New Haven: Yale University Press, 1950).

Rosenau, James N. "A pre-theory revisited: World politics in an era of cascading interdependence." *International Studies Quarterly* 28, No. 3 (1984).

Schaff, Adam. *Marxism and the Human Individual* (New York: McGraw-Hill, 1970).

Seton-Watson, Hugh. *The East European Revolution* (New York: Praeger, 1961).

Seewann, Gerhard. "Minority question seen from Budapest's viewpoint." *Suedosteuropa* 23, No. 1 (1984).

Tökés, Rudolf L. "Hungarian reform imperatives." *Problems of Communism* 33, No. 5 (1984).

Toma, Peter A., and Ivan Volgyes. *Politics in Hungary* (W.H. Freeman, 1977).

Toma, Peter A. "Revival of the communist party in Hungary." *Western Political Quarterly* 14 (March 1961).

The Truth About the Nagy Affair ; *Facts, Documents, Comments*. With a preface by Albert Camus (London: Published for the Congress for Cultural Freedom by Secker and Warburg, 1959) also (New York: Frederick A. Praeger, 1959).

Tucker, Robert C. *The Marxian Revolutionary Idea* (New York: W.W. Norton, 1969).

———. *The Marx–Engels Reader* (2nd ed.; New York: W.W. Norton, 1978).

U.S. House of Representatives, 80th Congress, Select Committee on Communist Aggression, Special Report No. 10. *Communist Takeover and Occupation of Hungary* (Washington, D.C., GPO, 1948).

Vajda, Mihály. *The State and Socialism* (London: Allison and Busby, 1981).

Valenta, Jiri. "Post-intervention normalization," in Teresa Rakowska-Harmstone, ed., *Communism in Eastern Europe* (2nd ed.; Bloomington: Indiana University Press, 1984).

Zinner, Paul, ed. *National Communism and Popular Revolt in Eastern Europe: A Selection of Documents on Events in Poland and Hungary, February–November 1956* (New York: Columbia University Press, 1956).

Index

About the Author

PETER A. TOMA is a professor of political science and international relations at the University of Arizona. He is a former director of an area program on Europe and the USSR at the National War College and a director of an EPDA institute in international affairs at the University of Arizona which investigates the changing face of communism in Eastern Europe. Professor Toma has authored or coauthored eight books and monographs. In addition, he has contributed chapters to nine books and published articles in numerous scholarly journals. His publications include *Politics in Hungary* with Ivan Volgyes (1977) and *Introduction to International Relations* with Robert Gorman (forthcoming).